Designing the
Modern Interior

Designing Modern

From the Victorians

—

**Edited by
Penny Sparke
Anne Massey
Trevor Keeble
Brenda Martin**

the
Interior
to Today

Oxford · New York

First published in 2009 by

Berg

Editorial offices:

1st Floor, Angel Court, 81 St Clements Street, Oxford, OX4 1AW, UK

175 Fifth Avenue, New York, NY 10010, USA

Berg is the imprint of Oxford International Publishers Ltd.

Library of Congress Cataloging-in-Publication Data

Designing the modern interior : from the Victorians to today / edited
by Penny Sparke ... [et al.].

    p. cm.

  Includes bibliographical references and index.

  ISBN 978-1-84788-287-5 (pbk.) — ISBN 978-1-84788-288-2 (cloth)

1. Interior architecture—Social aspects. 2. Interior decoration—Social

aspects. 3. Space (Architecture)—Social aspects. I. Sparke, Penny.

  NA2850.D47 2009

  729—dc22   2009009833

British Library Cataloging-in-Publication Data

A catalogue record for this book is available from the British Library.

ISBN 978 184788 288 2 (Cloth)

ISBN 978 184788 287 5 (Paper)

Typeset by Apex CoVantage, LLC, Madison, WI, USA

Printed in Great Britain by the MPG Books Group, Bodmin and Kings Lynn

www.bergpublishers.com

Contents

General Introduction

Penny Sparke

The greatest part of our modern existence takes place in an interior

Stéphane Mallarmé[1]

Mallarmé's statement, made in the 1870s as part of an attack on the *plein air* approach of the Impressionist painters, implied the existence of a direct link between modernity and the interior. If that were the case, the French poet went on to ask, why were modern painters preoccupying themselves with 'outside'? Writing from the vantage point of the 1930s, the German cultural critic, Walter Benjamin, also perceived a link between the interior and the modern, nineteenth-century world. Inasmuch as it represented, for him, the modern separation of the worlds of the private and the public, for the latter writer it was the bourgeois domestic interior which, in spite of its stylistic historicism and clutter, stood for modernity. 'Under Louis Philippe', he wrote,

The private individual makes his entrance on the stage of history ... for the private individual, the place of dwelling is for the first time opposed to the place of work. The former constitutes itself as the interior. Its complement is the office. The private individual, who in the office has to deal with reality, needs the domestic interior to sustain him in his illusions ... his living room is a box in the theatre of the world.[2]

This anthology of essays about the design of the modern interior in the period 1870 to the present is as strongly rooted in the ideas of Mallarmé and Benjamin as it is in the writings on the subject by architectural and design historians. The latter have tended to think of the term 'modern' either as a simple style descriptor, or they have associated it with the movement known as architectural and design 'modernism', a term—also utilised in the context of other creative practices, such as fine art, literature, drama, music and dance—used to denote a cultural response to modernity which made an appearance in the years between 1890 and 1930 and dominated discussions about architecture for decades after that as well. This book sets out, rather, to portray the modern interior as both linked to the experience of modernity in all its complexity and as it was addressed by architects, decorators and others who sought to find visual, material and spatial means of expressing that modernity, the modernists among them. In adopting this approach the book's main aim is to provide students of the late nineteenth- and twentieth-century interior, practitioners who intervene in the design of interiors, and anyone else interested in the spaces we inhabit, with an understanding of· why they look as they do and convey the meanings that they do, and with a sense of both the context of, and the key themes that informed, the development of the interior in the period in question.

To ensure that both breadth and depth are covered, both overviews and detailed case studies have been included in this publication. Whilst the introductions to the four sections set out to provide a broad picture of the periods in question and to offer historiographical introductions for future students of the subject, the case studies, provided by a number of experts in the field, illustrate, in some detail, the themes that have driven this book. The case studies cover the chronological span of the book and demonstrate that the study of the modern interior depends as much on the understanding of the particularities of a specific interior, or set of interiors, as it does upon the establishment of an appropriate theoretical and historical framework.

Whilst the history of the interior has been part of the territory of the architectural and the design historian of the modern era, it has, in some ways, tended to fall into the gap that exists between those two disciplines. Architectural history, the elder of the two disciplines, has, where an account of the period 1870 to the present is concerned, tended to adopt a modernist perspective and, following that movement's prejudices and preferences, to marginalise the interior, seeing it as a poor relation to architectural structure and space. Equally, design history, born in the 1970s out of late modernism and only fairly recently free of its ideological shackles and able to look at the impact of consumption as well as that of production, has focused on the material, mass-produced object and largely ignored the spatial and the idea of the 'ensemble', both key characteristics of the interior. That double marginalisation makes the study of the design of the modern interior an imperative task, and this book aims to make a significant contribution to implementing it.

In the resurrection of the interior that has been taking place over the last decade or so, the primary emphasis has been upon its links with domesticity. The influence of nineteenth-century social history, the growth of gender studies, the move away from modernism and towards all that it suppressed, post-1970s nostalgia, and an expanding interest in architectural heritage have all underpinned an expanding interest in the Victorian home and in domesticity in general. Whilst this book embraces the domestic interior, and indeed it is the subject of eleven of its seventeen chapters, it also wishes to move beyond it. The remaining six chapters—which address an exhibition, hotels, a concert hall and an ocean liner—are offered as an important balance to the focus on the home and provide ways of thinking about the modern interior as a phenomenon which exists both within and beyond the domestic sphere. Chapter 14, written by design historian David Crowley, adopts a slightly different means of moving beyond the contemporary obsession with domesticity. Instead of presenting it as a 'cosy' family-supporting concept, he offers a very different reading of 'home' that stands in opposition to the idea of the 'domestic utopia as marker of modernity', which is linked, rather, to a more dystopian idea of 'trash' or 'debris' in the home. Adopting yet another means of sidestepping 'cosy' domesticity in Chapter 17, design theorist Anne Chick offers a reading of the early twenty-first-century home which is, through its allegiance to the principles of sustainability, functionally, rather than psychologically or aesthetically, defined, and offers a model of the domestic space which lies outside 'design' as it is defined here.

Given its allegiance to both architectural and design history, as well as, as was noted at the beginning of this introduction, to literary and cultural history and criticism, the modern interior has to be positioned in a multidisciplinary context. Given the breadth of its manifestations, meanings and influences—the modern interior can be linked to architecture, which is visible in plans, axonometrics and photographs etc.; to the idea of theatre, as, that is, a 'stage set' for its occupants which invokes discussions about interiority; as an extension of the body, linked to the world of fashion; and as a represented, mediated ideal connoting a modern lifestyle—it is impossible to limit a study of it to a single discipline. The range of the modern interior's meanings can be seen, for example, by comparing Chapter 4 in this book, in which the art historian, Christopher Reed, links the modern interior to the world of *Vogue* magazine, with, say, Chapter 9 in which Peter Blundell Jones looks at the way in which the German architect Hans Scharoun handled the interiors of his buildings.

The definition of the modern interior as it is presented in this book is, therefore, very broad. It is not restricted to the élite work of reforming, modernist architects or designers. Nor is it limited to the vast numbers of interiors realised in popular modern styles over these years—from 'modernist' to 'moderne' to 'modernistic' to 'streamlined' to 'surreal' to 'contemporary' to 'retro' to 'minimal'. All

those terms were used at one time or another to denote different versions of the 'modern' style in the century under scrutiny. Nor will the writers in this anthology only deal with realised interiors. Idealised and represented spaces will prove equally important as it is in those forms that modern interiors openly revealed their messages and meanings.

The breadth permitted by this approach permits the authors of the essays offered here to include interiors created by amateurs and professionals as well as others presented in what, at first sight, look like historical styles. Indeed, as Sabine Wieber suggests in Chapter 3, 'Things that don't look modern now could have looked modern then'. If the intention of the 'designer'—be she or he a housewife or a professional decorator or architect—was to address modernity in however open-ended a way, the work produced qualifies for consideration in this study. Apart from dress-making, the design of the interior is unique among design areas in that it can be, and often was, created by amateurs. This fact continually stimulated much debate about the design agency of the modern interior, and some of the essays in this book address that theme which runs throughout the period in question. Just as, in an earlier era, architects sought first to create and then to protect their professional status, so through the twentieth century interior decorators and designers have locked horns with each other seeking to legitimise their respective activities and to protect themselves from amateurism and the appropriation by the mass media of the modern interior as a marker of popular taste and identities. The anxieties caused by these tensions have surfaced frequently and continue to preoccupy many people. This theme will appear recurrently as a leitmotif throughout the book.

Another important theme that pervades the pages of this book is the relationship of the worlds of the public and private—dubbed by historians 'the separate spheres'—in the formation of the modern interior. It was, as Benjamin noted, in the middle years of the nineteenth century that the middle-class interior was formed and took on its modern character—as, that is, the location of feminine modernity and interiority, as a supporting space for the family, as a refuge, for men, from the world of work, and a site for social aspiration and fashion-consciousness. At the same time, the public sphere became the site of the expanding practices of public display, leisure, consumption, as well as being the location of the 'rational' worlds of work, finance and production. In the first section of the book, design historians Trevor Keeble and Fiona Fisher address the late nineteenth-century interior inside and outside the home, respectively, whilst also demonstrating how they influenced each other. In Chapter 1, Keeble focuses on the desire of design reformers to eliminate the link between the domestic interior and fashion and to introduce into it a level of 'common sense', borrowed, perhaps, from the rational world of manufacturing, whilst in Chapter 2, Fisher explores the social relationships created by the manipulation, or indeed the 'modernisation' of space, within the aptly called 'public house'. It is clear from the beginning of the period under consideration in this book that, whilst the worlds of the public and private interiors had their own characteristics and languages, they did not confine them to one sphere only but, in fact, moved freely across them as the social and cultural conditions relating to categories such as class and gender changed and as modernity itself was transformed. Fisher reinforces this idea by showing that changes within the interior space of the nineteenth-century public house were linked to social fragmentation and increasing urban mobility.

Modernity is a complex phenomenon, however, as many writers on the subject have noted, and its interface with the development of the modern interior has reflected that complexity.[3] As well as witnessing the onset of professionalisation in this field, and encouraging a subtle and evolving relationship between the public and private spheres, it was also characterised by, among many other things, a progressive relationship with technology; a hyperconsciousness of what it meant to live in the present with an eye to the future; its positive embrace of the mass media, mass consumption and the marketplace; its emphasis on individualism, interiority and the self; and its acknowledgment of the importance of taste as marker of distinction and social status.

The first of those themes—the relationship with technology—was most visible in early twentieth-century modernism's articulation of the interior. Although the late nineteenth-century household had responded positively to many of modern technology's new offerings—gas and electric lighting and power, the ice box, the suction sweeper etc.—that later movement went one step further by adopting the machine as a key metaphor. The modernist architects and designers saw in what they believed to be the underlying rationalism of the machine a means of escaping from what they perceived to be the 'irrationality' of the middle-class Victorian domestic interior which, in their eyes, had brought in its wake all the 'evils' associated with feminine taste, domesticity, fashion and conspicuous consumption. Linked as it was to the public world of work, the machine, many of them felt, could save the dwelling from the same fate. Le Corbusier's famous statement that 'the house is a machine for living in' was widely supported. A positive relationship with progressive technology was more than a metaphor for modernist rationality, however. It also fed in to the broader culture of modernity and into a number of different formulations of the modern interior, both domestic and otherwise. Embracing technology and all that it could offer signified, on the part of the consumers, occupants and users of interiors, an acknowledgement of modern life. Thus the American housewife in her 1930s home developed a special relationship with her bulbous, streamlined refrigerator. Miami's 'glamorous' hotels of the 1950s, as Alice Friedman explains in Chapter 12, also 'prided themselves … on their new technology, offering quests access to telephones, elevators, radios, efficient plumbing, chilled water, heating and, of course, the latest in nautical engineering', whilst 1980s Japanese love hotels, described by the architectural/cultural historian Sarah Chaplin in Chapter 15, 'were early adopters of western furnishings and consumer technologies long before they were incorporated into the average Japanese home', a confirmation of the fact that they were, in Chaplin's words, 'progressive and modern'. The links between technology and modernity in this context were indubitably strong and defining ones.

In that it expressed many of the defining characteristics of that social and cultural condition the modern interior can be seen as a reflection of modernity. In Chapter 3, Sabine Wieber describes the constructed interiors at Munich's Seventh International Art exhibition of 1897 as 'cultural responses to the conditions of modernity and modern life' and as reflecting the 'accelerated pace of life and a sense of fragmentation … a break with the past brought about by modernisation'. The link between modernisation and modernity is a critical one as the former led directly to the latter, whilst modernism emerged as an artistic/cultural response to that condition. Several of the chapters point to the sense of a heightened awareness of the 'here and now' and of the closeness of the future that was one of modernity's characteristics and was frequently expressed in the modern interior. In many instances, that was represented by a rejection of historicism and the adoption of contemporary images, patterns and motifs. The protomodernist interiors designed by Theodor Fischer and others at the 1897 exhibition, described by Sabine Wieber, for example, expressed their contemporaneity by depicting flora and fauna of the local area, thereby also emphasising their strong commitment to regionality, yet another characteristic of late nineteenth-century modernity.

One of the modern interior's most consistent characteristics in the period under scrutiny is as a representation dependent upon various forms of mass dissemination. In that role it inevitably developed strong relationships with the mass media, mass consumption and the marketplace, themselves defining characteristics of industrial modernity. This theme underpins many of the chapters of this book, from Trevor Keeble's (Chapter 1), which demonstrates its inclusion in books written by design reformers; to Sabine Wieber's (Chapter 3), which discusses constructed interiors in an exhibition; to Christopher Reed's (Chapter 4), which locates its subject within a fashion magazine; to Pat Kirkham's (Chapter 10), which unpacks a photograph of the interior in the home of Charles and Ray Eames; to my account (Chapter 11) of the Italian domestic landscape between 1945 and 1972, that focuses on the modern interior as represented in Italian exhibitions and design journals. One face of the development of the modern interior has been through its relationship with forms of mass dissemination. In that context it has been used to convey multiple messages, importantly among them those of national identity and prowess, as discussed in a number of chapters in this book (3, 11 and 13 among them).

Through modernity's relationship with the mass media and mass consumption, a new emphasis on self-identity emerged which also manifested itself in, and indeed helped to define, the modern interior. An analysis of the interior from this perspective requires a dependence on work undertaken in the field of cultural studies where the theme of identity has been much discussed, especially in relationship to class, gender, sexuality, ethnicity, race and age. This extensive work necessarily informs a study of the modern interior which, from one perspective, can be seen as the site for the expression of the identities defined by these cultural categories. This is widely acknowledged in the pages of this book. In Chapter 4, for example, Christopher Reed discusses 'the rise of self-identified subcultures—especially youth cultures and cultures based on sexual identity—enabled by urbanisation and the mass media', whilst, in the following chapter, Elizabeth Darling addresses the way in which 'notions of identity manifest in the "daily drama of personal life" are formed in and seek to reform an existing built environment'. Later, in Chapter 16, Alison Clarke highlights 'the undermining of self through the loss or redistribution of personal possessions'. Beyond identity the modern interior also takes one into the psychoanalytically defined area of 'interiority' which has been much discussed by literary critics and which lends another dimension to the study of the subject addressed in this book.[4]

A discussion of 'taste', expressed in the interior, as a marker of social distinction is also included in this publication. Influenced by the theoretical work of the French sociologist/anthropologist, Pierre Bourdieu, a recognition of the sociocultural role of taste, especially in the modern interior, which has the role of expressing identities of various forms, is fundamental to a study of the interior which moves beyond modernism, both as an architectural and design movement but also as an ideology which has influenced historical and critical writing on the subject. In Chapter 1, Trevor Keeble tells us that the reformers disapproved of the attempt on the part of consumers to gain social standing through an expression of their tastes. One could argue that that same resistance went on to characterise the whole of the modern movement and that it was, first and foremost, in an attempt to side-step taste that its protagonists undertook their work.

Linked to the importance of taste in these discussions the concept of popular culture and its relationship with one face of the modern interior is also revealed in the pages that follow. Popular leisure and entertainment took place within modern interiors as Fiona Fisher, Alice Friedman, Anne Wealleans, Sarah Chaplin and Alison Clarke all explain. A strong link between studies of everyday life and the work presented here needs to be acknowledged, therefore. The taste theme is picked up again, in combination with a discussion of the everyday, in Clarke's essay in a quotation she offers from Raphael Samuel. He has written about the potential for banality to be transformed through social aspiration which he describes as a 'distinct hankering for dreamscapes, discovering decorative possibilities in the most unpromising settings, aestheticising the most humdrum objects of everyday life and beautifying kitchens and bathrooms'.

Despite the fact that discussions about modernity and the interior which fall outside the modernist canon make up much of this book, a strong interest in modernist architecture still pervades several of the essays, especially those presented by Elizabeth Darling, Irene Nierhaus, Hilde Heynen and Charles Rice. All four architectural historians have, however, addressed their subjects with perspectives which owe much to writings relating to modernity in general. Indeed their shared decision to focus on the interior, a subject largely avoided by modernists themselves, already points to the novelty of their approach. The interest in all that

modernity brings with it, and with the broad literature that addresses it, inevitably allows them to view modernism, and specifically the modernist interior, through a new lens. Irene Nierhaus, who addresses the interiors of the arch modernist Mies Van der Rohe, and Hilde Heynen, who is interested in modernism's — and indeed, in her view, modernity's — lack of sympathy with the concept of domesticity, both have recourse to ideas that originate within the field of cultural studies, rather than traditional architectural history, to support their discussions and analyses.

The chapters in the book are presented chronologically. Although its focus is not on interior styles for their own sake, the conventional, modernist story of dramatic stylistic change — i.e. of the historicist, backward-looking Victorian interior being replaced in the early twentieth century by a simple, modern style inspired by the machine — has not completely vanished. It has, however, been rendered more complex, contextualised and broadened. Indeed the sense of freedom that was expressed by many people in the early twentieth century, with regard to the rejection of Victorian clutter and the arrival of simplicity and 'light and air', is visible in the text, expressed, for example, by among other voices, that of the English actress, Elsa Lanchester. 'The spacious bareness around me', Lanchester writes, and Elizabeth Darling reports to us in Chapter 5, 'was heavenly after a childhood spent among thick carpets and pictures in ponderous gilt frames'. That experience, which was replicated in many spaces by many people, can be seen as fundamental to modernity as a whole and is linked to the hyperconsciousness of the present that was part of it. Although, of course, not everyone suddenly threw out their chintz and embraced the machine in their inside spaces, the adoption of 'light and bright' historical styles, such as Louis XV and XVI, also offered an escape from the heaviness of the Victorian interior and had, therefore, a modernising effect.

The book begins with a section on the late nineteenth century that addresses the modern interior in Britain and Germany and presents a number of the themes which are readdressed in later chapters. From there, in Part Two, it moves on to the first four decades of the twentieth century, years in which the tension between modernism and other modern styles was at its strongest. The essays presented in this section reflect the two sides of the interior coin—Mies's austere settings, for example, in which decoration is provided only by the shadows that fall on their white walls and unornamented surfaces, are contrasted with Duncan Grant's colourful and patterned interior spaces. It is at this moment that the interior most nearly disappears from view, however, absorbed by the power of the modernists' architectural propositions. Yet even they, as the essays demonstrate, featured complex interiors which, for their inhabitants, were redolent of modernity and of their self-identities, as Elizabeth Darling explains in her account of examples of the interior work of the modernist architect Wells Coates.

Things changed fairly dramatically after 1940, as Part Three of the book reveals. The most important change, perhaps, was the loss of what seemed at the time to be a clear demarcation between the ideology of modernism and the alternative modern interior styles available in the marketplace. That occurred, for the most part, as a result of the widespread, international dissemination of modernism, its appropriation by new groups of aspiring consumers and its presence, in the marketplace, as a modern 'style' first and foremost. As Christopher Reed explains in Chapter 4, 'modernism was a style that, like the other styles, served as a signifier; modernist housing [and its interiors] looked practical, rational and functional'. At the same time, the forms of the modernist interior were softened and humanised and, at least in the domestic sphere, lost their prewar austerity. As a result, the edges between modernist and modern became blurred. The adoption and modification of prewar modernism that was undertaken by Charles and Ray Eames, especially in the interior, as described in Chapter 10, in the new context of what Charles Rice calls, 'mid-century modernism', exemplified that shift and provided a new modern aesthetic which, in turn, both informed the decoration of the popular home and entered into the public sphere in the form of the modernised office. Outside Europe and the United States, the relatively late importation of modernism had created a hiatus, and, when it finally arrived in a country such as Australia in the postwar years, its appearance and meanings related to those expressed in Europe and the United States a little earlier, rather than to the new setting in which it found itself. Describing that phenomenon in the context of his account of the interiors of the Rose Siedler house in Sydney, Charles Rice talks about 'the arrived appearance of the modern world'. A similar situation presented itself in Italy, which, in the interwar years, had been held back by the autarchy promoted by the country's fascist regime. Whilst modernism made an initial impact in Italy in the interwar years, it was in the postwar years that it came into its own, influencing furniture and product design in particular.

Another feature of the post-1940 years was, in contrast to the denial of it expressed by its interwar manifestation, mid-century modernism's open acknowledgment of the interior as an important agent of change in its own right. Linked, openly now, to the concept of lifestyle in the domestic setting, and to fantasy fulfilment in the public sphere, the interior had the potential, its creators now fully understood, to encourage modern experiences and behaviours. That sense of open acknowledgment of the interior within architecture was clear, as Peter Blundell Jones explains in Chapter 9, in the work of the German architect Hans Scharoun. The interior of the Berlin Philharmonie building is, for example, described as a 'cosy, private world', a phrase which recalls descriptions of the mid nineteenth-century bourgeois domestic sphere, now present, however, in the public sphere.

Whilst in the early twentieth century, interiors dedicated to semipublic and public leisure and display, as a strategy for letting (usually female) consumers feel 'at home' outside the home, often borrowed and adapted the language of the late nineteenth-century domestic interior, that phenomenon was not so much in evidence in years after 1940. Instead, given the growing confidence of consumers and others to inhabit it, the public sphere began to cannibalise itself. The Fontainebleau hotel in Miami, analysed by Alice Friedman in Chapter 12, for example, borrowed its forms from another public sphere interior, that of the ocean liner, a typology which was already associated with the qualities of glamour, leisure and pleasure that the architect, Morris Lapidus, wished to inject into his dramatic interior spaces. The range of, by then, sophisticated languages, or styles, of the modern interior thus had the potential to move increasingly, within the democratised world of postwar consumer culture, from first-level to second-level signs, in the language of semiotics as described by the French theorist Roland Barthes. In that context, the 'stage-set' view of the modern interior—the one in which the fact that the outside of a building and its inside had no obvious relationship with each other—came to the fore. This presaged the arrival of the postmodern interior—visible in the shopping malls and hotel interiors of Las Vegas and, later, the branded spaces of franchised interiors, such as those of the McDonald's hamburger restaurant chain and the fantasy interior spaces of Disneyland—and the 'hyper-reality' observed by the French cultural critic, Jean Baudrillard.

That notion of the interior as a fantasy was sustained, in the context of popular culture and of the popular home, in years after 1970. Increasingly, the modern interior presented itself in a plurality of possibilities expressing diverse identities, from domestic stage sets to Japanese love hotels to the 'unloved' spaces in Soviet communal housing blocks to, most recently, spaces which expressed our desire to develop, and to manifest within our homes, a new ethically rooted relationship with the world and its limited resources. In some ways things have gone full circle. The Victorian middle-class interior described by Walter Benjamin had been a site in which the morality associated with the life of the Christian family had been expressed. By the early twenty-first century, the secularism that modernity had brought in its wake had been replaced by a new 'religion'—that of sustainability.

This book takes readers through a rich, and hopefully engaging, journey that embraces many of the themes which penetrate the very heart of what it has meant to inhabit the modern world. The designers of the modern interior, in their different and sometimes conflicting ways, understood the experience of modernity at its most complex and, as this book demonstrates, created the interior settings in which that experience was and continues to be expressed. Geographically, *Designing the Modern Interior* covers work created in Britain, Europe—Germany, Italy, France and Russia in particular—the United States, Australia and Japan. As such, it goes a significant way to presenting a global overview of the impact of modernism and modernity in the context of the interior. Its editors, all of them members of Kingston University's Modern Interiors Research Centre, would like to thank all the contributors to the volume, their support team in their home institution, especially Fran Lloyd and Maureen Hourigan, and the editorial team at Berg.

Notes

1. S. Mallarmé, quoted in D. Riout, *Les écrivains devant l'Impressionisme,* Paris: Macula, 1989, p. 94.

2. Quoted in H. Eiland and K. McLaughlin, tr., *The Arcades Project: Walter Benjamin,* Cambridge, Mass. and London: The Belknap Press of Harvard University Press, 2004 [1999], pp. 8–9.

3. Writers on the subject of modernity include M. Berman, *All That Is Solid Melts into Air: The Experience of Modernity,* London: Verso, 1983; M. Daunton and B. Rieger eds., *Meanings of Modernity: Britain from the Late Victorian Era to World War II,* Oxford and New York: Berg, 2001; and R. Felski, *The Gender of Modernity,* Cambridge, Mass: Harvard University Press, 1995.

4. Interiority has been addressed in D. Fuss, *The Sense of an Interior: Four Rooms and the Writers That Shaped Them,* New York and London: Routledge, 2004, and V. Rosner, *Modernism and the Architecture of Private Life,* New York: Columbia University Press, 2005.

Part One

The Late Nineteenth-century Interior (1870–1900)

Part 1 Wickham Hall, Kent. Harold Palmer 1897.

Introduction

Emma Ferry

… in modern houses one seldom finds a room which makes a harmonious whole.[1]

The word 'modern' is among those discussed by Raymond Williams in *Keywords: A Vocabulary of Culture and Society* (1976). Sandwiched alphabetically (and rather aptly) between 'medieval' and 'monopoly', 'modern' has developed from its Latin root, *modo,* meaning 'just now', to encompass a range of related words including the more specialised 'modernise', 'modernisation', 'Modernism', 'modernist' and 'modernity', which form the common keywords of this book.

In his brief but beautifully clear essay, Williams notes the shifting and historically specific meanings of 'modern', particularly the persistence of 'unfavourable' and 'comparative' uses of the word and its associates, before highlighting a 'strong movement the other way, until modern became virtually equivalent to improved, or satisfactory or efficient'.[2] He notes that this 'strong movement' from negative to positive nuance began in the nineteenth century; however, it is a shift that is often difficult to detect in the publications about the interior produced by architects, designers, decorators and aesthetes towards the end of this period. For many of them, the word 'modern' was used to critique the contemporary, and this is especially evident in the design advice literature aimed at the domestic market.

Best known for its 'Design Reforming' discourse, Charles L. Eastlake's *Hints on Household Taste* (1868) contains a wealth of critical references to the 'modern'. For example 'the conventional ugliness of the modern drawing room'[3] and 'the extravagant and graceless appointments of the modern boudoir' which are 'mirrored on the modern canvas'[4] are denounced in the introduction. Subsequent chapters continue to criticise most things 'modern' from the 'legalized evils of modern house building'[5] to 'the hackneyed portraits of tame lions and grinning satyrs which have been adopted as types of the modern door-knocker'.[6] 'Modern' even appears in the index to *Hints* as a less-than-favourable subject for discussion:

Modern houses, inferior construction of, 32
Modern furniture, shabbiness of, 83

Several of the writers contributing to Macmillan's *Art at Home* series also condemned the 'modern'. A simple quantitative analysis of Rhoda and Agnes Garrett's *Suggestions in House Decoration* (1876) identifies the word twenty-two times, whilst a qualitative analysis demonstrates that, on each occasion, it is employed unfavourably.[7] The same is true of the often-quoted book *The Drawing Room*

(1877), written by Lucy Orrinsmith for the same series. In this case, 'modern' appears thirty-six times, again, in negative phrases such as:

> It must have been remarked that great artists never choose to represent an ordinary modern English house, either inside or out; the 'why' is obvious. Our houses are crowded with ugly shapes disguised by meretricious ornament. The general forms are usually so bad as to require to be loaded with excrescences, which, while they blunt the critical power of the eye, leave the mind dissatisfied.[8]

In 'Making the Best of It' (1880), a lecture that bears a striking similarity in both its scope and advice to *The Drawing Room,* William Morris uses the '*m* word' eight times, and, with the exception of his hopes for 'modern civilised society', the tone is once again decidedly unfavourable.[9] Queen Anne and Georgian houses, he told his audiences:

> are at the worst not aggressively ugly or base, and it is possible to live in them without serious disturbance to our work or thoughts; so that by the force of contrast they have become bright spots in the prevailing darkness of ugliness that has covered all modern life.[10]

Morris, that well-known 'pioneer of modern design', went on to complain that 'there is no dignity or unity of plan about any modern house, big or little,' and, when discussing the proportions of the rooms, commented that 'it will be great luck indeed in an ordinary modern house if they are tolerable; but let us hope for the best.' Moreover, whilst floors were one of the 'chief disgraces to modern buildings', and decorative treatments he proposed for ceilings were unlikely to be achieved in 'our modern makeshift houses', this was as nothing to the rant occasioned by the modern fireplace, which he condemned as 'mean, miserable, uncomfortable, and showy, plastered about with wretched sham ornament, trumpery of cast-iron, and brass and polished steel, and what not—offensive to look at, and a nuisance to clean'.[11]

Oscar Wilde's lecture, 'House Decoration', is also distinctly unfavourable when it comes to things 'modern.' Written hastily, with the aid of copies of W. J. Loftie's *A Plea for Art in the House* (1876) and Haweis's *The Art of Dress* (1879) whilst on tour in the United States, the man who was the persona of the Aesthetic Movement commented variously upon 'the abominations of modern fashionable attire', the coarseness and vulgarity of 'modern jewellery' and even described a contemporary museum as 'one of those dreadful modern institutions where there is a stuffed and very dusty giraffe, and a case or two of fossils'.[12]

This critique of the modern continued in the work of Mary Eliza Haweis, who, in *The Art of Decoration* (1882), used 'modern' ninety-nine times, again more often than not in an unfavourable and comparative manner: 'however well a thoroughly modern room is arranged, it wearies, and wants freshness.'[13] Like Eastlake, Morris, Wilde and the writers from the *Art at Home* series, Haweis urged readers to study models from the past, and, with the hope that her 'strictures on modern English decorations' would 'open the eyes of a few to the remediable flaws in taste'[14], she criticised all aspects of 'modern' architecture, design, furniture, the decorative arts, books, dress, workmanship and trade. Interestingly, though, 'modern science', 'modern mechanisms' and 'modern teaching' receive more favourable comments. Usefully, Haweis also defines what she at least meant by 'modern':

The Modern time must be defined as extending from 1700 to 1880, but for clearness' sake we will make a distinction between the Modern time (say up to 1850) and the present day.[15]

This somewhat baffling distinction between the 'Modern time' and the 'present day' demonstrates how problematic the word with its shifting meanings can be for the historian and highlights the often negative connotations the word carried during the last three decades of the nineteenth century.

The thirty-year period, 1870 to 1900, which forms the historical scope of the first section of *Designing the Modern Interior,* has received a great deal of attention from historians, critics and theorists working from within the disciplines of the histories of art, design and architecture. However, it is important to understand that the architecture and design of the Victorian period—'modern' or otherwise—has not always been looked on favourably. The best overview of Victorian architectural and (by extension) interior design history is to be found in David Watkin's *The Rise of Architectural History* (1980), which includes a chapter on 'Victorian and Neo-classical Studies' that charts the 'gradual rise of a sympathetic re-assessment of Victorian architecture' over a fifty-year period. From the 'amused affection'[16] fashionable among Oxford undergraduates in the 1920s to 'the

great variety of serious studies of Victorian architecture published in the 1960s and 70s'[17], Watkin considers the influence of the work of architectural historians and writers including H. S. Goodhart-Rendel, Kenneth Clarke, John Betjeman, Osbert Lancaster, Henry-Russell Hitchcock, Christopher Hussey and John Summerson.

Within Watkin's discussion, a number of important factors emerge that surround the 'modern', which have had a direct impact upon why and how the nineteenth century interior has been studied. First is the long-lasting influence of Nikolaus Pevsner's *Pioneers of the Modern Movement from William Morris to Walter Gropius* (1936), which Watkin describes as:

architectural history with a mission on a scale that had scarcely been seen since the days of Pugin. It was an attempt to persuade the English to accept the Modern Movement as the only style in which a modern man ought to express himself. It led to an historical approach which granted recognition to buildings or objects regarded as in a Line of Progress to the Authentic Modern Movement.[18]

The dominance of this approach explains the early tendencies of architectural and design historians working on the nineteenth century to focus upon the use of new materials and building types; to highlight the work of designers like Morris and Mackintosh; and to trace the emergence of the avant-garde rather than popular revival styles.[19] Indeed, lamenting the fact that the Modernist agenda focussed only upon the 'progressive aspects of the story', Peter Thornton, former

Keeper of the Department of Furniture and Woodwork at the Victoria and Albert Museum, commented, 'everyone knows something about William Morris, the Aesthetic Movement, Arts and Crafts, Art Nouveau, the Viennese *Secession,* Hoffmann, Frank Lloyd Wright and the Bauhaus.'[20] Despite Thornton's hopes that, from a critical evaluation of the Modern Movement, 'a rather more balanced assessment of the alternatives will emerge'[21], this version of nineteenth-century interior design history endures. In *Victorian and Edwardian Furniture and Interiors: From the Gothic Revival to Art Nouveau* (1987), Jeremy Cooper follows the Pevsnerian model with eight specialist chapters on A.W.N. Pugin, William Burges, 'Geometric Gothic', Aestheticism, Morris and Co., the Arts and Crafts Movement, 'New Art', ending with 'Heal's and Liberty's'. Although the taste for the exotic and Renaissance Revival styles are mentioned briefly in the introduction, Cooper's aim is to highlight the 'modern'. He concedes that 'Not all homes, of course, were progressive and modern in their design' but comments that:

> Unlike today, the designers of the best furniture between 1830 and 1915 were mostly practising architects and much of what they produced was progressively modern, so much so that even now chairs by Pugin, for instance, retain an air of elemental originality.[22]

So keen is Cooper to demonstrate that, 'despite his medievalism', Pugin was 'almost an early modern'[23], he fails to explore the range of revival styles, which should also be interpreted and analysed as a direct response to the forces of modernity and the threats posed by modern life. Fortunately, studies such as Simon Jervis's *High Victorian Design* (1983); Joanna Banham, Julia Porter and Sally MacDonald's *Victorian Interior Style* (1995); Charles Newton's *Victorian Designs for the Home* (1999) and *Design and the Decorative Arts: Victorian Britain 1837–1901* (2004) edited by Michael Snodin and John Styles have deliberately attempted to redress the balance and discussed the styles often missing (or simply dismissed as vulgar) from the history of nineteenth-century interiors. These include the Oriental styles (Chinese, Moorish and Indian); the Renaissance styles (Flemish, French, German and Italian); Egyptian, Pompeian and Greek styles (the latter often referred to as 'modern'); the Antiquarian or Early English (Elizabethan and Jacobean) styles; the Old French styles known as *Tous les Louis;* the 'Cottage' or Vernacular styles; the 'Queen Anne' Revival style; the Colonial Revival style that became popular in the United States after the Philadelphia Centennial Exposition of 1876 and the Neo-Georgian styles (Regency Revival, Empire Revival and neo-Biedermeier) that reappeared at the end of the century. Examining objects, designs and interiors, these studies allow for an investigation of the nineteenth-century interior as a cultural response to modernity in its broadest sense. Very often the use of revival styles is at the centre of the discussion. Indeed, Charles Newton asks:

> Why did the Victorians employ a mixture of styles from the past instead of inventing something totally new? They had invented an impressive range of completely new things in other areas,

and had immense confidence in their radically new designs for engineering for example. Why did they not also find a completely new style of decorative art appropriate to the age?[24]

Given that the majority of these more recent publications have been produced by curatorial staff and scholars from the Victoria and Albert Museum, it is not surprising that another factor that has encouraged the study of the nineteenth-century interior is the exhibition of collections of nineteenth-century furniture and decorative arts from the 1950s onwards. Watkin identifies *Victorian and Edwardian Decorative Arts,* which was held at the Victoria and Albert Museum (V&A) in 1952 as the first and one of the most significant of these exhibitions, but stresses that the exhibits were chosen 'in accordance with Pevsnerian orthodoxy in which special emphasis was placed on what was regarded as sincerity and originality'.[25] Indeed, Peter Floud's introduction to the catalogue noted:

We have deliberately eliminated what was merely freakish or grotesque. At the same time we have purposely left out a whole host of Victorian designers whose work was unashamedly based on the copying of earlier styles.[26]

Nevertheless, this exhibition gave impetus to the collection of nineteenth-century objects and furnishings and was succeeded by other Victorian exhibitions organised by the V&A during the 1970s, which drew on the expertise of curators who had all written on aspects of Victorian design and decorative arts.[27] The importance of these later exhibitions, *Victorian Church Art* (1971–2); *'Marble Halls':*

Drawings and Models for Victorian Secular Buildings (1973) and *High Victorian Design* (1974–5) 'consisted in their emancipation from the ambition of excluding from our understanding of Victorian design anything that in 1952 would have been considered insincere, grotesque or imitative'.[28] The high-profile exhibitions, particularly those organised at the V&A, such as *Pugin: A Gothic Passion* (1994), *William Morris* (1996), *Art Nouveau* (2000), *The Victorian Vision* (2001), *Christopher Dresser 1834–1904: A Design Revolution* (2004), *Thomas Hope: Regency Designer* (2008) and the permanent collections displayed in the refurbished British Galleries 1500–1900 continue to be significant to the study of both the nineteenth century and the interior.[29]

As well as providing a focus for exhibitions, a number of museums play an important role in the study of the late nineteenth-century interior. The archives, collections and National Art Library at the V&A offer historians a wide range of research materials and expertise. Similarly, smaller London-based museums, such as the Geffrye Museum and the Museum of Domestic Architecture and Design, offer access to a range of objects, period room displays and archival materials as well as hold exhibitions and produce publications that are specific to aspects of the interior.[30]

The third important factor that has affected the study of the nineteenth-century interior is the development of the preservation movement. Watkin stresses the significance of the foundation of pressure groups such as the Victorian Society (f. 1958) and Marcus Binney's SAVE Britain's Heritage (f. 1975), whose popular, though sometimes unsuccessful, campaigns to save monuments, buildings and interiors threatened by postwar urban redevelopment and modernisation have helped raise the profile of existing nineteenth-century buildings and interiors.[31] The work of the Victorian Society, which celebrated its fiftieth anniversary in early 2008, today encompasses a range of activities at national, regional and personal levels. For example, under the Town and Country Planning Act (1969), the Society comments upon all applications involving demolition and it continues to campaign to save threatened Victorian sites; it organises local events including architectural walks and visits to important Victorian buildings and it offers advice to Victorian home owners through lectures and study days and a range of publications, such as the Society's journal, *The Victorian,* a series of booklets titled *Care for Victorian Houses* and Kit Wedd's book *The Victorian Society Book of the Victorian House* (2002).

The preservation movement and the debates surrounding 'heritage' and 'conservation' have generated a tremendous amount of literature—some practical, others polemical. Focusing upon the work of organisations like the Society for the Protection of Ancient Buildings (f. 1877), the National Trust (f. 1895), the Historic Houses Association (f. 1973) and English Heritage (f. 1984), a number of scholars have considered the display of the historic house interior.[32] Here, the emphasis is often on museological concerns rather than 'the interior', and the debates consider the various techniques employed by these organisations and private owners such as the creation of the 'country house' look,

academic restoration projects, 'preserve as found' or the preservation of 'layers of occupation'.[33]

The final important factor that emerges from Watkin's discussion is found in his concluding chapter, 'Some Recent Tendencies'. Writing in 1980, Watkin commented upon the 'increasingly determined attempts', prompted by an interest in Marxist theories in the 1960s and 1970s, 'to relate buildings to the society in which they were produced, and for the way of life for which it is believed that they and their contents were originally intended.'[34] This shift in architectural history was complemented by the emergence of design history as a separate discipline in the 1970s. Of particular importance for the present study, Watkin noted that this 'interest in the interlocking patterns of environment and social activity' was reflected 'in the study of interior design and furnishings, including the use and arrangement of furniture'.[35] Linked closely to the development of the preservation movement and the emergence of heritage tourism, the earliest studies of the interior also reflect an interest in the country house, perhaps inspired by the exhibition, *The Destruction of the English Country House*, held at the V&A in 1974. According to Clive Wainwright, this 'epoch-making' exhibition aroused 'public anger at such wanton destruction' and 'focussed attention upon the history and the surviving documentation of both destroyed and surviving houses'.[36] The country house interior became the subject of pioneering work by John Fowler and John Cornforth, whose work was the direct result of the authors' concerns 'about the problems of preservation, restoration and presentation of country houses'.[37]

This early interest in the country house also indicates the partial nature of the study of the nineteenth-century interior. As the authors of *Victorian Interior Style* (1995) remark:

> the majority of working-class people in both Britain and America could not afford to decorate and furnish their homes with new and fashionable products. Few writers wrote for working-class readers or bothered to describe working-class homes. Few artists or photographers chose to record them. Surviving interiors, even individual items of furniture are rare; in poorer homes most things were used until they were worn out.[38]

Thus, the dominance of Modernist design histories of the nineteenth century since the 1930s, influential exhibitions of nineteenth-century art, architecture and design from the early 1950s and the emergence of the preservation movement combined with shifts in architectural and design histories from the mid 1960s onwards have all impacted upon the study of the 'modern' interior. However, as Penny Sparke has commented, 'significant studies of the history of the design and decoration of the interior are few and far between'[39]. They become fewer and even further between once the historical scope is limited to a single century.

Fortunately, whilst the interior is still emerging as a fruitful field for historical enquiry, the last thirty years has seen growing interest in nineteenth-century culture. Influenced by critical theories, the period has become the subject of rich multi and interdisciplinary work by historians and scholars from a wide range of disciplines, which, in addition to art, design and architectural history, include literary history, gender studies, philosophy, sociology, cultural geography and anthropology. The fascination with an era of high imperialism, emerging nationhoods, religious revivals and crises of faith, contested gender and class politics and public debates on sexuality has resulted in the publication of more nuanced and complex analyses of the late nineteenth-century interior, both public and private, which move beyond simple discussions of style to highlight the connection between the interior and consumption, taste and identity. Whilst Adrian Forty's classic text, *Objects of Desire: Design and Society 1750–1980* (1986), includes an important chapter on 'The Home', which stressed the importance of gender and class identities in the construction and maintenance of the domestic interior, this shift in emphasis has been made explicit in more recent publications such as *Interior Design and Identity* (2004) edited by Suzie McKellar and Penny Sparke and in *Intimus: Interior Design Theory Reader* (2006) edited by Mark Taylor and Julieanna Preston, both of which aim—in very different ways—to make interior design history *and* its theories conspicuous as an emerging discipline.[40] Both studies highlight the many challenges the interior poses for historical and theoretic analysis and the centrality of gender to that analysis.[41] Indeed, Taylor and Preston comment:

> any book on theory surrounding interior design can not escape discussion about feminism, gender, race and sexuality, if not because of interior design's own history as a practice

stemming from the upholsterer's trade then for its alliances (or stereotype associations) with domestic, residential and feminine decorative practice.[42]

What follows is an attempt to offer a broad survey of publications relevant to the study of the late nineteenth-century interior published since the mid 1980s. It is not intended as an exhaustive bibliography, but instead an overview of studies produced from within this emerging field of research that are interesting and inspiring. The publications included here demonstrate the diversity of source materials and historical evidence left behind by the makers of the late nineteenth-century interior; some of them also highlight the range of methodological approaches and tools of analysis which can be employed.

There are a number of books based on the collection, organisation and analysis of nineteenth-century visual culture which incorporate a range of media: painting, drawing, engravings and the new medium of photography.[43] The type of images considered includes designs, plans, advertisements, cartoons and caricature, magazine illustrations, interior views and portraiture. This wealth of visual materials reflects the fascination with the interior and the objects and ideas contained within it during this period. Inspired by the work of Mario Praz (1964),[44] Peter Thornton's seminal study, *Authentic Décor: The Domestic Interior, 1620–1920* (1984), devotes an entire chapter to the period 1870 to 1920, which, in an attempt to counter the dominance of Modernist discourse, includes a wealth of images of 'delightful, extremely comfortable and in no way despicable interiors' in the popular styles that sprang from neoclassicism to evolve into what is sometimes termed 'Free Renaissance'.[45] Geographically, this visual survey covers the western world, and the images of domestic interiors that Thornton discusses have been selected from a range of sources—magazine illustrations; advertisements in trade catalogues; plates from influential publications written by architects, designers and upholsterers; room plans; paintings of interiors and photographic collections.

Along similar lines, Charlotte Gere's *Nineteenth Century Decoration: The Art of the Interior* (1989) is a collection of exclusively nineteenth-century imagery. Divided into twenty-year periods from 1800 to 1900, this study examines a range of domestic interiors; it also very usefully includes a bibliography of nineteenth and early twentieth-century works and a biographical index of artists, designers, decorators and architects.

However, unlike Frances Borzello's study, *At Home: The Domestic Interior in Art* (2006), neither Thornton nor Gere offer readers art historical interpretations of the interiors reproduced; instead, the images are discussed as fairly straightforward historical evidence. Whilst Thornton's assertion that 'these illustrations show rooms as they actually were'[46] will continue to be contested, both *Authentic Décor* and *Nineteenth Century Decoration* remain essential reading for the study of the interior. In contrast, the problems of interpreting representations and the changing meaning of the domestic interior in its broadest sense are placed at the very centre of *Imagined Interiors:*

Representing the Domestic Interior since the Renaissance (2006).[47]

Whilst the main emphasis of these studies is visual evidence, other historians have interrogated texts taken from a wide range of nineteenth-century publications. Occupying a position somewhere 'between fact and fiction', domestic design advice is a complex source, often more concerned with the formation of class and gender ideologies than with suggestions about interior decoration.[48] Indeed, as Elizabeth Langland has commented, 'these non-literary materials did not simply reflect a "real" historical subject, but helped to produce it through their discursive practices.'[49] Similarly, in her introduction to that quintessential advice book, *Mrs Beeton's Book of Household Management,* Nicola Humble stressed the value of studying this type of nonfictional text but added a note of caution:

> It is precisely because they are an ephemeral, market-led form of writing that cookery books reveal so much about the features of a particular historical moment. We must remember, though, that like any other text they consist of constructed discourse, and can never be clear windows onto the kitchens of the past.[50]

However, few scholars have made clear the distinction between advice and evidence or between prescription and practice. Some have commented on this difficulty. Jane Rendall for example has noted that the 'proliferation of all kinds of advice manuals … has left historians at times confused as to the extent to which such advice was ever taken, even practicable'.[51] Other scholars,

whilst acknowledging this dilemma, have nonetheless emphasised the popularity of the genre, suggesting that 'it is hard to over-estimate the role of the household book in promoting the ideal pattern of middle-class life.'[52]

Following the organising principles of the domestic advice manual, Judith Flanders's hugely successful popular history, *The Victorian House: Domestic Life from Childbirth to Deathbed* (2003), is a gendered account of Victorian urban domestic space that describes the functions and arrangement of the middle-class home whilst relating different rooms in the house to events in the female life cycle. Focusing on the period 1850 to 1890, this book aims to compare the 'theoretical' domestic space prescribed by advice manuals and described in contemporary novels with the 'reality' of Victorian diaries and memoirs. However, whilst she acknowledges that these represent an ideal, she nonetheless treats them simplistically as historical evidence rather than considering them as a literary genre.

A special issue of the *Journal of Design History* (2003), edited by Grace Lees-Maffei, examined domestic design advice literature and included several articles that considered the role this type of literature played in the formation of the nineteenth-century domestic interior and the writers associated with this type of literature. Moreover, providing a methodological context, the editor's essay, 'Studying Advice: Historiography, Methodology, Commentary, Bibliography', considered the problems of using advice literature.[53] My own contribution to this special issue, '"Decorators May Be Compared to

Doctors": An Analysis of Rhoda and Agnes Garretts' *Suggestions for House Decoration* (1876)', argues that domestic advice manuals cannot be used as conventional historical evidence, and suggests that they need to be understood both as historical documents that engage with contemporary notions of design and taste *and* as a genre of Victorian literature.

Offering arguably clearer windows on to the interiors of the past, other studies have examined examples of nineteenth-century texts that relate to the construction of the interior, sometimes quite literally. The number of publications aimed at the artist, the decorator, the furniture maker or retailer, the architectural profession and building trades that were published during the course of the nineteenth century is quite staggering: the number of magazine titles that appeared in this period is particularly noteworthy. These include, alphabetically: *The Architect* (f. 1869), *Architectural Review* (f. 1896), *Art and Decoration* (1885–6), *The Art Designer* (f. 1884), *Art Journal* (1839–1911), *Art Union* (1838–49), *Art Workman* (1873–83), *The Artist* (1880–92), *Artist and Journal of Home Culture* (1880–94), *British Architect and Northern Engineer* (f. 1874), *The Builder* (f. 1843), *Building News* (1855–1926), *Cabinet Maker and Art Furnisher* (f. 1880), *Cabinet Maker's Assistant* (f. 1853), *Cabinet Maker's Monthly Journal of Design* (f. 1856), *The Craftsman* (1901–16), *Decoration in Painting, Architecture, Furniture etc.*, (1880–93), *The Decorator* (1864), *The Ecclesiologist* (1841–68), *The Furnisher* (1899–1901), *Furniture and Decoration* (1890–98), *Furniture Gazette* (1872–93), *Hobby Horse* (1884–8), *The House* (1897–1902), *House Furnisher and Decorator* (1872–3), *Journal of Decorative Art* (1881–1937), *Journal of Design and Manufacturing* (1849–52), *Magazine of Art* (1878–1904), *The Studio* (f. 1893) and *The Workshop* (1869–72).[54]

This long list, for which I apologise, is intended to highlight the wealth of periodical material available for the study of the interior that a number of scholars have drawn upon to produce interesting and informative studies.[55] For example, Helen Long's *Victorian Houses and Their Details: The Role of Publications in Their Building and Decoration* (2002) draws upon publications that include architectural pattern books, trade manuals, decoration and home manuals, trade catalogues, pattern books of designs and journals of architecture, building trades and home furnishing. Set in the context of the nineteenth-century publishing world and the development of illustrative printing techniques in these types of publications, this study explores their importance in the transmission of practical advice and taste and demonstrates the profusion of published materials available for the study of the interior in this period.[56]

Other types of textual materials, such as inventories, probate records, private letters and diaries, have also been subject to critical investigation. Margaret Ponsonby's *Stories from Home: English Domestic Interiors 1750–1850* (2007) uses lists of houses' contents as its main type of documentary evidence. Just outside the period covered by this volume, the methodological discussion within this study provides an interesting and useful addition to fuel current debates surrounding source material and the methods of analysis and interpretation employed by scholars working in this fascinating field.[57] A number of the essays published in *Women and the Making of Built Space in England, 1870–1950* (2007), edited by Elizabeth Darling and Lesley Whitworth, also draw upon texts of a private nature. In his essay '"Everything Whispers of Wealth and Luxury": Observation, Emulation and Display in the Well-to-do Late-Victorian Home', Trevor Keeble, who has edited and contributed to the present study, draws upon the diary of Emily Hall and the letters of Maud Messel in order to explore the extent to which late-Victorian domestic space was both a gendered and a fluid social construction. In 'Women Rent Collectors and the Rewriting of Space, Class and Gender in East London, 1870–1900', Ruth Livesey uses the diary of Beatrice Webb in a case study of the women rent collectors at the Katharine Buildings, a block of model flats in the East End of London.[58]

There are also a few thought-provoking studies that are based on an analysis of the 'interior' as it has been represented in nineteenth-century fiction. The first of these studies was Philippa Tristram's *Living Space in Fact and Fiction* (1989), which considered the domestic interior of very different types of buildings described in a range of nineteenth-century novels, including Jane Austen's *Sense and Sensibility* (1811), Charles Dickens's *Bleak House* (1852–3), George Eliot's *Middlemarch* (1871–2), Thomas Hardy's *Far from the Madding Crowd* (1874), and Henry James's *The Spoils of Poynton* (1896). Sharon Marcus's *Apartment Stories: City and Home in Nineteenth Century Paris and London* (1999), *Domestic Space: Reading the 19th*

Century Interior (1999) edited by Janet Floyd and Inga Bryden and Thad Logan's *The Victorian Parlour: A Cultural Study* (2001) have also used literature, art historical and other sources to explore and interpret the interior. Fiction is, however, an incredibly problematic source as is demonstrated in 'The Domestic Interior in British Literature', an issue of *Home Cultures* (2005) edited by Charlotte Grant.[59]

The mediated nature of these types of primary materials has meant that the use of images and texts as design historical evidence has prompted a great deal of critical debate. Similarly, analytical work has been published in the field of architectural history, which also has implications for the study of the interior. The nineteenth century was a period that saw the development of a range of new building types that emerged as a direct result of industrialisation accompanied by resultant political, economic, social and religious changes and made possible by new technologies, materials and construction techniques. These new building types include sites of production, exchange and consumption: the factories, warehouses, office buildings, financial institutions and department stores; places of entertainment: hotels, clubs and music halls; and the spaces of culture and collection such as board schools, exhibition halls, libraries, art galleries and museums. Significantly, many of these buildings were directly affected by legislation at both national and local levels. Moreover, the period also saw the development and re-formation of older building types such as places of worship, army barracks, hospitals and asylums, prisons and theatres. During this period, each of these new or redeveloped building types required and acquired specialised forms of interior design, many of which persist today. Consequently, there are a number of informative and well-researched studies based upon an examination of surviving nineteenth-century buildings, topographical collections, photographic surveys, architectural drawings and plans. These offer either broad chronologies of Victorian architecture, case studies of particular building types or monographs of individual architects and designers. However, in *Buildings and Power: Freedom and Control in the Origin of Modern Building Types* (1993; 2004), Thomas A. Markus analyses the form, function and space of a range of buildings in what is a fascinating and inspirational study that offers the historian of the modern interior much to think about.[60]

The late nineteenth-century interior: Three new essays

The essays in this section of *Designing the Modern Interior* make new contributions to the historiography of the late-nineteenth-century interior. In '"Plate Glass and Progress": Victorian Modernity at Home', Trevor Keeble draws upon Lewis F. Day's lecture 'Commonsense House Decoration', which was published by the *Furniture Gazette* in 1883, to demonstrate the ways in which a dialogue of 'progressive' domestic furnishing and arrangement was unfolding during this time. The chapter considers the ways in which design professionals and householders jostled for position within this rhetoric and

the role that 'style' and 'presentation' played in the negotiation of tradition and modernity. Whilst 'Commonsense House Decoration' and the broader discourse of furnishing within the *Furniture Gazette* clearly anticipates early twentieth-century discussions of modernism, Keeble's chapter rejects an interpretation of this as protomodernism. Instead, he suggests that this discussion should be read as symptomatic of a nascent modernity that might have yielded possibilities for the following century other than those that coalesced into modernism.

In 'Privacy and Supervision in the Modernised Public House Interior, 1872–1902', Fiona Fisher examines the spatial and visual relations of the late Victorian public house. Set within the context of contemporary concerns surrounding alcohol consumption and intemperance, through an examination of surviving plans, Parliamentary papers, government legislation, contemporary photographs, newspaper reports and trade publications such as the *Barman and Barmaid* and the *Licensed Victuallers' Gazette,* Fisher demonstrates how the interiors of London's late nineteenth-century public houses were adapted to moderate and mediate social activity. In particular, this chapter highlights the use of visual and spatial divisions such as curtains, counter screens and partitions to negotiate a period of rapidly changing custom and instability in urban social relations.

Finally, in her chapter 'The German Interior at the End of the Nineteenth Century', art historian Sabine Wieber considers the two rooms designed by Martin Dülfer (1859–1942) and Theodor Fischer (1862–1938) displayed in the *Glaspalast* at Munich's Seventh International

Art Exhibition in 1897. Recognised as the first manifestation of Germany's *Jugendstil,* the two rooms have been celebrated as the eagerly anticipated arrival of a truly modern style of interior design in central Europe. Drawing upon the contemporary rhetoric surrounding the exhibition published in a range of German-language magazines such as *Deutsche Kunst und Dekoration, Pan* and *Kunst und Handwerk,* Wieber interrogates the meanings of the terms 'modern' and 'modernity' used to describe Dülfer's and Fischer's interiors to uncover the complex and often contradictory nature of this modernity.

Highlighting the problems associated with the word 'modern' in this period, all three essays demonstrate the range of materials available for the study and analysis of the late nineteenth-century interior; moreover, this diversity in subject matter, source materials, methodology and interpretation emphasises the rich and exciting possibilities of this developing field of research.

Notes

1. R. Garrett and A. Garrett, *Suggestions for House Decoration in Painting, Woodwork and Furniture* (Macmillan, 1876), p. 6.
2. R. Williams, *Keywords: Vocabulary of Culture and Society* (Fontana Press, 1983, revised and expanded edition), pp. 208–9.
3. C. L. Eastlake, *Hints on Household Taste in Furniture, Upholstery and Other Details,* 4th edition (Longmans, Green, 1878), p. 6.
4. Ibid., p. 7.
5. Ibid., p. 29.
6. Ibid., p. 45.

7. For a comparison of Eastlake's *Hints* with the Garrett's *Suggestions,* see my article '"Decorators May Be Compared to Doctors": An Analysis of Rhoda and Agnes Garrett's *Suggestions for House Decoration* (1876)', *Journal of Design History* 16/1 (2003). An excerpt (pp. 26–9) has been reprinted together with an extract from Eastlake's *Hints* in M. Taylor and J. Preston, *Intimus: Interior Design Theory Reader* (John Wiley & Sons, 2006), pp. 110–116.
8. L. Orrinsmith, *The Drawing Room: Its Decoration and Furniture* (Macmillan, 1877), p. 6. For an overview of the production of Macmillan's Art at Home series and a discussion of the dangers of using this type of literature as historical evidence, see my chapter '"… Information for the Ignorant and Aid for the Advancing …" Macmillan's "Art at Home Series", 1876–1883' in J. Aynsley and K. Forde, *Design and the Modern Magazine* (Manchester University Press, 2007).
9. W. Morris, 'Making the Best of It', December 1880. The production of this familiar publication is complex. On 13 November 1880, Morris delivered a version of this lecture (then titled 'Some Hints on House Decoration') before the Trades Guild of Learning in the lecture hall of the Society of Arts, John Street, Adelphi. On 20 November 1880, *The Architect* published a summary of Morris's lecture as 'Making the Best of It' (p. 318). A second version of 'Making the Best of It' was published in *The Artist* in December 1880. In December 1880, Morris delivered 'Some Hints on House Decoration' at the Royal Society of Artists, Birmingham, and on 18 December 1880, *The Architect* printed the first instalment of 'Making the Best of It' as 'Hints on House Decoration' (pp. 384–7). The second part appeared on 25 December 1880 (pp. 400–2). The essay was finally published in *Hopes and Fears for Art,* which is a collection of talks given by William Morris during the late 1870s and early 1880s. The talks were first published in book form by Ellis and White in 1882 and were reissued

in 1883, 1896, 1898, 1903, 1911 and 1919. It was reprinted in Bristol by the Thoemmes Press in 1994. A version taken from the 1919 Longmans, Green and Co. Pocket Library edition, originally prepared by David Price for Project Gutenberg and converted to XHTML by Graham Seaman, is available online at www.marxist.org.uk.

10. W. Morris, 'Making the Best of It' (December 1880).

11. Ibid.

12. O. Wilde, 'House Decoration', in *Essays and Lectures by Oscar Wilde* (Methuen, 1908). This lecture was delivered in the United States during Wilde's tour in 1882. Announced in the US press as 'The Practical Application of the Principles of Aesthetic Theory to Exterior and Interior House Decoration, With Observations upon Dress and Personal Ornaments', the title of Wilde's lecture on interior decoration varied between 'House Decoration' (first delivered in May 1882) and 'The House Beautiful', reflecting the popularity of the American Clarence Cook's successful advice manual, *The House Beautiful* (1876). The earliest date on which the lecture is known to have been given is 11 May 1882.

13. M. E. Haweis, *The Art of Decoration* (Chatto & Windus, 1881), Book 1, Chapter 1, p. 16.

14. Haweis, *The Art of Decoration,* Book 3, Chapter 11, p. 396.

15. Haweis, *The Art of Decoration,* Book 2, Chapter 1, p. 60.

16. D. Watkin, *The Rise of Architectural History* (Architectural Press, 1980), p. 165.

17. Ibid., p. 174. Chronologically, these publications include P. Ferriday, ed., with an introduction by Sir John Betjeman, *Victorian Architecture* (Jonathan Cape, 1963); R. Furneaux-Jordan, *Victorian Architecture* (Penguin, 1966); J. Summerson, *Victorian Architecture, Four Studies in Evaluation* (Columbia University Press, 1970); M. Girouard, *The Victorian Country House* (Yale University Press, 1971); R. Macleod, *Style and Society,*

Architectural Ideology in Britain 1840–1914 (Royal Institute of British Architects, 1971); P. Stanton, *Pugin* (Thames & Hudson, 1971); P. Thompson, *William Butterfield* (Routledge & Kegan Paul, 1971); J. M. Crook, *The Greek Revival: Neo-Classical Attitudes in British Architecture 1760–1870* (John Murray, 1972); S. Muthesius, *The High Victorian Moment in Architecture 1850–1870* (Routledge & Kegan Paul, 1972); N. Pevsner, *Some Architectural Writers of the Nineteenth Century* (Clarendon Press, 1972); M. Girouard, *Sweetness and Light, the 'Queen Anne' Movement 1860–1900* (Yale University Press, 1977); M. Girouard, *Life in an English Country House, a Social and Architectural History* (Yale University Press, 1978); and R. Dixon and S. Muthesius, *Victorian Architecture* (Thames & Hudson, 1978).

18. Watkin, *The Rise of Architectural History,* p. 170.

19. See for example E. Aslin, *The Aesthetic Movement: Prelude to Art Nouveau* (Elek Books, 1969); N. Pevsner, 'Art Furniture of the 1870s', in *Studies in Art, Architecture and Design* (Thames & Hudson, 1969); M. Girouard, *Sweetness and Light;* G. Naylor, *The Arts and Crafts Movement: A Study of Its Sources, Ideals and Influences on Design Theory* (Trefoil, 1990); E. Cumming & W. Kaplan, *The Arts and Crafts Movement* (Thames & Hudson, 1991); M. Richardson, *Architects of the Arts & Crafts Movement* (Trefoil/Royal Institute of British Architects, 1983); I. Anscombe & C. Gere, *Arts and Crafts in Britain and America* (Academy Editions, 1978); S. Escritt, *Art Nouveau* (Phaidon, 2000); P. Greenhalgh, ed., *Art Nouveau: 1890–1914* (Victoria and Albert Museum, 2000).

20. P. Thornton, *Authentic Decor: The Domestic Interior 1620–1920* (Weidenfeld & Nicolson, 1993), p. 308.

21. Ibid.

22. J. Cooper, *Victorian and Edwardian Furniture and Interiors: From the Gothic Revival to Art Nouveau* (Thames & Hudson, 1987), p. 7.

23. Ibid., pp. 7–8, quoting from W. R. Lethaby's *Philip Webb and His Work* (Oxford University Press, 1935).

24. C. Newton, *Victorian Designs for the Home* (V&A Publications, 1999), p. 8.

25. Watkin, *The Rise of Architectural History,* p. 174.

26. P. Floud, 'Introduction', *Victorian and Edwardian Decorative Arts* (Victoria and Albert Museum, 1952), p. 5, quoted in Watkin, *The Rise of Architectural History,* p. 174.

27. These notable curators include Elizabeth Aslin, Simon Jervis and Clive Wainwright. See for example E. Aslin, *Nineteenth Century English Furniture* (Faber & Faber, 1962); E. Aslin, *The Aesthetic Movement: Prelude to Art Nouveau* (Elek Books, 1969); S. Jervis, *Victorian Furniture* (Ward Lock, 1968); S. Jervis, *Nineteenth Century Papier Mâché* (Her Majesty's Stationery Office, 1973); S. Jervis, *High Victorian Design* (Boydell, 1983); C. Wainwright, 'A.W.N. Pugin's Early Furniture', *Connoisseur* 191/767 (1976) pp. 3–11; C. Wainwright, *George Bullock: Cabinet-Maker* (Murray, 1988); C. Wainwright, *The Romantic Interior: The British Collector at Home 1750–1850* (Yale University Press, 1989); P. Atterbury and C. Wainwright, eds, *Pugin: A Gothic Passion* (V&A Publications, 1994).

28. Watkin, *The Rise of Architectural History,* p. 174. *High Victorian Design* toured Canada but was not displayed in London. Watkin also highlights *Victorian and Edwardian Decorative Art,* an exhibition of the collection of Charles and Lavinia Handley-Read (both d. 1971) held at the Royal Academy of Arts in 1972.

29. These exhibitions and new galleries have been accompanied by lavishly illustrated books and catalogues, which include essays written by curatorial staff and other scholars of international repute working in these areas.

30. See for example C. Gere, with L. Hoskins, *The House Beautiful: Oscar Wilde and the Aesthetic Interior* (Lund Humphries/Geffrye Museum, 2000), which was published on the occasion of the exhibition *The House Beautiful: Oscar Wilde and the Aesthetic Interior* at the Geffrye Museum 18 July 2000 to 21 January 2001.

31. Founded by the Countess of Rosse at 18 Stafford Terrace (Linley Sambourne House) with the support of Sir John Betjeman and Christopher Hussey, among the high-profile but ultimately unsuccessful campaigns launched by the Victorian Society were the 'Save the Arch' campaign led by Betjeman to preserve the Euston Arch built by Philip and P. C. Hardwick (1835–9) and the attempt to save J. B. Bunning's Coal Exchange (1847–9); both were demolished in 1962. More successful campaigns include 'the Battle of Bedford Park'.

32. English Heritage, officially known as the Historic Buildings and Monuments Commission for England, was founded following the passing of the National Heritage Act in 1983.

33. The following studies relate to the presentation of historic houses in Britain, Europe and America rather than the wider heritage industry debates or histories of the preservation movement: E. Barker, 'Heritage and the Country House', in E. Barker, ed., *Contemporary Cultures of Display* (Yale University Press, 1999); G. Chitty and D. Baker, eds., *Managing Sites and Buildings: Reconciling Presentation and Preservation* (Routledge, 1999); J. Cornforth, *The Country Houses of England, 1948–98* (Constable, 1998); J. F. Donnelly, ed., *Interpreting Historic House Museums* (Altamira Press, 2002); J. Fawcett, ed., *The Future of the Past: Attitudes to Conservation 1174–1974* (Thames & Hudson, 1976); V. Horie, ed., *The Conservation of Decorative Arts* (Archetype Publications, 1999); G. Jackson-Stops, ed., *The Treasure Houses of Britain* (National Gallery of Art, Washington, DC, 1985); P. Mandler, *The Rise and Fall of the Stately Home* (Yale University Press, 1997); G. W. McDonald, *Hearth and Home: Preserving a People's Culture* (Temple University

Press, 1982); M. Ponsonby, *Stories from Home: English Domestic Interiors 1750–1850* (Ashgate, 2007); A. Tinniswood, *The Polite Tourist: A History of Country House Visiting* (National Trust, 1998); P. West, *Domesticating History: The Political Origins of America's House Museum* (Smithsonian Institution Press, 1999).

34. Watkin, *The Rise of Architectural History,* p. 183.

35. Ibid., p. 186.

36. C. Wainwright, *The Romantic Interior: The British Collector at Home 1750–1850* (Yale University Press, 1989), p. 2. Other notable publications that relate to this area include M. Girouard, *The Victorian Country House* (Yale University Press, 1971; 2nd edition,1980); M. Girouard, *Life in the English Country House* (Yale University Press, 1978); and J. Franklin, *The Gentleman's Country House and Its Plan* (Routledge & Kegan Paul, 1981).

37. J. Fowler and J. Cornforth, *English Decoration in the 18th Century* (Barrie & Jenkins, 1974; revised edition, 1978); J. Cornforth, *English Interiors 1700–1848: the Quest for Comfort* (Barrie & Jenkins, 1978); and Louise Ward's critique of English Country House style in 'Chintz, Swags and Bows: The Myth of the English Country House Style', *Things* 5 (Winter 1996–7), pp. 7–37, reprinted in S. McKellar and P. Sparke, eds., *Interior Design and Identity* (Manchester University Press, 2004).

38. J. Banham, J. Porter and S. MacDonald, *Victorian Interior Style* (Studio Editions, 1995), p.10 [first published by Cassell as *Victorian Interior Design* in 1991].

39. P. Sparke, 'Introduction', in McKellar and Sparke, *Interior Design and Identity,* pp. 1–9.

40. Both publications contain essays that consider aspects of the late nineteenth-century interior. See McKellar and Sparke, *Interior Design and Identity,* and Taylor and Preston, *Intimus.*

41. Gender is the dominant tool of analysis in a number of important books that relate to interior design in the nineteenth century. See for example the early chapters of Penny Sparke's *As Long as It's Pink: The Sexual Politics of Taste* (Pandora, 1995), which examines domesticity and feminine taste in the context of the design reform movement in the period 1830–90, highlighting the importance of the home and its much-contested decoration to middle-class identity and status, and Juliet Kinchin's essay, 'The Gendered Interior: Nineteenth Century Essays on the "Masculine" and the "Feminine" Room', in Pat Kirkham, ed., *The Gendered Object* (Manchester University Press, 1996), which examines the gendered nature of the middle-class dining room and the drawing room of the Victorian home. Interestingly, *A View from the Interior: Women and Design* (Women's Press, 1995), edited by Judy Attfield and Pat Kirkham, which presents the subject of design history from a feminist perspective, uses 'interior' within the title 'as a metaphor for the archetypal feminine position'. See J. Attfield and P. Kirkham, eds., 'Introduction to the Second Edition' in Attfield and Kirkham, *A View from the Interior,* p. 1.

42. Taylor and Preston, *Intimus,* p. 10.

43. See N. Cooper, *The Opulent Eye: Late Victorian and Edwardian Taste in Interior Design* (Architectural Press, 1979).

44. M. Praz, *An Illustrated History of Interior Decoration, from Pompeii to Art Nouveau* (Thames & Hudson, 1964).

45. Thornton, *Authentic Decor,* p. 308.

46. Ibid., p. 8.

47. Edited by Jeremy Aynsley and Charlotte Grant, *Imagined Interiors: Representing the Domestic Interior since the Renaissance* (V&A Publications, 2006), is the product of the Arts & Humanities Research Council Centre for the Study of the Domestic Interior, which completed its project in 2006.

48. G. Lees-Maffei, 'Introduction—Studying Advice: Historiography, Methodology, Commentary,

Bibliography', *Journal of Design History* 16/1 (2003), p. 1.

49. E. Langland, *Nobody's Angels: Middle-class Women and Domestic Ideology in Victorian Culture* (Cornell University Press, 1995), p. 24.

50. N. Humble, 'Introduction', *Mrs Beeton's Book of Household Management* (Oxford World Classics, 2000), pp. xv–xvi.

51. J. Rendall, *The Origins of Modern Feminism: Women in Britain, France, and the United States 1780–1860* (Macmillan, 1985), p. 206.

52. D. Attar, *A Bibliography of Household Books Published in Britain 1800–1914* (Prospect Books, 1987), p. 13; P. Branca, *Silent Sisterhood: Middle Class Women in the Victorian Home* (Croom Helm, 1975), pp. 16–17, also noted that advice 'was widely purchased'.

53. Lees-Maffei, 'Introduction', p. 1.

54. See J. Don Vann and R. T. VanArsdel, eds., *Victorian Periodicals and Victorian Society* (Scolar Press, 1994).

55. See also M. Beetham and K. Boardman's anthology, *Victorian Women's Magazines* (Manchester University Press, 2001), for information about periodicals aimed at women readers, many of which—for example *The Queen, The Englishwoman's Domestic Journal, Myra's Journal* and *Sylvia's Home Journal*—contain information about the domestic interior. To these specialist journals and women's magazines should be added the more general nineteenth-century periodical publications, which often include valuable articles on buildings and their interiors: magazines such as *Punch,* the *Pall Mall Gazette, The Athenaeum, The Graphic* and the *Saturday Review* are all worth exploring.

56. H. Long, *Victorian Houses and Their Details: The Role of Publications in Their Building and Decoration* (Architectural Press, 2002). For a slightly later period, see Long's, *The Edwardian House* (Manchester University Press, 1993).

57. See M. Ponsonby, 'Introduction', in *Stories from Home: English Domestic Interiors, 1750–1850* (Ashgate, 2007), pp. 1–19, for a methodological discussion that warns against the use of narrative paintings, advice books, prescriptive literature and other equally 'mediated' sources and which notes the limitations associated with the technique of quantitative analysis.

58. E. Darling and L. Whitworth, eds, *Women and the Making of Built Space in England, 1750–1950* (Ashgate, 2007). My own contribution, 'A Novelty among Exhibitions', examines the Loan Exhibition of Women's Industries held in Bristol in 1885 and considers the interior space of a public exhibition held by women in a domestic villa in Clifton through a range of contemporary newspaper and magazine articles, published locally, nationally and in the suffrage press.

59. C. Grant, ed., 'The Domestic Interior in British Literature', *Home Cultures* 2/3 (November 2005), pp. 229–32, This special issue of *Home Cultures* also contains five other relevant articles.

60. T. A. Markus, *Buildings and Power: Freedom and Control in the Origin of Modern Building Types* (Routledge, 1993; 2004) considers a range of buildings that includes schools; baths and wash houses; clubs, hotels and assembly rooms; institutions such as prisons, workhouses, hospitals and asylums; cultural buildings such as libraries, museums, art galleries, exhibitions, panoramas and dioramas, mechanic's institutes and lecture theatres; and those used for production and exchange such as mills and factories, markets, shops and exchanges.

Chapter One

'Plate glass and progress': Victorian modernity at home

Trevor Keeble

Throughout the nineteenth century, design reformers and professionals conducted a systematic campaign to reform the standards and conditions of middle-class domesticity. During the second half of the century, the burgeoning ranks of middle-class homemakers found models of taste and style in international exhibitions, museums, magazines and an increasing number of domestic design advice texts. These models went to great lengths to provide new ways of creating a home of appropriate taste and judgement, and, whilst many of them demonstrated tangible ways in which a 'modern' home might be achieved, the drive to understand the home within the context of modernity remained a largely rhetorical exercise which was often resisted by homemakers. This chapter considers a brief moment within this discussion exploring how notions of taste, sense and, perhaps more particularly, common sense, were used by professional designers to develop an argument for progressively modern homemaking. It considers the ways in which design professionals and householders jostled for position within this rhetoric and the manner in which domestic modernity became increasingly projected as a socially meaningful condition negotiated by individuals both within and beyond the home. The chapter also suggests that the call for common sense in regard to domestic taste represented a subtle shift in the reformist discourses that had proliferated previously and that this shift in both thinking and talking about domestic design underpinned a very particular understanding of the home as 'modern'.

On Friday 15 June 1883, Lewis Foreman Day addressed the National Health Society Exhibition on the subject of 'Commonsense House Decoration'.[1] By the 1880s, Day was an increasingly prolific designer and author.[2] Having initially worked in the stained glass industry during the 1860s, Day had established his reputation during the 1870s working on high-profile and expensive interior decoration projects with the firm of Heaton, Butler and Bayne, which had included various civic projects led by the architect Alfred Waterhouse.[3] At this time he also began designing for two prominent retailers: Howell and James, a retailer of fancy goods, drapery and other items for decoration of Regent Street, and W. B. Simpson, a retailer of domestic ceramics and metalwork, wallpapers and stained glass.[4]

In 1878 Day began writing an occasional series entitled 'Decorative Art Notes' for the *British Architect,* and, in the following two decades, he became a prolific contributor to the art and design press, publishing work in the *Magazine of Art,* the *Art Journal* and, during the early 1880s, the *Furniture Gazette.* Much of his journalism was based on his lectures and papers delivered on the expanding public lecture circuit in Britain, and much of his writing eventually found its final form in single-authored volumes published by B. T. Batsford.[5] 'Commonsense House Decoration', reproduced over a number of weeks by the *Furniture Gazette,* attempted to explain and characterise the role of common sense within the decorating process. The progressive nature of Day's venue and audience was noteworthy. However, the paper showed little concern for the more explicitly health-related discourses about domestic decoration.

Whilst acknowledging that the recent years had witnessed an improvement in domestic decoration, Day quickly moved to suggest that 'already there are signs of the ebbing of that wave of—shall we call it taste?—that passed over our society.'[6] He proposed a dialectical opposition between the influences of common sense and fashion upon choice:

The difference between fashionable and common-sensible decoration is not superficial but radical. They start from two distinctly opposite positions, and are propelled and regulated by two distinctly opposite considerations. Fashion concerns itself first and last with what certain other folk do, or are likely to do, and accommodates itself accordingly. Common sense considers what it itself wants, and goes as straight as it can to the accomplishment of its desire. Men and women do not, of course, divide themselves into persons of fashion and persons of sense. The most rigidly sensible of us have been known to carry on a flirtation with fashion (more or less dangerous, perhaps, but none the less delightful on that account), and the most fashionable of us have intervals of sense. But everywhere, from the choosing or the building of the house we inhabit to the smallest nicknack with which we furnish it, the two considerations are at war within us— the considerations, namely, of what we want, and what is supposed to be 'the thing'.[7]

Although somewhat simplistic in his definitions, Day's attempt to express the conflicting impulses that surrounded choice and intention within domestic design established a number of key propositions: that is that fashion and common sense were direct opposites to each other; that, whilst fashion sought its object in the choices of others, common sense found its object from within its own logic; and that, whilst the choices of fashion would be subject to eternal change, those made by common sense would be unchanging and enduring. In many ways such a characterisation of 'fashion' was commonplace in the design reform agenda of the time. However, what seems particularly interesting is that, in this attempt to explain the choice-making processes of the sovereign consumer, Day acknowledged the dualistic tension between fashion and common sense that lay at the heart of all decisions, and, if fashion could be characterised quite effortlessly by Day, its opposite position of common sense was perhaps much more difficult to define.

Day's choice of the word 'taste' to describe recent improvements in domestic decoration is unsurprising given the increasing centrality of that term to contemporary design reform debates. However, its semantic relationship with his use of the term 'commonsense' is worth considering. Both terms convey an ambiguous suggestion of both the bodily and the intellectual experience of domesticity and decoration, and yet the couching of domestic choice within the realm of common sense seems to emphasise this as a question of depersonalised rational judgement. Raymond Williams's investigation of the etymological development of the word 'sensibility' suggests ways in which the terms 'sense', 'judgement' and 'taste' came to be used in such an intimately related, yet subtly differentiated, way. He demonstrated how meanings of 'sensibility' developed during the fourteenth and fifteenth centuries from being concerned with 'physical feeling or sense perception' to a more objectified understanding of 'good sense' or 'good judgement' as conveyed by the term 'sensible'.[8] That transformation of meaning was not, however, exclusive, and during later centuries 'sensibility' came to describe 'tender' or 'fine' feeling. Williams suggested this latter interpretation went beyond what might commonly be described as 'sensitivity', 'a physical or an emotional condition', to become a 'social generalization of certain personal qualities, or, to put it another way, a personal appropriation of certain social qualities'.[9] He argued that it was in that context that the word 'sensibility' needed to be understood in an 'important formation' which included terms such as 'taste', 'cultivation' and 'discrimination'.

Whilst much of the domestic design advice and rhetoric of the late nineteenth century attempted to inculcate taste, judgement and discrimination through recourse to principle and rule as 'knowledge', it is clear, when looking back, that, with regard to the ways in which it used the terms 'sense', 'sensibility' and 'taste' interchangeably, it trod a far more ambiguous line. This was evident in the preface to *A Plea for Art in the House,* of 1876, by the Rev. W. J. Loftie:

> *The following chapters are an attempt to put some practical rules and anecdotes into colloquial language. Almost all that has hitherto been published on Art, either at home or abroad, has been written in a manner which may almost be called poetical, so far does it differ from the plainness of what is practical. I hope I have succeeded in showing, on simple grounds, the advantages of cultivating a love for art, especially art in the family and household. I am under the persuasion that common-sense arguments may be found powerful with many people to whom high flights are unpleasant.*[10]

Whilst it seems for Loftie that common sense might relate to the rhetoric of his discussion through references to plainness and practicality, it is clear that those discussions still served to emphasise the cultivation and aesthetic appreciation of art.

Given the rather high-flown popular discourse of aestheticism that marked the period in which he was writing, it is possible that, in an attempt to remove from his work any trace of the stigma that was rapidly becoming attached to much consideration of decoration and style, Loftie sought to characterise his discussion as arising from common sense.

It seems, upon reading subsequent volumes of Loftie's *Art at Home* series, that the opposition between the notion of common sense and the aesthetic became very firmly entrenched. Writing of *The Drawing Room: Its Furniture and Decoration,* Lucy Orrinsmith made very clear her address to people, and perhaps the Reverend Loftie as her editor, who chose to use common sense as an argument against aesthetic cultivation:

> At the outset of this attempt to lead our readers into what we consider to be the right way, arises the difficulty of dealing with those excellent contented folk who say: 'We are not artists; we are people of plain common sense, wishing to be comfortable, and knowing what we like, without reference to any aesthetic asceticism'. If there be any such people, and they care to proceed with this book, they must forgive our reminding them that if an Englishman's home is his castle, he has no right to make it a suite of artistic 'chamber of horrors', nor is the fiction that a man may do as he likes with his own to blind him to the fact that our rooms are decorated and pictures hung, not only for our pleasure, but for the delectation of our friends and guests. It therefore becomes a social duty to strive to attain to some guiding principles which may prevent an exhibition distressing to a visitor of, perchance, more educated taste than our own.[11]

Orrinsmith's suggested conflict between common sense and the aesthetic is one which might proudly have been written on either side of the argument. However, we find yet again the call for the use of principle in the realm of perception and taste.

Some months prior to the publication of Day's 'Commonsense House Decoration', the *Furniture Gazette* published the John D. Crace lecture 'Household Taste'.[12] That paper, presented before the Ascham Society in the spring of 1882, had previously been published by the *Gazette*'s contemporary, the *Builder.*[13] At the outset of his task, Crace provided a definition of what the term 'taste' might mean:

> I have said in passing that 'taste' is difficult to define. The difficulty is not lessened by the word being made to cover such a large field, — not only all the arts, but even social demeanour; still, some definitions will cover even its widest range. We may fairly say that 'good taste' is the sympathetic perception of fitness and proportion. It is, in fact (whether applied to art or manners), 'the refinement of good sense.' It is better thus to start with a clear understanding of what we mean, lest we get lost among the many spurious claimants to the title. 'Tastes' are even changing; fashion is mistaken for taste; and 'public taste,' as it is called (that 'mongrel product'), is ever ready to warp our judgement.[14]

Explaining his intentions further, Crace made clear that his subject was the 'household taste' of the 'great' middle classes, which, he noted, constituted perhaps the best and the worst of examples. Like many writers before him, Crace suggested that taste required a lifetime of study and that it would be best achieved by having 'the groundwork laid in youth'.[15] That emphasis upon the progressive development and inculcation of a domestic taste and sensibility was used to ascertain that taste needn't be dependent simply upon great wealth:

In some homes, with very modest means, there is an evident expression of a desire to satisfy some craving of the eye for form and colour. In a few cases this attempt is sufficiently successful to awaken a sense of gratification, sometimes imperfect, but occasionally thorough. In the latter case, the sense of pleasure is renewed with each visit, and may be said to assist in permanently raising our opinion of the owner.[16]

Whilst, on the one hand, that explanation allowed for a certain, if patronising, democracy of household taste which spread beyond the extremely moneyed classes, it also asserted that great amounts of money would not simply facilitate good taste. That factor firmly reinforced the hierarchical implications of household taste and the extent to which the household may be considered the measure of the householder.

In other homes, again, a similar attempt is obvious, but excites immediately our critical faculties–not our spontaneous goodwill, nor any sense of contentment. In such instances we become critical the more often we enter the house; and, whilst allowing that there is much to admire, we invariably fail to like it as a whole, and cannot avoid searching for defects. If we are not very good-natured, our verdict on the occupants is perhaps that they seek credit for more taste than they possess, that fact probably being, that instead of following any consistent aim, they have copied more or less imperfectly results intended for the expression of an entirely different intention. We may be pretty sure in this case that our hosts have no very genuine taste, unless it be the taste for such mild flattery as is conveyed by those expressions of surprise to which their quests politely give the sound of praise.[17]

Given Crace's profession as a decorator, his emphasis upon consistent intention in order to reinforce an understanding of the domestic interior as a totality is not surprising. His socially determined notion of taste reveals a multitude of motivations. However, Crace's principal concern was against the wilful and ill-advised attempt to gain social standing through taste. This led to an objectified understanding of taste in terms of a 'genuine' authenticity and as a means of policing class division and social standing. The deployment of taste to transgress those divisions was clearly measured by Crace in terms of a 'personal' vanity rather than personal achievement, and such observation justified his championing of 'reservation' in domestic decoration. Noting the need for reserve in all households, rich and poor alike, Crace noted that 'nothing is so fatal to good effect as to produce an impression that you have done all you can afford to do. If your room once becomes a silent "bit of brag," all is lost.'[18]

Throughout 'Household Taste', Crace reiterated the role of the householder. Most commonly, the householder was a depersonalised, if well-meaning, member of the masses, who, through 'slovenly observation', furnished his or her home and person with 'those innumerable grotesque travesties of well-designed originals'.[19] Crace acknowledged that the ability of the householder to decorate a house in one go was rare. He suggested that the taking up of a new property already decorated or the accommodation of existing possessions kept 'not because they are admired' might limit the independence of the householder's choice. Indeed Crace proposed that those existing styles or possessions need not mar the overall effect of the interior.

> If retained these objects must become part of the scheme and not left to become casual excrescences. Should they be important in kind or numerous, they may largely influence the choice of style; for it will be well to avoid absolute incongruity, though they may be themselves unsatisfactory, or even ugly. As part of a whole, which has been consistently thought out with them, they may, in effect, be dragged up to a higher level by association with better things, just as we find uninteresting persons who happen to associate with amusing or intelligent people reflect something of the interest of the latter. Certainly a good deal may be done in the direction of making common-place objects take their place in a house without giving direct offence.[20]

Such an anthropomorphic characterisation of individual objects within a greater scheme reflected the extent to which these objects might be read as part of a broader and legitimate hierarchy of taste. Crace's writing, however, acknowledged the humanistic and personal qualities of a lived-in space,

and it is perhaps in that respect that his characterisation of taste was most sensuously perceptive. Writing that 'a really cosy room must *seem* to be a low room', he introduced a factor less certain than the general principles of decoration.[21] Admitting the difficulty of tracing 'the chain of association' which leads to such an understanding, he suggested that 'it may almost be called essential to the "sentiment" of the place if it be a room of quiet retirement.' His discussion of sentiment led Crace to explore the manner in which various domestic spaces constructed and represented meanings beyond those simply related to social status:

> We may certainly be said to attach certain sentiments to certain rooms. One room is associated in the mind with the daily reunion of the family, with hospitality and the more social moments of one's days. It is here that one localises the ideal "hearth." It is the centre of the family home, and as such, there attaches to it certain a [sic] sentiment of what is lasting and venerable, no less than what is warm and hospitable, which seems to call for expression. To gratify this sentiment seems to me quite reasonable; nor is it necessary in doing so to make the room a mere "imitation antiquity".[22]

By the mid eighteenth century, the word 'sentimental' was widely used to describe both opinion and emotion, and it was that use of it to describe 'a conscious openness to feelings, and also a conscious consumption of feelings' that brought the word into much disrepute during the Victorian era. Raymond Williams has suggested that the word was permanently damaged by conservative, moral and radical complaints against people who felt 'too much' and who 'indulge their emotions'.[23] In his *Studies of Complex Words,* William Empson cast this particular interpretation of 'sensibility' in the context of taste:

> *If you have good taste you will be easily disturbed; you can no more help having a brainstorm or a flood of tears when disturbed than you can help seeing what is before your eyes; and you are particularly praised by the word if you take a somewhat passive attitude to life, open to impressions, for example if you easily feel pity and tenderness.*[24]

To discuss the attachment of sentiment to the domestic space is to partially acknowledge the extent to which the domestic space was understood in the nineteenth century as an expression of a sensual or evocative nature. Recognising this, Crace criticised the excessive formality of a drawing room prepared for and presented to guests according to principle. Suggesting that such attention to presentation often lessened the 'certain individual domesticity which should be its best charm', Crace's writing revealed a tension between principled judgement on the one hand and everyday life and dwelling on the other—a tension that was also evident in the writing of Day.

Discussing the progressive modernity of plate-glass windows, Day's writing demonstrated that tension in the complex and sometime contradictory terms 'commonsense' and 'sentimentality', with regard to domestic furnishing:

> *The common sense in house decoration is not all on the side of modernism. For instance, there is an idea amongst those who most pride themselves on their common sense, that leaded glass is a barbarism – an anachronism in these days of progress and patent plate – and that it is only the narrowness of the antiquary and the sentimentality of the aesthetic that can prefer the patchwork of small glass pieces of only partially transparent glass to one big sheet of absolutely clear glass. But reason is not so entirely on the side of such reasoning. Plate glass and progress are not so entirely inseparable. There may even be something of prejudice in the preference, everywhere and under all circumstances, for big, plain, naked window-sashes. The old-fashioned glass and glazing distinctly recommends itself, at least wherever transparency is not to be desired. The modern habit of first being at pains to manufacture a faultlessly clear material, and then proceeding to dull it, is progress with a vengeance—two steps forward and one step back again—three steps in all. Big plate-glass windows have these defects—that from the exterior the windows look like so many gaps in the architecture, and passers-by see far too plainly into the sanctity of your dwelling; and from inside you miss the comfort and cosiness and the sense of privacy.*[25]

Although couched in the design reformer's rhetoric of 'barbarism', Day's example revealed the extent to which his particular formulation of progressive 'modernism' was established within an empirical culture of everyday use—a culture most appropriate for the discussion of the domestic space. Central to his concern was a conception of comfortable domestic privacy. Day's commentary on windows showed that his attempts to reform the domestic space were not simply abstract 'aestheticised' principles but rationalised considerations rooted within consumption and use. Just as he had asserted the individual's inner compulsion towards both common sense and fashion, his writing revealed the tension between the dogmatic design reform that emanated from the professional sphere of production and a more reasoned discussion based on the experiences of domesticity. Yet, writing on the subject of domestic ornament, he provided a starkly protomodernist account:

> An Englishman of simple tastes has some excuse for a pronounced dislike to all ornament. The truth is that when the manufacturer breaks out into ornament, he mostly breaks out into revolt against all that is restrained. It follows – partly out of ignorance about what is really art, and partly from the common love of ostentation – that only the plainest and simplest manufactures are likely to be inoffensive in respect to taste. We can scarce be too chary about the introduction of ornament. We want less of it, but we want what there is to be really good. To insist rigorously upon the quality of ornament would be the surest way of limiting it in quantity.[26]

In many instances Day's writing embodied an ambiguous dichotomy between the concerns of the design professional and those of the decorating householder. Whilst revealing the commonsense nature of his approach to matters of design, it reflected Day's reformist impulses, which ultimately

sought to regulate the taste of the amateur decorator or householder. Nevertheless, his use of the term 'commonsense' to explain a rationalised, intellectual exercise of judgement rather than a personal, principled or aesthetic one suggested a utilitarian approach to domestic modernity. Perhaps most importantly, however, the deployment of 'commonsense' as a term in the design reform lexicon of the late Victorian era represented a fundamental move away from earlier aspirational strategies of improving taste according to aesthetic judgement, education and principle. By suggesting that common sense was the basis on which judgement was made, Day's writing placed the domestic design reform agenda firmly within the grasp, possibility and responsibility of the masses.

Notes

1. L. F. Day, 'Commonsense House Decoration', *Furniture Gazette* (16 June 1883), pp. 415–7. The fact the *Furniture Gazette* began publication of this address the day after its delivery indicates that Day made his paper available for publication. Despite his Arts and Crafts connections, Day worked extensively as a commercial designer and has come to be regarded as such. S. Durant, *Victorian Ornamental Design* (Academy Editions, 1972). Day maintained a lifelong friendship with Walter Crane, who he met at the Quibblers Sketching Club in the early 1870s. E. Rycroft, 'Lewis F. Day 1845–1910', MA thesis (Royal College of Art, 1980), p. 52.

2. J. Cooper, *Victorian and Edwardian Furniture and Interiors. From the Gothic Revival to Art Nouveau* (Thames & Hudson, 1987), p. 180; G. Naylor, *The Arts and Crafts Movement: A Study of Its Sources,*

Ideals and Influences on Design Theory (Studio Vista, 1971); P. Stansky, *Redesigning the World. William Morris, the 1880s, and the Arts and Crafts* (Princeton University Press, 1985). For a discussion of the Arts and Crafts Exhibition Society's influence during the early twentieth century, see T. Harrod, *The Crafts in Britain in the 20th Century* (Yale University Press, 1999), pp. 15–28.

3. Cooper, *Victorian and Edwardian Furniture,* p. 93.

4. Rycroft, 'Lewis F. Day', p. 54.

5. These publications include *Every-Day Art* (1882), *The Anatomy of Pattern* (1887), and *Nature in Ornament* (1892). In addition, Day was one of the first design writers to retrospectively consider the work of William Morris, publishing a monograph upon his late friend in a special edition of *Art Journal* in 1899.

6. Day, 'Commonsense House Decoration', p. 416.

7. Ibid.

8. R. Williams, *Keywords: A Vocabulary of Culture and Society* (Fontana Press, 1976), p. 280.

9. Ibid.*,* p. 281.

10. W. J. Loftie, *A Plea for Art in the House* (Macmillan, 1876). I'm most grateful to Emma Ferry for bringing these *Art at Home* examples to my attention.

11. L. Orrinsmith, *The Drawing Room: Its Decoration and Furniture* (Macmillan, 1877), pp. 5–6.

12. J. D. Crace (1839–1919) entered the family decorating firm of Crace & Sons in 1854. He assumed partnership with his father in 1873 and took control of the company in 1889 on his father's death. Crace travelled widely and worked in numerous styles, including, most prominently, Italian Renaissance, Italian Gothic, French Renaissance and Classicism. His most prominent work was for the International Exhibition of 1862 and the Houses of Parliament during the 1860s. See M. Aldrich, 'The Victorian Craces, c.1830–1899', in M. Aldrich, ed., *The Craces. Royal Decorators 1768–1899* (John Murray & the Royal Pavilion, Art Gallery & Museum, 1990), pp. 53–136.

13. Lectures by Crace were published by the *Gazette* on other occasions. These were often concerned specifically with colour in the interior. 'Colour Decoration, a paper by Mr. J. D. Crace', *Furniture Gazette* (23 February 1884), pp. 164–6 (originally delivered to the Architectural Association); 'Colour in Interior Decoration by John D. Crace', *Furniture Gazette* (1 August 1888), p. 251 (originally delivered to the Society of Arts); 'Nature and the Study of Colour Decoration', *Furniture Gazette* (23 June 1877), pp. 409–11. Though unpublished in the manner of a number of his contemporaries, Crace's lectures were evidently quite prolific and widely reported. In 1883, a speaker before the Liverpool Architectural Association took particular issue with a number of ideas expressed. 'Some Notes on Furniture and Decoration', *Furniture Gazette* (17 February 1883), p.109.

14. J. D. Crace, 'Household Taste', *Furniture Gazette* (11 March 1882), p. 151.

15. Ibid., p. 151.

16. Ibid., p. 151.

17. Ibid., p. 151.

18. J. D. Crace, 'Household Taste', *Furniture Gazette* (18 March 1882), p. 167.

19. Ibid., p. 167.

20. Ibid., p. 167.

21. Ibid., p. 167.

22. Ibid.

23. Williams, *Keywords,* p. 282.

24. W. Empson, *The Structure of Complex Words* (Chatto & Windus, 1951), p. 258.

25. L. F. Day, 'Commonsense House Decoration', *Furniture Gazette* (30 June 1883), p. 451.

26. Ibid.

Chapter Two

Privacy and Supervision in the Modernised Public House, 1872–1902

Fiona Fisher

This chapter examines the development of London's public house interiors in the thirty years between the Licensing Acts of 1872 and 1902, a period in which many of the capital's businesses were rebuilt or remodelled to create drinking environments of greater spatial, material and aesthetic complexity than those that preceded them. Implicated in debates on social order, poverty and working-class health, the late nineteenth-century public house was a problematic and highly contested site. In their efforts to minimise the harmful social consequences of the liquor trade, one of the strategies adopted by the late nineteenth-century authorities was to intervene in the design of licensed premises with the aim of improving order and regulating consumption. Design, as this discussion will show, was seen as an agent of social reform. Regulatory interventions took the form of national licensing legislation and local licensing policies that governed the spatial organisation of public house interiors and the materials that could be used within them. Local regulations, which varied according to licensing district, were enforced through the practice of publicans petitioning

magistrates for approval of their development plans in advance of building work. Much of the legislative drive to reform the public house focused on opening up the interior and exposing drinkers to greater scrutiny, but emerging consumer preferences for privacy whilst drinking and dining conflicted with these regulatory objectives. In the post-1872 period, the public house interior became a site in which tensions between supervision and privacy, regulation and the market, were negotiated through the process of modernisation. That process forms the focus for discussion here.

Throughout the nineteenth century, most of London's public houses functioned as homes as well as businesses, with the majority of publicans and their families residing on site. For much of that period, public and private life intersected and overlapped in spaces that fulfilled both domestic and commercial functions, but, by the beginning of the twentieth century, the domestic/commercial relationship had been radically transformed. Central to that transformation was the development of the commercial interior as a distinct and independent region, dedicated to retail sales and separate from the publican's private accommodation. Although the roots of the commercial interior lie in the first half of the nineteenth century, the Licensing Act of 1872 marks a critical point in the clarification of the domestic/commercial relationship. The Act required businesses applying for a licence to sell beer and spirits for consumption on the premises to provide two rooms for the use of the drinking public; these were to be over and above any rooms used by residents for domestic purposes.[1] The separation of commercial activities and spaces from the domestic arrangements of the licencee made public houses easier to control, situating customers within a clearly defined public environment where police could observe and intervene in their activities.

National legislation and the local policies that supplemented it not only imposed tighter control over licensed sites and the individuals who managed and frequented them, but also created a climate in which it was hard to obtain new licences and it became profitable to improve and enlarge existing businesses.[2] Opponents of the licensed trade argued that the larger and more attractive public houses that had begun to evolve in response to these circumstances represented a serious temptation to the temperate, but the trade defended its alterations as improvements and placed responsibility for them firmly in the hands of legislators. In a submission made to the Select Committee of the House of Lords on Intemperance, in the late 1870s, the Licensed Victuallers' National Defence League described the 1872 Licensing Act as 'the real creator of the modern bar system' and claimed that, as a result of it, publicans were 'expected and required to do, or to prevent the doing, of things which are humanly speaking impossible to do or prevent in houses of old construction'.[3] The 'winding passages, out-of-the-way closets, and dimly-lighted, many-doored rooms' of these older businesses made them difficult to oversee; greatly preferable, claimed the trade, was the 'modern' bar system that was being introduced in their place, which improved supervision and demonstrated its commitment to good order.[4] The most significant aspect of the 'modern' system, in terms of the spatial organisation of the interior, was the introduction of counter service and the arrangement of the drinking bars around the service space.

'Inside a Public House on a Saturday Night' (Fig. 2.1) appeared in *Living London*, an edited collection of writings on the capital, and depicts a modernised interior of the multiple bar type, with a central service area and a number of radiating drinking compartments. The image draws on a Victorian artistic tradition of social realism and spectacular representation, but also calls to mind contemporary institutional spaces based on Jeremy Bentham's panoptical model.[5] For many of London's licensing magistrates, this would have represented the ideal drinking environment: an interior without hidden corners within which to conceal illicit activities, such as prostitution or gambling, and without cover for the unruly customer or habitual drunkard.[6] Penalties for committing licensing infringements were high, and the trade claimed to favour the radiating plan because it allowed the publican to assess his customers and see 'at a glance what they are, in what state they are, and what they are doing'.[7] The reality of most modernised

INSIDE A PUBLIC-HOUSE ON SATURDAY NIGHT.

Fig. 2.1. A modernised public house interior with central servery, bar stillion and radiating drinking compartments. *Source:* Graham Hill, 'Bar and Saloon London', in George R. Sims, ed., *Living London: Its Work and Its Play, Its Humour and Its Pathos, Its Sights and Its Scenes* (Cassell and Co., 1902), volume 2, p. 287.

interiors was somewhat different from the magisterial ideal and image of continuous surveillance promoted by the licensed trade in support of their adaptations. Few public houses exposed customers to the degree of scrutiny suggested by the image. Partitions and counter screens, coloured glass and ornamental door and window glazing, portières and curtain walls (in the most literal sense of the term) combined to create environments in which visual contact between customers was carefully regulated, but visual control over drinkers was rarely uniform. Visual obstructions within the interior

were a particular target for intervention by licensing magistrates, and, in some districts, the use of coloured or opaque glass was restricted.[8] Publicans complained that these policies were detrimental to trade, as their customers desired privacy and were afforded it by commercial rivals who were free from interference in their businesses.[9]

The Prince Alfred in Maida Vale, which was built in the 1850s and refitted in the 1890s, has one of the best preserved late nineteenth-century public house interiors in London and contains a variety of features that were typical of businesses of the period. The visual dynamics of the interior are complex. Five drinking compartments ring the central servery; each is divided from the next by half-height wooden partitions with decorative glazed panels that restrict the view from one compartment to the next (Figs. 2.2, 2.3 and 2.4). One of these compartments is fitted with a swivelling counter screen which, when fully closed, conceals occupants from staff and from customers drinking in other parts of the interior (Fig. 2.5). Within the servery, a central bar fitting, or stillion, used to house liquors and bar accoutrements, creates a further visual interruption, inhibiting the view from one side of the public house to the other. Curtains were sometimes used to similar effect, dividing the service space to screen drinkers in opposing bars. The flexibility of divisions of this type suggests that trading conditions may have determined the level of privacy that was desired by customers or permitted to them. Curtains were also employed in other locations. Portières in lobbies kept out the dirt and dust of the street, but were also used to screen dining rooms from adjacent drinking spaces. In better class establishments of the 1890s, seating areas in alcoves or bay windows were draped to create public environments comparable to the cosy corners that were popular in domestic drawing rooms at that time. These partially screened subsidiary spaces incorporated customers within the wider drinking environment, usually of the saloon bar, creating an intimate setting and vantage point from which its activity could be observed.

The proliferation of fixed and flexible forms of screening, which is evident in the interiors of the 1880s and 1890s, is broadly concurrent with significant changes in public house custom. In an important historical account of drink in Victorian society, Brian Harrison suggested that, by the 1830s, London tradesmen had withdrawn from public drinking. John Tosh, drawing on Harrison's study, has associated the departure of better-class customers with an emerging cult of domesticity.[10] Late nineteenth-century sources suggest that London's public house custom began to broaden in the 1870s and had expanded significantly by the 1890s.[11] Diverse in totality, but particular to each district and individual business, the broad picture that emerges from contemporary accounts is of a large working-class base supplemented by a smaller but notably expanding contingent of lower middle-class drinkers. Some distinctly well-to-do customers patronised businesses in high-class residential districts, but this appears to have been rather unusual.[12] Men outnumbered women in most locations, but that was not the case everywhere.[13] Female custom grew significantly in the final third of the century, and contemporary accounts represent it as being of a better or more respectable class than had formerly been the case. London's public houses catered for different types of social use as well as different categories of user. The custom of most fluctuated according to the time of day or day of the week, and some businesses experienced significant seasonal variations in response to changing patterns of urban leisure.[14] Public houses close to amenities such as municipal parks or the zoological gardens attracted recreational users; commuters supported the licensed buffets at

Fig. 2.2. Half-height timber and glass screening at the Prince Alfred, Maida Vale. Photograph: Fiona Fisher.

Fig. 2.3. Partition and service door between drinking compartments at the Prince Alfred, Maida Vale. Photograph: Fiona Fisher.

Fig. 2.4. Partition and service door between drinking compartments at the Prince Alfred, Maida Vale. Photograph: Fiona Fisher.

Fig. 2.5. Swivelling counter screen at the Prince Alfred, Maida Vale. Photograph: Fiona Fisher.

London's railway stations; women shoppers formed a significant portion of the trade of public houses in and around London's main street markets; business diners patronised city establishments; and, in residential areas, domestic customers used the jug-and-bottle compartment of their local public house for the purchase of off-sales.

The development of the jug-and-bottle compartment offers some insight into the way in which interiors evolved in response to new trading patterns and emerging consumer preferences and demonstrates the significance that privacy had for customers who began to use London's public houses from the 1870s onwards. Some public houses of the first half of the century had retail or off-sales compartments, but these became more widespread after the introduction of the Wine Licensing Bill of 1860, which allowed shopkeepers to sell small quantities of alcohol and increased the competition faced by publicans.[15] The jug-and-bottle or off-sales compartments were aimed at the respectable lower middle-class and working-class trade that the architects of the bill hoped would buy foreign wines from the grocer and would consume moderately, with a meal, in the morally uplifting environment of the home. Jug-and-bottle compartments often had their own entrance and were usually isolated from other parts of the interior, particularly the main public bar that was used by lower-class customers. This separation of domestic customers from on-site drinkers materialised and spatialised the ideological distinction made between the public and private consumption of alcohol in the period. Domestic consumption was a barometer of respectability and a public house with a strong jug trade was understood to be indicative of the superior status of the surrounding district.[16] However, the jug-and-bottle compartment was, for some time, a problematic site. In the 1870s, John Weylland, District Secretary of the London City Mission, observing recent changes in London's public house custom, commented that 'ladies and women' and 'the more respectable men' had begun drinking in the compartments that publicans provided for the service of off-sales.[17] Weylland, who viewed this evidence of on-site consumption as a worrying sign of social deterioration, described the jug-and-bottle compartment as a 'sly corner'.[18] Commentators of the 1890s, such as G. C. Whiteley, clerk to the licensed justices of Newington, regarded the jug-and-bottle compartment as an aid to morality that shielded domestic users, particularly vulnerable servant girls, from potentially corrupting sights and sounds in the public bars.[19] These differences in opinion are a reflection of the significant developments that took place within the public house in the intervening period. Customers of the 1870s were fairly restricted in the choice of drinking spaces available to them, but, as public houses expanded, so did the variety of bars and dining rooms incorporated within them. By the time that Whiteley made his comments, many of London's public houses had introduced comfortably furnished bars and saloons aimed at lower middle-class customers; in the 1890s, discussion about the design of the interior and the regulation of consumers became more focused on these newer spaces.

The jug-and-bottle compartments of the 1870s offered respectable customers an acceptable point of entry to the public house, allowing them to preserve the private or domestic status that was a marker of that respectability. Theoretical writings on privacy have suggested that one of its functions is to allow individuals freedom to deviate from social rules or customs in protected fashion and, critically, without threatening those rules or customs in the way that a public or visible contravention of them would.[20] At a time when barriers to public consumption of alcohol remained high, off-sales compartments not only protected the status of domestic customers, but also provided a new public context in which respectable individuals could drink in privacy and, significantly, without threatening the ideology of respectability upon which their social status rested.

The jug-and-bottle or off-sales compartment was not the only part of the interior in which customers of the 1870s could drink in conditions of 'public privacy'.[21] Private bars were becoming more common, and the history of these two spaces appears closely entwined. In the 1850s and 1860s, the term 'private bar' was used in connection with off-sales, where it signified the area or compartment that served the needs of domestic customers, and in connection with the bar parlour, where it identified the partially domestic status of the space.[22] Lack of clarity in the terminology of the 1850s and 1860s is a reflection of ambiguities within the interior at that time and of the complex ways in which privacy and domesticity intersected within unmodernised public house sites. Through the process of modernisation, these ambiguities began to be resolved, and, in the 1870s, the term 'private bar' started to be used more consistently to describe drinking compartments that were designed for privacy and intended for on-site consumption. Similar in character to jug-and-bottle compartments, these private bars were usually separated from other spaces and were either screened or discreetly located. The practice of on-site drinking in the jug-and-bottle compartment probably contributed to the development of the private bar as a discrete drinking environment aimed at better-class customers.

Counter screens were a particular feature of the private bar (Fig. 2.5). It is difficult to be specific about the date or location of their introduction. In one of the earliest architectural studies of the public house, Maurice Gorham and H. McG. Dunnett suggested that counter screens were first used around 1860, but they offered no firm evidence in support of their view.[23] A recent national study questioned whether counter screens were, in fact, that common a feature of nineteenth-century public house interiors.[24] Few counter screens survive, but contemporary sources show that they were not unusual and could be found in a variety of metropolitan locations. The earliest textual evidence of the use of a counter screen in a London public house appears as a reference to 'a small glass frame, over the bar' in a report of a theft at a public house in King's Cross in 1870.[25] More extensive evidence of counter fittings of this type can be found in sources of the 1880s and 1890s, the period in which lower middle-class custom appears to have been expanding most rapidly. A comment about counter screens in the private and saloon bars of a public house in Islington appears in one of the police notebooks that form part of the Charles Booth Archive.[26] Screens are also indicated on a variety of architectural plans, including those for the Angell Arms in Brixton, the Artichoke in Newington Causeway and the Feathers in Lambeth Walk.[27] Further evidence of counter screens can be seen in contemporary visual representations, such as an advertisement for the Diamond Soda Water Machine Company that appeared

in *Licensed Victuallers' Gazette and Hotel Courier* in 1902.[28]

The limited evidence that exists about how London's magistrates responded to counter screens suggests that they were prepared to tolerate them as long as adequate supervision could be maintained.[29] The right to privacy that was granted to the customers of the private bar was not, however, extended to all occupants of the interior. In contrast to public houses frequented by lower middle-class drinkers, parts of the interior used by lower-status customers were becoming more open to inspection in this period. In older premises, the main public room that served poorer customers was often located to the rear of the ground floor and was either separated from the service area or linked to it by a hatch or internal sash window, which made supervision difficult.[30] Rooms of this type were regular casualties of modernisation, and the public bars that replaced them were usually located in a more prominent position, where drinkers could be more easily observed.

The presence of growing numbers of respectable women in London's public houses of the 1890s complicated this class-based hierarchy of privacy and supervision and raised specific concerns about the design of modern drinking environments and the regulation of women's consumption. Lady Henry Somerset, an important witness to the Royal Commission on Liquor Licensing Laws, stated in her evidence:

I think that the greater facilities for privacy that are afforded by the arrangement of public-houses at present have been a great inducement for women to drink. The private saloons and bars, and other matters which have arisen lately, undoubtedly give a greater facility, and certainly have produced a larger amount of drinking among women.[31]

When asked whether she felt that secrecy was one of the attractions of 'the modern public-house', she replied:

I think in the construction of public-houses that has been taken into consideration, viz., the greatest possible amount of privacy during the consumption of drink and secrecy as to company; and the ground floor of the large London public-houses in itself is, I think, a reflection of the different classes of people whose custom it is striving to obtain. There is a great change in the plan of the public-houses lately.[32]

Following extensive debate within the context of the Royal Commission, the subject of visual control became a matter for national legislation in 1902. The Licensing Act of that year incorporated the following clause, placing further restrictions on the development of the interior:

Any alteration in any licensed premises for the sale by retail of intoxicating liquors to be consumed thereon, which gives increased facilities for drinking, or conceals from observation any part of the premises used for drinking, or which affects the communication between the part of the premises where intoxicating liquor is sold and any other part of the premises or any street or other public way, shall not be made without the consent of the licensing justices.[33]

The commercial interiors that developed in London's public houses of the post-1872 period were products of a complex of social, cultural and legislative factors. The manner in which the design of these interiors evolved is not straightforward. There is no designer; rather, their design was a collective, although not always a co-operative, enterprise. Highly controlled, yet permissive of new forms of social activity, it is perhaps helpful to consider these interiors as sites that express tensions between social autonomy and regulation that are characteristic of modernity and which represent concerns for social status and identity that are a distinguishing feature of consumer culture.

Notes

1. The Licensing Act of 1872, 45b.
2. On the political and economic context for development in London, see M. Girouard, *Victorian Pubs* (Yale University Press, 1984), pp. 62–4.
3. Select Committee of the House of Lords on Intemperance, Fourth Report 1878, Appendix A.
4. Ibid.
5. J. Bentham, *Panopticon: or, the inspection-house* (T. Payne, 1791).
6. As James Kneale has noted, when key nineteenth-century government enquiries considered public house design, 'their discussions had already been framed by a set of assumptions about the organization of space for disciplinary ends.' J. Kneale, '"A Problem of Supervision": Moral Geographies of the Nineteenth-Century British Public House', *Journal of Historical Geography* 25 (1999), p. 335.
7. Select Committee.
8. Royal Commission on Liquor Licensing Laws (1897–1899), C.35600.

9. *Licensed Victuallers' Gazette and Hotel Courier* (7 June 1895), p. 361.

10. B. Harrison, *Drink and the Victorians: The Temperance Question in England, 1815–1872* (Faber and Faber, 1971), p. 45; J. Tosh, *A Man's Place: Masculinity and the Middle-class Home in Victorian England* (Yale University Press, 1999), p. 125.

11. The following discussion of London custom draws on a variety of late nineteenth-century sources, including national newspapers, licensed trade journals, the minutes of evidence of the Royal Commission on Liquor Licensing Laws and the extensive information on local drinking habits contained in the police notebooks that form part of the Charles Booth Archive at the London School of Economics and Political Science.

12. One such district was St. John's Wood; on its 'peculiar' and 'highly profitable' clientele, see The Charles Booth Archive, Police Notebook B352, p. 30.

13. Some businesses in working-class districts were so heavily patronised by women that they were known locally as 'cowsheds' or 'women's houses'. Booth Archive, B346, p. 41 and B348, p. 75.

14. For example, the Lovat Arms in the Stepney area depended on strong off-sales in winter but had more passing trade in summer, when it benefited from trippers heading for the GER railway to Southend or for Victoria Park or Epping Forest. Booth Archive, B350, p. 235 and p. 237.

15. Select Committee.

16. Booth Archive, B346, p. 141.

17. Select Committee, C.9204.

18. Ibid.

19. Booth Archive, B348, p. 173 and p. 185.

20. B. Schwartz, 'The Social Psychology of Privacy', *American Journal of Sociology* 73 (1968), pp. 741–52; A. F. Westin, *Privacy and Freedom* (Atheneum, 1967), pp. 32–9.

21. As used here, the term 'public privacy' derives from Richard Sennett's discussion of social experience in the Parisian café, in which he suggested that 'invisible walls' divided the crowds of drinkers and that 'silence made it possible to be both visible to others and isolated from them'. R. Sennett, *The Fall of Public Man* (Penguin Books, 2002), pp. 216–7. The problematic cultural standing of the English public house made visual privacy a greater issue for customers, particularly for those least secure in their social status.

22. On off-sales, see Girouard, *Victorian Pubs,* p. 67. On the bar parlour, see *The Times* (10 February 1857), p. 9 (16 February 1857), p. 9.

23. M. Gorham and H. McG. Dunnett, 'Inside the Pub', *Architectural Review* 106 (1949), p. 242.

24. G. Brandwood, A. Davison, and M. Slaughter, *Licensed to Sell: The History and Heritage of the Public House* (English Heritage in Association with CAMRA, Campaign for Real Ale, 2004), p. 106.

25. *The Times* (7 January 1870), p. 9.

26. Booth Archive, B348, p. 79.

27. These plans form part of the Drawings Collection of the Royal Institute of British Architects. See PA1190/9, PA1190/10 and PA1191/22.

28. *Licensed Victuallers' Gazette and Hotel Courier* (26 September 1902), p. 662.

29. Evidence comes from a widely reported case of the 1890s in which a barman, unsighted by a counter screen, served an on-duty policeman in contravention of licensing regulations. Magistrates, rather than demanding the removal of the screen, suggested that it be adapted to improve supervision. See *The Times* (13 July 1896); *Licensed Victuallers' Gazette and Hotel Courier* (17 April 1896, 24 April 1896 and 17 July 1896) and *Westminster and Pimlico News* (17 April 1896).

30. Service windows appear in elevation on a number of late-nineteenth-century architectural plans, which suggests that they were of particular interest to magistrates. See, for example Royal Institute of British Architects, PA1190/24 and PA1190/28.

31. Royal Commission, C.31297.

32. Ibid, C.31478.

33. The Licensing Act of 1902, 11.2.

Chapter Three

The German Interior at the End of the Nineteenth Century

Sabine Wieber

Design historians characterise German nineteenth-century interiors as a virtually uninterrupted succession of historicist revivals. This trajectory begins with the Biedermeier's adaptation of a French-inspired classicism and culminates in the embrace of Neo-Rococo and Neo-Baroque interiors in the late 1880s. The 1890s, it is argued, were plagued by an eclecticism of stylistic revivals that anticipated historicism's death knell and left contemporary reformers and progressive critics anxious about Germany's design future.[1] Luckily, a new generation of craftsmen and designers based in Munich began to spread their wings from the mid 1890s onwards and liberated the German interior from its historicist impasse. This story of the birth of modern German design practices was inscribed into design history as early as 1908, when the German architectural critic Joseph August Lux enthused that 'the year 1898, being a year of revolution, may be described as the official birth year of the modern movement in Germany.'[2] This 'modern movement' had been christened Jugendstil and represented Germany's manifestation of Art Nouveau.

The genesis of the modern German interior at the close of the nineteenth century thus seems to present a rather straightforward narrative. This is reflected in subsequent discussions of these events, which primarily focus on the issue of style when trying to determine whether the Jugendstil represented Germany's last historicist style or indeed its first truly modern design language.[3] Without intending to question the validity of these debates, this essay argues that a preoccupation with style misses an important point: namely, how these 'modern' interiors were received at the time and how they were postulated as cultural responses to the conditions of modernity and modern life. By taking a close look at the rhetoric of the critical reception of Munich's early Jugendstil interiors and contextualising these responses within a larger cultural landscape, it becomes evident that the notion of the modern interior actually presented a highly contested and inherently unstable ideological territory.

In 1897, Munich's official artists' association, the *Künstlergenossenschaft,* joined forces with the Munich Secession to organise the Seventh International Art Exhibition in the city's premier exhibition space, the Glaspalast. This exhibition was remarkable on a number of levels because it not only attracted an international gathering of visual artists from across central Europe and England, but it also represented a first rapprochement of two often antagonistic bodies of artists: the traditional *Künstlergenossenschaft* and the progressive Secession. The 1897 exhibition also included sections on the decorative and applied arts. These entries were featured in two historicist interiors: an 'Arabian Room' by Ferdinand Bredt and an 'Empire-Style Vestibule' by Martin Dülfer.[4] In addition, a group of young Munich designers had convinced the exhibition organisers to allow them to showcase some of the most recent developments in local design practices. Although relatively small in scope (a mere two rooms in one of the outer corners of the Glaspalast) and quite contentious in its inception (exhibition organisers refused to contribute any funding towards their cost), these two rooms became an unforeseen critical success, and design historians have since christened them cradles or *Keimzellen* of modern design in Germany.[5]

These two rooms were conceived as Wagnerian total works of art, and each design feature stylistically harmonised with its surroundings. That is to say that an overall aesthetic vision determined the material composition of each interior. *Room 24* at the Seventh International Art Exhibition was designed by the architect and stage designer Martin Dülfer (1859–1942) and *Room 25* by the architect and urban planner Theodor Fischer (1862–1938).[6] A special committee oversaw the selection process for these two interiors, and applicants were asked to focus on 'the best that modern applied arts has accomplished' and to choose objects that 'fulfil the requirements of our modern

life … and exclude everything that appears as thoughtless and false copy or imitation of past and foreign styles.'[7] After this committee accepted a range of objects from Munich's up-and-coming young designers, Dülfer and Fischer were asked to arrange them into modern interiors. Both presented audiences with unified architectural environments that could have served as actual living quarters in a modern Munich home. Fischer's *Room 25*, for example, was designed as a modern salon (Fig. 3.1). This photograph suggests that, in addition to the stylistic coherence of the interior's objects, Fischer had also manipulated colour and atmosphere to create a sense of overall unity. Contemporary descriptions of this room reveal, for example, that the panelling was painted in dark blues and greens and that the borders were decorated with small flowers.[8] The palette of Richard Riemerschmid's large wall painting depicting a gently sloping river's shore as well as his elaborately framed tempera painting *Wolken-gespenster* echoed the blues and greens of the panelling. By extension, the room's timbered ceiling softened the atmosphere through its golden beams and deep blue interstices featuring delicate foliage. Heavy curtains and wall carpets combined with the room's dark wooden pieces of furniture, such as Riemerschmid's sideboard and Hermann Obrist's chest (not shown in the photograph but now in the collection of the Munich Stadtmuseum), further diffused the light from the Glaspalast's window panels. Fischer's conscious manipulation of colour and atmosphere did not escape contemporary critics such as Wilhelm von Bode, who praised *Room 25* in his exclusive art journal *Pan* for its 'coherent painterly effects'.[9] Bringing into play the notion of the painterly signals Bode's understanding of Fischer's intended interplay between the physical and the psychological in the creation and experience of his interior's totalising aesthetic.

As already mentioned, the two applied arts interiors at the Seventh International Art Exhibition proved a big success with progressive critics. A survey of Germany's leading art and design journals of the day reveals that Dülfer's and Fischer's interiors were praised as trailblazers for a new and distinctly modern development in contemporary design practices. To this day, they are celebrated for their daring embrace of a distinctly modern *Wohnkultur* that not only rejected Germany's hitherto dominant historicist revivals but advocated a design language that was deeply rooted in the present. Whilst conceding that the exhibition's applied arts section occupied somewhat of a 'Cinderella status' among the Glaspalast's vast number of exhibits, Bode hailed these two interiors as 'breeding grounds for an independent development of very modern art forms that are deeply rooted in the conditions of modern life'.[10] Hans Eduard von Berlepsch, who had served on the applied arts section's committee for the 1897 exhibition, wrote an influential article in Alexander Koch's new applied arts journal, *Deutsche Kunst und Dekoration,* in which he saluted his fellow craftsmen and designers as courageous instigators of a design revolution: 'Facta loquuntur! The modern movement has done pioneering work. The ball has finally been set into motion and nothing at all can stop it now!'[11] Berlepsch's plaudit was echoed

50. Aus der Kleinkunst-Abtheilung der VII. internationalen Kunstausstellung in München. Gesammtanordnung von Architekt Theodor Fischer, Wandmalerei von Richard Riemerschmie

Fig. 3.1. Theodor Fischer, Room 25 at the Seventh International Art Exhibition in Munich, 1897 (from *Kunst und Handwerk* 47 (1897). Museum für Kunst und Gewerbe, Hamburg).

in Wilhelm Rolfs's closing remarks of the 1897 exhibition, in which he acknowledged the group of young designers involved in the successful applied arts section for their Herculean efforts to make 'Munich the feeding ground for a growing and prospering applied arts scene'.[12]

It might not be surprising that progressive critics such as Bode and von Berlepsch as well as vanguard publishers such as Alexander Koch celebrated the Munich exhibition's modern interiors.[13] Yet, even more conservative observers conceded that Dülfer's and Fischer's interiors represented a conscious break with the kinds of historicist design practices these critics tended to support (Fig. 3.2). One such critic was Leopold Gmelin, who had regularly defended historicism and whose views carried great weight because he was the editor of the Bavarian Applied Arts Association's internationally renowned journal *Kunst und Handwerk* from 1887 onwards. In his aforementioned review of the 1897 exhibition, Gmelin credited Dülfer's and Fischer's interiors with bringing 'modern applied arts to bloom and to the attention of the visitors' and implied that the most recent historicist revivals of the neo-rococo and the

neo-baroque might have run their course, although he cautioned his readers to not disregard the past.[14]

This albeit too brief an examination of the overall positive reception of the 1897 exhibition's interiors across a range of print media and ideological positions unveils a recurring rhetoric of the 'modern'. Despite the frequent and quite self-conscious use of the term 'modern' during the 1890s, it can be a misleading concept if not put into its proper context. At this time, German writers regularly used the terms 'modern' and 'modernity' in an attempt to come to terms with the many bewildering shifts in cultural, historical, economic and sociopolitical conditions that were seen to characterise the fin de siècle. Across Europe, the 1890s were permeated by an atmosphere of uncertainty, if not crisis, and virtually no aspect of everyday life was exempt from this feeling. Within this context, thinkers and writers evoked the idea of modernity to describe an accelerated pace of life and a sense of fragmentation experienced by individuals living in these modern conditions. Modernity, 'this bewildering jumble of transformations', thus represented an attempt to describe a break with the past inherent in the new social experiences that modernisation had brought about.[15] For progressive artists, designers and intellectuals, the heterogeneous manifestations of modernity served as a rejuvenating force and propelled a wide range of aesthetic and literary responses. Yet not everybody celebrated this newfound state of flux and transience, and, for many, these were 'years of ambivalence: of great expectations and disappointments, of relinquishing old convictions and groping for new myths.

Fig. 3.2. Joh. Behr, dining room in the style of the Renaissance (from *Illustrirte Kunstgewerbliche Zeitschrift für Innendekoration* 8 (1897). Museum für Kunst und Gewerbe, Hamburg).

Few were able to discern, in Robert Musil's words, what was moving forward and what was moving backward.'[16] Yet, despite its many discontinuities and ruptures, modernity served as a powerful theoretical construct during the 1890s to articulate one's position in the present as different from the past and from other contemporaneous positions.

Dülfer's and Fischer's interiors at the 1897 exhibition and their contemporary reception as distinctly 'modern' should thus be viewed as one response to the conditions of modernity briefly outlined above. However, despite their regular use of the term 'modern' in relation to these two interiors, reviewers remained somewhat ambiguous, if not misleading, over its precise meaning. Indeed, the interiors' modernity was delineated more by negation (i.e. that which they were not) than by definition (i.e. that which they were). Critics primarily based their pronunciations on the observation that these spaces consciously broke with previous historicist styles, which had dominated the German applied arts scene since the early 1870s. Modern design was called upon to be 'of the present' or 'up to date,' which, by implication, signalled a rupture with the past and its conventions. Gmelin, for example, demanded that modern designers 'take into account modern technologies, modern lifestyles and modern needs and outlooks'.[17] Furthermore, craftsmen and designers involved in the conception and realisation of the Munich exhibition's modern interiors were credited with a clear awareness of the latest national and international cultural developments. It was argued that this participation in international artistic trends set the exhibition's modern designers apart from the previous generation of German designers. In fact, reviews abound with rhetorical constructions of the 'young' versus the 'fathers', the 'new' versus the 'old' and the 'contemporary' versus the 'traditional'. Modern design was thus seen as being firmly anchored in the present and no longer weighed down by historicism's servitude to the past. 'Modern artists', and by extension modern designers, 'are modern people, and vice versa'.[18]

It is with this understanding of the modern in mind, that one should reassess how Dülfer's and Fischer's interiors at the 1897 exhibition could signal a path into the future by being 'of the present'. In his careful evaluation of these interiors, Gmelin provided insight into the contemporary understanding of the modern when explaining that 'two essential features characterise applied arts' modern direction: first, the spurning of anything that smacks of even the slightest touch of surrogacy or bragging … second, the confraternity with local plants and animals, which goes hand in hand with a preference for unpretentious materials coupled with a simplicity of construction'.[19] An anonymous colleague writing for the journal *Kunstchronik* stipulated that the displays in the Munich exhibition's applied arts section were modern because they 'rejected the kind of historicist ornament prevalent in earlier styles, kept in mind a practical usability and functionality and thus focused primarily on their building components.'[20] Both critics were adamant in their rejection of historicist design practices and their reliance on the revival past styles. Interestingly, the rhetoric of a truthful use of materials (*Materialechtheit*) and a formal language that was conditioned by an object's function (*Zweckmässigkeit der Form*) seen here as characteristic of Jugendstil design was absorbed into discussions of modernist design practices emerging out of the German Werkbund and the Bauhaus, despite the latter's adamant rejection of Jugendstil ornament and decoration.

A comparison of two other interiors designed around the same time and within the same cultural context illustrates how proponents of the modern Jugendstil interior positioned themselves in relation to historicist interiors, which continued to prosper in late nineteenth-century Germany interior design manuals and practices. Indeed, both historicist interiors and modern interiors regularly appeared in the Bavarian Applied Arts Association's journal *Kunst und Handwerk*. A photograph of Emanuel von Seidl's historicist reception room (Fig. 3.3) and that of another modern interior designed by Martin Dülfer, this time furnished with objects from the Munich Board for Art in Handicraft and exhibited in 1898 (Fig. 3.4), are cases in point. Viewed next to Seidl's historicist interior, Dülfer's modern interior serves a powerful visualisation of some of the rhetorical claims made by proponents of the Jugendstil: the development of one's own artistic language (vs copying of past forms), the advocacy of simple organic forms (vs misplaced ostentation and luxury), the honest employ of material (vs surrogates and pretence) and, most importantly, the ability to address the conditions of modern life (vs historicism's denial of the evolution of time).

The comparison of Seidl's historicist interior with Dülfer's Jugendstil interior raises

yet another important point. Namely, that during the 1890s, the idea of 'being of the present' lent itself to a range of ideological positions and generated a diverse array of material articulations. This is to say that Seidl's historicist reception room could be viewed as equally of the present as Dülfer's Jugendstil interior. This points to some interesting fissures and ruptures of the seemingly hermetically constructed category of fin de siècle modernity. Such an approach allows for a more complex and modulated approach to this historical moment by not simply positing the modern versus the antimodern, the optimists versus the pessimists. By departing from Fritz Stern's influential paradigm of 'cultural pessimism', a paradigm that posited powerful antimodern forces as the source of German society's descent into irrationality and crisis, the model offered here envisions the fin de siècle as a place and a space in which often contradictory paths into the future coexisted and offered multiple responses to modernity.[21] Viewed from this perspective, the 'modern' did not simply register one's divergence from the past, but actually delineated a sense of difference within the present. It could therefore be argued that the modern interiors at the 1897 exhibition represented but one possible response to living in the modern world and that indeed diverse design languages could lay claim to being 'of the present'.

So who was to say that the kinds of historicist interiors embraced by a majority of fin-de-siècle producers and consumers of culture could not engender a modern subjectivity? As a matter of fact, a survey of contemporary applied arts journals published

127. Empfangsfaal in einem Münchener Haufe. Architekt Prof. Eman. Seidl.
Wandbezug in rothem Seidendamaft von J. Ebner & Co., Vergolderarbeit von Barth & Co., Stukfaturen von Rappa und Giobbe.

Fig. 3.3. Emanuel von Seidl, reception room in a Munich house (from *Kunst und Handwerk* 47 (1897). Museum für Kunst und Gewerbe, Hamburg).

from the late 1880s onwards attests to a continued momentum of historicist *Wohnkultur* that supporters of the 1897 exhibition so adamantly rejected. A careful look beyond the new generation's battle cries of 'away with the old' reveals that members of Germany's historicist circles also responded in a critical and self-conscious way to the conditions of modern life and were actively engaged in developing an appropriate material response.[22] This implies that during

the 1890s in Germany, interiors that do not look modern to our twenty-first century eyes might have had equal stakes in being 'of the present'.

The rhetoric of the birth of a modern movement through Dülfer's and Fischer's interiors at the 1897 exhibition thus warrants further consideration, as does the familiar art historical narrative positing producers and supporters of the exhibition's Jugendstil interiors as Germany's design avant-gardes

586. Fenster-Sitz; Architekt M. Dülfer.
Möbel nach Entwürfen von B. Pankok, München.

Fig. 3.4. Martin Dülfer, window seat 1898 with furniture by B. Pankok (from *Kunst und Handwerk* 48 (1898). Museum für Kunst und Gewerbe, Hamburg).

and advocates of historicism as *arrière-gardes.* This is not to advocate a revisionist endorsement of historicist design practices, because it certainly holds true that historicism had run its course by the mid-1890s and produced little more than a succession of futile stylistic revivals. And yet the persistence of historicist interiors both in design manuals and actual home decors (*Wohnkultur*) complicates discussions of Wilhelmine modernity. As a matter of fact, some of the fundamental concerns articulated by the modern movement picked up and reformulated key objectives that previous generations of designers had been struggling with since Germany's unification in 1871.

For example, the search for a national design language that, whilst in tune with international developments, represented a truly German cultural identity fuelled design debates from the 1870s onwards. Despite the obvious disagreement over the appropriate visual and material solutions to this fundamental question, both camps, modern and historicist, were invested with German nationalism. Ironically, this common ground tied both groups to a fairly conservative agenda. When discussing the 1897 exhibition's modern interiors, critics consistently evoked the notion of the painterly, which was understood at the time as an effective design strategy that infused interior spaces with a certain mood and atmosphere. The distinctly German atmosphere borne forth by painterly interiors was one of *Gemütlichkeit.* Although Wölfflin's discussion of the painterly was not published until 1915, the importance of ambience and psychological effects anticipated some of Wölfflin's key tenets, in particular the painterly eye's 'abandon [of] tangible

design … the apprehension of the world as a shifting semblance'.[23] In 1884, for example, the then director of the Frankfurt Applied Arts School Ferdinand Luthmer published a visual sourcebook for contemporary interior design entitled *Malerische Innenräume moderner Wohnungen* in which he described light and colour as two of the key ingredients of a successful painterly interior:

These days, one forgoes large and equally disposed amounts of light in favour of a more painterly appearance of a room. The latter is achieved by arranging windows not on the long wall of a room, but on one of its smaller ones instead. Now light has to cover an even longer distance to reach the opposite small wall, while the two long walls are now merely brushed by a focused and effective lighting. This kind of lighting is particularly popular in our modern time … since the images that are created by this sharp and concentrated light are always painterly and full of effect.[24]

As a visual comparison between Seidl's reception room (Fig. 3.3) and Fischer's 1897 interior (Fig. 3.4) shows, the manipulation of light and surfaces to create a painterly interior did not come to an end with historicist design practices, and the painterly continued to feature in modern interiors and their new design language of the Jugendstil.

Another design strategy that tied Dülfer's and Fischer's interiors to earlier historicist practices was their shared indebtedness to the Wagnarian notion of a total work of art. The clever exhibition tactic of presenting audiences with carefully constructed domestic environments that were intended to conjure up actual living spaces was first tested at Germany's First National Art and Design Exhibition in 1876, which had also been staged in the Munich Glaspalast under the auspices of the Bavarian Applied Arts Association's twenty-fifth jubilee. This landmark exhibition introduced a stylistically driven display concept that presented objects in their formal and functional relationships rather than their regional and temporal alliances. In other words, objects were no longer displayed as clusters of the same category or shared point of origin, but played a crucial role in stylistically unified, historically situated room ensembles that critics promptly christened *Gesamtarrangements.*[25] The 1876 exhibition's most famous *Gesamtarrangement* was undoubtedly Gabriel von Seidl's *German Room,* a historicist fancy, with serious nationalistic implications, in the style of the neo–Northern Renaissance.[26] Although Dülfer's and Fischer's 1897 modern interiors adamantly rejected the historicism of earlier *Gesamtarrangements,* they reinscribed these earlier exhibition strategies' innovative presentation of paintings, sculptures and applied arts in stylistically unified architectural environments.

The painterly composition and the display of a stylistically unified space are only two examples drawn from a range of complex interrelations between historicist and modern interiors in late nineteenth-century Germany. Yet these two links suggest that, despite their divergent stylistic languages, both historicist and Jugendstil designers shared a desire to develop a *Wohnkultur* that could address the conditions of modern life. Although historicist interiors produced during the 1880s and well

into the 1890s might not look 'modern' to our eyes since we have been conditioned to see them as products of the *arrière-guard* by modernist art history, they should be viewed as a potentially viable cultural response to late nineteenth-century modernity. Therefore, the possibilities they offered contemporaneous beholders to envision and negotiate a modern world should not be ignored. Much like their Jugendstil counterparts, these historically inspired spaces participated in debates around the articulation of a modern subjectivity. By unhinging modernism as a cultural practice from modernism as a stylistic category, a complex and often contradictory picture of late nineteenth-century discussions of the 'modern' emerges. Far from attempting to retrieve historicist design practices, this essay advocates a more nuanced interpretation of the meaning of modernity in late nineteenth-century German design practices. The reception of Dülfer's and Fischer's interiors as 'modern' by contemporary critics thus not only marked their difference from the past, but tried to actively stake out a territory in Germany's fraught present.

Viewed from a historical perspective, Jugendstil interiors eventually toppled historicist *Wohnkultur,* but the ever-present contestations over the meaning of modernity soon claimed Jugendstil designers as their next victim. After the founding of the German Werkbund in 1907, a purist, antiornamental rhetoric began to take hold of German applied arts reformers and turned the tide against the Jugendstil. Whilst some might argue that this 'ontological discontinuity' lies at the very heart of modernity, the repercussions for Jugendstil interiors, and even more so for historicist interiors, were serious.[27] They were written out of the design historical canon for decades to come and did not seem worthy of attention until Friedrich Ahlers-Hestermann's cautious overture in 1956.[28] Today, we seem to have come full circle in that Dülfer's and Fischer's interiors are once again posited as the starting point or *Keim Zelle* of the modern German interior, with Jugendstil exhibitions proving as guaranteed crowd pleasers across Europe and North America.

Notes

1. For surveys of German nineteenth-century interiors, see, for example M. Forkel, *Wohnen im 'Stil' des Historismus* (Museumsdorf, 1990); H. Kreisel and G. Himmelheber, eds., *Die Kunst des deutschen Möbels: Möbel und Vertäfelungen des deutschen Sprachraums von den Anfängen bis zum Jugendstil,* iii, Georg Himmelheber, *Klassizismus, Historismus, Jugendstil,* new and rev. ed. (Beck, 1983); L. Niethammer, ed., *Wohnen im Wandel: Beiträge zur Geschichte des Alltags in der bürgerlichen Gesellschaft* (Hammer, 1979).

2. J. A. Lux, *Das neue Kunstgewerbe in Deutschland: Ein Versuch* (Klinkhardt & Biermann, 1908), p. 116.

3. For the dominant position on Jugendstil as Germany's first modern style, see, for example, G. Fahr-Becker, *Der Jugendstil* (Könemann and Ottomeyer, 1996); H. Ottomeyer, ed., *Wege in die Moderne: Jugendstil in München, 1896 bis 1914* (Klinkhardt & Biermann,1997). For a more nuanced position on Jugendstil as Germany's last historicist style, see, for example, F. Schmalenbach, *Jugendstil: Ein Beitrag zu Theorie und Geschichte der Flächenkunst* (Triltsch, 1935).

4. E. Rathke, *Jugendstil* (Bibliographisches Institut, 1958), p. 16.

5. S. Günther, *Interieurs um 1900* (Wilhelm Fink Verlag, 1971), p. 21.

6. Theodor Fischer was a pupil of the famous Munich architect Friedrich von Thiersch, but he soon turned away from his teacher's historicism. Fischer became a founding member of the German Werkbund in 1907 and the German Garden City Society, which led to his close involvement in the realisation of Germany's first garden city, Hellerau. For more information on Fischer, see U. Kerkhoff, *Theodor Fischer: Eine Abkehr vom Historismus oder ein Weg zur Moderne* (Karl Krämer Verlag and Nerdinger, 1987). Martin Dülfer is primarily known for his theatre architecture and as an important Jugendstil architect. See D. Klein, *Martin Dülfer: Wegbereiter der deutschen Jugendstilarchitektur,* 2nd ed. (Bayerisches Landesamt für Denkmalpflege, 1993).

7. K. Bloom Hiesinger, *Art Nouveau in Munich: Masters of Jugendstil* (Prestel Verlag, 1988), p. 169.

8. L. Gmelin, 'Die Kleinkunst auf der Kunstausstellung zu München 1897', *Kunst und Handwerk* 47 (1897), pp. 17–29, 50–9.

9. W. von Bode, 'Künstler im Kunsthandwerk: Die Abteilung der Kleinkunst in den Internationalen Ausstellungen zu München und Dresden, 1897', *Pan* 3/2 (1897), p. 113.

10. W. von Bode, *Kunst und Kunstgewerbe am Ende des Neunzehnten Jahrhunderts* (Bruno & Paul Cassirer, 1901), p. 94.

11. H. E. von Berlepsch, 'Endlich ein Umschwung', *Deutsche Kunst und Dekoration* 1 (1897), p. 3.

12. W. Rolfs, 'Alte Gleise—Neue Pfade', *Kunst und Handwerk* 48 (1897/98), p. 6.

13. Alexander Koch first supported progressive design practices in his interior design journal *Illustrirte Kunstgewerbliche Zeitschrift für Innen-Dekoration* (1890–1944, from 1900 as *Innendekoration: Mein Heim, Mein Stolz*), which served an important forum for the rejection of historicist styles. He continued his crusade against historicism in the even more progressive journal *Deutsche Kunst und Dekoration* (1897–1932). Koch saw himself as a mediator between designers, intellectuals and consumers. Koch's publishing house exists to this day (as part of the Verlagsgruppe Weinbrenner).

14. Gmelin, 'Die Kleinkunst auf deer Kunstausstellung', p. 17.

15. K. Repp, *Reformers, Critics and the Paths of German Modernity* (Harvard University Press, 2000), p. 21.

16. S. Marchand and D. Lindenfeld, eds, *Germany at the Fin de Siècle: Culture, Politics and Ideas* (Louisiana State University Press, 2004), p. 6.

17. Gmelin, 'Die Kleinkunst auf deer Kunstausstellung', p. 17.

18. A. Freihofer, 'Die Münchner Kunstausstellung III', *Der Kunswart* 7/1 (1893), p. 11.

19. Gmelin, 'Die Kleinkunst auf deer Kunstausstellung', p. 17.

20. Anonymous, 'Internationale Kunstausstellung im Glaspalast in München' *Leipziger Kunstchronik* 9/33 (1898), p. 532.

21. F. Stern, *The Politics of Cultural Despair: A Study in the Rise of the Germanic Ideology* (University of California Press, 1961).

22. Gmelin, 'Die Kleinkunst auf deer Kunstausstellung', p. 18.

23. H. Wölfflin, 'Principles in Art History', in D. Preziosi, ed., *The Art of Art History: A Critical Anthology* (Oxford University Press, 1998), p. 116.

24. F. Luthmer, *Malerische Innenräume moderner Wohnungen: In Aufnahmen nach Natur* (Heinrich Keller, 1884), p. 9.

25. F. Pecht, 'Aus dem Müncher Glaspalast', *Beilage zur Allgemeinen Zeitung,* 15 June 1876, p. 2551.

26. For a discussion of the 1876 exhibition's impact on new trends in interior design, see S. Muthesius, 'The "altdeutsche" Zimmer, or Cosiness in Plain Pine', *Journal of Design History* 16/4 (2003), pp. 269–90; and, for the neo–Northern Renaissance's implications in Germany's quest for a national design style, see S. Wieber, *Designing the Nation: Neo-Northern Renaissance Interiors and the Politics of Identity in Late Nineteenth-Century Germany, 1876–1888,* PhD dissertation, University of Chicago, 2004.

27. W. R. Everdell, *The First Moderns: Profiles in the Origins of Twentieth-Century Thought* (University of Chicago Press, 1997), p. 11.

28. F. Ahlers-Hestermann, *Stilwende: Aufbruch der Jugend um 1900,* 2nd ed. (Mann, 1956). This book was initially published in 1941, but its second edition in 1956 initiated the above-discussed reassessment of the German Jugendstil.

Part Two

The Early Twentieth-century Interior (1900–1940)

Part 2 Interior staircase in Le Corbusier's Villa Savoye, Poissy, France, 1929. Photograph: Penny Sparke.

Introduction

Penny Sparke

The years 1900 to 1940 represented a crucially important period for the formation and dissemination of the concept of the modern interior as it manifested itself in the Western industrialised world. However, during those years, it was both vociferously repudiated and enthusiastically embraced. Whilst in their frantic attempts to eradicate nineteenth-century bourgeois domesticity and all that went with it—conspicuous consumption, the self-consciously artistic interior, the dominance of 'feminine' taste, visual clutter etc.—many of the architects and designers who were working under the banner of modernism in those years sought to deny the existence of a separate concept of 'the interior', other groups of aesthetic practitioners, with different backgrounds and experiences, set out to redefine its parameters and those of the professionals who would specialise in forming it. The modernists saw the interior as intrinsically linked to the architectural shell and belonging exclusively to the domain of the architect, whilst others—amateur housewives with responsibility for the decoration of their homes, the professional interior decorators/designers emerging in the United States and elsewhere, the French ensembliers and commercial industrial designers among them—focused their attentions directly on the discrete interior, imbuing it with a life of its own beyond the architecture that contained it and understanding the important role it had to play within modernity and modern life.

The deep-seated dualism that underpinned the way in which the interior was understood in those years—as something that is either to be eliminated or embraced depending on whether it was being discussed or experienced within the context of architectural and design modernism or within a wider frame linked to a broader understanding of what it meant to be 'modern'—was reflected in both the rich variety of styles of the interiors that came into being and the frameworks—the academic discourses, the educational context, the media promotional material and the commercial context—that supported them. Given the strikingly divergent views about the modern interior in those years, the literature that addressed it, both within the period and beyond, was unsurprisingly fragmented and failed to provide a clear and consistent picture of it between 1900 and 1940.

The dominant accounts of the modern architecture and design of the period, written from within the ideology of modernism, paid scant attention to the interior in and for itself. Whilst, for example, in his influential *Pioneers of Modern Design: From William Morris to Walter Gropius* of 1936, Nikolaus Pevsner devoted considerable attention to the subjects of painting, engineering and to the individual components of the interior—carpets, wallpaper, chairs, chimney pieces etc.—he only referred to complete interiors in passing. Although he included a number of illustrations of interiors—among them Victor Horta's hallway at 6 rue Paul-Emile Janson, Brussels; a Plumet interior; a flax-spinning mill in Shrewsbury; Boileau's St. Eugène in Paris; the Halles des Machines in Paris; St. Jean de Montmartre, Paris; C.F.A. Voysey's The Orchard; Mackintosh's Glasgow School of Art and tearooms; Wright's Larkin Building; a Loos shop interior; and Wagner's Post Office Savings Bank—the text failed to reflect that fact and focused instead on their structural and spatial, that is their architectural features, rather than on their specific characteristics as interior spaces intended for occupation.[1] In essence, Pevsner adopted the *Gesamtkunstwerk* (total work of art) approach towards the interiors of the architects and designers he had chosen to discuss and focused on their architectural characteristics.

Sigfried Giedion's *Mechanization Takes Command: A Contribution to Anonymous History,* published just over a decade after the first edition of Pevsner's text, did acknowledge the existence of certain kinds of interiors— particularly those within factories, Pullman trains, ocean liners and kitchens—but that historian's emphasis was firmly focused on the rational processes that, he claimed, led to their formation rather than on the values underpinning the idea of modern 'interiority'.[2] In keeping with the views of the modernists he admired so much, he emphasised what he believed to be the evils of bourgeois domesticity and praised their rational, scientific approach. Giedion's perspective on the modern interior directly mirrored that

of several of the pioneering architects of the Modern movement—Bruno Taut, Walter Gropius and Ernst May among them. They had borrowed ideas about scientific management from men such as Frederick Winslow Taylor and applied them to the domestic arena as a strategy for counteracting what they saw as the emotionally charged approach of the amateur housewife and the decorator—the contaminators, they believed, of domestic architecture. Also, once again emulating the modernist practitioners, Giedion pointed a finger of blame for the 'problem' of the bourgeois domestic interior at the housewife and her alliance with commerce and trade. 'Women whose husbands had recently acquired means', he explained, were, he felt, responsible for the decorative excesses of the nineteenth-century domestic interior.[3]

In its account of modern architecture in the period 1900 to 1940, Reyner Banham's 'Theory and Design in the First Machine Age', published a little later in 1960, was also not committed to the interior for its own sake.[4] Like Pevsner's, Banham's text acknowledged the importance of the legacy of avant-garde painting and sculpture and of nineteenth-century engineering to modern architecture. Like Pevsner, he included illustrations of a number of interiors—that of Max Berg's Jahrhunderthalle in Breslau for example—but referred only to their structural properties, in that case reinforced concrete.[5] Paralleling Pevsner once again, Banham also included an image of the interior of Frank Lloyd Wright's Larkin Building but captioned it 'an achievement so far out of step with progressive architectural thought at the time', thereby demonstrating his interest in it as radical architecture first and foremost.[6]

The interior of Le Corbusier's iconic Pavillon de l'Esprit Nouveau, shown at the 1925 Exposition des Arts Décoratifs Modernes et Industriels in Paris was also included. To show that it was entirely rationally and functionally conceived, and that it had not been left to the whim of an amateur housewife or a decorator, it was described as being 'furnished with equipment from manufacturers' catalogues'.

Within modernist accounts of modernist architecture, therefore, the interior had a significant visual presence but was largely unacknowledged nonetheless. It was only included to evidence rational thinking and structural innovation rather than to show that the interior could mirror modernity in terms which went beyond the remit of architecture. Another, less well known, body of literature written in the first half of the twentieth century adopted a different approach, however; one that granted much more independence to the modern interior as a phenomenon in its own right. In 1916, for instance, an American, Hazel Adler, published a book entitled *The New Interior: Modern Decoration for the Modern Home.*[7] Building on the work of the Weiner Werkstätte, which had been imported to the United States, Adler's text was directed at an amateur audience and written with the assumption that the new decoration was a democratic possibility. Her aim was to 'suggest new possibilities and open new trains of thought by setting forth those fresh and stimulating currents which are influencing the creators of what has been called "the new taste" in interior decoration'.[8] Filled with illustrated exempla, the book supported the idea of a craft-based modern interior aesthetic. The idea that a modern decoration existed that paralleled modern architecture

was embraced by a number of texts written in the late 1920s and 1930s. Paul Frankl's *New Dimensions: The Decorative Arts of Today in Words and Pictures* of 1928, Dorothy Todd and Raymond Mortimer's *The New Interior Decoration: An Introduction to Its Principles,* and International Survey of its Methods of 1929 and Hans Hoffmann's *Modern Interiors in Europe and America* of 1930, among them, all promoted the idea of modern interior decoration and adopted a very different approach towards the work of the international modernist architects to the apologists of that movement.[9] Their mission was to explain how, within modernism, the interior had been transformed and that a modern form of interior decoration, characterised by 'simplicity and clear, defined lines' had emerged.[10] Embracing the late work of the Werkstätte designers and of both modern and modernist architects across the globe—from Josef Franck in Vienna to Josef Gočar in Prague; to Rava and Larco in Milan; to Duncan Grant and Vanessa Bell in England; to Alvar Aalto in Finland; to Pierre Chareau, Djo-Bourgeois, René Herbst, Le Corbusier, Pierre Jeanneret and Charlotte Perriand, Paul Follot and Jean-Michel Frank in France; to Bruno Paul and Ludwig Mies van der Rohe in Germany, and many more besides—they showed that, whether the modernists chose to acknowledge it or not, a new modern interior decoration could be seen to have emerged, the mission of which was to be expressive of a new age. Recognising no significant distinction between residential and commercial spaces, nor between the most austere and the most decorative ends of the modern visual spectrum, these writers celebrated the emergence of the new interiors which, through their shared simplicity, clear lines, emphasis on spatial articulation and use of new materials, such as tubular steel, set out to reflect modernity first and foremost. Whilst the same relief felt by the modernists that nineteenth-century bourgeois domesticity had finally disappeared was expressed by those writers, they, in sharp contrast, openly welcomed the arrival of an interior that, in their views, had been visually and conceptually renewed rather than allowing itself to be subsumed within architecture and lost as an autonomous concept.

The two distinct bodies of literature that emerged were, in effect, two sides of the same coin. The interiors they addressed were largely the same ones, but their approaches were fundamentally different. On one hand, the modernist critics and historians extended the ideas they found within modernist treatises; but another group of writers, linked more closely to the mass media and to the commercial world of interiors, saw a new era dawning within which the interior played an important role. As Todd and Mortimer explained, 'It is essential to realise that our decoration is as much a characteristic product of our civilisation as our newspapers, our poems, our dances and our morals.'[11] To a considerable extent, therefore, the same interiors were being viewed through different lenses, and, whilst there was a clear stylistic spectrum—from overtly decorative at one end to austere and minimal at the other—the same spaces were being interpreted very differently by different observers.

Whilst one of the many differences of perspective that defined the modern interior of the first four decades of the twentieth century developed within the critical literature that addressed it, or indeed failed to do so, another was rooted in the diverse range of 'agents' of the design of the interior who emerged in those years and vied with each other for attention. As we have seen, architects, amateur housewives, professional decorators, *ensembliers* and industrial designers were among the many interior 'agents' who were active in that area in those years. Where progressive modern interiors were concerned, the architects undoubtedly dominated the picture. Their commitment to the idea of the *Gesamtkunstwerk* meant that they included fitted and built-in furniture wherever possible and defined free-standing furniture items as pieces of 'equipment' rather than as providers of physical or psychological comfort. Their interior spaces emphasised transparency, inside/outside ambiguity, lightness, the open plan and space over mass. As such, they were visually innovative and overtly modern.

In addition to architects, amateur housewives also continued to create interiors in those years, especially in the domestic context, as they had been doing through the last decades of the nineteenth century. As she had been at that time, the amateur housewife continued to be helped in her tasks by advice books which expanded in number after 1900. They were written by a range of people from journalists to decorators and, whilst they all had subtly different messages to convey, shared a commitment to helping the housewife create a modern home in which she could express both her own self-identity and the social status that her family had either achieved or to which it aspired. Self-identity and expression were, for the housewife, more important than the specificity of the style of decoration through which that expression occurred. As the pioneer American interior decorator, Elsie de Wolfe, explained to women readers of her 1913 book, *The House in Good Taste,* 'you will express yourself in your home whether you want to or not.'[12] In their best-selling book of 1897, *The Decoration of Houses,* as a means of escaping Victorian clutter, the novelist Edith Wharton and the architect Ogden Codman had promoted a return to the French and Italian styles of the eighteenth century.[13] Their advice had created a vogue for those styles in the United States, and, a little later, Elsie de Wolfe extended the popularity that they had established for the Louis XV and Louis XVI styles to a much wider audience, advocating it as a modern idiom that would help women create their modern self-identities. Rather than promoting a form of historicism, however, the decorator was offering a light, bright and, relatively speaking, simple, modern alternative to Victorian decoration. Her late nineteenth-century refurbishment of her East 17th Street home in New York had exemplified the transformation from voluptuous cosy corners to painted wooden furniture in a range of pastel colours that she went on to recommend to her readers a decade or so later. Typically, her book contained a double level within it, suggesting, on the one hand, that housewives could achieve such a transformation themselves whilst, on the other, making it clear that the easier route would be to employ an interior decorator. A later advice book of 1936, *What's New in Home Decorating,* written by Winnifred Fales, advocated a decorating

style which was much more overtly modern and owed much to the French Art Deco style and to the American Streamlined Moderne idiom. Styles apart, however, Fales's advice had much in common with that of de Wolfe three decades earlier.[14] 'The trend in design', she wrote, 'is unmistakable: simplicity of form; fewer colours.'[15] According to Fales, historical styles continued to be acceptable at that later date, however, and, alongside contemporary ones, were considered just as modern as the 'machine style'. 'But if your preference … is Colonial, or one of the Old World styles', Fales wrote, 'and your tastes in furnishings revolve around fine old highboys and four-posters, wing chairs and mellow-toned English chintzes … rest assured, you will have no difficulty in obtaining suitable designs.'[16] In the end, style was seen as being less important than the ability of a decorative scheme to express identities and project 'modernness'. 'Indeed, as it appears to me', explained Fales, 'a free, intelligent, well considered expression of *individuality* is the keynote of modern living and of modern decoration.'[17] Through the words of de Wolfe, Fales and others, housewives were encouraged to modernise their homes and, in the process, the decoration of the interior came to have more and more in common with the world of haute couture and fashion, about which the architectural modernists were open in their condemnation. A marker of feminine identity and expression, like clothes, the interior came to be seen, from this perspective, as a stage set within which identities were formed and re-formed.

The professional lady decorator emerged in the United States in the early twentieth century, therefore, and worked like a couturier, supplying clients with modern lifestyles through the material and spatial environments they inhabited. De Wolfe had spent her early career on the stage in New York modelling couture gowns, and, when she switched to interior decoration, she took with her her 'good eye', her understanding of 'good taste' and of what modern women wanted. She established a direction of travel which others—among them, in the United States, Ruby Ross Wood, Rose Cumming and Francis Elkins and, in the United Kingdom, Syrie Maugham and Sibyl Colefax—developed further. Their role was to select interior items and arrange them in complete interior settings which conformed to the taste and aspirations of their clients. Their desire to please, and their close links to fashion and to trade and commerce, evoked condemnation on the part of the modernists who took a diametrically opposed approach to the interior—one which grew from, and was determined by architecture, which was based on functionality and rationality and which was not compromised by the marketplace. When, after 1940, the idea of the male interior designer emerged, he defined himself in sharp contradistinction to the lady decorators who became, as a result, marginalised and relegated to the background as conservative forces.

Whilst the interior decorator dominated the commercial world of the interior in the Anglo-Saxon world in the first four decades of the twentieth century, in France the *ensembliers* took on an equal significance. Rooted in cabinet-making and the luxury trades, they also saw the interior as an independent phenomenon and set out to redefine it as an important mirror and agent of modernity. As Katherine Kahle explained in her 1930 study, *Modern French Decoration,* the *ensembliers* included some who reached maturity between 1900 and 1910, among them Leon Jallot and Maurice Dufrêne; some who had emerged between 1910 and 1914, including Francis Jourdain, Emile-Jacques Ruhlmann and the partnership of Louis Sue and Andre Mare; Pierre Chareau and René Prou, who had become visible in about 1919; and some younger designers, among them Edouard-Joseph Djo-bourgeois, Etienne Kohlmann, Maurice Matet and Charlotte Perriand.[18] Kahle's account of their work divided them into the traditionalists (Ruhlmann, Jallot, Follot and Prou among them) and the rationalists (notably Djo-bourgeois, Pierre Chareau and Mallet-Stevens). The latter produced interiors containing furniture pieces they had designed that were characterised by their use of metal and glass and geometric forms, which related to the high modernist designs of German designers associated with the Bauhaus and the 'machine aesthetic' of the French architect-designer, Le Corbusier. The former group, whilst producing interiors which were indubitably modern, retained, nonetheless, numerous references to the past (especially the eighteenth century), used surface pattern and ornament to varying degrees and worked in traditional materials, predominantly wood.

Above all, Kahle believed that all the interiors shown at the 1925 exhibition, at which the *ensembliers* came into their own, represented a 'complete expression of the Modern French Spirit'.[19] They were, she explained, characterised by their simplicity, efficiency, usefulness and comfort. Their origins, she claimed, lay in Cubism and the work of the École Boulle, a furniture-making school founded in 1889 by the Society for the Encouragement of Art and Industry.[20] Importantly, after about 1910, as Kahle also explained, the idea of the interior as an *ensemble* came into being. As a direct result, 'the architect', wrote Kahle, 'is forced into second place for a time.'[21] Above all, the French *ensembliers* aligned themselves enthusiastically with the commercial sector, several of them joining forces with the new department stores—Dufrêne with Galeries Lafayettes to create La Maitrise; Paul Follot (another traditionalist) with Au Printemps to form Primavera; and René Prou with Bon Marché to create La Pomone. Sue et Mare formed La Compagnie des Arts Français in 1919; two decorators named Joubert and Petit named their company DIM; whilst another, Robert Block, established Studio Athelia.

The final group of 'agents' of the interior of the middle years of the twentieth century were the industrial designers who emerged in the United States as the stylists for industrially produced goods. Their definition of the interior was one which was shaped by the material objects within it and which acted as a promotional and theatrical frame for their products. The diversity of the agents of the designed interiors of the first four decades of the twentieth century was reflected in the support systems which underpinned them. Different magazines promoted different kinds of interiors—architectural journals such as *The Studio* and *Architectural Review* dealt with the *Gesamtkunstwerk* and the modernist interior, whilst *Vogue* magazine dedicated many of its pages to the work of the decorators, illustrating them alongside

examples of haute couture, and *Good Housekeeping* reported on scientifically planned kitchens which owed much to Taylorism. Exhibitions also focused on particular kinds of interiors. Whilst the Paris 1925 exposition featured the work of the *ensembliers,* the Weissenhofsiedlung of 1927, held in Stuttgart, was dedicated to white, flat-roofed modernist buildings and their interior spaces. More popular events, such as Britain's annual Ideal Home exhibition, showed a more eclectic range of interiors designed in a variety of styles from Tudor Revival to Moderne. The examples of modern interiors, expressed through a variety of styles which were exposed to the public, were many and varied, therefore, in the years leading up to the middle of the twentieth century. That pluralism was also expressed in the ways in which interior decorators and designers were educated. Whilst the former frequently learned their trade through correspondence courses or by simply learning on the job, interior design courses became more formalised and linked to architectural education as the century progressed.

The relatively small number of books published over the last few decades which have set out to map the story of the design of the twentieth-century interior have attempted to capture the pluralism of the early twentieth-century interior. The first five chapters of Anne Massey's *Interior Design of the Twentieth Century* for example focus on 'Reforming Victorian Taste', 'The Search for a New Style', 'The Modern Movement', 'Art Deco and the Moderne' and 'The Emergence of Interior Decoration as a Profession'.[22] These chapters offer a narrative of the modern interior which starts with the 'problem' of

Victorian bourgeois domesticity and then moves on to describe the alternatives that emerged as potential 'solutions' to it. Whilst the tensions and ambiguities that arose are inevitably not explored fully in this general survey of the subject, a much richer story than one simply focused on the contribution of modernism is offered, and a clear sense of the pluralism that characterised the design of the interior in the years leading up to 1940 is presented. Stanley Abercrombie's *A Century of Interior Design, 1900–2000: The Design, the Designers, the Products, and the Profession,* covers similar ground.[23] His survey covers the work of the early *Gesamtkunstwerk* modernists, the emergence of the 'New Interior' that accompanied the development of Art Nouveau and Jugendstil, the lady decorators, the influence of architecture, the hegemony of modernism and the growth of Art Deco and of Streamlined Moderne. The pluralism of the area is emphasised and the sense of the different versions of the modern interior coexisting alongside each other is exposed. Once again the scope of the study does not allow for a critical engagement with the contradictions, the tensions or the exclusions that inevitably resulted from that complex picture.

Over the last couple of decades, alongside the surveys which have demonstrated the breadth of activity going on in the area, a body of critical literature on the subject of the modern interior has also emerged. To account for some of the tensions, ambiguities and anomalies in the area, to redress the denial of the interior which characterised modernist accounts of modernist architecture and to explain why some areas have been marginalised by others, it has drawn on a range of approaches. My own 1995 study, *As Long as It's Pink: The Sexual Politics of Taste,* for example, looked at the cultural gendering of Victorian domesticity and of modernist architecture and design, emphasising the hegemonic nature of the former and the marginalised nature, within modernism, of the latter.[24] A similar theme provided the focus for a collation of essays published in the following year. *Not at Home: The Suppression of Domesticity in Modern Art and Architecture* was edited by Christopher Reed, a case study contributor to this book.[25] Essays in that compilation included one by Lisa Tiersten that looked at home decorating in turn-of-the-century Paris and another by Susan Sidlauskas, who discussed the relationship of the body to the interior and the meaning of interiority. 'In representations of the body within the domestic space', she wrote, 'we are contending not with one interior but with two: the body itself and the container that surrounds it.'[26] An image of the modern interior which was not architecture-dependent was thus being constructed through a reexamination of domesticity, seen, first and foremost, as a gendered concept.

Another essay in Reed's book was provided by the American architectural historian, and another case study contributor to *Designing the Modern Interior,* Alice T. Friedman. Her case study in Reed's book, which focused on the anxiety experienced by Edith Farnsworth, the client of Mies van der Rohe's Farnsworth House, by that architect's extensive use of glass and transparency in what was meant to be her home, formed the basis of one of the chapters of Friedman's 1998 book, *Women* and the Making of the Modern House.[27] By focusing on the relationship of clients to their architecturally designed, modernist buildings—their interiors in particular—Friedman was able to show the gap that existed between intentions and effects and the complex roles of gender and sexuality in that problematic relationship. By looking at modernist architecture from a fresh perspective, the author was able to provide a critique which highlighted the marginalisation of domesticity and feminine culture by modernism. Irene Nierhaus, yet another contributor of a case study to this anthology, published a book in German in 1999 entitled *Raum, Geschlecht, Architektur* (Space, Gender, Architecture) which addressed a similar theme. In 2005, Hilde Heynen, a further case study contributor to this book, and Gülsüm Baydar picked up, yet again, the theme of the relationship of modern architecture to domesticity and feminine culture in their edited book, *Negotiating Domesticity: Spatial Productions of Gender in Modern Architecture.*[28] Two other contributors of case studies to *Designing the Modern Interior,* Elizabeth Darling and Charles Rice, provided essays for the Heynen and Baydar anthology. The emphasis in the book was upon what the two editors felt to be the essential antipathy between both modernity and modernism and being 'at home'. 'In so far', they wrote in the introduction, 'as modernity means change and rupture, it seems to imply, necessarily, the leaving of home.[29] Theirs was a very particular definition of modernity, however—one that derived from the world of literary criticism. Other definitions of the same concept, linked to other aspects of the experience of the

modern world—among them the impact of the mass media, the separation of privacy from publicity, the rise of interiority etc.—could be seen as more compatible with domesticity. Heynen and Baydar's book built on ideas expressed in Heynen's earlier 1999 text, *Architecture and Modernity: A Critique,* which was an extended discussion, from the perspective of critical theory, about the ways in which architecture and modernity interfaced with each other.[30] The aim was to unpack the 'differences' between modernism and modernity that the modernists had tried to 'smooth out'.[31] Focusing on the work of Walter Benjamin in this context, Heynen was led to address ideas about the exterior versus the interior, the private versus the public.

In 2005, I published a study of the work of the pioneer American interior decorator, Elsie de Wolfe, in which I focused on the way in which she addressed the issues of domesticity and feminine culture in the interior through a decorating strategy which crossed the domains of the amateur and the professional, thereby reconstituting the relationship between them.[32] The relationship between the public and the private spheres had underpinned Beatriz Colomina's 1998 study, *Privacy and Publicity: Modern Architecture as Mass Media,* one of the first studies of modern architecture to foreground the importance of the interior in that context.[33] Colomina's chapter in the book entitled 'Interior', which also recalled Walter Benjamin's views on the subject, focused on the inside spaces of buildings by Adolf Loos and demonstrated the ways in which that architect arranged the furniture pieces to create complex theatrical effects that confounded the relationship between private and public. 'Upon entering a Loos interior', Colomina wrote, 'one's body is continually turned around to face the space that one has just moved through, rather than the upcoming space or the space outside.'[34] My 2008 publication entitled *The Modern Interior* builds on Colomina's focus on the relationship between the public and the private and suggests that it is the constant shifting of their relationship, and the reworking of the boundaries between them, that defines the modern interior. Also, like Colomina's, my study posits a link between the rise of the mass media within modernity and the emergence of the modern interior that leads to a difficulty in distinguishing between its idealised and its realised forms.

Three more books which address the problematics of the modern/modernist interior are worth mentioning in this context. To coincide with the exhibition of modernism, held in London's Victoria and Albert Museum in 2006, the architectural historian, Tim Benton, penned a small book on the subject of *The Modernist Home*.[35] The aim of his study was to analyse the extent to which the modernists could be said to have been successful at domestic design; that is did they design 'homes' or merely 'houses'? The life they expected to go on in their 'homes' was, in Benton's words, 'more active and austere, less passive and comfortable'.[36] Benton claims that the modernists did design homes but that they were directed at people who wanted to experience a new lifestyle that was not dependent on 'the snug, cosy, satisfied homes of their parents'. Whilst this may have been a satisfactory solution for some, it clearly did not, as Friedman has shown us,

work in the case of Edith Farnsworth, nor, as Benton admits, of Madame Savoye. Charles Rice's study, *The Emergence of the Interior: Architecture, Modernity, Domesticity,* offers a theory of the modern interior which builds on the work of both Benjamin (modernity) and Sigmund Freud (interiority) whilst also acknowledging its links with architecture, primarily through the medium of the plan.[37] Elizabeth Darling's book, *Re-forming Britain: Narratives of Modernity before Reconstruction,* of 2007 looks at modern architecture in Britain in the interwar years. Her emphasis upon 'dwellings' takes her into domestic interiors, as does her discussion of the work of the modernist architect, Wells Coates, who undertook a number of interior projects.

The five case studies that constitute the second section of this book all relate to the debates and discussions concerning the nature and meaning of the modern interior that have been taking place over the last decade and a half through the texts described above. They all have their roots in the history of modern (indeed mostly modernist) architecture and have developed through studies of that subject that have focused on the marginalised themes of domesticity and feminine culture. Addressing these themes has led the five historians in question—art historian Christopher Reed and architectural historians Elizabeth Darling, Irene Nierhaus, Hilde Heynen and Charles Rice—to undertake research into areas that have allowed them to develop new ideas about the modern interior in the period in question. Reed's chapter, 'Taking Amusement Seriously: Modern Design in the Twenties', addresses a marginalised area of interior decoration executed in Britain in the 1920s by members of the Bloomsbury Group, which was widely reported in *Vogue* magazine and which stood out 'against the hegemony of modernist design'. According to the author, that marginalisation occurred as a result of anxieties relating to sexuality and gender. The work itself aligned itself more readily with 'modernity' than with 'modernism', characterised as it was by its use of theatricality and its lack of certainties. Reed argues that this work could be seen as a prelude to postmodernism. '"The Scene in Which the Daily Drama of Personal Life Takes Place": Towards the Modern Interior in Early 1930s Britain', Darling's chapter, focuses on some interior projects undertaken by the English modernist architect Wells Coates. She argues that this work—one interior for George Russell Strauss and another for the actors Elsa Lanchester and Charles Laughton—can be read as sets for identity formation rather than simply as modernist interiors in the conventional sense of the term. Darling sees the manipulation of space in the interior as a 'process' and, like Reed, stresses the bohemianism of the clients in question.

Whilst Darling is arguing for a rereading of the modern interior, Heynen, in 'Leaving Traces: Anonymity in the Modernist House', suggests that modernist architecture and domesticity stand at opposite ends of a spectrum and that the work of Mies van der Rohe, for example, and of the Russian revolutionary architects, was antipathetic to privacy and intimacy. She describes Benjamin's view of the modern interior, one which contends that inhabitants needed to adopt, along the lines that Benton has described, an active relationship with their environment. Like others who have also focused on it, Heynen posits Rietveld's house for Truus Schröder as an example of a successful modernist home as a result of the fact that the inhabitant's lifestyle values were aligned with those that underpinned the modernist utopia. In 'The Modern Interior as Geography of Image, Space and Subject', Nierhaus adopts an alternative view about the interiors of Mies van der Rohe and Lilly Reich to that of Heynen, arguing that they do contain levels of intimacy and privacy but that they have to be read in a particular way. Indeed she suggests that there are still images present in Mies's houses but that there is 'a change of images rather than their eradication'. Her contention is in tune with Reed's idea that modernist houses were decorated; it was just a different form of decoration. Once again, the Rietveld house is offered as an example of a successful modernist house/ home, as is one commissioned by Sibyl Moholy-Nagy. Charles Rice offers a reading of the Rose Seidler House in Sydney which, although strictly beyond the time frame of this section of the book, represents, as he argues himself, a late Australian implementation of ideas which had been developed in Europe in the interwar years under the banner of modernism which tended to 'do away with' the interior. These five chapters either explore marginalised modern interiors or they offer new readings of mainstream modernist ones in the light of ideas that have emerged from recent debates about gender and modernity. They all have much to offer to the ongoing discussion about the design of the modern interior.

Notes

1. N. Pevsner, *Pioneers of Modern Design* (Penguin Books, 1960 [1936]).

2. S. Giedion, *Mechanization Takes Command: A Contribution to Anonymous History* (W. W. Norton, 1947).

3. Ibid., p. 452.

4. R. Banham, *Theory and Design in the First Machine Age* (Architectural Press, 1960).

5. Ibid., p. 58.

6. Ibid., p. 169.

7. H. A. Adler, *The New Interior: Modern Decoration for the Modern Home* (Century Company, 1916).

8. Ibid., p. 1.

9. See P. Frankl, *New Dimensions: The Decorative Arts of Today in Words and Pictures* (Payson & Clarke, 1928); D. Todd and R. Mortimer, *The New Interior Decoration: An Introduction to Its Principles, and International Survey of Its Methods* (B. T. Batsford, 1929) and H. Hoffman, *Modern Interiors in Europe and America* (The Studio, 1930).

10. Todd and Mortimer, *The New Interior Decoration,* Plate 4.

11. Ibid., p. 21.

12. E. De Wolfe, *The House in Good Taste* (Century Company, 1913), p. 5.

13. E. Wharton and O. Codman, Jr., *The Decoration of Houses* (B. J. Batsford, 1897).

14. W. Fales, *What's New in Home Decorating?* (Dodd, Mead, 1936).

15. Ibid., p. 8.

16. Ibid., pp. 8–9.

17. Ibid., p. 173.

18. K. M. Kahle, *Modern French Decoration* (G. P. Putnam's Sons, 1930), p. 32.

19. Ibid., p. 21.

20. Ibid., p. 29.

21. Ibid., p. 35.

22. A. Massey, *Interior Design of the Twentieth Century* (Thames & Hudson, 1990).

23. S. Abercrombie, *A Century of Interior Design, 1900–2000: The Design, the Designers, the Products, and the Profession* (Rizzoli, 2003).

24. P. Sparke, *As Long as It's Pink: The Sexual Politics of Taste* (Pandora, 1995).

25. C. Reed, ed., *Not at Home: The Suppression of Domesticity in Modern Art and Architecture* (Thames & Hudson, 1996).

26. Ibid., p. 67.

27. A. T. Friedman, *Women and the Making of the Modern House: A Social and Architectural History* (Harry N. Abrams, 1998).

28. H. Heynen and G. Baydar, eds., *Negotiating Domesticity: Spatial Productions of Gender in Modern Architecture* (Routledge, 2005).

29. Ibid., p. 2.

30. H. Heynen, *Architecture and Modernity: A Critique,* (MIT Press, 1999).

31. Ibid., p. 5.

32. P. Sparke, *Elsie de Wolfe: The Birth of Modern Interior Decoration* (Acanthus Press, 2005).

33. B. Colomina, *Privacy and Publicity: Modern Architecture as Mass Media* (MIT Press, 1998).

34. Ibid., p. 234.

35. T. Benton, *The Modernist Home* (V&A Publications, 2006).

36. Ibid., p. 16.

37. C. Rice, *The Emergence of the Interior: Architecture, Modernity, Domesticity* (Routledge, 2007).

Chapter Four

Taking Amusement Seriously: Modern design in the twenties

Christopher Reed

The hegemony of modernist design in the third quarter of the twentieth century depended, as hegemonies do, on misperceiving ideology as fact. That modernism was rational and functional was—and in some quarters still is—taken to be true despite the overwhelming evidence of modernist design schemes that, simply, did not work. In a forthright debunking of modernist claims more than two decades ago, Witold Rybczynski pointed out that the mechanics of Corbusian houses were no more advanced than vernacular domestic architecture of the twenties, whilst their construction materials (rust-prone metal fittings abutting blank white surfaces), exterior design (flat roofs in rainy or snowy climates) and organisation of interior space (tiny kitchens up many stairs) rendered them often less practical than conventional houses.[1] A second ideology that developed early and lingered late around modernist design is exemplified in Julian Holder's 1990 essay 'Promoting Modernism in Britain', which begins by taking it 'as axiomatic that a major concern of British Modernism, like their European counterparts, was with what was variously termed social, workers', or mass housing. New materials and methods of production were thought to

be employed most appropriately on mass housing.'[2] As Holder acknowledges and the evidence visible to anyone walking British city streets confirms, however, the public and private bodies that built worker housing in the twenties and early thirties found conventional brick construction and neo-Georgian style less expensive and more appropriate.[3]

Contrary to the axioms of design history, in short, modernist design was not the rational, functional outcome of needs for worker housing. As Rybczynski and other polemicists for postmodernism have shown, modernism was a style that, like other styles, served as a signifier; modernist housing *looked* practical, rational and functional. And the evidence of the design publications and BBC architecture broadcasts of the twenties and thirties reveals that, despite awareness of modernist workers' housing in Europe, the modernist look in Britain was strongly associated with the bourgeoisie.[4] In a typical BBC broadcast of 1933, printed in *The Listener* under the title 'Modern Dwellings for Modern Needs', Wells Coates presented modernism as appropriate to a 'we' with a family history of home ownership and habits like playing golf, driving motor cars and enjoying the leisure in which to 'read, write, play the piano or listen to the gramophone or wireless' but who now found themselves challenged by keeping house with fewer servants. Coates's solution is that this 'we' should treat their houses like their cars: as appliances with built-in furniture. 'We' can forego older modes of domesticity in favour of a high-tech future, Coates reassures, secure in the knowledge that 'our real possessions' are 'good manners' and 'good taste'.[5] Modernism this may be, but concern for the worker it is not.

This disjunction was clear at the time, as is shown by the *Daily Express*'s 1937 'Change Homes with Me, I May Turn Socialist' feature on Coates's redecoration of George Russell Strauss's mansion, discussed by Elizabeth Darling in this volume. Although by the mid thirties, Maxwell Fry—and his overlooked collaborator Elizabeth Denby, as Darling elsewhere shows—began to expand the focus of modernist designers to include working-class housing, the battle to bring International-style modernism to Britain was not initially fought in the name of the workers.[6] It was waged within the bourgeoisie, with the verbal and visual rhetorics of rationality and functionality deployed as solutions to problems associated with middle-class domesticity.

At this point I should be frank about my own axioms. To me it seems axiomatic that the history of design—and domestic interior design in particular—has been strongly inflected by broader anxieties over gender and sexuality, especially and specifically as these played out among members of the middle classes for and by whom design histories are generally produced. These anxieties were particularly acute in the late twenties and early thirties, in the wake of political changes signalled by women's achievement of the vote, cultural shifts embodied in the androgynous generation of Bright Young Things and the economic tensions that followed the Great War, worsening, of course, with the worldwide economic depression of the 1930s. The anxiety over the role of women designers that prompted Elizabeth Denby's contributions to be written out of the story of Maxwell Fry's modernism is not incidental to the history of modernist design. On a very fundamental level, the 'problem' for which modernist design proposed the look of rationality and functionality as a solution was not the needs of workers, but deviation from traditional middle-class norms of sex and gender.

An obvious, and highly influential, source of modernism's conservative gendered rhetorics is Le Corbusier's *Towards a New Architecture*. This manifesto opens by linking 'houses and moth eaten boudoirs' as feminine spaces that undermine the masculinity of the men who live in them, leaving them 'sheepish and shrivelled like tigers in a cage'. Imputations of effeminacy fused with rehearsals of the homophobic rhetorics generated around the Wilde trials as Le Corbusier condemned conventional architecture schools as 'hot-houses where blue hortensias and green chrysanthemums are forced, and where unclean orchids are cultivated'. All this to contrast, of course, with his own designs inspired by the heroic figure of the 'healthy and virile' engineer.[7]

Le Corbusier's appeals to anxieties over sexuality and gender were seized upon in the first British manifestoes for modernism. John

Betjeman's '1830–1930—Still Going Strong, A Guide to the Recent History of Interior Decoration', published in the *Architectural Review* in 1930, is still widely lauded for its prescient advocacy for modernist design. Betjeman's essay is equally prescient of the repressive gender rhetorics that accompanied modernism's introduction in Britain. His opening lines invoking a 'British public' summoned by dinner gongs address modernism to the bourgeoisie. Far from attending to worker housing, modernism, as Betjeman presented it, confronted the problem of the 'recent permission that was given to Germany to thicken English design' with what he called the 'awf'lly modern' style, 'started in 1920 and known as "jazz"'. And who granted this permission for a promiscuous internationalism embodied in 'cushions, whose colours resemble the allied flags … strewn about [the] parlor'? The culprits were our 'healthy daughters in simple frocks': 'With fingers busy at last, after long emancipation, they do "batik-work," "poker work," stencilling, "fret-work," "copper-work," "metalwork," "lampshade-work" and any other kind of "work" that can be devised. The harm they have done is terrific, for now the truly simple efforts of Le Corbusier and Dufy are hardly appreciated.' Betjeman's nationalist ideology, which turned British women working in the Arts and Crafts tradition into a foreign threat to a Britishness embodied by Continental designers, culminates in his conclusion warning that 'French, German, and Swedish' manufacturers, by following Le Corbusier, have usurped a truly British legacy, 'when we bear in mind the axioms of Soane in that their simplicity is the result not of whim but of logic'. To right this wrong, Betjeman asserted, Britain must turn to 'intelligent designers'—that is to professional men who could suppress the international jazz aesthetic of their amateur daughters (more likely, sisters) by deploying an essentially British style embodied in a Swiss architect.[8]

This illogical manifesto for logic would be funny—well, it is funny—but it would be funnier if it had not been taken so seriously at the time and for decades afterwards. Betjeman's rhetoric was part of a full-bore assault on what, during the twenties, was actually a homegrown style of British modernism, an assault successful enough to consign this style—simply called modern or contemporary in its own day—to an oblivion so complete it does not have a name in design history.[9] The characteristics of this style include theatricality, humour and an emphasis on artifice and playfulness exactly opposite to the claims for functional rationality that were used to promote the competing version of modernism of the thirties. To identify this suppressed form of modernism, I have proposed to rehabilitate a ubiquitous adjective of approbation of the twenties, by coining the term 'Amusing style'.[10]

The ubiquity of 'Amusing' is attested to in Paul Nash's 1932 *Room and Book,* which described the early twenties as a time when 'the adjective "amusing" started on its endless flight from lip to lip.'[11] By 1932, Nash intended this to be pejorative, for he was part of the trend towards the masculine professionalisation of design. Like Betjeman, Nash invoked the spectres of both national and sexual boundary violation in his description of the twenties as a time when 'charming young men and formidable ladies were hopping backwards and forwards between England and the Continent,' importing 'a piece of stuff from Paris, a German lamp, a steel chair, or just a headful of other people's ideas'. Borrowing from Betjeman for his survey of 'Modern English Furniture' in *Room and Book,* Nash analysed the 'not altogether happy ... after effects' of the Omega Workshops. In the twenties, he explained, 'vulgar adaptations' engulfed 'the charming inventions of the Omega ... in the new vogue of Jazz which lingers in Suburbia to this day'.[12] Ratcheting up the rhetorics of *Room and Book* in an admiring review in the *Architectural Review,* R. H. Wilenski invoked Wyndam Lewis's condemnation of the 'queerer' qualities of the 'amusing' fondness for 'stuffed birds, wax flowers, and so forth'. For Wilenski, too, the solution to the 'parlour pastimes' and 'dilettantish activities' characterising modern British interior design was to be found in the figure of the 'creative professional designer'.[13]

To judge from the invective against it, the Amusing style was promiscuous in its mixing of media and colours no less than in the attitudes towards gender manifested by those 'charming young men and formidable ladies'. Worse still, it was popular, particularly among emancipated young women. These were the problems for which, in its critics' view, a stern new fraternity of experts was the solution. But what if we allow the Amusing style to speak for itself? To that end, we might turn to the interior design features of British *Vogue,* the primary—through far from the only—forum for coverage of the Amusing style in the mid twenties. Here we find the

aesthetic of Amusement was promoted as—well, as promiscuous and popular, particularly among emancipated young women. But these qualities were not seen as problems. Promiscuity and popularity were key values for *Vogue,* which in the mid twenties expanded the rubric of 'fashion' far beyond clothes. Editorials in 1925 announced, 'Vogue has no intention of confining its pages merely to hats and frocks. In literature, the drama, art, and architecture, the same spirit of change is seen at work,' and asserted: 'The modern woman ... looks to Vogue for the most up-to-date ideas of the modern world.'[14] Freely mixing media, frankly admiring foreign trends, asserting the emancipation of both women and men from traditional gender roles—this was modernity for *Vogue* in the twenties.[15]

When it came to domestic design, the modernity that up-to-date women found in *Vogue* included Corbusian high-tech as one possibility.[16] But *Vogue* also presented as modern the commedia dell'arte murals commissioned from Gino Severini by the Sitwell brothers ('A Modern Fresco Painter') as well as whimsical painted furniture and murals by Vanessa Bell, Duncan Grant and other British artists ('The Contemporary Style of Decoration', 'Modern English Decoration' and 'The Work of Some Modern Decorative Artists').[17] *Vogue* defined these interiors as 'modern' in contrast to the 'period rooms' in historical styles promoted by large retailers: 'From Elizabeth to Victoria, whole rooms decorated in the style of any stipulated monarch can be bought wholesale by anyone with money to pay.'[18] The new style was modern also in relation to new forms of concert music ('Satirical Tendencies in Modern

Music'), poetry ('Modern Free Verse') and the prose of Gertrude Stein as explicated in articles by Edith Sitwell.[19] As the titles of these articles indicate, the 'modern' in *Vogue* was characterised by freedom from conventional constraints and a taste for satiric amusement. This was not simply a matter of subject matter, but also of style. Sitwell's two articles on Gertrude Stein present stylistic freedom for women writers as a break from domestic norms, contrasting Dorothy Richardson's 'warm household style … seldom telling you anything' with Stein's 'strange, wild' writing. Stein's importance, Sitwell says, lies in her revivification of 'our language', in which words conventionally are 'grouped together in little predestined families, bloodless and timid'. Stein 'breaks down the predestined groups of these words, — their sleepy family habits'.[20]

Before design historians accept the erasure of the Amusing style from the history of modernism, we ought to pause to consider these characteristics — freedom from convention, expressions of individual wit, feminism and new forms of family life — as characteristics of modernity at least as important as the technological innovations in the uses of concrete that justified Le Corbusier's appeals to the disciplined, standardised, authority of the heroic engineer. Although — no, because — the Amusing style did not submit to the rational imperatives of truth to materials and the look of functionality, it claims a legitimate place alongside humanistic histories of modernism in music, poetry and literature.

To exemplify the dynamics of the Amusing style of interior design, let me take as a case study the Chelsea home of the Sitwell brothers, Osbert and Sacheverell, as it was featured in

Vogue in 1924 under the headline 'Unity in Diversity'. *Vogue* was not the only magazine to manifest an interest in the dwelling of these young men, who had organised the first exhibition of modernist French painting in London after the war. The *Illustrated London News* in 1926 carried a colour photograph of their sitting room above the caption, 'A well known Modernist Poet's taste in furniture and decoration' (see Fig. 4.1). *Vogue*'s coverage was more complete, however, and presented itself as a manifesto for the Amusing style as the look of the modern: 'There are two ways of furnishing a house, the grimly historical and the purely whimsical,' the article begins. The modern man's alternative to the grimness of backwards-looking revival styles is to play with history amusingly: 'For now nothing will be in a room for any reason save that it amused the owner the day he put it there. It is his character, not his possessions, that gives

Fig. 4.1. *Illustrated London News, 1926.*

reigns supreme, and mathematical exactness is joined to daring and imagination.'[22] Instead, a dynamic model of identity is embodied in the diversity of what *Vogue* called the Sitwells' 'most unco-ordinated of worlds,' different on any given day. The photo captions draw our attention to the unexpected juxtapositions of an 'extremely modern silver statuette' and 'fruit in Victorian shell-work' that 'jostle each other strangely', the 'ormulu Dolphin table' before the 'little gallery of pictures by Severini' (see Fig. 4.2) and the 'primitive art of the negro heads and figures in dramatic contrast with the modern theatre audience depicted by the French artist', Thérèse Lessore (see Fig. 4.3).[23]

Some of the elements in the Sitwells' decor—African carvings and Cubist paintings—today fall within the established modernist canon, which, as perceptively analysed by Tanya Harrod, during the 1930s was narrowed to 'a restrictive mixture of advanced fine art, mass-produced goods, and mostly non-European art and craft', the latter category constituting a 'primitive' foil for the modernity of easel paintings and machine-made home furnishings designed by professionally trained European men.[24] But the Sitwells' promiscuous inclusion of craftwork by nonprofessional women (the Victorian bibelots concocted of shells that come 'as a bit of a shock', *Vogue* says, juxtaposed with Cubist and Futurist art) along with artefacts from the more exuberant periods of European history (that baroque dolphin-legged table) clearly exceed the restrictions modernists like Paul Nash and Herbert Read would soon use to define modernist design. In the mid twenties, however, designers like Allan

Fig. 4.2. The Sitwell house, illustrated in 'Unity in Diversity', *Vogue* [London], Late October 1924, p. 53. [in GLQ article]

the room its quality. Hence if his character be sufficiently amusing his room will also be lovable.'[21] Here personal identity and its aesthetic manifestation in domestic design are linked, but not as an expression of sober, professional, masculine selfhood on the model of Le Corbusier's 'Engineer's Aesthetic' appropriate to the 'big business men, bankers, and merchants' for whom 'economic law

Walton promoted a very different model of the modern. In a 1923 *Vogue* essay, 'The Use of Decorated Furniture in England', Walton situated an appreciation of the Sitwells' baroque furniture (not identified as theirs) as both modern and British. Like Betjeman, Walton allied 'the temperament of our race' with the stately restraint of traditional British design. But Walton then used this history of decorum to authorise modern Britons who amused themselves with 'silver baroque furniture in grotto style,' carved with 'twisted dolphins and silver shells' and 'touched here and there with coral', against 'walls covered with sea-green tinsel'. 'To-day in England', Walton explained, 'we can be amused by ... the more elaborate of these foreign styles because we do not feel on looking at them a shudder of familiarity. They are things from abroad, and their exotic flavour is both novel and interesting.'[25]

The Sitwells' promiscuous play with foreignness, with women's work, with amateur work—all those 'works' Betjeman disdained—set in rooms that, when they were not the dining room's 'sea-green tinsel', were painted what *Vogue* described as 'Marie Laurencin pink', was exactly what subsequent modernists' policing of national and gender boundaries sought to prevent. This restrictive version of modernism was not constructed, as is claimed by its proponents at the time and since, to answer the need for a modern style in the absence of anything appropriate to the conditions of modern life, and still less with ideas of housing the working classes. Rather, the rhetorics of what became mainstream modernist design responded to what came to be seen as the wrong kind of modernism,

Fig. 4.3. The Sitwell house, illustrated in 'Unity in Diversity', *Vogue* [London], Late October 1924, p. 54.

the kind that featured bachelor brothers painting their walls, not just pink, but a pink evocative of a painter both female and foreign. Allusions to Laurencin, specifically, invoked her other appearances in *Vogue* at this era, when she was praised as a 'sister of Sappho' whose art displayed 'a sort of wittiness mixed with wantonness. She will emphasize a pout, an attitude, an expression, a gesture, as character, which is witty; and also as a perverse physical attraction, which is wanton. The spectator is continually being reminded of the peculiar perverse desirability of women.'[26] Challenges to the conventions of masculinity, of professionalism, of Britishness were here linked to the androgynous promiscuity of the Bright Young Things in a compelling conception of what it meant to be modern.

What would it mean to take Amusing domestic design seriously? To analyse it

Fig. 4.4. Cabinet painted by Duncan Grant, illustrated in 'Modern English Decoration', *Vogue* [London], Early November 1924, p. 44.

Davidson brothers, whose Sitwellian home was prominently illustrated in both *Vogue* and the *Architectural Review* (see Fig. 4.4). *Vogue*'s article in 1924 illustrated the cabinet with a long caption under the photograph, which read in part:

> *Mr. Duncan Grant has restored fantasy to furniture. What—one immediately wonders— does this corner-cupboard contain? Raisins and oranges, wines from Xeres and Oporto? Or music, and the manuscripts of unforgotten songs? Or love-letters, perhaps—for the cupboard has a key? Our questions stay unanswered—still the lover sings, and still the lady listens, and beneath their spell we forget our curiosity. For Mr. Grant has turned a cupboard into a romance. He has transformed this Cinderella among furniture into poetic loveliness.*[27]

What to make of this? The pastiche of references clearly does not describe the iconography of Grant's design. Rather, it playfully—amusingly, one might say—rehearses a range of plots associated with love and eroticism, asserting a kind of equivalence to the cupboard that it says has been turned into a 'romance'. The allusion is not to a specific coupling, but to a genre of narrative that is recognised as such by sophisticated modern viewers who—like jazz musicians or stream-of-consciousness novelists—find formal pleasure in riffing through variations on a familiar theme. Compare *Vogue*'s photo caption to a passage from the famous dinner-party scene in Virginia Woolf's *To the Lighthouse,* published three years later, in which Mrs. Ramsay ruminates over the table's centrepiece:

stylistically, for instance, in comparison to canonic works of modernist literature. Let me experiment with a last case study, a cabinet painted by Duncan Grant for the

Rose's arrangement of the grapes and pears, of the horny pink-lined shell, of the bananas, made her think of a trophy fetched from the bottom of the sea, of Neptune's banquet, of the bunch that hangs with vine leaves over the shoulder of Bacchus (in some picture), among the leopard skins and the torches lolloping red and gold ... [l]t seemed possessed of great size and depth, was like a world in which one could take one's staff and climb up hills, she thought, and go down into valleys.[28]

Even if we accept that *Vogue*'s prose performs a recognisably modernist response to Grant's cabinet, however, we are still justified in asking whether the cabinet justifies that reaction. Let me suggest some of the visual characteristics of the Amusing style that might prompt exactly this kind of reading. To begin, Amusing motifs are often framed by curtains, reinforcing a theatricality evocative of scripts and the repetition of stylised plots. This is true in the cabinet and also in the mural that embellished what a 1925 *Vogue* feature called 'A Bachelor Flat in Bloomsbury', which just happened to be the residence of its own theatre and literature editor, Raymond Mortimer (see Fig. 4.5).[29] This effect of quotation is furthered by other characteristics of the Amusing style, among them plays with scale, either blatantly incongruous, as in an overmantel Grant also painted for the Davidsons and illustrated in *Vogue* (see Fig. 4.6), or coy in the way the musician on the cabinet door is scrunched into his space on the panel so as to emphasise that this is an image applied to a surface, thus asserting a reference to other images rather than to musicians in real

Fig. 4.5. Mural by Duncan Grant and Vanessa Bell, illustrated in 'A Bachelor Flat in Bloomsbury', *Vogue* [London], Late April, 1925, p. 44.

life. Such visual quotation marks set off the imagery as invocations of preexisting genres that can be played with by the artist to the delight of the viewer.

This emphasis on the artist's sensibility is reinforced by the Amusing predilection for what *Vogue* called 'écriture': traces of the maker's hand manifest in sponged and scrawled wallpapers as well as in painted surfaces enlivened with the marks of brushes, palette knives, even fingerprints. Such records of the artist's gestures, very much at odds with the conventions of disciplined craftsmanship that were carried into mainstream modernist design, were later incorporated into the most canonic forms of modernist easel painting as evidence of primal, 'morbid and extreme'— that is *not* Amusing—masculine authenticity.[30] In contrast, Clive Bell's description of Grant's paint surfaces emphasised their playful sensuality. Grant's 'sensibility of touch', Bell

which were used to dismiss the Amusing style from the modernist canon. The modernists' insistence that things look like exactly what they are—no secret-concealing painted surfaces, but the masculine engineering know-how of the machine with each component revealed—is diametrically opposed to a cupboard conceived as a 'romance'. But there is no reason for design history to accept the pseudo-logical essentialism of the chrome-and-leather tool for sitting as the only legitimate form of modern furniture, to the exclusion of alternatives related to habits of thought other humanistic disciplines are quite accustomed to conceiving as modernist. The exclusion of the Amusing style from histories of modernist design, I'm afraid, says less about the history of the twenties than about the disciplinary blinders of most design history.[32]

Design historians' blindness to the clear archival evidence of modernism's diversity in the twenties bespeaks a continuing defensive reaction to the imputations of modernists of the thirties, who pejoratively associated it with femininity and non-normative sexuality. Stripped of their pejorative intent, however, these associations provide another compelling reason to take the Amusing style seriously as a form of modernism. Social historians have emphasised, as one of the distinctive features of modernity, the rise of self-identified subcultures—especially youth cultures and cultures based on sexual identity—enabled by urbanisation and the mass media. Although these social formations flourished in the second half of the twentieth century, they have their roots in the twenties in places like London and magazines like *Vogue*. *Vogue's*

Fig. 4.6. Overmantel painted by Duncan Grant, illustrated in 'Modern English Decoration', *Vogue* [London], Early November 1924, p. 45.

said, has the quality of a thrilling caress' and 'the quality of his paint is often as charming as a kiss.'[31]

This emphasis on eroticism and artifice flies in the face of prescriptions of 'truth to materials', 'fitness for purpose' or 'the spirit of living in mass production houses', all of theatre coverage and society pages promoted as 'modern' new attitudes that relished plays with identity, especially gender identity. Its cartoons—perhaps the locus classicus of the Amusing sensibility—play constantly on the twin themes of youth and androgyny. A typical series, *Baring the Secrets of the Turkish Bath* juxtaposes one vignette of the young using the old as rubber rafts, with another showing Gustave, confused by encountering in the men's area 'Bertie Caraway, one of those plump youngsters whose figure and gestures are just too girlish for anything. Which proves that girls sometimes simply *will* be boys.'[33] Another cartoon, 'Courtship in a Variety of Modes', plays on various scripts of heterosexual romance, poking fun at the subversive secrets that lurk outside the conventional frame. The perspective is youthfully irreverent: the central vignette, titled 'The Conventional Way', illustrates the proposition, 'Strange, how a shadow seems to fall across two young lives at the exact moment Father gives his blessing.' In the vignette titled 'The Spanish Way', a troubadour sings to his lady at a high window, oblivious that 'the Señorita … happens to have preferred the supine student on the left who has been stabbed by the musician on the right' (see Fig. 4.7).[34] The humour here relies on the same foreknowledge—and the same irreverent attitude towards that knowledge—presumed by Grant's painted cabinet. Domestic interiors in the Amusing style manifest a youthful subcultural sensibility prescient of episodes in the history of design in the 1960s and after.

The implication of this last example may be that the Amusing style belongs to the

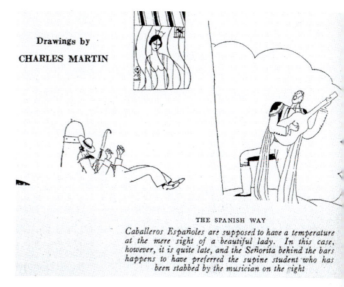

THE SPANISH WAY

Caballeros Españoles are supposed to have a temperature at the mere sight of a beautiful lady. In this case, however, it is quite late, and the Señorita behind the bars happens to have preferred the supine student who has been stabbed by the musician on the right

Fig. 4.7. Charles Martin, detail from 'Courtship in a Variety of Modes', *Vogue* [London], Late May 1924.

prehistory of postmodernism rather than to the history of modernism per se. But this proposition uncritically accepts the restrictions applied to modernism in the 1930s, as memorably visualised in the famous 1936 Museum of Modern Art chart winnowing all the various in modernist styles down to one form of architecture (and two modes of abstraction in painting: 'geometrical' and 'non-geometrical'). This chart, originally polemical—perhaps even a little, dare I say, amusing—quickly became pedagogical, as this ideology of modernism established itself as fact.[35] The triumph of this version of modernism during the 1930s—whether for the bourgeoisie or, later, for working-class housing—undoubtedly reflects this uncertain era's desire for certainties about issues of gender and family life. Rhetorics of modernist standardisation in the 1930s fused with invocations to familial normality that insisted on nuclear families in which labour was clearly divided by gender.[36] But we need not go on accepting the erasure of modernism's preceding history of diversity.

The twenties really were different. This is clear in Elizabeth Darling's contribution to this volume, locating the origins of Wells Coates's career as a modernist architect in the theatrical circles of slightly aging Bright Young Things around Elsa Lanchester and Charles Laughton. That his modernist interiors were compatible with theatricality should not surprise us. So saturated in the rhetorics of Amusement were Britons in the twenties that their first response to Corbusian minimalism was to see it as yet another kind of whimsy. This is true even of a sober-sided professional magazine like the *Architectural Review,* whose reporter, on first encountering Le Corbusier's now-famous *Pavillon de l'esprit Nouveau* in 1925 at the Art Deco show in Paris, saw it not as a manifestation of the rational functionalism of the Engineer but as a new mode of play:

> *Is not every wall patterned by sunlight and shadow; is not the whole filled with fanciful reality? Ghostly grey at dawn, changing with every fleeting iridescent colour of the sunrise, blatantly, cruelly brilliant at high noon, soothing with restful and deepening tones at the close of day, who is there to say that this room is not decorated?*[37]

As Anglophones were introduced to the terms with which Le Corbusier promoted his aesthetic, such responses disappeared. Modernists, we learned, were not Amused. To return to the origins of canonic modernist design, however, is to find it competing with other ideologies of what it meant to be modern. To understand that Corbusian modernism competed in the twenties with the already-established Amusing style helps explain—although perhaps not excuse—the modernists' more pernicious gendered rhetorics.[38] Understanding the productive diversity of modernisms that flourished in the twenties may also help design history forge much-needed links with other humanistic disciplines dedicated to the understanding of modernism and its legacies.

Notes

1. W. Rybczynski, *Home: A Short History of an Idea* (Viking/Penguin, 1986), p. 173, pp. 189–90. Elizabeth Darling's *Re-Forming Britain: Narratives of Modernity Before Reconstruction* (Routledge, 2007), notes that modern plans and equipment lurked behind the 'debased Arts and Crafts or Tudorbethan' vernacular facades of new houses in Britain in the 1920s (p. 82; see also p. 92) as well as behind the 'neo-Georgian house style' of worker housing into the early 1930s (p. 127).

2. J. Holder, 'Promoting Modernism in Britain', in P. Greenhalgh, ed., *Modernism in Design* (Reaktion Books, 1990), p. 126.

3. The modernist prototype of Wells Coates's 1934 Isokon flats was explicitly rejected by the Chair of the London County Council as not cost-effective. Darling, *Re-Forming Britain,* p. 106.

4. Malcolme Yorke's *The Modern House* (Architectural Press, 1934) opens by regretting that 'this book concerns the individual villa type of house' despite the fact that 'the author does not pretend that the building of villas is a good or even possible solution to the problem of housing people' (p. 1). Yorke's theoretical preferences for housing blocks, however, ceded to his recognition that extant modernist domestic design was manifested primarily in the houses of the bourgeoisie.

5. Wells Coates in G. Boumphrey and W. Coates, 'Modern Dwellings for Modern Needs', *The Listener* (24 May 1933), reprinted in C. Benton, ed., *Documents: A Collection of Source Materials on the Modern Movement* (Open University Press, 1975), pp. 72–5. The Isokon Flats, which Coates was designing at this period, were explicitly conceived for middle-class 'businessmen and women who have no time for domestic troubles' (publicity pamphlet quoted in Darling, *Re-Forming Britain,* p. 96).

6. E. Darling, 'Elizabeth Denby or Maxwell Fry: A Matter of Attribution', in B. Martin and P. Sparke, eds., *Women's Places: Architecture and Design, 1860–1960* (Routledge, 2003), pp. 149–70. Darling's *Re-forming Britain* devotes a very useful chapter to British modernists' promotion of worker housing, noting that this issue was 'put ... to one side' in 1931 (p. 113) and that it returned first in 'Fry's writing ... rather than Coates' (p. 116).

7. Le Corbusier, *Towards a New Architecture,* F. Etchells, tr., 1927, reprinted (Praeger, 1960), pp. 18, 20, 23. For feminist critiques of Le Corbusier, see B. Colomina, 'The Spilt Wall: Domestic Voyeurism', in B. Colomina, ed., *Sexuality and Space* (Princeton Architectural Press, 1992), pp. 73–130; and M. Shinar, 'Feminist Criticism of Urban Theory and Design', *Journal of Urban and Cultural Studies* 2 (1992), pp. 29–39. Flora Samuel's *Le Corbusier: Architect and Feminist* offers a spirited counter-argument but ignores the sexist rhetoric of his manifestos, making only passing reference to his highly influential *Towards a New Architecture.* As Penny Sparke notes in her review, Samuel does not explore the contradictions between 'Le Corbusier's views of "real" women ... and the way he uses the "ideal" of womanhood in his work', *Journal of Design History* 18 (2005), p. 218.

8. J. Betjeman, '1830–1930—Still Going Strong: A Guide to the Recent History of Interior Decoration', *Architectural Review* 67 (May 1930), pp. 231–40.

9. To the extent that design histories acknowledge that International style modernism competed with any other form of modern design, they cite Art Deco, the sleek, high-finish style named for the 1925 Exposition des Arts Décoratifs in Paris. This binary renders invisible the style I am discussing, although it was widely publicised as 'modern' by 1925.

10. C. Reed, *Bloomsbury Rooms: Modernism, Subculture, and Domesticity* (Yale University Press, 2004), pp. 236–8. In describing the Amusing style as British, I am signalling its roots in the amateur traditions and whimsical iconographies of the Arts and Crafts movement. Like the Arts and Crafts movement, however, the Amusing style was quickly disseminated by magazines with international readerships, and British *Vogue* highlighted manifestations of the aesthetic in France (R. Mortimer, 'Paris Fashions in Furnishing', *Vogue* [London] (Late August 1924), pp. 27–31) and in the United States ('Modern Murals for a House in Florida Painted by Robert Loecher', *Vogue* [London] (Late September 1925), p. 70).

11. P. Nash, *Room and Book* (Scribners, 1932), p. 26. Laurence Whistler also emphasises the use of this term at the period in his *The Laughter and the Urn: The Life of Rex Whistler* (Weidenfeld and Nicolson, 1985), p. 97. Casual references abound in period sources.

12. Nash, *Room and Book,* pp. 25–8.

13. R. H. Wilenski, in R. H. Wilenski, and J. Gloag, 'Two Points of View', *Architectural Review* 71 (April 1932), p. 149.

14. Editorials, *Vogue* [London] (Early April 1925), p. xiv; (Late May 1925), p. liii.

15. On British *Vogue* in the 1920s, see my 'Design for [Queer] Living: Sexual Identity, Performance, and Décor in British *Vogue,* 1922–1926', *GLQ*

12 (2006), pp. 377–404. 'A *Vogue* That Dare Not Speak Its Name: Sexual Subculture during the Editorship of Dorothy Todd, 1922–26', *Fashion Theory* 10 (2006), pp. 39–72. Some material original to this chapter appeared in the first of these articles.

16. 'A Modern French House', *Vogue* [London] (Late March 1926), pp. 59–61. 'A Modern House in the Provinces' features the work of Peter Behrens (Early December 1926), pp. 88–9.

17. 'A Modern Fresco Painter', *Vogue* [London] (Early September 1922), pp. 66–7, 92. 'The Contemporary Style of Decoration', *Vogue* [London] (Early January 1924), pp. 50–1, 74. 'Modern English Decoration', *Vogue* [London] (Early November 1924), pp. 43–5, 106. 'The Work of Some Modern Decorative Artists', *Vogue* [London] (Late August 1926), pp. 27–31, 68.

18. 'The Contemporary Style of Decoration', p. 50.

19. R. Aldington, 'Modern Free Verse', *Vogue* [London] (Late September 1925), pp. 57, 90; (Early December 1925), pp. 95, 130. E. Evans, 'Satirical Tendencies in Modern Music', *Vogue* [London] (Early May 1925) pp. 52, 90.

20. E. Sitwell, 'Three Women Writers', *Vogue* [London] (Early October 1924), p. 81; 'The Work of Gertrude Stein', *Vogue* [London] (Early October 1925), p. 73.

21. 'Unity in Diversity', *Vogue* [London] (Late October 1924), p. 53.

22. Le Corbusier, *Towards a New Architecture,* p. 22.

23. 'Unity in Diversity', pp. 53–5.

24. T. Harrod, 'House-Trained Objects', in C. Painter, ed., *Contemporary Art and the Home* (Berg, 2002), p. 64.

25. A. Walton, 'The Use of Decorated Furniture in England', *Vogue* [London] (Early August 1923), pp. 39, 69.

26. Polly Flinders, 'Marie Laurencin', *Vogue* [London] (Late January 1925), p. 40. The pseudonym (for Mary Hutchinson) evokes a nursery rhyme—'Little Polly Flinders/Sat among the cinders/Warming her pretty little toes./Her mother came and caught her/And whipped her little daughter/For spoiling her nice new clothes'—that suggests an antagonism towards conventional feminine decorum in behavior and dress.

27. 'Modern English Decoration', p. 44. The serenade motif echoes the imagery in a painting in the same room of a woman at a balcony, visible in the photograph of the sideboard. The same cabinet appeared in an uncaptioned full-page photograph in an *Architectural Review* special double issue on 'Modern English Interior Decoration' (vol. 67, May 1930, p. 222).

28. V. Woolf, *To the Lighthouse* (Hogarth Press, 1927), pp. 150–1.

29. 'A Bachelor Flat in Bloomsbury', *Vogue* [London] (Late April 1925), pp. 44–5.

30. Clement Greenberg's characterization of Jackson Pollock is quoted from his 'The Present Prospects of American Painting and Sculpture', 1947, reprinted. J. O'Brian, ed., *Collected Essays and Criticism* (University of Chicago Press, 1986), vol. 2, p. 166. On the importance of asserting masculinity for abstract expressionists, see A. Eden Gibson, *Abstract Expressionism: Other Politics* (Yale University Press, 1997), pp. 1–17.

31. C. Bell, *Since Cézanne* (Chatto and Windus, 1922), p. 109.

32. Excepted from this generalization about design history is Alan Powers's 'A Zebra at Villa Savoye: Interpreting the Modern House', *Twentieth Century Architecture* 2 (1996), pp. 16–26. Powers's linguistic sensitivity to architectural metaphor allows for an analysis that links the Surrealist elements in modernist domestic architecture of the 1930s to the eroticism of the Amusing style, although Powers does not make that connection. As with Surrealist art and literature, the effect of 'strangeness' achieved by this architecture is often a forceful imposition of masculinity—'imagery derived from alien building types such as industrial buildings or hospitals'—over the feminine, at odds with the playful androgyny of the Amusing style.

33. FISH, 'Baring the Secrets of the Turkish Baths', *Vogue* [London] (Late October 1925), pp. 66–7.

34. C. Martin, 'Courtship in a Variety of Modes', *Vogue* [London] (Late May 1924).

35. This diagram by Alfred H. Barr, Jr., originally appeared as the cover of the catalogue for the 1936 Museum of Modern Art show *Cubism and Abstract Art.* Some photo credits for this often-reproduced image cite its reproduction by the Works Project Administration for classroom use by the later 1930s.

36. Maxwell Fry insisted that functionality was the only appropriate architectural form for 'poor but otherwise normal people. Anything less than this is an indulgence of private taste at someone else's expense' ('The Architect's Problem', *Architects' Journal* 77 (1933), in Darling, *Re-forming Britain,* pp. 115–16). Darling describes the design of his

and Denby's Kensal House flats as 'a device through which each member of the family could (re)learn specific familial roles' (p. 143), preparing men and women for gender-specific forms of exemplary 'citizenship' in accord with the essentialist 'New Feminism' that supplanted the political and social imperatives to break down gender barriers in the 1920s (p. 154).

37. Silhouette, 'The Modern Movement in Continental Decoration. IV—The Living Room,' *Architectural Review* 60 (September 1926), p. 123.

38. Le Corbusier's most direct acknowledgement of this competition may be his reproduction of publicity for a *Vogue*-like French magazine titled *Flirt,* which is illustrated in Le Corbusier's 1925 *The Decorative Art of Today,* published on the occasion of the Expositions des Arts Décoratifs, with his caption, 'Here, without comment, is the little song of a cabin-boy sitting astride the masthead of a ship that is going to be torpedoed this fine autumn afternoon' (J. I. Dunnet, tr. (Architectural Press, 1987), p. 44.

Chapter Five

'The scene in which the daily drama of personal life takes place': Towards the modern interior in early 1930s Britain

Elizabeth Darling

This chapter considers two interiors by the British-Canadian modernist architect Wells Coates, whose description of the function of the interior forms the epigram of its title.[1] The first is the series of rooms in the mansion owned by a young Labour politician, George Russell Strauss, at 1 Kensington Palace Gardens, London, which were completed in May 1932. The second is his commission from the actors Elsa Lanchester and Charles Laughton to redesign their flat at 34 Gordon Square, London—a project completed in 1933. Today, these interiors are little known, and Coates is most associated with the three blocks of flats he designed in the thirties: the Isokon Flats at Lawn Road of 1934, Embassy Court at Brighton of 1936 and the flats at Palace Gate, Kensington, of 1937. Yet the Isokon scheme was completed seven years after Coates had begun his practice, and it was as an architect of interiors that he would specialise throughout that time; indeed, the Isokon design was first exhibited as an interior at the Exhibition of Industrial Art in the Home held at Dorland Hall in spring 1933.

According to the conventions of architectural history, the opening of an 'actual monument' in the Isokon flats would usually be seen as the moment when Coates's modernism achieved maturity.[2] Now something complete, permanent and worthy of serious consideration, his architecture had overcome the ephemeral, mutable and frivolous phase of the interior.[3] But downplaying the significance of interiors overlooks the sites where the rearrangement of space is foregrounded. The sites where things are taken away and added and new spaces created and from which we gain the clearest statement of how notions of identity manifest in 'the daily drama of personal life' are formed and seek to re-form an existing built environment, creating a space in which those identities, those dramas, can be accommodated. In other words, interiors allow us to see very clearly the processes through which space is made.

It is these processes which this chapter traces. Its analysis begins with these two domestic interiors in Bloomsbury and Kensington—interiors which will be treated as complete works in their own right, not steps towards the achievement of an 'actual monument'. It will also consider the other interiors which made these re-formed interiors, the spaces where the sensibilities which made Elsa Lanchester's and George Strauss's daily dramas jar with their existing environments and thus demand new ones, and the spaces in which Coates developed the sensibility to articulate these dramas spatially and formally. Finally, it will acknowledge another set of spaces through which interiors were articulated: those of the periodical press.[4]

Geographies of transformation

The first of these interiors is London itself, although not all of our protagonists were born there. Laughton was a Scarborough lad, whilst Coates was born in Tokyo. Strauss and Lanchester were both Londoners, although from rather different sides of the track. Strauss grew up on 'Millionaires Row', Kensington Palace Gardens, adjacent to Hyde Park. Lanchester was raised in a series of rented rooms in south London. By the early 1920s, they would come together and meet in the hinterlands of London's main thoroughfares: the narrow streets of Soho, a mews off Gower Street, the bedsits of Charlotte Street and Fitzroy Square. Their geography was primarily that of Bohemian Fitzrovia, a site which has been largely ignored in accounts

of architectural modernism in Britain but in whose interiors they found a gathering ground, common cause and a place to forge identities in opposition to the lingering Edwardianism of the 1920s.

The Fitzrovian bohemian is epitomised, perhaps almost caricatured, by Elsa Sullivan Lanchester. A bohemian by birth, her parents refused to marry and were socialists and vegetarians.[5] Brought up in Clapham Common, she attended a progressive school before a talent for dance led her to spend three months in Paris at Isadora Duncan's School of Dance in 1914. On her return to London, she taught dance at the Margaret Morris School in Chelsea and pursued a career as a singer and actress.[6] In 1921, in partnership with the painter John Armstrong and the actor Harold Scott, she set up a club called the Cave of Harmony, first in Charlotte Street and then in a former Territorial Army hall in Chenies Mews, Gower Street. Here they hosted cabaret, one-act plays, including Chekov and Pirandello, as well as dancing. Attendees ranged from Alec and Evelyn Waugh, Cedric Morris and Anton Dolin to a young man, new to London, Wells Coates.[7] The Cave of Harmony was also Lanchester's home, and it is important to acknowledge the elision of art and life that this arrangement caused. She recalled:

I lived at the studio and slept in a kind of balcony-loft which I had built at one end; I climbed up a ladder and through a trap door to get to it. In this comfortable den I really felt independent and secure. I could see down on to the dance floor through a little square window, and could retire if I wanted to and just listen to the music and general babble.[8]

This sense of ad-hocism and security conveyed in Lanchester's prose was not unique. Rather it formed part of a broader process of rethinking where and what might constitute home in the early 1920s, as is evidenced in the Sitwell brothers' interior discussed by Christopher Reed elsewhere in this volume, and in this description of another Bohemian home, that of the painter Kathleen Hale. Her Fitzroy Square bedsit may have been furnished with only a fourth-hand table and a bed, a chair, bucket and jug, but, for her, it was liberating:

Early each morning I would blissfully survey my humble possessions. The spacious bareness around me was heavenly after a childhood spent among heavy furniture, thick carpets and pictures in ponderous gilt frames ... the sense of freedom, the lack of responsibility, was quite wonderful.[9]

By the early 1920s, then, Lanchester, and others like her, had established both a modus vivendi and a modus operandi. Their bohemian practices could not be accommodated within a conventional interior, so they made new ones. But Lanchester's loyalties were not confined to the Cave of Harmony; she also attended another club for those of non-establishment inclinations, one where a political, rather than cultural, bohemianism flourished. This was the 1917 Club which had been set up by Leonard Woolf and friends to celebrate the Bolshevik Revolution. Located at 4 Gerrard Street in Soho, it was described by Douglas Goldring as 'a home of political idealism, democratic fervour and serious progressive thinking', where Lanchester was 'one of its shining lights'.[10] In any one evening, one might encounter there Clement Attlee, Osbert Sitwell or H. G. Wells, and it was, 'an environment in which Aldous Huxley and Ottoline Morrell could go unremarked'.[11] This was a club also frequented by Wells Coates and, almost certainly, another young man, George Russell Strauss.

Strauss's background was very different from Lanchester's. He was the son of Minna Cohen and Arthur Strauss, a metal merchant, founder of the London Metal Exchange and Conservative Member of Parliament. Educated at Rugby, he entered the family firm at age 20 and had substantial personal wealth: estimated at £40,000 to £50,000 a year in 1930.[12] Politically, at least, Strauss would depart dramatically from this background, and he made an early commitment to socialism, remaining on the far left of the Labour Party for much of his life. From 1925 onwards, he represented North Lambeth on the London County Council and became its MP from 1929 to 1931 and again from 1934 to 1950. This political radicalism, and break with his Conservative father, would be paralleled by a willingness to commit to dramatic transformations of space.

Wells Coates

The common denominator between Lanchester and Strauss was Wells Coates. He, with their patronage, would be at the forefront of the development of the modernist interior in Britain. He was able to translate their desire for 'new scenes', in which the daily drama of their lives could be enacted, into a new spatial and formal language—a facility which he developed from both his family background and the interiors he navigated in the 1920s.

Coates was born and educated in Tokyo and throughout his life would reference the influence of Japanese domestic architecture on his design sense. After service in the Great War, and the award of a degree in engineering from McGill University College, Vancouver, Coates came to England in 1922 to study for a doctorate which explored the gases of the diesel engine. The award of his degree in 1924, however, rather than signalling the start of a brilliant career in the field of mechanical engineering, saw, in fact, its end. A thorough disillusionment with this work had set in, and he elected, instead, to re-educate himself. In a letter of 1926 he described this process:

I was working one day a week in Fleet Street. They made me an offer, so I accepted three hours a day at a special job, and with about seven guineas a week coming in altogether—including special work for the Sunday—this enabled me to supply myself with all my personal necessities, and moreover it gave me a very useful residuum of time, which I profited by enormously. I did all the reading which I had hoped some day I might be able to do. I did not spare myself, and did a great deal of work ... The fellows in the office were amazed at me ... [but] I was learning and perfecting myself. I was laying up 'capital'—spiritual capital, a background—which would be of far more value to me than all the money they thought I could make. [13]

Elsewhere he explained how he:

followed carefully every development of modern knowledge and culture, combining

this study with a rediscovery of knowledge and culture of the past according to a well-defined plan. And quite appropriately I found myself moving easily in the most advanced intellectual circles of Bloomsbury in London. But I had not yet reached my goal. [14]

It is clear that when Coates wrote these letters, in 1926 and early 1927, he was not quite sure to what end this 'training' would be applied. In August 1927, however, he married Marion Grove, a young graduate of the London School of Economics, whom he had met at the Cave of Harmony and who now worked for Francis Meynell at the Nonesuch Press. The establishment of their marital home finally gave him his answer. Grove would later recall:

We rented two rooms in a Bloomsbury square close to the Nonesuch ... Conveniently I had £100 from a grandmother. Wells went to Heals and chose the plainest furniture and haircord carpet and had plain curtains made of corduroy with a line design painted on them by John Banting, who painted another on a cupboard. Wells took aluminium sheeting and covered the fireplace. [15]

A visit to the newly redesigned flat by the painter Arthur Lett-Haines led to his recommendation to a friend that Coates design them some furniture, and thus was a career born and a vocation found. Through other friends came an introduction to Alec Walker, who ran Crysede Silks and for whom he would design a shop in 1928 in Cambridge. This commission in turn led, in 1929, to a fruitful association with Cresta, the firm founded by Tom Heron, who had been sacked from Crysede. Over the next four years, Coates would design a factory at Welwyn and a series of shop interiors across the southeast of England for Heron. Soon a distinct formal language evolved which comprised plywood panelling to create sleek and bare wall surfaces, open plans divided by sliding screen doors, built-in furniture where necessary and muted colour schemes of browns, whites and creams.

In the early 1930s, Coates began to write and theorise his practice. Among the first published expressions of this work was an article for the *Architectural Review* called 'Furniture To-day—Furniture To-morrow—Leaves from a Meta-Technical Notebook'.[16] Despite its title, this was really a discussion about the reform of the interior. Its tone suggests we add Le Corbusier's texts to his well-defined plan:

The intricacies of the houses of our fathers was a museum-type intricacy, and one of the chief occupations of our mothers was that of curator and guide. How barbaric their habit of overloading was! How seldom an object stands in the place which correlation appoints to it! How obtrusive their pictures and ornamental bric-a-brac! And how rarely were they aware that a room exists for the man, and not vice-versa; that he, and not the curtain or the picture, is to be given the best possible setting.

He continued:

The dwelling scene of tomorrow will contain as part of its structure nearly all that today is carried about for the purpose of 'furnishing' one house after another ... Thus furniture ... will take its place in the logic of construction, becoming an

integral part of architecture. For the rest, clothing, bedding, crockery, utensils, books, pictures and sculptures will have the select value of a personal environment: will be, in fact, the only 'furniture' (personal belongings) in use.[17]

The article formed part of a supplement to the *Review* called, in an interestingly yet-to-be-updated phrase, 'Decoration and Craftmanship'. This included a further article on modern interiors and furniture by Coates, which referenced designs by contemporaries such as Rodney Thomas and Serge Chermayeff and which had as its climax a four-page spread of what Coates called 'illustrations [which] show the "museum-type" of furnishing of a Victorian house, and a contemporary treatment of the problem of living equipment and environment at No.1 Kensington Palace Gardens, London'.

A modern fairy palace[18]

The scheme was Coates's most significant and substantial commission for an interior in the first decade of his career and comprised the remodelling of large parts of the mansion which George Russell Strauss had inherited from his father. The house had originally been built in the 1840s, and its interiors were first remodelled, presumably at Arthur Strauss's behest, in 1893, in extraordinary taste.[19] The subsequent reconstruction of the house, which cost something in the region of £4,000, coincided with Strauss's marriage in March 1932, and we might understand the commission as the mark of his separation from his family, socially now as well as politically, and a setting for his new life.[20]

Fig. 5.1. The waiting room at 1 Kensington Palace Gardens, before and after its redesign by Wells Coates, 1932. *Source:* Royal Institute of British Architects photographs collection.

The *Review* article documented this process of separation and transformation in a series of fascinating before and after photographs. Coates's fusion of the anti-Edwardian, anti-stuff sensibility of Fitzrovian Bohemia with his Japanese-derived sense of space and order, had replaced the dark interiors packed with heavy furniture, festooned with ornament and draped with antimacassars, with a series of calm, sophisticated and (in comparison) empty interiors, as the images reproduced here show.

Each pair of images was accompanied by a description of what had been replaced and the new fixtures and fittings. Of the house's Waiting Hall (see Fig. 5.1) before the cleansing hand of Coates was applied, it is recorded that it contained a:

> *photogravure after Maude Goodman, a pair of Italian majolica brackets with figures; a ditto pilgrim bottle; two Worcester pattern jardinieres with aspidistras; a statuary marble figure of Venus di Milo … a 42 inch verde antique marble spiral column on octagonal base … and a set of ten Swiss cow bells on chain, forming a dinner gong.*

Now, with all mouldings removed, the surfaces repainted and sliding doors to the living and dining rooms installed, the only decoration was a frieze by John Armstrong.

All the space held was 'a telephone cabinet which encloses the bell-boxes and other equipment … and a set of push buttons for the four extension lines; an illuminated electric synchronome clock over'.[21] Such a magnificent transformation of a home should be understood as a 'showpiece' both for the Strausses' new life and Coates's career, and, as this chapter will discuss below, it would continue to advertise the latter's work throughout the rest of the decade.

An open, liveable place[22]

I turn now to a similar process of transformation and the interiors which Coates fashioned for Strauss's fellow bohemians, Elsa Lanchester and her husband the actor Charles Laughton. As mentioned, Lanchester had already experimented with the spatial expression of new modes of life at Cave of Harmony, a practice she would continue in partnership with Laughton, whom she married in February 1929. After a few years in a small flat in Percy Street, Fitzrovia, in 1934 Lanchester found the couple a larger flat.

On the north side of Gordon Square (now demolished), Bloomsbury, she bought the top three floors of number 34. Coates, a friend from the Cave of Harmony and 1917 Club days, was appointed their architect. From Lanchester's recollections, it seems that they asked him to design a relatively informal

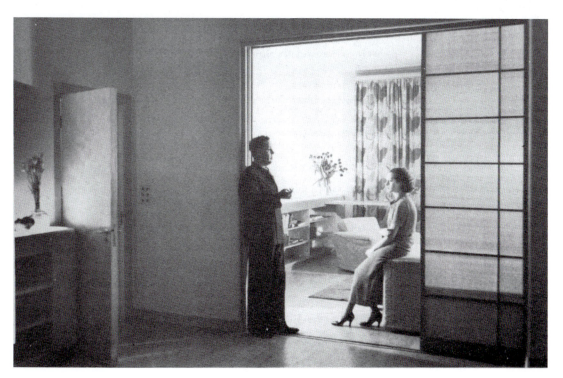

Fig. 5.2. The drawing room of 34 Gordon Square designed for Elsa Lanchester and Charles Laughton by Wells Coates, 1933.

Fig. 5.3. The dining room of 34 Gordon Square designed for Elsa Lanchester and Charles Laughton by Wells Coates, 1933. Door panels by John Armstrong. *Source:* Untraceable.

environment for, as she wrote, 'Charles has very definite ideas about how to live in comfort.'[23] There is also the suggestion that the interior should form a backdrop both to themselves and their pastimes; Lanchester noted how the built-in bookshelves that Coates designed for the new living room served as a stage on which to make her flower arrangements.

Coates's ideas about built-in furniture and 'the select value of a personal environment' clearly corresponded well to such demands,

and Lanchester would report that Coates had created from another dreary Victorian interior, a flat that 'is airy and white, and so simply furnished that even a bull could do little damage if let loose in it'.[24] Such simplicity also served as an appropriate setting for Laughton's collection of paintings, which included a Renoir, a Rousseau and a Utrillo. But for some, the selectedness of this environment was a little confusing. Lanchester commented wryly, 'the flat was rather unfurnished but not quite as unfinished as most people thought.'[25]

Although this interior was not on the scale of that for the Strausses (he was not commissioned to design all the furniture and fittings, as had been the case at Kensington) and perhaps not quite such a personal triumph for Coates, he nevertheless succeeded in creating an environment in which Lanchester and Laughton could perform their lives; it remained their London base until they relocated to Hollywood permanently in 1939. It was clearly something through which their identities were expressed, and it occupies several pages in Lanchester's 1938 book, *Charles Laughton and I*. Despite this, it seems to have been an interior they were reluctant to share with anyone but their friends, and it does not seem to have been photographed or reproduced to any significant extent.

Conclusion: the interior mediated

It is the interior reconstruction at number 1 Kensington Palace Gardens which was most heavily reproduced in the spaces of the contemporary media. It is clear from other projects on which he worked that Coates was highly skilled in setting up photography deals with the editors of the architectural press to ensure publicity for his projects.[26] The *Review* articles of 1932 seem likely to have been his first foray into this process, and they were a masterpiece of promotional work with their carefully choreographed series of texts, culminating in the account of the new rooms, and the device of the contrast deployed carefully to exaggerate the shift between old and new.[27]

The Kensington interiors would go on to be reproduced at regular intervals over the next decade in newspaper articles, pamphlets to accompany BBC broadcasts and books on the new architecture. Such mediation set in motion a powerful force for change for, although such work was relatively rare in Britain, its constant reiteration was in the sort of media which were read by the progressives who would ultimately lead cultural debates in wartime and establish the cultural politics of postwar Britain. Such a process can be seen in an article in *The Weekend Review,* a paper founded by Gerald Barry, a man who would be a central 'cross-over' figure from the 1930s to the 1940s, as the driving force behind that definitive statement of postwar modernity, the Festival of Britain. In December 1932, an article entitled 'Explaining the Photo's, Pre-war and Present Day', was published and accompanied by four pages of photographs linked by the theme of 'the growth of order and simplicity in twentieth-century British design'. Amongst these were the before-and-after shots of the living and dining room of number 1 Kensington Palace Gardens. The text explained:

In the next group of pictures we come back for a moment to a domestic interior, to note a spectacular change. Each pair represents the same house, and exactly the same view of the same house, photographed as it was and as it has recently been remodelled by the eye of genius. Few more astonishing and satisfactory instances can exist of the revolution that has been wrought in domestic design and decoration since the frills and fussiness of style illustrated in the two left hand of these four pictures passed away.[28]

Notes

1. W. Coates, 'Furniture To-day, Furniture Tomorrow: Leaves from a Meta-Technical Notebook', *Architectural Review* 73 (July 1932), p. 31.

2. The term is Henry-Russell Hitchock's. See H-R. Hitchcock and P. Johnson, *The International Style, Architecture since 1922* (W. W. Norton, 1995 [1932]), p. 37.

3. By way of example, Sherban Cantacuzino, in his 1978 study of Coates, *Wells Coates, a Monograph* (Gordon Fraser), places his discussion of Coates's designs for interiors in a chapter entitled 'Designer and Propagandist' and Coates's designs for buildings in one called 'Architect'.

4. A detailed elaboration of this process can be found in my book, *Re-forming Britain, Narratives of Modernity before Reconstruction* (Routledge, 2007), on Chapter 1 of which this discussion partially draws.

5. R. McWilliam, 'Lanchester, Elsa Sullivan', in the *Oxford Dictionary of National Biography* (Oxford University Press, 2005).

6. E. Lanchester, *Charles Laughton and I* (Faber & Faber, 1938).

7. D. Goldring, *The Nineteen Twenties, A General Survey and Some Personal Memories* (Nicholson & Watson, 1945), pp. 147–8.

8. Lanchester, *Charles Laughton and I,* p. 51.

9. Kathleen Hale cited in Virginia Nicholson, *Among the Bohemians, Experiments in Living 1900–1919* (Penguin, 2003), p. 101.

10. Goldring, *The Nineteen Twenties,* p. 145.

11. Ibid.

12. *Daily Express,* 'Kensington Socialist Sits for Lambeth' (24 October 1934), press cuttings book in the Wells Coates Archive (WCA), Canadian Centre for Architecture, Box 16.

13. Letter to Marion, March 1926, WCA Box 35/A.

14. Letters to Marguerite Broad, September 1927 to January 1928, WCA Box 35/B. Coates includes a very long list of what he consulted; this included the following: Einstein, Bertrand Russell, Wittgenstein, Freud, Jung and Adler, Virginia Woolf and James Joyce, Cezanne, Van Gogh, Picasso, Derain, Matisse, Duncan Grant, Braque, Epstein, Dobson, Brancusi, Maillol. Youthful bragging might have caused some exaggeration, but there can be little doubt that Coates had read a significant amount of the most advanced cultural literature of the day.

15. Marion Grove, 'About Wells', typescript memoir, February 1970, WCA Box 35/C.

16. This was published in July 1932.

17. Coates, 'Furniture To-day', p. 32.

18. *Daily Express,* 'Kensington Socialist Sits for Lambeth'.

19. F.H.W. Sheppard, *Survey of London, Northern Kensington* (Athlone Press, 1973), pp. 151–62.

20. Specification for 1 Kensington Palace Gardens, WCA Box 7. By way of contrast, the Isokon Flats—a five-story block of flats—cost £14,850. A. Grieve, *Isokon* (Isokon Plus, 2004), p. 10.

21. Coates, 'Furniture To-day', p. 35.

22. Lanchester, *Charles Laughton and I,* p. 191.

23. Ibid, p. 190.

24. Ibid.

25. Ibid, p. 200.

26. For example Coates provided the *Architectural Review* with directions on how to photograph the Isokon block, which were followed to the letter. See my *Re-forming Britain,* Chapter 3.

27. Strauss must have been happy for this coverage, but it did not necessarily have a positive effect for him. The right-wing *Daily Express* made frequent reference to the contrast between his home and that of his constituents in North Lambeth, one of London's poorest working-class boroughs. A 1934 headline read 'Kensington Socialist Sits for Lambeth. His home is a mansion. His income £40,000 a year. The "capitalist" who could buy up the socialist party'; a theme resumed in 1937 when an article entitled 'Change Homes with Me, I May Turn Socialist', contrasted the home of his constituent Mrs Rose Marshall, a war widow with two sons who lived in Newport-street, North Lambeth, with Strauss. *Daily Express* (26 February 1937).

28. 'Explaining the Photo's, Pre-war and Present Day', *Weekend Review* (10 December 1932), pp. 708–12.

Chapter Six

The Modern Interior as a Geography of Images, Spaces and Subjects: Mies van der Rohe's and Lilly Reich's Villa Tugendhat, 1928–1931

Irene Nierhaus

In the nineteenth century, the notion of the 'private sphere'—understood as the locus of the social and political formation of the individual, of the family and of gender difference—became the site of the development of the modern subject and of people's emotions and feelings. It was thus transformed into a 'complex geography of intimacies'.[1]

This chapter deals with the living space as a 'given-to-be-seen', a concept which refers to the social and cultural fields that determine the hegemonic possibilities of the visible, which we as spectators and spectated are tuned into and which is focused on the formation of the social subject.[2] In the nineteenth century, perception—understood as a historically and socially determined system of relationships between the subject and its surroundings—became an object of negotiation linked to the complex structures that underpinned emotions, sensations, states of mind and the social positions ascribed to them. Thus, the nineteenth century saw the ascription

of certain character traits of perception to social, ethnic and gender groups: femininity and distraction versus masculinity and concentration, or the *flâneur*'s wandering gaze versus the fixed gaze of women walking in the streets.[3] That system of differences was extended to living spaces. Whilst the lady's drawing room was a space for those who did not 'strive for serious contemplation', the man's study was a 'place of work' where he could 'collect his thoughts'.[4]

In this chapter I aim to illustrate the perception that was created between the inhabitant and the furniture of the living space. I will use the example of the nineteenth-century interior but, more importantly, its transition into the modernity of the twentieth century as shown through the example of the Tugendhat Villa in Brno, which was planned, built and furnished between 1928 and 1931 by Mies van der Rohe in collaboration with Lilly Reich. In that context, the furnishings—the walls, the wallpaper, the view from the window, the furniture and the appliances—were conceptualised as an ordering of the private sphere in which the social and the subject encountered each other.

Things of history

What are those strategies of spatialisation and visualisation that (re)present the 'complex geography' of the private sphere? I will focus mostly on the strategy of involving somebody in the abundance of images and things—literally a drawing in, a covering and a wrapping of them in ensembles of images and spaces. In the nineteenth century, the newly created living spaces (dining rooms, living rooms etc.) were mixed with images (furnishings and decoration in historical styles, figures, ornaments etc.). Life took place within a continuum of spaces and images arranged in screens and displays.[5] I am defining screens, or displays, in this context as linked groupings which expressed social meanings and whose prerequisites were expressed through narratives. They worked as codes, as 'certain types of the already-read, already-seen, already-done'.[6] Such groupings consisted of constellations of objects, of relationships between objects, of perceptions and of the positions of the spectator. Expressed spatially we can employ the term 'display' to denote a meaningful grouping of associated constellations, images, that is, worked in conjunction with the materiality and the spatiality of rooms. A dining room, for example, was an amalgamation of its furniture, the decorative elements chosen for it, the central position of the table and the gathering of the inhabitants

as a family—images which, on the one hand, extended to the kitchen and to the economic conditions of the home and, on the other, to the sofa, and to the novel or film. The 'dining room' display became the spatial nexus in a complex set of images that created a pictorial space, which could also be found in elements of the living space, such as the space above the sofa. In the nineteenth century, historical styles, ornaments and figurines were used to create ensembles of images and spaces that, in turn, generated the pictorial display of the bourgeois living space. Because of the increased sensitivity towards texture, colour, light and odours, and because of their reproduction and repetition, which existed in the last quarter of the century, the living space became a sensual world created by the interplay of the inhabitants, motifs and the material items contained within it. In conjunction with figures from history and culture, the abundance of things developed a narrative flow that communicated with the inhabitants of the dining room. It told stories of the Renaissance and of the Orient. In the Rococo-style drawing room, it spoke of distraction, and in the old German-style library, it talked about contemplation. The role of things was extended to become narratives. Merleau-Ponty has said of the thing/object, that it is rendered a 'nexus of qualities', a 'principle of identity'.[7] The ensemble of things is visualised as *atmosphere* and dramatised to be an *event.* This eventlike quality makes the interior seem like the subject's latent exterior, almost like the subject's surface. As the Viennese writer Peter Altenberg explained in 1896: 'What I have put on my side table, on my walls, is mine, just like my hair and my skin.' Here we can understand the screen/ display as 'the curling in of the visible into the seeing body'.[8] 'Therefore that which remains visible of the things and of the ego is by no means their secret and profound essence, but rather their surface—the innocent and precarious silence of their surface,' says Starobinski.[9] In the context of the living space, the precarious is mostly associated with the uncanny. In the nineteenth century, the uncanny was defined in the new genres of gothic and crime fiction and was located, in particular, in the catastrophic domesticity and the animated world of objects of the living space, which was a location bordering on the *Kluft zum Unsichtbaren,* the abyss to the invisible.[10] Freud's 1919 publication about the uncanny starts with an analysis of language, referring to the shift from *Heim* (the home) to *heimlich* (secretly) to *unheimlich* (uncanny). Modernists criticised the horror of the living space with its overabundance of things. Le Corbusier spoke about its craziness and nonsense and wanted to tidy up. This remains the dogma of modern architecture: it supposedly emptied surfaces, liberated humans and placed them in a neutral, transparent space free of (pictorial) representations. Modernism's plain and monochrome walls and its lack of ornaments allegedly stopped the narrative flow and the noise to create silence. In particular, Mies van der Rohe's buildings are considered to be new, abstract rooms of 'eloquent silences'.[11] In this context, the abundance of things acquires a femininity which is almost always seen as negative, as tempting *frivolités de la mode* and as *mascarades*—against which a huge gesture of liberation is made by the

hands of a male master with a superior 'moral attitude'.[12] This echoes the tricky relationship between the image and space in the modern avant-garde. *In extremis* it leads to an ethical devaluation of the image as being merely illusionary in contrast with space as truth and fact. In the twentieth century, this rhetoric had its starting point in the codification of the avant-garde as being *without pictures*— and in the narrative of modern architecture representing a moralising rupture of illusionist image and transparent space. Referring negatively to the image was part of the avant-garde's belligerent rhetoric against the imagery of nineteenth-century architecture. Instead of this dualism, images and spaces can also be understood as performative social configurations, as Foucauldian 'figures of knowledge'. This implies a reading of images and spaces as interacting, social and medial situations of localising or of refusing territory, of rendering visible and invisible.

I have been working on a new analysis of the status given to images within modern architecture which considers its unadorned nature and the antifigurative world of objects as a *transformation* of tendencies that were typical of the late nineteenth century; as a change of images, that is, rather than of their eradication. Linked to this is the question of how the rearrangement of the screen shifted the display and its structure of spectatorship.

At the historical point of media conflict between the *tempting* image and the *straightforward* space, the filled living space of the nineteenth century is contrasted with the emptied living space of the twentieth century. The untamed old pictorial rooms filled with horror have supposedly been replaced by rooms free of gloom ... Yet it is just the nineteenth century's very intensity of things and images which works to differentiate the bourgeois subject's ability to perceive and to imagine, and thus become a spectator—and which became the basis of modernity and the potential of the images which it brought with it. Moreover, we have to ask whether the horror was really eradicated or simply transformed.

Things as nature

Around 1900 we can detect a change in the central motif of the notion of the private. Whilst the living space of the nineteenth century was crafted from history and culture—from the neo-Gothic wardrobe to the historical novel— the modernity of the twentieth century used figures from the social imagery of nature, that is *naturalness* as an emergence of the *actual, the true, the profound.* Since the nineteenth century, this recourse to nature has been part of the sentiment of existence and of overcoming the bourgeois subject's self-alienation by the means of relaxation and contemplation; leisure has become a social category. When Art Nouveau began with its style inspired by flora and fauna, a reevaluation of classical modernity was initiated. Thus wrote Le Corbusier:

> *And maybe, at this moment of leisure, of relaxing in the home, we feel like thinking about something? Here's the pivotal point; thinking of something ... Life offers so many opportunities of collecting things that can become objects for reflection: This little pebble from the bottom of the sea, this pretty pine cone, this butterfly, this beetle, this shiny piece of steel ... this piece of ore.* [13]

Accordingly, screens/displays function through the essentialisation of surfaces and materials in their "natural" forms (the glow of a bright wall, for example, or the presence of the lines in a piece of wood, and of the relief and texture of that material): 'That which endows things with their solidity, yet at the same time also with their growing sensuality, causes the colour, the sound, the density, and the massiveness that is the texture of the things.'[14] Loos speaks of the 'deification' of the material as a 'mysterious substance' which needs to be 'felt'.[15]

Pictures in motion

In the Tugendhat Villa, the surfaces and the colours of the wood, the glass, the fabrics and the steel determine the structure of its interior space. It is as though nature had entered the house in the grain of the wood, the fibres of the fabrics, the design of the cut onyx, the surface of the water in the winter garden, and in the view of the garden and of the cityscape from the panoramic windows. However, nearly all of these surfaces are smooth, gleaming and they often reflect light (see Fig. 6.1). This implies that they are less about the haptic mediation of the material than about its visual presence and variety. They include the opaque and transparent glass, the veins of the cut stone and the grains of the woods which range from pear to Zebrano wood. One aspect of this way of dealing with the material and its appearance which we must not leave out are the experiences Mies van der Rohe and Lilly Reich had made at craft exhibitions, among them, significantly, their way of presenting materials in an isolated and classifying manner. An important question to ask in this context would be how far it was that these experiences with exhibiting and arranging things in a display in an open exhibition space substantially influenced the design of the open rooms in the domestic sphere. Thus, the division of rooms by curved walls that was in evidence at the Gallery of Velvet and Silk at the 1927 Berlin Fashion Exhibition immediately preceded the semicircular form of the Villa Tugendhat's dining niche, although the material was changed from fabric to wood. Whilst they were planning and building the Villa Tugendhat, Mies and Reich were also actively working on exhibitions, ranging from the 1927 *Werkbundausstellung* to the pavilions at the 1929 World Fair in Barcelona.

What we encounter in the surfaces of the Villa Tugendhat is a visual eventlike quality that affects the disposition of the entire living space. It is organised as a synthesis of image and space which works to set the inhabitant in motion and—through various movements of the gaze and images; through looking close and then further away; through the macroscopic zoom and the miniature-rendering panorama, the fragmented and the entire view, as a framing to enclose tableaus or an unframing of units—to create visual complexity. All of this works to evoke various positions of the gaze and movements of the

Fig. 6.1. Living room in Villa Tugendhat, Brno 1929–31, Mies van der Rohe/Lilly Reich. Photograph: Irene Nierhaus, 2000.

spectator; thus framing becomes a fixating localisation in space.[16] The panoramic window is transformed into a picture wall: 'In fact, these modern glass homes are not really open; quite on the contrary, outside, nature, landscape permeate into the private sphere from the exterior through the glass and its abstraction and then are perceived as part of the living space atmosphere ... The whole world is connected to the private universe like a stage set.'[17] In the 1930s, panoramic windows brought into houses the drama of the mountains and of the sea in cinemascope. Paintings, hitherto conventional components of living rooms, were replaced by the experience of framed nature. 'Just like in Davos', was what the inhabitants of Villa Tugendhat said about their view. In front of the panoramic window a screen could be lowered for the projection of films. From what the former nanny recalls, it appears that the films that were projected

showed pictures of plants and the stages of their growth, resembling the ones made by Carl Blossfeldt.[18] The enclosing frame in Mies's panoramic window was reduced in order to increase the effect of presenting the immediacy of nature (see Fig. 6.2), an analogy to the onyx wall. Photographs exist showing that, in the drawings of the Resor House of 1938, a mountain landscape covered the entire (glass) house front. He gave one side of the house a panoramic view of a monumental mountain range and the other a close-up view of a river. In the Villa Tugendhat, the views, and the relationships between them, were put in a hierarchical order. It was primarily the master and lady of the house who, in their bedrooms,

Fig. 6.2. View from the living room in Villa Tugendhat, Brno 1929–31, Mies van der Rohe/Lilly Reich. Photograph: Irene Nierhaus, 2000.

owned the view through the windows. It was like a tableau—a framed, vedutelike view of the skyline of the city. The view from the children's bedroom was limited by the patio and the pergola which was covered with foliage. The nanny's room—the only employee who lived in the house with the family—had a window to the side. It was the only room in the family's living quarters that did not permit a full view since it was divided several times by mullions (like the other rooms in which the servants worked during the day, such as the kitchen). Large-scale, unframed viewing was restricted to the representative space of the living room.

Inside the house, macroscopic, zoom-in views on to the surfaces of the objects contrasted with the distant view from the windows; for instance the unframed view of the grain of the wood, such as that of the veneer of the piece of furniture which appeared to have been cut from one piece of material. The large mirror in the anteroom also worked with close-up views: In the small niche where the wardrobe was located, the mirror wouldn't permit a distant view of bodies; rather, it offered details of hairstyles, of close-fitting collars and of closed buttons. Bodies, fragments of body images and the room melted together as a result of the proximity to the image reflected in the mirror. The different ways in which the gaze was being directed—close-ups and distance views, panoramas and zooms, peeks and surveys—seem to parallel those used in film. This has encouraged art historians to speak of a 'cinematographic dispositive of perception' of the house.[19] Thus the mobility of the gaze was awakened, and, in fact, the room was transformed into an ensemble of screens which could be turned into a chain as a result of the view and the movement of the inhabitants.

Another view of the Resor House shows the interior as a combination of rectangular spaces: a window, a piece of cut wood veneer and a painting by Paul Klee. This imagelike quality evoked the criticism of contemporaries: 'Because the pattern of the marble and the grain of wood have replaced art', there was no place for paintings in the building (see Fig. 6.3).[20] The wall of frosted glass in the living room, which could be illuminated from behind, was turned into a tableau, into a framed picture. The family often came together in that room to play cards. A glowing screen created the backlighting against which the inhabitants were turned into shadow play. From the eighteenth century onwards, silhouettes and shadow pictures made from portraits and scenes of genre pictures had been a popular art associated explicitly with the home. That art form was renewed in the twenties in the new media of photography and especially in film. Another relationship with film can be found in another possibility of shadow play in the Tugendhat House. When seen from the street at night, the hall and staircase, lit up behind frosted glass, made the inhabitants passing by appear to be floating, blurry shadows on a cinema screen. It recalled scenes from Marcel Herbier's film *L' inhumaine* (1924; set designed by Fernand Léger)—which Adolf Loos had praised very highly.

The reflections of light on the shiny surfaces must be considered in that context, too (see Fig. 6.4). They made objects and

Fig. 6.3. Living room in Villa Tugendhat, Brno 1929–31, Mies van der Rohe/Lilly Reich. Photograph: Irene Nierhaus, 2000.

Fig. 6.4. Living room in Villa Tugendhat, Brno 1929–31, Mies van der Rohe/Lilly Reich. Photograph: Irene Nierhaus, 2000.

people flicker as though in a kaleidoscope and endowed the geometry of the room with a certain blurriness that created a pictorial effect. In certain parts of the living room, its pure geometry seemed to vanish completely among the shimmering and reflecting chrome-plated pillars, the reflections on glass, the view on to the green outside and the gathered curtains. The photographs of light and shade effects taken by the owner of the Villa Tugendhat in his living room in the 1930s clearly follow the same rhetoric. He had repeatedly taken pictures of the water-filled vase on his desk with mirror images reflected on its surface, and he integrated the reflections on the surfaces of the furniture. He also took backlit pictures of the living room winter garden, thus completely turning that end of the room into a play of shadow and light with all sorts of plant figures. He thus created yet another wall screen image with nature-as-nature motifs which complemented the view from the panoramic window, the stone lineament of the onyx wall, and the grain of the Makassar wood used in the dining niche. In his film *Les mystères du chateau du dé* (F 1929), Man Ray included a long shot of the house's swimming pool which was shown as a dynamic play of light as a result of the reflections of the rays of sunshine that played on its surface. Reflected on the wall, they transformed it into a picture wall. The surfaces of the house were thus developed not only as defined image spaces, but also as potential ones on which the inhabitants could see silhouettes, shapes and movement, depending on the light, the time of the day and their mood. Meanwhile, fragments of the mirror images of the inhabitants flickered in

the reflective surfaces in the Villa Tugendhat as though, reflected through itself, the private sphere was looking back at the living space. The potentiality of the appearance and disappearance of shapes became an issue in photography and in film, whilst cross-fades of bodies and of objects were also popular (e.g. in films by Man Ray and Edmund Kesting). The effects of the mirror images focused on the inhabitants themselves, making them appear in a flash and then vanishing again.[21] A central motif in Freud's definition of the uncanny was the *doppelgänger,* which he introduced in his anecdote about a door that suddenly opened in a sleeper cabin, revealing a mirror image which was read as 'Other'. This confusion recalled the horror of the language of things in the 'old' interior. Siegfried Kracauer has described Mies's glass room displayed at the 1927 Stuttgart *Werkbundausstellung:*

A glass box … Each appliance and each movement … makes shadow play appear on the wall, body-less silhouettes which float in the air and mingle with the mirror images of the glass room itself. The conspiracy of this intangible, glass haunting which changes like a kaleidoscope just like the reflections of the light, is a clear sign that the new residential house does not mean ultimate fulfillment.[22]

Appearing and disappearing thus brought into being a new force of the uncanny whose *abyss to the invisible* engraved itself into the centre of the living space. In his text about his visit to the Barcelona pavilion, which was originally built in 1929 (and reconstructed in 1986), Victor Burgin has stated: 'The pavilion haunts me.'[23] Burgin's concept of 'sequence-image' described a process of the nonlinear and asynchronous associative transport of the image. Into his observations he wove memory fragments. Thus the hand gesture of a young woman in his documentary of the Spanish Civil War recalled the gesture of a figure by Georg Kolbe. The transfer of images is also virulent in the Villa Tugendhat, when, for instance, the architectural photographs empty of inhabitants blend with the emptying of the Villa due to the inhabitants' emigration to Venezuela forced on them by National Socialism.

As reflections and shades, the inhabitants enter the image and become part of the living space surface. Here a correlation exists between the cross-fades of the body and the image typical of photography and film shows. In art, since Impressionism this had been developed as an intricate equivalence of figure and background: 'Flatness may serve as a powerful metaphor for the price we pay in transforming ourselves into images.'[24] The new equivalence of figure, ornament and background made the body, part of the surface of the image, at one with the structure of material. The Villa Tugendhat works as an example to show that the defigurisation of modernism is followed by a refigurisation and that we can detect image transformation rather than image elimination, a transformation of the screens/display which had been newly elaborated in the nineteenth century into a potential, essentialised imagelike quality which resembles nature. The narrative flow of the old interior was replaced by the new, simultaneous coexistence of parts of images

and movements of the gaze which deployed cropped views, close-ups and long shots, the appearance and disappearance of the inhabitants, in order to define the inhabitant as an active body of perception: 'It is necessary ... to let your gaze be drawn into the calligraphy of the patterned marble and its kaleidoscopic figures, to feel yourself enmeshed in a system of planes in stone, glass and water that envelops and moves you through space.'[25] In the display as a texture of image–movement–space, the inhabitants are entangled and wrapped in screens which exist in a structurally reciprocal relationship with the contemporary visual cultural forms of painting, photography and film. The eventlike quality of the modern interior sent the inhabitants on their way. It combines the montage of gaze with parts of images and of rooms and spaces to create a loosely woven background story in which they can observe themselves as protagonists.

Notes

1. G. Barbey, *WohnHaft. Essay über die innere Geschichte der Massenwohnung* (Vieweg, 1993), p. 89.

2. The 'given-to-be-seen' is a figure of speech which has been taken from Merleau-Ponty and Lacan and adopted by image theory (particularly gender-analytical image theory).

3. Perception is socially structured, and all privileges of, and participation in ways of viewing and observing, as well as the visual technologies, are permeated by the entire system of social differences; for instance certain constellations of the panoramic are linked to power, the seizing of power and masculinity.

See L. Hentschel, *Pornotopische Techniken des Betrachtens. Raumwahrnehmung und Geschlechterordnung in visuellen Apparaten der Moderne,* Studien zur visuellen Kultur, Vol. 2 (Jonas, 2001); I. Nierhaus, 'BIG-SCALE. Zum Dispositiv von superlativem Blick und großem Raum,' in I. Nierhaus and F. Konecny, eds., *RÄUMEN. Raum, Geschlecht, Visualität und Architektur* (Selene, 2002), pp. 117–145.

4. This differentiation in terms of gender is then transferred to the furniture as well as to its arrangement in the room. See I. Nierhaus, *Arch6: Raum, Geschlecht, Architektur* (Sonderzahl, 1999), pp. 103 and 10.

5. When referring to the arrangements of the given-to-be-seen and their constellations of spectatorship, I will make use of the doubling of screen/display—a somewhat vague couple, or one that can only be differentiated in a spatial constellation. My use of *screen* here is that of a certain form of *screen-likeness,* which relates to screen theory. See, for example, K. Silverman, *The Threshold of the Visible World* (Routledge, 1996), pp. 41–64.

6. R. Barthes, *Das semiologische Abenteuer* (Suhrkamp, 1988), p. 292.

7. M. Merleau-Ponty, *Das Sichtbare und das Unsichtbare, gefolgt von Arbeitsnotizen,* C. Lefort, ed. (Fink, 1994), p. 312.

8. Ibid., p. 191.

9. Starobinski referring to Rousseau. J. Starobinski, *Rousseau. Eine Welt von Widerständen* (Fischer Taschenbuch, 1993), pp. 386–7.

10. G. C. Tholen, 'Einleitung. Der befremdliche Blick', in M. Sturm, ed., *Ausstellungskatalog Phantasma und Phantome. Gestalten des Unheimlichen in Kunst und Psychoanalyse* (1997), p. 13.

11. My translation of: C. Martí Arís, *Silenzi eloquenti. Borges, Mies van der Rohe, Ozu, Rothko, Oteiza* (Marinotti, 2002).

12. Le Corbusier quoted in W. Oechslin, *Stilhülse und Kern. Otto Wagner, Adolf Loos und der evolutionäre Weg zur modernen Architektur* (gta-Verlag, 1994), p. 37.

13. Le Corbusier [1929], 'Das Abenteuer der Wohnungseinrichtung', in Le Corbusier, *Feststellungen zu Architektur und Städtebau* (Ullstein Verlag, 1964), p. 105.

14. M. Heidegger [1935/36], 'Das Ding und das Werk', in M. Heidegger, *Holzwege* (Klostermann, 1990), p. 11.

15. A. Loos [1924], 'Von der Sparsamkeit', in A. Opel, ed., *Die potemkin'sche Stadt. Verschollene Schriften 1897–1933* (Prachner, 1983), pp. 205, 209. This statement also recalls the intensive eventlike quality of the counting of things typical of the old interior.

16. Brian O'Doherty elaborates extensively on the relation between image, frame and wall (see B. O'Doherty, W. Kemp, eds., *In der weißen Zelle. Inside the White Cube* (Merve, 1996); and M. Foucault discusses the spatiality of the image in its frame using Manet's work (see M. Foucault, *Die Malerei von Manet* (Merve, 1999).

17. J. Baudrillard, *Das System der Dinge. Über unser Verhältnis zu den alltäglichen Gegenständen* (Campus-Verlag, 1991), p. 56.

18. In a personal telephone conversation in 2003.

19. K. Sierek, 'Vorschrift und Nachträglichkeit: Zur Rhetorik von Bauen und Filmen', *Daidalos* 64 (June 1997), p. 116.

20. Criticism formulated by architecture critic Justus Bier in the debate revolving around the question: 'Is it possible to live in Villa Tugendhat?' (*Kann man im Haus Tugendhat wohnen?*) Quoted in D. Hammer-Tugendhat and W. Tegethoff, eds., *Ludwig Mies van der Rohe. Das Haus Tugendhat* (Springer, 1988), p. 29.

21. In this, they evoke the effect of the Lacanian tin can (the experience of a boat ride on the sea and the sudden flash of a can as the light shines on it) which is relevant for the concept of the gaze and which, turned the concept of the self being under observation into a topic for discussion.

J. Lacan, *Die 4 Grundbegriffe der Psychoanalyse, Das Seminar von Jacques Lacan* 11 (1987 [1964]), Berlin.

22. S. Kracauer's *Das neue Bauen,* 1927, quoted in H. Brüggemann, *Das andere Fenster. Einblicke in Häuser und Menschen. Zur Literaturgeschichte einer urbanen Wahrnehmungsform* (Fischer-TB.-Verlag, 1989), pp. 254–5.

23. V. Burgin, 'Mies in Maurelia', in V. Burgin, *The Remembered Film* (Reaktion Books, 2004), p. 75.

24. D. Joselit, 'Notes on Surface: Toward a Genealogy of Flatness', *Art History* 23/1 (March 2000), p. 20.

25. I. de Solá Morales, Christian Cirici et al., eds, *Mies van der Rohe. Barcelona Pavillon* (Gustavo Gili, 2002), p. 39, concerning the Barcelona Pavilion. Another argument to support the importance to Mies of the idea of the moveable body in the house is offered by his proposal to include sculptures of figures in motion in his houses.

Chapter Seven

'Leaving traces': Anonymity in the modernist house

Hilde Heynen

Modernity and homelessness

The literature of modernity focuses on the idea of change and discontinuity, stating that, in a modern condition, change is paramount and nothing can remain fixed or stable. The basic motivation for this struggle for change is located in a desire for progress and emancipation, which can only be fulfilled if the containment within the stifling conventions of the past can be overcome. The usual depictions of modernity thus present it as a heroic pursuit of a better life and a better society, which is basically opposed to stability, tradition and continuity.[1] The conceptualisation of modernity is therefore at odds with home and domesticity. In as far as modernity means change and rupture, it seems to imply, necessarily, the leaving of home. This theme, which was already present in the discourse of the interwar period, became all the more prominent in the postwar period.

A metaphorical 'homelessness' indeed is often considered the hallmark of modernity. For a philosopher such as Heidegger, it is clear that modern man has lost the knowledge of 'how to dwell'[2]. Theodor Adorno is of the same opinion: 'Dwelling, in the proper sense, is now impossible ... The house is past.'[3]

Although Adorno's perspective is very different from Heidegger's, both philosophers share the fundamental assumption that modernity and dwelling are at odds and cannot be reconciled. The metaphor is also recurrent in sociological studies, as can be inferred from the 1974 book by Peter Berger, Brigitte Berger and Hansfried Kellner, *The Homeless Mind. Modernization and Consciousness.*

In architecture, this sense of homelessness is probably best captured in the works of Mies van der Rohe. His transparent glass buildings do away with the privacy and intimacy long associated with domesticity. His work, states Cacciari, has one dominant characteristic: 'a supreme indifference to dwelling, expressed in neutral signs ... The language of absence here testifies to the absence of dwelling.'[4] Indeed, looking at the picture of a living room in Mies's Lake Shore Drive apartments (see Fig. 7.1), one perceives elegance, openness and sobriety. The openness, however, turns into exposure whilst the sobriety somehow equals glamour—thus erasing any feelings of warmth or enclosure that signal 'home' for most people. The dominant sense produced by this image closely resembles, somewhat surprisingly, the effect of Edward Hopper's

Fig. 7.1. Interior of Mies van der Rohe's Lake Shore Drive apartment, Chicago. Photographer unknown.

painting *Western Motel* (see Fig. 7.2). In both cases, a woman is sitting in front of a window, in a posture that makes clear that she is ready to leave. She is not nestling comfortably in her chair, she is not involved in conversation or reading; she is simply waiting for the moment to depart. Both women are in a space where they seemingly do not

Fig. 7.2. Edward Hopper, Western Motel, 1957. Courtesy of Yale Art Gallery.

belong. They clearly do not *inhabit* these interiors—although it might very well be that the woman in Mies's interior is living in this apartment. Both images produce a sense of imminent departure rather than a welcoming feeling of home. They thus resonate with Ernst Bloch's description of modern houses:

> These days houses in many places look as if they are ready to leave. Although they are unadorned or for this very reason, they express departure. On the inside they are bright and bare like sickrooms, on the outside they seem like boxes on moveable rods, but also like ships.[5]

Old and new dwelling

Modernist architecture was really caught up in the paradoxes of home and homelessness. Aiming towards the future, battling convention and tradition, modern architecture pursued the ideals of purity, functionalism and heroism. Notwithstanding its masculinist rhetoric, however, which glorified ascetism, authenticity and integrity, the focus of modernist architects was to a very large extent oriented towards the home. The genealogy of modernism in architecture indeed goes back upon a culture focusing on dwelling and domesticity. The Arts and Crafts movement of William Morris, the *Wiener Werkstätte* of Josef Hoffmann and the books by Muthesius on the art of living—all three of them repeatedly mentioned in history books as important sources of modernism in architecture—centred on the design of beautiful, comfortable and modern homes. A lot of artists interested in abstract art also explored the abstract implications of the applied arts and investigated how the decorative arts could contribute to pure form. They experimented with 'abstract interiors' that would transfer the objective, universal qualities they strived for in their art to the spatial realm of home or studio.[6] This kind of practice clearly undermines the supposedly clear-cut opposition between the heroic pursuit of an abstract ideal on the one hand and the narrow-mindedness associated with domesticity on the other. As a consequence, these practices occupy an uneasy position between the different domains of art and everyday living.

In Walter Benjamin's work of the 1920s and 1930s on the *Arcades Project,* one can find some interesting attempts to theorise these paradoxes. Benjamin differentiated between two modes of dwelling: an old one based upon enclosure and security and a new one aiming towards openness and flexibility. The old mode of dwelling was paramount in nineteenth-century bourgeois interiors. It had to do with living as a process of 'leaving traces'.[7] Benjamin described this mode of dwelling relying upon the metaphor of the shell:

> *The original form of all dwelling is existence not in a house but in a shell. The shell bears the impression of its occupant. In the most extreme instance, the dwelling becomes a shell. The nineteenth century, like no other century, was addicted to dwelling. It conceived the residence as a receptacle for the person, and it encased him with all his appurtenances so deeply in the dwelling's interior, that one might be reminded of the inside of a compass case, where the instrument with all its accessories lies embedded in deep, usually violet folds of velvet.*[8]

As much as this description may convey a sense of love and appreciation, it nevertheless is consistent with Benjamin's condemnation, in his 1933 essay on 'Experience and Poverty', of these interiors as completely bound up with exploitation and injustice.[9] For Benjamin was convinced that these interiors were intimately linked with the capitalist values of property, ownership and ostentation. Their message to every visitor, he stated, was unmistakable: 'there is nothing here for you; you are a stranger in this house.' Because of this, he was convinced that this way of dwelling could not be made productive for the twentieth century. A new way of living had to be conceived, which would no longer follow the lines of bourgeois domesticity. This new way of living, he surmised, could be recognised in the experiments of the avant-garde in architecture. He thus supported the efforts of modern architecture to do away with the overstuffed and heavily ornamented Victorian interiors (see Fig. 7.3) and to devise an alternative. This alternative would give rise to a new mode of dwelling, more apt for a collective way of living in a classless society.

Benjamin's visit to Moscow in the winter of 1926–1927 had given him firsthand contact with the Russian living conditions at that particular time. It was an extraordinary moment, since the revolutionary attempts at restructuring the material world of daily life were visibly influencing the way people occupied their accommodations. Benjamin attested to how people were trying to get rid of the petit-bourgeois aspect of 'cosiness' that overshadowed interiors 'over which the devastating assault of commodity capital [had] victoriously swept'.[10] To annihilate the

Fig. 7.3. Poster announcing the Werkbund exhibition in Stuttgart, 1927. *Graphic design:* Willi Baumeister.

traces of cosiness, he accounted, they weekly rearranged the furniture in bare rooms, devoid of pictures on the walls, cushions on the sofas or ornaments on the mantelpiece. They could bear with this, because their real dwelling place was not their house, but the office, the club or the street. They had given up private life to fully indulge in collective life.[11]

The restructuring of daily life was advocated by avant-garde artists such as Vladimir Tatlin and Alexander Rodchenko, who promoted the so-called *novyi byt* (new forms of domesticity). This new way of life, which was also advocated by many feminists, would no longer be based upon the nuclear family, but upon a broader association of adults, with children living separately from their parents.[12] According to Olga Matich, this movement can be symbolically summed up in its rejection of the marital bed:

> the proponents of **novyi byt** replaced the double bed of generational continuity and social stability with the mobile single bed. It was an emblem of the new Soviet person who believed in the end of the family and in mechanized, accelerated everyday life. Culture in the traditional sense, handed down from one generation to the next, was abolished, to be replaced by the culture of the new Soviet person who either does not sleep or sleeps in keeping with scientific rules of physical revivification. The New Man and the New Woman do not have children, or if they do, they live separately from them, asserting the supremacy of the non-biological family.[13]

Walter Benjamin, who was deeply taken by his Moscow experiences, recognised a similar utopian impulse in the modern architecture of his contemporaries. He declared that, in the twentieth century, the days of the cosy interior were over, since dwelling as seclusion and security had had its day. Dwelling would no longer be recorded in ineradicable imprints, but was to be articulated in changeable constructions and anonymous, transitory interiors—which, one can assume, might be exemplified in Hannes Meyer's Co-op Zimmer (see Fig. 7.4). This new environment harboured an important promise, since its coolness represented the openness and transparency that were characteristic of a new form of society:

> For it is the hallmark of this epoch that dwelling in the old sense of the word where security had priority has had its day. Giedion, Mendelsohn, Corbusier turned the abiding places of man into a transit area for every conceivable kind of energy and for electric currents and radio waves. The time that is coming will be dominated by transparency.[14]

For Benjamin, modern architecture's transparency and porosity pointed forward to a classless society still to come; its coldness and sobriety were forbearers of an era in which it would no longer be necessary to seclude oneself from one's neighbours, an era where warmth and security would pervade the whole of social structure, and therefore need no longer be provided by one's individual home.

Benjamin thus constructed modern architecture as radically critical of conventional patterns of family life, sedimented in the bourgeois houses of the nineteenth century with their overfull interiors. According to his

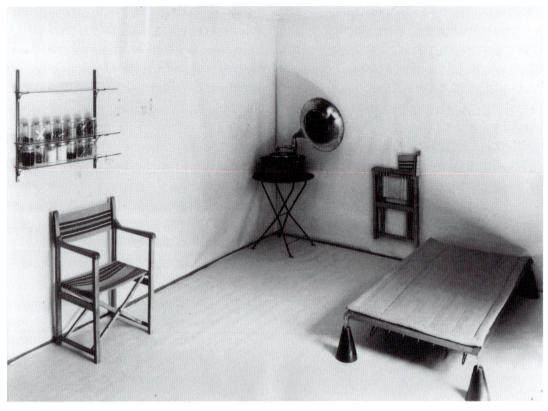

Fig. 7.4. Hannes Meyer, Co-op Zimmer, 1926. Courtesy of Collection Kieren, Berlin.

diagnosis, such interiors were deeply ingrained with capitalist commodity culture and corresponded to an oppressive, patriarchal, individualist and unjust social system. The new architecture, on the other hand, would, with its bare interiors and its open plans, instruct people that material belongings were less important than a social spirit. They would act as perfect accommodations for a life that would be much more mobile and flexible.

Inhabitation as appropriation

In many ways the battle for the abstract interior bore gendered overtones. It played out tradition and convention on the feminine side versus modernity and progress on the masculine side.[15] The caricature painted by the critics of the cosy interior had it that this interior was stifling and overwhelming, thus prohibiting its inhabitants to liberate and emancipate themselves. If one wanted to live one's life authentically, one had to do away with this interior's commodified object, bravely embracing the bareness of a naked interior, stripped of its decorative items and its abundant coverings. The abstract and bare utopian interior, on the other hand, was seen by its opponents as so rational and anonymous that it seemed totally inappropriate as a personal space where the inhabitant could feel 'at home'. In retrospect, one could claim that the discourse advocating this new way of dwelling was forging it on purely masculine terms, without any consideration of sensibilities and desires that are usually qualified as 'feminine': the caring for things invested with memories or cultural significance, the transmittance of private meanings and values to the next generation, the continuous arranging and rearranging of the necessities for daily life, the performance of family rituals and acts of emotional bonding. Modernist interiors were often blamed for their coldness and their abstract character, for doing away not only with sentimentality and kitsch but also with warmth and comfort.[16] Answering to some concerns about the modernist transformation of the Harvard architectural curriculum, dean Joseph Hudnut thought it indeed necessary to declare that the Faculty of Design would 'NEVER NEVER … take part in any effort to eradicate charm, hospitality, warmth, privacy, womanhood, or beauty from the American home'.[17] So it seemed that life called for a negotiation between modernity and domesticity.

In contrasting the utopia of daily life with the bourgeois cosy interior, however, two polar opposites had been constructed that hardly ever occur in a real-life situation. Both extremes—the bourgeois interior and the naked utopia—seem to deny one of the crucial qualities that is inherent to most people's experience of domesticity: the fact that 'making a home' is a continuous process that requires a lot of effort and work and that is obviously never 'finished'. It is this insight that seems to underline an enigmatic remark by Benjamin, which refers to dwelling as

some repetitive act—or rather process—of inhabitation: '"To dwell" is a transitive verb—as in the notion of "indwelt spaces"; herewith an indication of the frenetic topicality concealed in habitual behavior. It has to do with fashioning a shell for ourselves.'[18]

This means that Benjamin understood dwelling as an active form of interaction between the inhabitant and his environment, in which individuals and their surroundings adjusted to each other. In the German original, he referred to the grammatical connection between *wohnen* (dwelling) and *gewohnt* (customary, habitual), a connection that is found in English between 'habit' and 'inhabit' or 'dwell' and 'indwelt': dwelling, inhabiting, in this sense has to do with the formation of habits. To inhabit a house meant to go through a mutual process of moulding in which house and inhabitant become adapted to one another.

What is at stake is indeed the interaction between inhabitant and home. Following Benjamin's lead, one could state that, in the nineteenth-century bourgeois dwelling, the interaction was a rather slow and enduring process; the inhabitant settled in an interior as if enveloped in a case, a shell, leaving his or her traces slowly and continuously, which resulted in a static and stable situation. Modern life, however, significantly increased the pace of this process, because it required individuals to change and adapt themselves much more frequently. This resulted in dwelling as a sort of 'frenetic topicality', as Benjamin indicated. For me this phrasing suggests a mode of dwelling very much in tune with the modern condition of changeability and transparency. I read it as implying a continuing gesture, as if the shell is not fashioned once and for all, but rather again and again. This kind of dwelling involves, therefore, the constant shaping and reshaping of a shell.

A possible example of such a constant shaping and reshaping can be found in the Rietveld Schröder house (1924). Given the quite dramatic difference between this house and any other one designed by Rietveld, it has been argued that Truus Schröder played a major role in its conception and design.[19] The house is set up as a small living space for Schröder and her three children. The spaces on the ground floor are more or less conventional—enclosed rooms with four walls and a ceiling—although each of them has some remarkable details. The spatial qualities of the house really unfold on the first floor, which is conceived as one large space that can be subdivided according to the needs and wishes of the inhabitants. The house is famous in architectural history for embodying a *De Stijl* aesthetic in built form. Its resemblance to a contra-construction by Van Doesburg, its remarkable way of defining spaces by way of planes and lines instead of volumes and its use of primary colours have been commented upon extensively. It is thus one of the earliest icons of the Modern movement in architecture, and it was clearly a major achievement in experimenting with a new formal language.

Regardless of its purely architectural value, however, the house is also fascinating because it embodies a remarkable sense of domesticity. This is not immediately obvious from the famous pictures of the interior, which show abstracted spaces, appealing because of their colours and their interlocking planes and lines. A visit to the house (which is now a museum) reveals a multitude of little details, though, that speak of an intensive engagement with the concerns of everyday life and household arrangements. What is most striking to many visitors is how the interior has an almost shabby quality, which is not really perceivable in the photographs. The bookshelves and furnishings have a kind of do-it-yourself aspect that one wouldn't expect from the perfectionist and abstracted *De Stijl*. Truus Schröder herself confirmed that '"solidity" wasn't something Rietveld really cared for', tentatively talking about the 'fragility' of his work.[20] The surfaces indeed are often not completely smooth but speak of intensive use and bodily appropriation. This is a house in which inhabitants *did* leave traces, although it is at the same time one of the prototypical examples of the 'abstract interior'.

Details such as the shelf for hats and outdoor items in the hallway, the seat with the leather belt to lean against when removing one's shoes and the shoe rack and coat hanger that are provided at the other side of the entrance hall prove that the everyday business of how one comes in and what one leaves where has been carefully considered. In the upstairs space, each sleeping place has its own shelves and conveniences, and one can easily imagine how the actual inhabitation probably involved some cushions and plaids. One can assume that it must have been a tedious affair to fold and unfold the separating walls on a daily basis and to make the sleeping quarters each morning again acceptable and seemly for daytime appearance. The very flexibility that was thus provided, however, makes up what modern domesticity in a Benjaminian sense was all about. It is a house that, on the one hand, represents modernity's longing for openness and transparency but that, on the other hand, exhumes a sense of comfort and well-being, even in its present bare appearance.

The house had indeed been lived in intensively; Truus Schröder occupied it until she was over eighty years old (see Fig. 7.5). The interior bore the marks of an ongoing negotiation between art and life. In a 1982 interview, Truus Schröder recalled a very telling anecdote:

A delightful thing happened recently: some people visited me in connection with the future of this house. As they were leaving, one of them, a pleasant, older man, looked at that painting by Van der Leck and said, 'Look at that Van der Leck there … a fine work.' To which one of the others replied, 'Yes, and a fine mess underneath it.' 'Yes, but that's life,' was my reaction, to which the first man assented: 'Yes, that's life.' So enthusiastically—as if to say, that's allowed! That really gave me a fillip. To accept the state of things as they are: a painting by Van der Leck and underneath, the mess of life. Nothing you can do about it.[21]

Fig. 7.5. Truus Schröder with one of her daughters in the Rietveld Schröder house, ca. 1925. © Gerrit Rietveld, interior Schröder house, c/o Pictoright Amsterdam 2008–06–03.

In its easy accommodation of the 'mess of life', the Rietveld Schröder house was unlike many other modernist homes, which were known for their exacting restrictions on lifestyles and behaviours. Most notorious was probably the case of the Farnsworth house, which Edith Farnsworth thought incredibly difficult to live in.[22] And other modernist icons, like the Villa Savoye, were not exactly cherished family homes but rather showcases or second residences, used to entertain large parties rather than to accommodate the messiness of everyday reality.

The need for identification

Although the most severe criticisms of the abstract interior came from conservative sources, there were also within modernism voices that warned against neutrality and transparency as dominant characteristics of the home. Sibyl Moholy-Nagy fiercely disagreed with Mies van der Rohe, who applied the neutral grid without any distinction to public as well as private buildings, and with Richard Neutra, who advocated that 'the inner and the outer world should be fully meshed.'[23] She claimed that humans have a need for identification and that this need cannot be fulfilled by anonymous spaces that merge inside and outside. Whereas public buildings could fully engage in technological achievements such as the curtain wall, the home was something else altogether. The home should respect man's need for privacy and for identification. It should offer differentiated spaces with different characters, which offer a variety of possibilities

for identification. She echoes Benjamin's metaphor of the shell by discussing how successive rooms might vary 'as if a different personality had moulded the enclosing form like a cocoon'.[24] She thus advocated that the architect 'see himself not only as the builder of technological monuments but as the keeper of the matrix in which the individual is being cast'.[25]

It is through dissonant voices such as Truus Schröder's or Sibyl Moholy-Nagy's that one comes to suspect that not all modernist architects, nor the inhabitants of their houses, followed the purist and masculinist logic of the abstract interior to the full extent. Indeed, the most interesting modernist houses are those where this logic is modified or even disturbed by the intervention of feminine sensibilities that make them more complex, more layered and, ultimately, it seems to me, more inhabitable.

Notes

1. M. Berman, *All That Is Solid Melts into Air. The Experience of Modernity* (Verso, 1982), p. 15.
2. M. Heidegger, 'Building, Dwelling, Thinking' [1954], in M. Heidegger, *Poetry, Language Thought* (Harper & Row, 1971), p. 161.
3. T. W. Adorno, *Minima Moralia. Reflections from Damaged Life* (Verso, 1951), pp. 38–9.
4. M. Cacciari, 'Eupalinos or Architecture', *Oppositions* 21 (1980), p. 108.
5. E. Bloch, *The Principle of Hope* [translation of *Das Prinzip Hoffnung* 1959] (Blackwell, 1986), p. 733.
6. J. Beckett, 'The Abstract Interior', in *Towards a New Art: Essays on the Background to Abstract Art 1910–1920* (Tate Gallery, 1980), pp. 90–124.

7. W. Benjamin, (1978), 'Paris, Capital of the Nineteenth Century' [1935], in W. Benjamin, *Reflections. Essays, Aphorisms, Autobiographical Writings,* (Schocken, 1978), pp.155.

8. W. Benjamin, *The Arcades Project* [translation of Walter Benjamin, *Das Passagenwerk,* 1982], (Harvard University Press, 1999), p. 200.

9. W. Benjamin, 'Experience and Poverty' [1933], in W. Benjamin, *Selected Writings. Vol. 2* (Harvard University Press, 1999), pp. 731–6.

10. W. Benjamin, *Moscow Diary* (Harvard University Press, 1986), p. 48.

11. W. Benjamin, 'Moscow' [1927], in W. Benjamin, *Reflections. Essays, Aphorisms, Autobiographical Writings* (Schocken, 1978), pp. 108–9.

12. V. Büchli, *An Archaeology of Socialism* (Berg, 1999).

13. O. Matich, 'Remaking the Bed. Utopia in Daily Life', in J. Bowlt and O. Matich, eds., *Laboratories of Dreams. The Russian Avant-Garde and Cultural Experience* (Stanford University Press, 1996), pp. 59–78.

14. W. Benjamin, *Gesammelte Schriften. Werkausgabe Vol. 8* [Collected Writings. Work Edition Vol. 8] (Suhrkamp, 1980), pp. 196–7.

15. H. Heynen, 'Modernity and Domesticity: Tensions and Contradictions', in H. Heynen and G. Baydar, eds., *Negotiating Domesticity. Spatial Productions of Gender in Modern Architecture* (Routledge, 2005), pp. 1–29.

16. K. Van Herck, '"Only Where Comfort Ends, Does Humanity Begin": On the "coldness" of avant-garde architecture in the Weimar period', in H. Heynen and G. Baydar, eds., *Negotiating Domesticity. Spatial Productions of Gender in Modern Architecture* (Routledge, 2005), pp. 123–44.

17. J. Hudnut, 'Letter to the Editor', *Harvard Alumni Bulletin* (October 13, 1943).

18. Benjamin, *The Arcades Project,* p. 221.

19. A. T. Friedman, *Women and the Making of the Modern House: A Social and Architectural History* (Harry N. Abrams, 1998); L. Büller and F. Den Oudsten, 'Interview with Truus Schröder', in P. Overy a.o., *The Rietveld Schröder House* (MIT Press, 1988), pp. 42–103.

20. Büller and Den Oudsten, *The Rietveld Schröder House,* p. 79.

21. Ibid, p. 96.

22. Friedman, *Women and the Making of the Modern House.*

23. S. Moholy-Nagy, 'Steel, Stocks, and Private Man', *Progressive Architecture* (January 1958), pp. 128–129+.

24. Ibid, p. 192.

25. Ibid, p. 192.

Chapter Eight

The Geography of the Diagram: The Rose Seidler house

Charles Rice

When one considers the oppositional stance of the modernist avant-gardes, the domestic interior appears as one of the most charged sites of an anti-bourgeois antagonism. One might consider the famous poster for the Deutscher Werkbund exhibition *Die Wohnung,* in Stuttgart in 1927 (see Figure 7.3). An image of a cosy, complacent, overstuffed bourgeois interior is literally condemned with a red *x* daubed over it. The poster implies that, before the new could be realised, the old needed to be obliterated. Indeed, what seems to be done away with in modernism is the very idea of the interior itself, the interior as the provision of soft furnishing, as the covering of an inside space with pliable, impressionable stuff.

A year before the Deutscher Werkbund exhibition, Hannes Meyer forwarded his own image of a modernist domesticity with the Co-op Zimmer (see Figure 7.4). A room with the barest essentials for habitation, it provided for a nomadic, contingent domesticity—one not concerned with the maintenance of stable connections but rather embracing the flux of metropolitan life. This consciousness of flux was one of the main points of impetus for Meyer to reconceptualise architecture

within transformed modes of production and reception.[1] Yet Meyer's room was only ever an image of a room, a backdrop and a series of props that were assembled in order to capture a photograph. Whilst the interior in the Deutscher Werkbund poster and the Co-op Zimmer seem to be polar opposites, linked only by a narrative calling for the former to be obliterated and replaced with something like the latter, their existence as photographic representations unites them. Both of these interiors are lodged within a conceptual structure that came into being around the beginning of the nineteenth century with the emergence of a modern concept of the domestic interior. For the first time, the word 'interior' attained a domestic meaning, as not simply inside as distinct from outside—this is what it had always meant—but as the inside of a room and its artistic effect, the idea that an interior was a deliberate addition to a given architectural 'inside'. It also began to refer explicitly to representations that could be made of this condition, either in terms of the projection of a decorative scheme, or a recording of a room and its contents as themselves the primary subject of a painting or drawing.[2]

Avant-garde modernism did not simply 'get over' the interior by removing additional decoration and opening up to the space and flux of an external world. Rather, the interior's image form was redeployed to imply new spatial conditions, relying on exactly what made the interior prominent in the nineteenth-century—its condition of doubleness, its existence and reception as both image and space. In these terms, it is important to see that the interior is a conceptual apparatus marked by the temporal and experiential disjunctions of modernity. These disjunctions are not simply about a 'break' with the past that an avant-garde mentality might suggest. Rather, the newly outmoded illuminates the contours of a present within which a future possibility is projected.[3] In other words, the outmoded interior in the Deutscher Werkbund poster is made present at the moment its obliteration is projected. What is modern is the conceptual structure of this operation, one brought into being through the emergence of the interior.

Yet the very real articulation of difference at the level of interior images must be noted. With the obliteration of bourgeois 'stuff', what becomes prominent is an explicitly diagrammatic understanding of domesticity, which can be understood as a clarification of the contours of the domestic as they relate to the key modern technique of architectural design. If the interior articulated itself separately from architecture at the point of its emergence, then, with the advent of an explicit modernism, architecture begins to redescribe the interior within a logic of the diagram, the effect of which is to reveal the bourgeois interior as additional, and

hence superfluous to a future-oriented domesticity.

This chapter will discuss the relation between the domestic interior and the architectural diagram with reference to the Rose Seidler House, built by Harry Seidler between 1948 and 1950 for his mother in the suburbs of Sydney. This example is important for the way it is positioned relative to conditions of transformation in modernism. Temporally, it could be classed as mid-century modern, but it relates clearly to a European avant-gardism of the 1920s and 1930s. It sits at the geographical periphery of the major 'sources' of modernism but is also prescient in terms of how the discipline of architecture would investigate its avant-garde legacy in the postwar period.

In a brief observation about the Rose Seidler House, Anthony Vidler has gestured towards what is at stake in its particular positioning. Writing about a kind of double abstraction at play in modernist diagrammatics, Vidler writes:

Modernist diagrams have not, however, been received without their own diagrammatic transformation at the hands of followers, epigones and revivalists ... Other followers of the first generation of modernists built diagrammatic buildings to exemplify modernist principles—among the best known would be Philip Johnson's quasi-Miesian Glass House in Connecticut of 1949 (itself a codification of Johnson and Hitchcock's own codification of modernism as 'international style') and Harry Seidler's post-Marcel Breuer house for his mother of the same year in Sydney, a perfect composite model of a villa with elements from Le Corbusier's Poissy, Breuer's early Connecticut houses, and Oscar Niemeyer's sense of colour and space.[4]

Seidler's own geographically inflected modernist 'formation' is revealed here. He had fled Vienna for England as a teenager, before being interned in Canada during the Second World War. He completed his undergraduate studies in architecture in Manitoba, before going on to study at Harvard under Walter Gropius and Marcel Breuer and at Black Mountain College under Josef Albers. For two years, he was an assistant to Marcel Breuer in New York. Seidler's mother Rose invited him to Australia with the commission for a house, and he made his way there via Brazil, where he spent a period of time with Oscar Niemeyer. This biographical account of the house's design will prove insufficient, however, and it is necessary to elaborate Vidler's position on the diagram in order to consider more fully what the Rose Seidler House's particularity suggests about modern architecture's relation to the interior.

Following Robert Somol, Vidler describes the diagram as '"the matter of architecture" itself, as opposed to its representation'.[5] Vidler goes on to claim that, in this way, architectural drawing might be cast more generally as diagrammatic, as a tool to get to a building, rather than recording what already exists. At the turn of the nineteenth century, J.N.L. Durand's rationalisation of classical architecture in terms of a diagrammatic logic based on metric comparison and financial viability represents the emergence of a modern diagrammatic logic. It is crucial to note that the modern concept of

the domestic interior also emerges at this moment.

It is possible, then, to argue for a parallel trajectory of domesticity's development through the nineteenth century. On the one hand, a diagrammatic logic takes hold of the planimetric organisation of domesticity. This is especially prominent in Britain, where this architectural technique joined with a social reform agenda to do with the spatial constitution and division of the nuclear family. On the other hand, there is the fact that, increasingly through the nineteenth century, upholstery and interior decoration manifested themselves as distinct professions that dealt with the interior in a way separate from architectural concerns. The representation of the interior became the concern of these professions, whilst a diagrammatic arrangement of domesticity became the concern of architects.

In this light, it is interesting to look at a figure such as Robert Kerr, who is credited with having codified what Robin Evans refers to as 'room and corridor' planning.[6] Kerr's 1864 treatise *The Gentleman's House* outlines a fully formed technique of the plan, which revolved around the key concepts of comfort, convenience and privacy. Whilst operating within a very different architectural culture and stylistics from those of Durand half a century earlier, Kerr's account of the development and values of the asymmetrical domestic plan marks a crucial development in architecture's diagramming of the domestic.

Kerr himself was aware of the parallel, or split, trajectory of domesticity's development. In *The Gentleman's House,* he remarked that 'the architect must not venture to reckon without in the first place his client, and in the second place his client's upholsterer.'[7] This comment signals a tension that reached a climax around the turn of the twentieth century in a culture that promoted the dwelling, and one's existence within it, as a total work of art. Seen from an architectural perspective, Art Nouveau and Jugendstil's attempts to reunite all levels of design can be seen as the reunification of architecture and the interior, but one, according to Walter Benjamin, that led to the interior's liquidation.[8] As a consequence of this crisis, Benjamin saw the possibility for architectural modernism to contribute to a reordering of the domestic based on the potential of new social and political organisations of life.[9] Architecture would become prototypical, its abstractions reorganising domesticity in a post-interior world.

One can see the role played by diagrammatic abstraction in the 'emptying out' of traditional signs of the domestic, such as those that marked the plush environs of the bourgeois domestic interior. Referring to Le Corbusier's neo-Platonic polemics on the purity of form, space and geometry, Vidler argues:

> Transparency, infinity, ineffability, liminality, and the expansive extensions of the post-Nietzschean subject demanded as few boundary conditions as possible; the thinner the line, the more invisible the wall. Succinct and economical, the architect's 'épure' [diagram] reduced a project to its essentials; it described the fundamental organization of a building tersely and in terms that seemed to correspond to the scientific tenor of the times; it was, in some sense the essence of the project,

> at once a correct and analytic representation of relations and a formal analogue to the built structure itself.[10]

These values and uses of the diagram were directly opposed to the 'misleading' and seductive nature of Beaux Arts–type renderings, which, according to Le Corbusier, were made merely to please clients and thereby promote the false ambition of architects. The interior, consolidated through the nineteenth century as much as 'seductive' representation as spatial condition, could not adapt to the logic of the diagram. Indeed, the prehistory of the interior's emergence is one of the insufficiency of conventional architectural drawings—such as plan and section and the short-lived hybrid, developed surface drawing—to come to terms with the spatiality of the interior.[11] The interior is condemned by the thinness and operativity of the diagrammatic line and the abstraction this diagram implies. It is this focus on the diagram as the 'formal analog of the built structure itself' that vetoes the interior as a space to be added to an 'inside' already provided architecturally.[12] The line of the diagram seems to hold the promise of a direct translation from drawing to building.

In this way the Rose Seidler house confirms, or at least conforms to, the logic of the modernist diagram, and Seidler's own writing about his early houses upholds the developments of an avant-garde modernism.[13] Yet there is the potential to see the Rose Seidler House's existence within what might be called a second-order diagrammatics, one that brings back the question of the interior as representation. As Vidler writes:

'Modernist diagrams have not, however, been received without their own diagrammatic transformation at the hands of followers, epigones and revivalists.'[14] Whilst one might think that a diagram of a diagram would be a further abstraction, a further distillation of the operative quality of lines, it serves to make of the first diagram an image. It does so because this supposed 'first' diagram exists as that which is imagined or recalled. In itself it is no longer operative, whether by force of time or distance. With the Rose Seidler House, the question of distance—or, more properly, geography—is the crucial issue concerning its second-order nature.

In this context, it is important to note how Australia has occupied a particular geographical positioning relative to the forces of modernity. As Tony Fry has argued:

Australia was first constituted by imposition. The slow progression to self-determination, in conditions of dependency, was bonded to models of the modern drawn from elsewhere— especially Britain and, later, the USA. Modernity was thus not a driving historical condition of transforming social and economical conditions and their cultural consequences. Rather, it was a regime of signs—the arrived appearances of the modern world of metropolitan capitalism … Objects, such as imported machinery and manufactured goods, and images, such as imported illustrated publications, acted to create a typology that registered the look and operation of the modern world.[15]

The Rose Seidler House is figured through such a regime of signs. It is the arrived appearance of the modern world, being a constitutive factor in the modernity of its location. In this light, it is interesting to revisit Seidler's geographical trajectory. His path to Australia was somewhat more convoluted than initially suggested. In 1948, unable to travel directly from South America to Australia, Seidler flew to Sydney via Los Angeles, where he met with John Entenza, editor of *Arts & Architecture* magazine, having met him previously at Breuer's office in New York.[16] That year, *Arts & Architecture* published a project for a house for a family with three young children designed by Seidler with an associate, Rolland Thompson. (Thompson was the nephew of Breuer's client for the lavish Thompson House in Pennsylvania of 1947–48, an architecture graduate of Harvard and an employee of Breuer.)[17] Represented through a plan and photographic views of a model, this project bears an uncanny resemblance to the Rose Seidler House to the extent that it is easily possible to say that it *is* the Rose Seidler House, even down to the site topography, which, as represented in the model, appears uncannily similar to the topography of the site in the northwest of Sydney Seidler found for his mother's house.

Seidler's biographer, Alice Spigelman, claims that 'The plan of his mother's house was based on one for the Thompson house in Foxborough, Massachusetts, which had never been built.'[18] It can be inferred that the project published in *Arts & Architecture* was this Thompson house, that the family with three children was Rolland Thompson's family, for whose house design Thompson is somewhat oddly named as associate. One could speculate on issues of authorship and its apportioning in a publication that Seidler himself would most likely have brokered with Entenza at their meeting; however, Spigelman casts the mismatch between a house for a family with three young children and a house for Seidler's parents (having adult children) in terms of the future viability of the Rose Seidler House: 'Seidler originally planned it as a three-bedroom home for a family, so that [Seidler's brother] Marcell could live there when he had children, and Rose and [Seidler's father] Max could move to Marcell's one-bedroom open-plan house on the [same parcel of] land.'[19] Seidler designed and built three houses on the land purchased for the Rose Seidler House. Marcell's one-bedroom house was sold to Julian Rose after Marcell and his new wife did not wish to live on the site, and it was completed to the original design in 1952.[20] This meant that Rose and Max Seidler lived in the Rose Seidler House until Rose's death in 1967. A third house on the same site was built in 1950 for Seidler's relative Marcus. In 1951, photographs of the completed Rose Seidler House taken by Marcell (some of which are reproduced here) were published in *Arts & Architecture*.

The point to be made from this historical detail is that the project is caught up in a complex weave of geography. An understanding of the second-order diagrammatics, bound up in what Fry calls a geography of power, illuminates the shifts and translations that underpin the project. This weave of geography is not simply about Seidler's personal formation within an international trajectory of modernism, but about how this weave created a series of possibilities for his architectural output. One of these possibilities was the publication of the scheme for the house with three young children prior to its transformation into the Rose Seidler House. This publication allowed a relationship to be set up with Entenza whereby the Rose Seidler House as built would also be published. At a larger scale, these publications projected Seidler's work within a magazine that would become most widely known for the Case Study House programme. Seidler could be said to have still been at the periphery of a programme that would become central in defining mid-century modernism, yet his very geographical marginality allowed what Fry refers to as 'an appeal to other means'.[21] These 'other means' included access to a steady stream of domestic clients in a context where modern architecture was a relative novelty.[22] Seidler completed thirty detached houses in and around Sydney between 1948 and 1960, all elegant variations on the themes first made visible in the Rose Seidler House. This was a volume not equalled by the output from the Case Study House programme, and Seidler was also able to assert his sole authorship over this oeuvre, free of both Breuer and Thompson.

Yet in a way that undercuts this very modernist projection of sole authorship, one might see how the position of the designer is itself transformed within such a geography of power. Fry suggests that: 'The designer in such a context [of geographical marginality] has to be named and interrogated not as a creative subject but as a deployed labourer.'[23] In other words, and in terms of a second-order diagrammatics, design is about the reorganisation of signs of the modern in relation to the geographical shifting of context. 'Labour' denotes the idea that nothing is invented in relation to the context of production or the reality of social change. Rather, the signs on the modern are made available as material to be configured. Given that this material, architecturally, is itself diagrammatic, a reduction of symbolic content to the authority and operativity of the line, a second-order configuration takes place.

A look at the house bears out this point. The plan is a clear adaptation of a Corbusian 'fourth' house type, the clearest example of

which is the Villa Savoye, where a taught exterior volume has outdoor space cut into it (see Fig. 8.1). Unable, because of scale, to incorporate the ramp of the architectural promenade within the floor plan, it is pulled to the exterior in a gesture that transforms the promenade, making it about a link to the surrounding garden and landscape, enabling them to be experienced physically rather than only visually (see Fig. 8.2). The stair from the ground-level arrival lobby, however, acts faithfully as the pivot around which the rest of the plan is arranged. Structurally, there is a strange equivocation between the Breuer-esque stone walls which keep

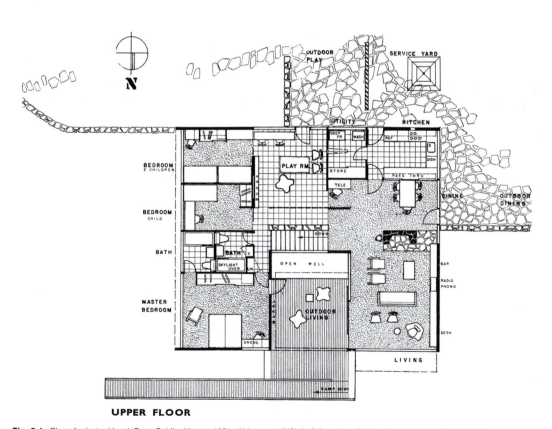

UPPER FLOOR

Fig. 8.1. Plan of principal level, Rose Seidler House, 1951, Wahroonga (NSW). © Penelope Seidler. Reproduced with permission.

Fig. 8.2. Exterior, showing ramp, Rose Seidler House, 1951, Wahroonga (NSW). Photograph by Max Dupain. Sir John Sulman award–winning buildings, 1934–1966, Royal Australian Institute of Architects. New South Wales Chapter. Collection of the State Library of New South Wales. © Penelope Seidler. Reproduced with permission.

the house anchored to the ground and Corbusian pilotis—here detailed as circular steel poles—which attempt to make the building levitate. The Niemeyer-esque mural which Seidler painted himself on the blind wall of the outdoor living space and which provides a map of the colour scheme of the entire house, seems designed to capture the intensity of southern hemisphere light (though the amount of glazing and lack of sun protection, especially on the house's eastern aspect, shows how removed the design is from local conditions) (see Fig. 8.3). All of the house's furniture was imported directly from Herman Miller and Knoll in New York, with Seidler designing the dining table, desks and other storage elements (see Fig. 8.4 and Fig. 8.5). The metal casement windows were also specially imported from England.[24] Due to its technological appointments, the kitchen was reputed to be the most advanced in Australia at the time. The house thus became a veritable advertisement for the equipment of modern living, and its success as the arrived appearance of the modern world was consequent upon its widespread publication in design, living and fashion magazines in Australia.

Fig. 8.3. Exterior, showing mural, Rose Seidler House, 1951, Wahroonga (NSW). Photograph attributed to Marcell Seidler. Sir John Sulman award–winning buildings, 1934–1966, Royal Australian Institute of Architects. New South Wales Chapter. Collection of the State Library of New South Wales. © Penelope Seidler. Reproduced with permission.

Fig. 8.4. Interior, lounge room with view from windows, Rose Seidler House, 1951, Wahroonga (NSW). Photograph attributed to Marcell Seidler. Sir John Sulman award–winning buildings, 1934–1966, Royal Australian Institute of Architects. New South Wales Chapter. Collection of the State Library of New South Wales. © Penelope Seidler. Reproduced with permission.

Fig. 8.5. Interior, lounge room with curtained windows, Rose Seidler House, 1951, Wahroonga (NSW). Photograph attributed to Marcell Seidler. Sir John Sulman award–winning buildings, 1934–1966, Royal Australian Institute of Architects. New South Wales Chapter. Collection of the State Library of New South Wales. © Penelope Seidler. Reproduced with permission.

Through the logic of the second-order diagram, the arrived appearances of the modern world are reassembled as an interior. It is precisely because the architectural enclosure of the house has become diagrammatic, reduced to the operativity of the single line, that the interior can take on a new impetus. Built-in and moveable furniture become what define this interior spatially. The potentials within their combination and recombination are recognised at the level of images that were crucial for ensuring the widespread understanding and uptake of this sense of the interior. If mid-century modern is

to designate anything, it is the reemergence of an architectural concern with the interior, this time not decrying it as the suffocating, sealed space of bourgeois complacency, but as the site for the domesticity of a rapidly growing and strengthening postwar middle class, who would be receiving images of this modern interior through the popular media at an unprecedented level.

There is another reading of the second-order diagrammatics of the Rose Seidler House which has to do with the way in which avant-garde modernism became a subject of increasing disciplinary self-awareness in the postwar period. In this context, the diagram became an analytical tool for the codification and critical examination of both classical and modern architecture, especially in the work of Peter Eisenman, but also for Rudolf Wittkower in his analysis of Palladian Villa Types circa 1952 (see Vidler) and, of course, for Colin Rowe.[25]

In his analysis of Eisenman's diagrammatic body of work—an analysis which is itself the function of the diagram's ability to analyse a body of work—Somol distinguishes between two sorts of repetition: one, which he aligns with Rowe, the copying of an original (this copying being subject to certain rules) and the other, which he aligns with Eisenman, the production of difference and distortion through repetition taking place in a series, where time would have a transformative effect.[26] The geographical, in dealing directly with images, with arrived appearances, is what clarifies the idea of repetition as difference, because there is no ability to 'check back' to a single original source. Geography as a context for production provides the conditions whereby any repetition is subject to a differing set of possibilities, some of which, as has been seen with Seidler's early works, relate to the possibility to instantiate the diagram as a series of built facts.

Seidler's differential repetitions have importance equally for both dominant accounts of postwar architecture: the lifestyle-based account of the mid-century modern on the one hand and, on the other, the account which develops an argument about disciplinary autonomy. That the discourse of the diagram has figured exclusively in the latter account does not mean it is irrelevant or antagonistic toward the former. The geographical makes both of these accounts graspable on the same plane of consistency. That Eisenman's early houses are devoid of an interior, and that Seidler's reinstate the interior, does not mean that these are, as with the Deutscher Werkbund poster and Co-op Zimmer, simply polar opposites. The diagram provides the conceptual structure for their productive, though differential, comparison.

Modernity and modernism need to be considered as discontinuous formations.[27] A conventional history of modern architecture would usually position the practices of those positioned on the periphery to be the outcome of an eventual diffusion from centres. The agency of this diffusion is normally ascribed to individuals whose experience is formed in or in relation to the centre. Biographically, the example of Seidler fits this framing, in that he can be seen personally as the conduit for modern architecture's arrival in Australia. Though the conditions of the arrival of the modern are crucial to consider in the context of Australia—in its modern form, a nation constituted through modernity as arrived appearance—a geographical consideration of modernity inscribes its movement within a complex weave of conditions rather than a narrative of the heroic and inevitable outcomes of individual intentions. Architectural modernism in Australia might then be considered as a construction of difference through repetition. The role and technique of the diagram is crucial in this consideration, as is the interior's relation to modern architecture. In addition, the condition of Australian modern architecture—and the Rose Seidler House as a particular example within a series of repetitions—might now be able to be seen to be crucial to these larger conditions and their interlinking.

Notes

Uncredited factual information about the Rose Seidler House has been taken from an undated and unpaginated leaflet supplied at the house by the Historic Houses Trust of New South Wales.

1. K. M. Hays, *Modernism and the Posthumanist Subject: The Architecture of Hannes Meyer and Ludwig Hilberseimer* (MIT Press, 1992).
2. C. Rice, *The Emergence of the Interior: Architecture, Modernity, Domesticity* (Routledge, 2007), p. 2.
3. W. Benjamin, 'Experience and Poverty,' in M. Jennings et al., eds., *Selected Writings,* Vol. 2 (Belknap Press of Harvard University Press, 1999).
4. A. Vidler, 'Diagrams of Diagrams: Architectural Abstraction and Modern Representation', / *Representations*/72 (2000), pp. 13–14.
5. R. Somol, 'Dummy Text, or the Diagrammatic Basis of Contemporary Architecture,' in P. Eisenman, ed., *Peter Eisenman: Diagram Diaries* (Thames & Hudson, 1999), p. 24; Vidler, 'Diagrams of Diagrams', p. 5.
6. R. Evans, 'Rookeries and Model Dwellings', in *Translations from Drawing to Building and Other Essays* (Architectural Association, 1997).
7. R. Kerr [1864], *The Gentleman's House: or How to Plan English Residences from the Parsonage to the Palace* (John Murray, 1871), p. 111.
8. W. Benjamin, *The Arcades Project,* R. Tiedemann, ed.; H. Eiland and K. McLaughlin, tr. (Belknap Press of Harvard University Press, 1999), p. 20.
9. Benjamin, 'Experience and Poverty'.
10. Vidler, 'Diagrams of Diagrams', pp. 1–20.
11. R. Evans, 'The Developed Surface: An Enquiry into the Brief Life of an Eighteenth-century Drawing Technique', in *Translations from Drawing to Building and Other Essays* (Architectural Association, 1997).
12. Vidler, 'Diagrams of Diagrams', p. 12.
13. H. Seidler [1954], 'Our Heritage of Modern Building,' in H. Seidler, *Harry Seidler: Houses & Interiors 1, 1948–1970* (Images Publishing, 2003).
14. Vidler, 'Diagrams of Diagrams', p. 13.
15. T. Fry, 'A Geography of Power: Design History and Marginality', *Design Issues* 6/1 (1989), pp. 24–5.
16. A. Spigelman, *Almost Full Circle: Harry Seidler* (Brandl & Schlesinger, 2001), p. 164.
17. J. Driller, *Breuer Houses* (Phaidon, 2000), p. 263.
18. Spigelman, *Almost Full Circle,* p. 175.
19. Ibid., p. 176.
20. Ibid.
21. Fry, 'A Geography of Power', p. 16.
22. Contrary to some of Seidler's own claims, Sydney was not devoid of modern architecture at this time. The work of local Sydney architects and Seidler's contemporaries Sydney Ancher and Arthur Baldwinson must be noted, as must their own 'mediated' reception of European modernism through publications, itself an 'appeal to other means'.
23. Fry, 'A Geography of Power', p. 24.
24. C. Abel, 'Early Years: The Tall Poppy,' in H. Seidler, *Harry Seidler: Houses & Interiors 1, 1948–1970* (Images Publishing, 2003), p. 8.
25. Vidler, 'Diagrams of Diagrams', pp. 14–15.
26. Somol, 'Dummy Text'.
27. P. Taylor, *Modernities: A Geohistorical Approach* (Polity, 1999).

Part Three

The Mid Twentieth-century Interior (1940–1970)

Part 3 Philharmonie Concert Hall, Berlin. Hans Scharoun 1956–63. Photograph: Peter Blundell Jones.

Introduction

Penny Sparke

The years 1940 to 1970 were also important ones for the development of the modern interior and took it into a new and rapidly changing context. Building on the shifts and tensions of the previous few decades and responding to the dramatic social, cultural and economic changes of the early post–Second World War years, the modern interior both consolidated itself and subtly transformed itself into a new entity at that time. Two main themes dominated the era where the modern interior was concerned in that period. Whilst, on the one hand, modernism was reworked and reshaped, the impact of the growth of mass culture in those years undermined that movement's prewar ideological baseline and offered an alternative cultural framework for the development of the modern interior which embraced pluralism and alternative sets of values.

Surprisingly, however, despite the significant developments that took place in the evolution of the modern interior in those years, they have, to date, been less than adequately documented. Whilst, as has already been noted, the key historical texts that have dealt with the visual, material and spatial culture of the period from 1900 to 1940 have focused heavily on architecture at the expense of the interior, those which have dealt with the later years, 1940 to 1970, have emphasised designed artefacts and

tended to ignore their spatial context— that is the interiors that contained them. The strong emphasis on 'good design' and its demise in the post–Second World War years served to prioritise the mass-produced designed object as a marker of national identity and cultural prowess, and historical accounts have followed that lead. Indeed the rise of the discipline of design history from the 1970s onwards can be seen to have reinforced that tendency and to have marginalised the historical study of the modern interior even further. Only in recent years has that marginalisation begun to be addressed. This book aims to play a role in that process.

Whilst the two overarching themes of reworked modernism and the rise of mass culture dominated the period in question, several other familiar themes within the evolution of the modern interior also continued to exert their influence, although frequently in new guises. The battle between the interior decorator and the interior designer continued unabated, for example, although the terms of reference changed somewhat; the tension between amateurism and professionalism in the field increased as the 'do-it-yourself' movement took a strong hold in a number of countries; and the mediation of the represented modern interior, through lifestyle magazines, journals, exhibitions and increasingly film, radio and television, also took an upward surge in this period.

Elsie de Wolfe, one of the leading American pioneering interior decorators died in 1950. Her legacy was clearly visible, however, in the work of subsequent generations of decorators who continued to work with wealthy clients who could afford their services, often in historical styles, especially in the United States and the United Kingdom but increasingly in other countries as well. More and more, however, in the years after 1945, the task was performed by men. Mark Hampton's book, *Legendary Decorators of the Twentieth Century,* has documented, in a somewhat anecdotal manner, the American work of Billy Baldwin and William Pahlmann, among others. 'He loved luxury', Hampton wrote of Baldwin, 'but he abhorred conspicuous richness. His aim was to be stylish at all times.'[1] In his 1946 book, *Inside Your Home,* the American decorating advisor, Dan Cooper, explained that, 'When you choose your decorator … here is the basic criterion by which you judge him: he should start by *asking* you, and not by *telling* you.'[2] Indeed that distinction seemed to be a key one as it was widely perceived that the designer came with an agenda whilst the decorator was more open to suggestion. In England, the work of men such as John Fowler and David Hicks sustained the decorating tradition established in the United States, the former promoting a reworked English country house style which quickly became fashionable on both sides of the Atlantic. In France, men such as Jean Royère worked in a similar way, although with a more overtly modern orientation. In the domestic arena, the work of decorators, designers and architects began to become blurred as many of them began to utilise modern decoration in their spaces. The arrival of educated, professional interior designers in the 1950s was felt most in the public arena, where they worked very closely with architects and within the aesthetic and ideological remit of modernism for the most part. Their training overlapped with that of architects to a considerable extent, and they saw their primary responsibilities as being with 'planning, scale, heating, lighting, surfaces, furniture, pattern and colour, thereby complementing those of the architect'.[3] There was a significant amount of criticism of decorators by men who called themselves 'designers'. In his 1944 book, *Goodbye Mr. Chippendale,* the interior designer, T. H. Robsjohn-Gibbings, for example, blamed Elsie de Wolfe for what he saw as the problem of the modern American interior. 'Decoratively speaking', he wrote, 'American women live in the shadow of Elsie de Wolfe and if it was the Chicago World's Fair that held American architecture back fifty years, it is she who did the same thing for American furniture design.'[4]

The tension that existed between decorating and designing the interior also characterised the relationship of amateur work with professional activities in that era. In simple terms, the former expanded enormously helped along by vast numbers of advice books, supplemented by magazines and television programmes. In the United Kingdom, a man called Barry Bucknell, who appeared on a weekly television programme, became a household name. He helped countless people to put up bookshelves and build new kitchen cupboards. In both the United States and Europe, the postwar years saw a vast increase in the numbers of middle- and upper-working-class owner–occupiers living in new housing developments who were not in a position to hire decorators and designers but who were committed, nonetheless, to modernising their domestic spaces as a marker of their engagement with modernity. Paralleling the growth industry in 'do-it-yourself', which spawned a literature and a retail sector to support it, art schools and universities across the globe began to offer courses in interior design, and numerous professional groups emerged to protect their interests. In London, for example, the Royal College of Art hired the architect, Hugh Casson, to set up an interior design course in that illustrious institution.

The strong links that existed between the modern interior and the media grew even stronger in those years as well. The female-oriented lifestyle magazine came into its own in that period, consolidating the links between the decoration of the domestic interior with fashion, make-up and family holidays. Increasingly, feature films emphasised the interior settings of their dramas, and popular exhibitions used the constructed interior as a means of attracting large audiences. The Ideal Home exhibitions held in London, for example, continued, as they had in the interwar years, to display interiors which could be experienced by the public. In her 1997 book, *The Ideal Home Through the 20th Century,* Deborah Ryan illustrated a number of examples, among them a 1955 interior which combined a living room with a bedroom to save space and a 1956 kitchen

which included one of Britain's first breakfast bars.[5] Above all, the British, as indeed was the American, public of those early postwar years was more committed than ever before to the idea of a modern interior.

In Britain, the United States, Europe and increasingly elsewhere as well, the years after 1945 saw the continuation of the impact of modernism at both an élite and a more popular level. The values that had underpinned that movement in the interwar years fed into the social housing schemes of the later period, whilst the modernist style fed into the popular imagination. In the process, at both ends of the social spectrum, it was softened and humanised and recognised openly as a style. In addition, the idea of the 'interior' within post-1945 modernism was acknowledged more directly, both in the domestic and in public contexts. Indeed, as mass public leisure expanded, a stronger sense of the interior in public-sphere buildings emerged. The expansion through the social spectrum of holidays, staying in hotels, participating in public leisure whether in dance halls, bowling alleys, cinemas, cafes, bars, restaurants or on cruise ships, travelling in the new forms of transport (aeroplanes among them) or shopping in the new supermarkets and malls led to an enhanced awareness of the 'modernity' expressed in those interior spaces. The case study provided by Anne Massey in this section of the book engages with the interiors of the *QE2,* an ocean-going liner which was designed for mass travel and public leisure. Increasing numbers of people wanted to engage in that public modernity and to emulate it in the more private spaces of their homes. Such was the experience of the mass media as well that the desire for modernity to be combined with 'glamour' in the private context was widely embraced. As a result, the desire for public leisure spaces to be 'homes from homes' as they had been in the nineteenth century receded, and a desire for nondomestic fantasy in those spaces became increasingly widespread. Alice Friedman's case study, which focuses on the hotels created by Morris Lapidus in Miami, provides an American example of 'glamorous' fantasy interior environments. Indeed it was in the United States that the public leisure fantasy interior emerged at its most extreme, as evidenced by the hotels and shopping malls in Las Vegas and at Disneyland. Whilst developments such as these occurred across the industrialised world, and, as a result of the influence of the mass media, a strong sense of internationalism emerged in those years, different countries also used the concept of the modern interior in different ways as a means of both unifying their populations under national banners and promoting themselves in the international marketplace with their own distinct 'modern' identities.

The links between national identity and the modern interior were inevitably multiple and complex in the years after 1945. In Britain, for example, it was used by the design reform body, the Council of Industrial Design (later the Design Council), formed in 1944, in both of the ways suggested above. If the domestic population could be encouraged to embrace modernity in their homes, the thinking went, they would want to consume modern designed objects which could also be sold in the international marketplace, thereby boosting the United Kingdom's postwar economy. The

Council implemented its strategy in a number of ways, including through exhibitions. *Britain Can Make It* was held at London's Victoria and Albert Museum in 1946. Numerous furnished interiors showing modern products were displayed. A book entitled *Did Britain Make It: British Design in Context, 1946–86,* edited by myself, was published in 1986 to celebrate the fortieth anniversary of the event. Jonathan Woodham's article in that book entitled 'Design Promotion 1946 and After' included a section on the 'furnished rooms' at the exhibition. 'The idea of furnished rooms as a means of design promotion in the public eye', Woodham explained, 'had long been used both at home and abroad. It was, however, generally agreed that the 1946 settings showed a greater sense of social awareness than had their predecessors in the design propaganda shows of the 1930s.'[6] He went on to describe a number of the rooms on display and illustrated Edna Mosley's 'Kitchen of a Cottage in a Modern Mining Village', just one of the many interiors which were constructed to convey a specifically social message.[7] A book from the period, published by the Council of Industrial Design in 1947, entitled *The Things We See: Houses* made a clear contrast between the British domestic interior of 1936, which 'found it easier to achieve the spaciousness than the cosiness', and its equivalent of a decade later, which, with its patterned rug, comfy armchair and vase of flowers, represented a 'reaction from austerity'.[8]

A number of studies have addressed British design of that period and included material on interiors within them. Lesley Jackson's two books—*The New Look: Design in the*

Fifties and *The Sixties: Decade of Design Revolution*—are international in scope but contain material on Britain in the period in question.[9] In the former, the interior work of the British design team, Robin and Lucienne Day, is highlighted, and a 1956 interior by the British architect, Keith Roberts, is illustrated. The vast majority of the book is, however, dedicated to individual artefacts, glass, ceramics and furniture, indicating the rather lowly role played by the interior in design historical texts of that era. An earlier text, which was more specifically Britain-focused, *1966 and All That: Design and the Consumer in Britain, 1900–1969,* was also object-centric in its coverage, but it did include an image of a supermarket interior; the Biba boutique in Kensington, designed in neo-Victorian style; an early shopping mall; and a show house in Runcorn New Town, suggesting that the interior—both private and public—played a significant sociocultural role at that time.[10]

The Scandinavian countries, especially Sweden, Denmark and Finland, developed their own national versions of the modern interior in those years which were hugely influential internationally. Design historians have subsequently given the impression that it was conceived as the sum of the parts, that is the decorative arts/craft objects— glass, ceramics, metalwork, textiles and furniture—that it contained, and that it was not promoted very strongly in and for itself. At the time, however, a rather different view was expressed. A popular exhibit at New York's World's Fair of 1939 had been an interior created by the designer Josef Frank who had lived and worked in Sweden for some years by that time. The living room he created

for that event, which contained upholstered furniture—one boasting a flowered print—a kidney-shaped desk, an open fireplace and rugs on the floor, was dubbed 'Swedish Modern', and it helped set the stage for postwar developments which built on Frank's commitment to the idea of 'humanised modernism'.

Building on traditions established in the early century, Sweden's version of the postwar modern interior was characterised by its emphasis on inhabitability. Filled with the products of its progressive decorative arts industries, it exuded light and air. Domesticity and the role of the family played key roles in Swedish modernity and were represented by the modern interior. The modern Swedish home was succinctly summarised in a 1948 publication entitled *Design in Sweden Today* as:

> *a friendly place light to the eye and to the mind, functionally furnished in a natural and unconventional manner. The light woods of the delicately scaled furniture give it a self-effacing quality against the light coloured walls—the personal touch being supplied by fresh flowers, small decorative objects, paintings and textiles in clean, clear colours. But these too are used restrainedly, to avoid any sense of oppressiveness in the interior, and to create instead a background against which the human beings, for whom it is designed, may feel themselves to their best advantage.[11]*

An illustration in the same publication featured a room with a table set, complete with plates, cutlery, glass and a vase of flowers, ready for a meal. In many ways, it was Sweden's version of the modern interior, created by architects for the most part, that set the tone internationally for the 1940s and 1950s. The use of wood, textures and textiles in a humanised domestic space was both modern and human and seemed to solve the problem of what had come to be seen as the dehumanised Germanic model of interior modernism that had been promoted in the interwar years.

Denmark's contribution to the modern interior followed on the heels of Sweden's and directed a spotlight on to its craft-produced furniture items. Given its strong traditions in that area, the emphasis in Denmark was more firmly on objects than on spaces, but the same sense of a humanised modernism was present. Although it had installed a housing exhibition at the 1957 Milan Triennale which had furnished rooms, it wasn't until the 1960s that Finland developed its own modern design movement, and, like Denmark, it tended to emphasise the designed interior artefact rather than the ensemble. By the late 1960s, however, under the influence of pop culture, a stronger sense of the interior environment emerged, as indeed it did in a number of other countries including the United Kingdom and Italy, and furniture items became less self-contained and more expressive of the spaces which housed them and the people who occupied them. Information relating to the nature of the postwar modern interior in Scandinavia was widely available in specialist magazines from the period—the Swedish *Form* and *Kontur* among them. More recent accounts, such as David McFadden's 1982 *Scandinavian Modern Design, 1880–1980,* have, however, removed the centrality of the

interior to the national cultures in question and emphasised the role of the decorative arts and designed objects.[12] This has tended to obscure the role played by the interior and to suggest that it was little more than the sum of its parts.

Whilst the Scandinavian countries, especially Sweden, provided a strong northern European model of the postwar modern interior—one which, as we shall see, was highly influential in the United States—Italy also played a significant role in that context. Once again, the discourse occurred within national boundaries, and the agenda which informed the development of the modern interior was one of modernisation at home and improved performance in the international marketplace through the creation of a strong national identity which had modern design at its core. As in Scandinavia, the interior was seen as both a designed space with its own special meanings and, in the case of Italy, a container for the strikingly modern industrially designed artefacts—furniture items and domestic machines—that brought that country a reputation as being the home of modern design in the years after 1945.

The Italian discussion about the interior began immediately after 1945 with the need to furnish the new homes that replaced those which had been bombed during the war. The solution was a neofunctionalist approach which stressed space-saving and aesthetic simplicity. The consumer culture that grew up a little later in Italy through the 1940s, 1950s and 1960s, however, reoriented the design emphasis towards the discrete designed artefact, presented as a modern work of art. That approach was visible in the photographs presented in design magazines of the time. Whilst the images of interiors in *Form* and *Kontur* had frequently included people eating or reading in them, *Stile Industria,* launched in Italy in 1954, pictured its objects in isolation, posed as if in an art gallery. My book, *Italian Design, 1870 to the Present,* published in 1988, took its direction from that approach and emphasised the designed artefact over the designed interior.[13] Whilst some interior images were included—among them one of Carlo Mollino's interiors for a private home in Milan of 1944, Gio Ponti's interior of the casino at San Remo of 1952, a few exhibition installations, a modern kitchen illustrated in *Domus* magazine in 1954 and Ponti's design for an office inside the Montecatini building—the vast majority of the images in the book were of sculptural lighting objects, furniture pieces, automobiles and domestic machines. This was in spite of the fact that the key designers under discussion— Ettore Sottsass, Vico Magistretti, Achille Castiglioni, Marco Zanuso, Joe Colombo and others—were all trained architects and they all worked on interiors through their long careers. My case study essay in this section of the book hopefully goes some way towards filling the gap that I left in 1988. As that essay demonstrates, the advent of pop culture engendered a new understanding of the domestic landscape, which encouraged Italy's architects and designers to create environmental furniture pieces and domestic 'pods'. The same shift occurred in the work place for which Ettore Sottsass and others began to create 'systems' rather than desks and chairs. It is ironic that, given their strong interest in lighting, it was to the 'lighting-

object', rather than to the effects of lighting in the interior, that Italian designers paid most attention in the 1950s and 1960s. The 'anti-commodity' mood of the late 1960s changed all that, however, and, as the image of Cini Boeri's 'Serpentone' seating in my book demonstrates, they began to think more about ensembles of objects.[14] More than anyone else, perhaps, in the 1970s Ettore Sottsass turned away from objects and towards representations of complete environments.

The United Kingdom, the Scandinavian countries and Italy were, of course, not the only European countries to develop a philosophy of, and a set of practices for the design of, the modern interior which matched their national agendas, but the impact of their programmes was felt most strongly internationally. Germany also developed a strong postwar design culture, rooted in interwar achievements at the Bauhaus and elsewhere, but, even more than Italy, it focused its energies on industrially produced designed artefacts and modern architecture. The strong emphasis on industrial culture tended to downplay the role of modern domesticity in German life and produce a dichotomy between the traditional private sphere and the modern public sphere. Thus, whilst modern work spaces and the insides of new transportation objects received plenty of attention, the home was a much more shadowy place in postwar Germany than it was, say, in Sweden and the United Kingdom, in terms, at least, of the design promotional material that emerged from Germany and the specialist design press of the day. Peter Blundell Jones's case study essay in this section of the book, which focuses on the interior of buildings by the German architect Hans Scharoun, breaks new ground, therefore, and brings a new perspective to the study of postwar German design and architecture.

It was, perhaps, in the United States where the most influential and radical ideas about the postwar modern interior were formed, however. Although they built on European ideas, American designers succeeded in transforming them into a wholly new interior design movement which affected both the home and the public-sphere interior, nationally and internationally. Ideas about the interior had begun to make a mark in the United States in the 1930s. Emigrés from Europe—among them Marcel Breuer, Walter Gropius and Walter Knoll from Germany and Eliel Saarinen from Finland—had brought functionalist ideas to the 'new world', and the furniture designs of men such as the Finn Alvar Aalto and the Swede Bruno Mathsson had been highly influential. Within that new context, however, their work underwent a reassessment and was reinterpreted in the US context. In a 1950 publication, the curator of design at New York's Museum of Modern Art, Edgar Kaufmann, Jr., included a short essay entitled 'What Is Modern Interior Design?' in which he set out to define 'the art of arranging objects for agreeable living'.[15] Kaufmann claimed that the modern interior had come into being about a century earlier and that, in 1950, its main traits were 'comfort, quality, lightness and harmony'.[16] He illustrated his essay with images which ranged from the work of William Morris in the United Kingdom through to that of the European modernists, Walter Gropius, Marcel Breuer, Mies van der Rohe and Le Corbusier, to that of Frank Lloyd Wright in the United States, through to more contemporary projects undertaken by US designers Edward D. Stone, George Nelson, Charles Eames, Alexander Girard and Florence Knoll. In his conclusion, Kaufmann returned to two examples of the work of Frank Lloyd Wright, commenting that 'Neither one is excessive in its emphasis on modern technology, nor on nature, for that matter. A close relationship between man and the natural world around him is assumed but not stressed.'[17] His message reflected the need for a middle ground which embraced technological modernism but which also linked the interior to the world of nature. Kaufmann's emphasis on the work of Frank Lloyd Wright in that context provided an American perspective on the modern interior which, in the postwar context, was represented by the work of Charles Eames, who, working with the Finn, Eero Saarinen, succeeded in bridging European modernism and the more humanistic idea of the American home. Pat Kirkham's case study essay in this section of the book emphasises the way in which Charles and Ray Eames developed between them a vision of the modern domestic interior which was technology-dependent but which, at the same time, embraced the need for human intervention and for decoration as a form of personal expression. Charles Eames moved easily between the domestic interior and the work space, seeing the same furniture objects, albeit realised in different materials, as being equally appropriate in both spaces. Florence Knoll, who took over Knoll Associates following the death of her husband Walter, also understood the level of interchangeability that was possible between the domestic interior and the work space. Working with 'classic' furniture items designed by Mies van der Rohe and others, she developed a new aesthetic for corporate America in the 1950s and 1960s which was based on a simple interior language made up of classic chairs, a coffee table and plants and other appropriate decorative items. Soon every reception area in every skyscraper office building boasted a Florence Knoll–style interior setting.

Books on the history of twentieth-century US design have recognised the centrality of the modern interior in the years after 1945. Jeffrey Meikle's 2005 publication, entitled *Design in the USA,* for example, included a number of illustrations to accompany its discussion of American design in the late nineteenth century but moved, in the section on the interwar years, towards the presentation of more discrete mass-produced objects, automobiles and domestic machines. In his account of American design after 1945, however, Meikle returned to a discussion about the interior, showing, among other images, the collection of Charles Eames's and Saarinen's furniture at the Museum of Modern Art's 1941 *Organic Design in Home Furnishings* exhibition and the 'Good Design' installation at the same museum in 1952.[18]

The 1950s American modern interior was visible in a number of different settings, including the home, the office reception area and the exhibition installation. A humanised version of modernism emerged which was style-conscious, comfortable, popular and of its time. It succeeded in providing an international model of the postwar modern interior which crossed the social spectrum and which introduced 'modernity' to an ever larger audience. As in Scandinavia and Italy, the modern interior in the United States was represented in the media and had its own specialist professional publication. From 1940, *Interiors* magazine, previously known as *The Upholsterer, The Upholsterer and Decorator* and *The Decorator,* addressed the area in depth and provided a forum for the new professional, the interior designer.

The modern interior was not only an American and European phenomenon in the years after 1940, of course. As Charles Rice demonstrated in his case study essay in the previous section in this book, it had reached Australia by this time as well. Japan was also influenced by Western design culture by the 1950s, but, ironically, in that the Western model of the modern interior owed much to traditional Japanese domestic spaces, that Eastern country took a while to emulate the Western model. When it finally did so in the 1970s, it contributed significantly to the emergence of the global model of the 'minimal interior' which had a huge stylistic impact on the modern interior and remained fashionable for several decades. In my 1987 book, *Japanese Design,* which focused on the new technological goods, graphics and fashion which emerged from that country in the postwar years, I included a few images of 1970s interiors, created by Japanese architects, which reflected indigenous traditions in that area, among them the living space in a domestic building designed by Kazuo Shinohara in 1975.[19]

Whilst the legacy of modernism remained strong through the 1940s and 1950s, it came under increasing scrutiny in the 1960s with the emergence of youth culture and consumer culture which, together, engendered the 'pop' revolution. Where visual, material and spatial culture were concerned, pop's greatest impact was on the ephemeral areas of graphics and fashion, but it also, as we have already seen in the context of Italy, had the effect of making some designers and architects think less about hard, long-lasting objects and more about softer, ephemeral environments. The result was a renewed focus on the interior for which ephemerality had always been a fact of life. The other effect of pop, and what came to be called the 'crisis of modernism', which can also be seen as the birth of 'postmodernism', was an opening of the stylistic floodgates and a renewed interest in historical styles. Thus, the hitherto upper-class-oriented country house look pioneered by John Fowler and others became popularised by retailers of household furnishings, such as Laura Ashley in the United Kingdom. Tradition was reinvented and a plurality of alternative styles became increasingly acceptable, the Japanese-inspired minimal interior becoming, for example, just one among many.

In many ways, the period from 1940 to 1970 is even less well served by historical accounts of it than the earlier period. Until recently, both architectural and design historians have avoided addressing the interior of those years. The 1980s were dominated by accounts of national design movements which focused on product and graphic design for the most part, with a huge emphasis upon chairs. The richest accounts of the modern interior of this period are, therefore, still to be found in journals and magazines of the period. The general accounts of twentieth-century interior design have also inevitably covered the years 1940 to 1970. In her 1990 survey, Anne Massey, for example, devoted two chapters of eight to the period. Entitled 'Postwar Modernism' and 'Consumer Culture', they addressed the two key themes of the era.[20] Fiona Leslie's Designs for 20th Century Interiors of 2000 dedicated a number of pages to the years in question, showing a range of designs, mostly furniture items and textiles rather than ensembles.[21] In his A Century of Interior Design: 1900–2000, Stanley Abercrombie emphasised the United States' contribution to the development of the modern interior after 1940.[22] More recently, the book Imagined Interiors: Representing the Domestic Interior since the Renaissance, the third section of which covers the period 1850 to the present, embraced the shorter period, 1940 to 1970, within its themed essays which cover the display of designs of the domestic interior and its presence in films, fiction and television.[23]

The earliest analytical design historical work to focus on the interior—the domestic space especially—came through studies which focused on the relationship between gender and design. Judy Attfield's essay, 'Inside Pram Town: A Case Study of Harlow House Interiors, 1951–1961', for example, published in the 1989 book, A View from the Interior: Feminism, Women and Design, edited by Attfield and Pat Kirkham, focused on the isolation of women in their kitchens which had been positioned at the front of their homes.[24] My 1995 book, As Long as It's Pink: The Sexual Politics of Taste, also focused on interiors (including those of the period in question) in its attempt to argue that feminine taste had been marginalised within modernism. *Women and the Making of the Modern House,* written by Alice Friedman and published in 1998 and which focused on the interior in her discussion about the relationship between clients and architects, included case studies of Mies's Farnsworth House designed in the 1940s, Richard Neutra's 1950s Constance Perkins House and Robert Venturi's Vanna Venturi House of 1961–4.[25]

The case studies in this section of the book represent, as we have seen, the main themes of the modern interior in the period in question and take a discussion of it into new, hitherto unexplored territories. In his essay, Peter Blundell Jones looks at the interiors of Hans Scharoun's architecture and notes a 'shift to space and light as opposed to building-as-object', an observation which relates to the idea that, in its postwar manifestations, modernism was more conscious about the role of the interior and acknowledged its presence than it had in the interwar years. Pat Kirkham's study focuses on the way in which Charles and Ray Eames were indebted to Japan in the construction of the interior of their home in Santa Monica, in which they brought tradition into contact with the modern— thereby, once again, humanising modernism in this period. My essay on developments in Italy emphasises the way in which the Italian home of these years also represented a merging of tradition and modernism and how Italy transformed architectural modernism into a luxury artistic ideal represented by its chic, mass-produced artefacts, which, in

turn, tended to obscure the importance of the development of the modern interior. In her study of the work of Morris Lapidus in Miami, Alice Friedman explores the effects of mass tourist culture on architecture and the emergence of an escapist, fantasy style of 'glamourous' architecture, at which Lapidus, with his store design background, excelled. Finally, Anne Massey looks at the impact of pop culture on the design of an ocean liner in 1960s Britain and shows how modernism was transformed into a fashionable style in that context. Although their strength lies in their attention to original detail, in their various ways all five essays help to provide an overview of the design of the modern interior in the years between 1940 and 1970.

Notes

1. M. Hampton, *Legendary Decorators of the Twentieth Century* (Doubleday, 1992), p. 111.

2. D. Cooper, *Inside Your Home* (Farrar, Straus, 1946), p. 53.

3. D. Rowntree, *Interior Design* (Penguin Books, 1964), p. 23.

4. T. H. Robsjohn-Gibbings, *Goodbye Mr. Chippendale* (Alfred A. Knopf, 1944), p. 25.

5. D. Ryan, *The Ideal Home Through the 20th Century* (Hazar, 1997), pp. 108, 109.

6. J. M. Woodham, 'Design Promotion 1946 and After', in P. Sparke, ed., *Did Britain Make It?: British Design in Context, 1946–86* (Design Council, 1986), p. 30.

7. Woodham, 'Design Promotion 1946 and After', p. 31.

8. L. Brett, *The Things We See: Houses* (Penguin Books, 1947), p. 47.

9. L. Jackson, *The New Look: Design in the Fifties* (Thames & Hudson, 1991) and *The Sixties: Decade of Design Revolution* (Phaidon Press, 2000).

10. See J. Harris, S. Hyde and G. Smith, *1966 and All That: Design and the Consumer in Britain, 1960–1969* (Trefoil, 1986).

11. *Design in Sweden Today* (Svensk Form, 1948), p. 39.

12. See D. R. McFadden, *Scandinavian Modern Design, 1880–1980* (Harry N. Abrams, 1982).

13. P. Sparke, *Italian Design: 1870 to the Present* (Thames & Hudson, 1988).

14. Ibid., p. 183.

15. E. Kaufmann, Jr, 'What Is Modern Interior Design?', in E. Kaufmann, Jr, *Introductions to Modern Design* (Museum of Modern Art, 1950), p. 3.

16. Ibid., p. 3.

17. Ibid., p. 29.

18. J. L. Meikle, *Design in the USA* (Thames & Hudson, 2005).

19. P. Sparke, *Japanese Design* (Michael Joseph, 1987), p. 89.

20. A. Massey, *Interior Design of the 20th Century* (Thames & Hudson, 1990).

21. F. Leslie, *Designs for 20th Century Interiors* (V&A Publications, 2000).

22. S. Abercrombie, *A Century of Interior Design 1900–2000* (Rizzoli, 2003).

23. J. Aynsley and C. Grant, *Imagined Interiors: Representing the Domestic Interior since the Renaissance* (V & A Publications, 2006).

24. J. Attfield, 'Inside Pram Town: A Case-Study of Harlow House Interiors, 1951–1961', in J. Attfield and P. Kirkham, eds., *A View from the Interior: Feminism, Women and Design* (Women's Press, 1989), pp. 215–38.

25. A. T. Friedman, *Women and the Making of the Modern House* (Harry N. Abrams, 1998).

Chapter Nine

Hans Scharoun and the Interior
Peter Blundell Jones

The interior of Hans Scharoun's Philharmonie building, rightly regarded as his masterpiece (see Fig. 9.1), is certainly a highly self-conscious construction, and its author made his intention clear that 'music was the focal point from the very beginning.'[1] The social question of setting up an appropriate relationship with the performers was at the heart of his thinking, and the terraced in-the-round organisation was hugely successful—in fact, it became the main twentieth-century precedent for the building type. The outside, though, has always been far more controversial. Sandy Wilson made much of the fact that, when asked about the elevations, Scharoun denied that it had any, and everyone has always felt that it seemed something of a beached whale. Heinrich Klotz even accused Scharoun of making 'dinosaurs in the urban landscape', and he became a principal object of scorn for the new urbanists.[2] Other buildings suffered similar insults: his girls' school at Lünen of 1958 was dismissed by Charles Jencks with the words 'but it's so ugly'.[3]

It had not always been so: in the late 1920s and early 1930s, Scharoun designed a series of shiplike buildings in the new white-clad and flat-roofed style that were admired for their exterior forms. It appears with some of them that the whole conception is in terms of external form, and the interior is unimportant. There seems little doubt about the turning point: in 1933, when Hitler came to power, modernist architecture was repressed, and Scharoun had to ghost for others on housing schemes, but he kept going as a creative architect by building private houses for friends and acquaintances like his brother-in-law Mohrmann, the painter Oskar Moll, the art dealer Ferdinand Möller and Fritz Endell, the son of the architect August Endell. More than twenty were designed, and about fifteen were built.[4] They all had to conform to a Nazi vernacular ideal by looking like normal houses, but their interiors were extraordinary and unprecedented, with flowing spaces, surprising transitions and angular planning geometries. They were the laboratory for Scharoun's new architectural vocabulary which he went on to develop in public buildings after the war, often with the consciously expressed intention of working from the inside outwards; in other words, they marked the domination of interior space as the primary constituent of architecture, or so it seemed. The exteriors of the 1930s houses have always been hard to take—for the Germans because they are associated

Fig. 9.1. Philharmonie interior, exterior and main entrance. Photographs: Peter Blundell Jones.

with Nazi folksy rusticity and for Italian historians Borsi and Koenig because of a lapse of taste 'worse than that of a provincial engineer', as they put it in their book on Expressionist architecture.[5] When one knows the stories of Scharoun's struggles with the Nazi planners and of his bold attempts to get things past them, one also recognises a certain irreverent humour. But to get away with these extraordinarily free interiors must have seemed both a triumph and a liberation: the creation of a cosy private world freed from the oppression and forced conformity of public life. From all this one might conclude that Scharoun was a great architect spoiled by the twelve years of Nazi repression. Once driven indoors to make secret private works, he lost all sense of balance and was thus never able to return properly to the civic realm, to contribute effectively to the city.

I do not believe this; it is too simplified a picture. For a start, it is not true that Scharoun ignored the context in his later work; the truth is quite the opposite. The Philharmonie is a misleading example because it was planned for another site then built in a wasteland, with few of its author's ideas for the intended future context carried through. From beginning to end, Scharoun's work was contextual, though in his sense of Stadtlandschaft—city landscape—rather than in terms of supplying elevations; a relationship with neighbours was always sought. Second, it is not true that the emphasis on the interior started with Nazi repression. The two works in which the new kind of interior space first emerged were both designed before 1933: the Schminke house at Löbau of 1932 and the Mattern house in Bornim completed in 1934.

The Schminke house, Scharoun's masterpiece of his early period, is more or less balanced between inside and out (see Fig. 9.2). It is difficult to decide which is more impressive, the solarium and balconies jutting out over the garden or the long light-filled living room with its pools of space defined by built-in furniture (see Fig. 9.3). The extraordinary innovation here was the adoption of a 26-degree angle given by the site and made to ricochet through the house, at the last minute adopted to give direction to the diagonal staircase. The stair was used to control the transition from the axis of entry to the main axis of the house, and the angle was picked up again in the solarium and external stairs. This marked a radical advance in Scharoun's handling of space and a permanent break with the orthogonal. The single angle shift at the Schminke house completely breaks the sense of being in a box and presents unusual perspectives and shifts of scale. In photographs it looks very different from the later house because of the style, but in reality the flowing spaces are very similar.

The other house for Scharoun's friends, the landscape architects Hermann Mattern and Herta Hammerbacher, was a much more modest affair but again very innovative. Because it was a single story and almost flat-roofed on a flat site, there was very little exterior to see, and it was almost impossible to recognise as an object, being appropriately dominated by the garden spaces which the Matterns—as great garden specialists—treated as a series of outdoor rooms.[6] The plan was largely orthogonal except for a great curved wall on the west side embracing

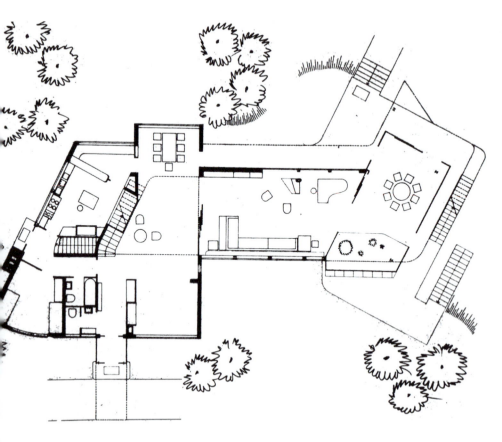

Fig. 9.2. Schminke House, main floor plan showing the open-plan living room, solarium and conservatory with built-in furniture. The 26-degree angle shift was prompted by the site. Courtesy of Akademie der Künste Berlin.

a built-in sofa which looked both across the house and outward. The roof was tilted up southward to a climax over a great multipane studio window to make the primary link with the garden (see Fig. 9.4). In its extreme modesty and lack of formal ambition, the Mattern house shows Scharoun's shift of interest to space and light as opposed to building-as-object at a time when the Nazi planning restrictions were not yet in force. The innovation of the sofa wall also makes the rectangular Schminke sofa look weak by comparison. Working with the Matterns was in itself significant, as nearly all the later houses were provided with Mattern gardens, and Scharoun went on to collaborate with

Mattern on many postwar projects, including the great ill-fated Kassel Theatre of 1952.[7] The consciousness that buildings must stand in some kind of landscape, often accompanied by controlled vegetation, added positively to the contextual concern of both architect and landscape architect. Exteriors were transitions into more rooms rather than flat facades.

To understand how these interiors developed and what they meant, it is best to look at one of the later examples, and I have chosen the tiny Möller house of 1937 because it has been painstakingly restored and I had the chance to photograph it. Ferdinand Möller was a Berlin gallery owner who specialised in Expressionist work. The

Fig. 9.3. Schminke House, living room. Photograph: Peter Blundell Jones.

house, which is about an hour from Berlin by train, was his weekend retreat. It now belongs to the Ferdinand Möller Foundation and is in use as a guest house, after a restoration funded and organised by art dealer Wolfgang Wittrock.[8] Photographs are always inadequate, though. First, one always feels that the imposition of the frame is arbitrary and the lens is never wide enough, for always one wants to look all around. Second, because of the strange angles, perspectives are distorted, and one's sense of scale is disrupted. Third, the important transitions of view and light between inside and out are destroyed by film's inability to deal with the contrast—you get one or the other, but not both. A site plan from a preliminary design stage reveals the essential relationships and angles to which Scharoun felt obliged to respond (see Fig. 9.5). To the right is the shore of a lake with good outward views, above the space is closed by a line of trees and north points away below right. The house is set to occupy a pivotal position on the hillside, with ringed contours dropping away from it. The outline of the house shows the larger, more ambitious first version, and the spread of angles exploiting the pivotal position is evident, as is the intention of turning a part of the living room south. The double image of

Fig. 9.4. Hans Scharoun, Mattern House, Bornim, 1934, interior view with rising ceiling and big window opening to garden, study left and built-in sofa to right. Photograph: Peter Blundell Jones.

the house's footprint shows how Scharoun has decided to move the house back on the site. There were struggles over permissions, and eventually a much smaller house was built. The thirty-degree angle shift deals with the pivotal site by projecting out the sunken dining bay to allow views in all directions, whilst on one side of it the study has a view to the west and the living room combines the view of the lake to right with south light from top right. The splayed wall and archway on the right complete the definition of a space spreading radially from the sofa in the living room. The key gesture in this plan is the curved wall, which not only embraces the sofa but also defines the beginning of the stair

leading to the open studio above. The main body of the house has a double-pitched roof running parallel with the outer walls, and its underside is exposed in the studio, the ridge running across to land on the small chimney by the stair. The expected geometry of the vernacular roof is thus denied internally by Scharoun, almost as if he wants to show what he can do in spite of it.

In the upper floor is a generous studio looking over a diagonal balcony rail into the living room (see Fig. 9.6). The rail and the stair set up a diagonal axis almost as strong as the main orthogonal one. This room receives extra light from the east, a direction cut off in the space below via a window and roof light. A tiny bedroom occupies the space over the study. The section is all about the relationship with the hillside and lake and the downward view both from the sofa via the main windows and from the balcony framed by an 'eyebrow window' in the roof. In Fig. 9.7, we stand at the door looking out to the terrace on the right and in to the living room on the left, with the dining area behind us. I had to reduce the contrast between the two sides, a perpetual problem when photographing from inside to out. It is interesting how both sides appear cut off, because Scharoun wants continuous space rather than a framed composition. On the terrace, Scharoun has used crazy paving to indicate the outside, and there is a bench of brickwork.

Further in, moving across to the entrance to the study we look back across the living room, and up towards the studio. The outside view is already killed in the film by overexposure, since photography can never reproduce the contrasts of light seen by the naked eye. Moving up to the studio, there is a view back towards the rising stair, over the balcony to right, and out through the eyebrow roof window. The exposed roof truss across the middle of the house presents itself on the diagonal. You can also look down from the studio to the sunken dining bay below, again showing a problem of light contrast for the photo which is no problem in reality. The photographs show the space as flowing and open and very four-dimensional in that it requires movement and time properly to be appreciated—in this respect, it was far ahead of the Bauhaus which Giedion used as his space/time example.[9] Indeed it is

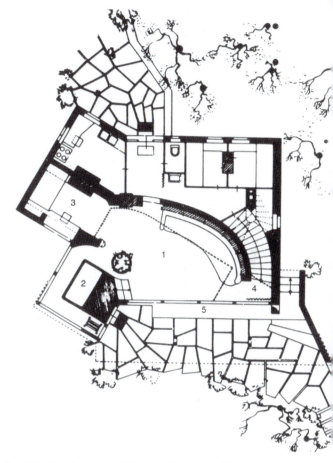

Fig. 9.5. Möller House, ground floor plan of the house as built. Photograph: Peter Blundell Jones.

already aperspectival, a term Scharoun did not actually use until more than ten years later when it appeared as the central concept in Jean Gebser's philosophy in his book *Ursprung und Gegenwart.*[10]

But, although the space is fluid, it is full of distinct places related to particular activities: the sunken well with its dining table, the study with its desk and window, the built-in sofa for enjoying the view (see Fig. 9.8) and the brick bench outside as a second version and the

Fig. 9.6. Möller House, upstairs and cross-beam view. Photograph: Peter Blundell Jones.

studio, with its strong light above. Space is not neutral and free-flowing but very much contained and centred; the sofa in its focal position taking the place perhaps of a hearth in a more traditional house. Although this looks like functional differentiation or zoning, the point of the open plan is to bring things together, not to break them apart, so, beside declaring their uses and suggesting the practices associated with them, the defined places are also set in a relation of proximity— adjacencies, polarities, centre and periphery—

and it is their particular combination with the site that makes the house. The spaces are so important that the building fabric is left in a subordinate role: it helps to frame and separate, but it does not assert its own physicality. It is often even deceptive, illusory. That is why there is no emphasis on façades: they are subordinate to the screening and manipulation of space, which is made to nurture and suggest activity.

In conclusion, let us return to the Philharmonie, which is definitely an interior,

Fig. 9.7. Möller House, external/internal view. Photograph: Peter Blundell Jones.

cut off from the outside world by soundproof doors and with no windows at all. But the foyer surrounding the hall has windows and doors; it makes connections with the outside world, and it is all about transition and movement. In its complexity and fragmentation is a wonderful anticipation for the fullness of the hall, but the concentration of stairs and landings leading one through makes it obviously a place of transition and a place for ritual display in the interval. Since the addition of the Chamber Music Hall and Museum of Musical Instruments, there has been a whole internal musical landscape which also starts to become external in the gardens and courts between the buildings, and the Scharounian city would presumably have continued in this vein, moving from indoor room to outdoor room and back again, a fluid series of spaces blending into one another without ever presenting a building as a detached object or having to confront you with a façade. But it would, of course, have a series of centres, of special places concentrating differentiated

Fig. 9.8. Möller House, sofa and diagonals view. Photograph: Peter Blundell Jones.

kinds of dwelling. It is this sense of centre, as opposed to the bland infinity of neutral Cartesian space, that makes Scharoun's work a matter of interiors.

Notes

1. From a statement by Scharoun published in a publicity leaflet for the opening of the building, 1963, in English in original. For a general account of the building and of the architect's work, see

P. Blundell Jones, *Hans Scharoun* (Phaidon Press, 1995).

2. H. Klotz, *Architektur in der Bundesrepublik* (Ullstein, 1977), p. 10.

3. Personal conversation with Jencks, c. 1973–74.

4. See P. Blundell Jones, *Hans Scharoun* (Gordon Fraser, 1978); P. Blundell Jones, 'Hans Scharoun's Private Houses', *Architectural Review* (December 1983), pp. 59–67; Blundell Jones, *Hans Scharoun*, 1995, Chapters 1 and 4.

5. F. Borsi and G. K. Koenig, *Architettura dell' Espressionismo* (Vitali e Ghianda, 1972).

6. For further detail on this not embraced by the above references, see P. Blundell Jones and J. Woudstra, 'Some Modernist Houses and Their Gardens Part 2, The House of the North and the Pleasure Pavilion', *Die Gartenkunst* 1 (2002), pp. 123–34.

7. Together on equal billing they won the competition for the new Kassel Theatre of 1952 and spent a year developing the design into working drawings, but when site work began some unknown foundations were discovered, and the consequent delay was exploited to unseat the architects in favour of Paul Bode, a local man who had been developing an alternative design in secret. This scandal marked the loss of one of the most progressive German works of the early 1950s and the most promising collaboration of Scharoun and Mattern.

8. Ferdinand Möller's career is described in E. Roters, *Galerie Ferdinand Möller* (Gebr. Mann, 1984). I thank Wolfgang Wittrock for allowing me access to the house and to photograph it in 2005.

9. S. Giedion, *Space, Time and Architecture* (MIT Press, 1941).

10. J. Gebser, *Ursprung und Gegenwart* (Novalis Verlag, 1978; first publication 1948). Translated as *The Ever Present Origin* (Ohio University Press, 1991).

Chapter Ten

New Environments for Modern Living: 'At home' with the Eameses

Pat Kirkham

The wife/husband design and film-making team of Ray and Charles Eames approached design in much the same way as they did entertaining. Taking the host–guest relationship as the basis of design as well as a civilised lifestyle, they thought of themselves as hosts designing for a guest whose every need they sought to anticipate.[1] The Eameses were also interested in how things were used, and this study is part of a wider one about how they used their home and items within it. In this chapter I discuss their innovative mode of interior design, advice they gave on home decoration, an evening 'at home' with Billy and Audrey Wilder and a Japanese-style tea ceremony within the context of the Eameses' interior design aesthetic—particularly 'extra-cultural surprise'—as well as broader political issues.

Modernism, proto-postmodernism and personal statements

Ray, a founder member of the American Abstract Artists (1936), was trained as a fine artist; Charles trained as an architect and was already involved in furniture design when they married in 1941. From then until Charles's death in 1978, they enjoyed a close personal and professional collaboration and headed one of the most famous design offices of the twentieth century. Their low-cost industrially mass-produced furniture—plywood (1946), plastic (1948) and metal (1951)—epitomised the Modernist ideal of using new materials and mass-production techniques to bring better housing and products within the reach of the majority of the population.[2] Modernism here refers to the antihistoricist and antidecorative movement in architecture and design that developed out of the interwar European Modern movement that was known in the United States, from 1932, as the International Style.[3] From the mid 1920s, 'rational', 'functional', minimal and abstract forms were deemed the most appropriate for, and symbolic of, the new 'Machine Age'; form was claimed to follow function, and many believed that style, like decoration, was a thing of the past.[4]

The Eames House (Pacific Palisades, California, 1945–49), a steel-frame and glass building made from prefabricated parts and designed as part of a programme seeking to give physical expression to new attitudes towards living whilst offering exemplars of low-cost single-family housing, was seen as epitomising Modernist ideals.[5] The interior (see Fig. 10.1), however, which owed much to Ray's interest in collage, was in certain ways antithetical to them, offering a 'human', personalised solution to living in a prefabricated space that might otherwise have seemed impersonal and 'cold'.[6] More than any other leading Modernist designer of the period, the Eameses saw the user of a space and the contemplator of the objects therein as an active maker of that environment; as someone who could transform an industrially produced structure into a 'personal statement' by filling it with 'the accessories of his or her own life'.[7]

This approach also distinguished the Eameses from most professional designers of interiors, including the seven 'experts' (including Raymond Loewy, Eero Saarinen and Freda Diamond) invited by *Family Circle* magazine in 1958 to respond to the proposition: 'If I could tell a woman one thing about furnishing a home …' With the exception of Charles (who almost certainly collaborated with Ray on the article), the professionals illustrated their contributions with their own work. Charles's contribution featured a Native American pueblo interior from the southwest United States in which rugs, blankets and other textiles served both decorative and functional ends (Fig. 10.2). Readers learned that Charles wanted 'to help people enjoy the richness of simple stuff' and that the interior was not meant as a model to copy but rather as a demonstration of 'a quality that can come from

a natural discipline combined with respect and affection for "things"'.[8] This affection for 'things', everywhere apparent in the interior of their home, is also evident in their exhibitions and films.[9]

Eclectic assemblages and 'extra-cultural surprise'

At the Eames House, hints of things to come inside were given by the folksy bell and potted geraniums by the front door as well as the boldly coloured Mondrian-like panels on the front façade which disrupted the very concept of a minimal Modernist 'glass box' such as Mies van der Rohe's Farnsworth House (1948–51) and Philip Johnson's Glass House (1949). The Eameses' term 'functioning decoration' described their carefully composed groupings of eclectic objects in space: startlingly juxtaposed items of cultural, material and visual diversity that differed in scale, size, colour, texture, type, age, materials and monetary value, amongst other things. An aesthetic of addition, juxtaposition, wit, whimsy and the de- and recontextualisation of objects and images, it personalised and humanised what might otherwise have seemed impersonal 'machine-age' spaces.[10] Floors, tables, sofas and even kitchen work surfaces were used to display what others considered knick-knacks. Nothing was sacred; or rather everything was—from pebbles, combs, candles, starfish and driftwood to toys, souvenirs, Mexican piñata, Christmas decorations and flowers. Many objects were handcrafted, vernacular, found, natural, commonplace and from cultures and countries 'other' to the United States.[11]

Fig. 10.1. Ray and Charles Eames in their living room, Eames House, c. 1958. Photograph: Julius Shulman. © J. Paul Getty Trust. Used with permission. Julius Shulman Photography Archive, Research Library at the Getty Research Institute.

Fig. 10.2. This image was chosen by Charles, almost certainly in consultation with Ray, to help illustrate the answer to a question posed to him and other designers by *Family Circle* magazine (March 1958): 'If I could tell a woman one thing about Furnishing a Home …'

The 'look' was widely accessible, because so many of the items could be acquired relatively cheaply or for nothing.

Many who admired the Eameses' Modernist architecture and furniture felt uncomfortable with the very notion of 'decoration' and did not know quite what to make of the display that greeted them inside the Eames House. A few perceptive onlookers, however, grasped that something exciting was happening. Discussing the Eameses' room setting at *An Exhibition of Modern Living* (1949), designer George Nelson noted that it was more about artistic statements and new ways of viewing objects than specific suggestions about placing furniture in a room.[12] In the

1960s, British architects Alison and Peter Smithson discussed the Eameses' decorating of surfaces and space in their home in ways that later would be described as postmodern, noting the odd juxtapositions and collagelike groupings of objects and pointing to 'extra-cultural surprise' and the 'wide-eyed wonder of seeing the culturally disparate together and so happy with each other'.[13] They credited the Eameses, particularly Ray, with the reintroduction of 'fresh, pretty, colourful ephemera' to interiors and with the shift within Modernism from the 'machine age' aesthetic to 'the world of the cinema-eye and … the layout man'.[14] In the early 1970s, postmodernist Robert Venturi recognised that what the Eameses were doing with interiors lay outside orthodox definitions of Modernism, referring to them as reinventing Victorian 'clutter': 'modern architects wanted everything neat and clean and they came along and spread eclectic assemblages over an interior.'[15]

Gender, 'second home' and 'shock absorber'

Exceptional for its time in that it was planned for two equal partners, the Eames House 'remains a model for working and living at home'.[16] But gender was inscribed therein even before it was built. In 1944, Charles sketched out the various activities a couple might engage in within a home.[17] The man saws wood, plays music, selects records, shakes cocktails, relaxes on a recliner, projects films, reads the newspaper, stands on his head, plays with a model airplane and dances and cuddles up with the woman. The only occupation the woman undertakes on her own is painting; otherwise, she cuddles and dances with the man and joins him and another person for a game of cards. No one cooks, yet cooking was, and remains, a major marker of domestic divisions of labour. Ray did most of the cooking at home, but from 1958 they employed a cook at the newly expanded work space where they spent most of their time and had all meals except breakfast.[18] Literally their 'second home', all mail went to the work place and it was there that clients were entertained, including executives of IBM, the Herman Miller Furniture Company and the United States Information Agency.

Charles and Ray envisaged their home as a 'shock absorber': a place of respite from the buffeting of work and life, with a living area for 'music, reading, watching the fire, talking, leaving a large unbroken area for pure enjoyment of space in which objects can be placed and taken away ... driftwood, sculpture, mobiles, plants, constructions, etc.'[19] The fireplace was omitted from the final design after architect Eero Saarinen, a close friend, convinced them that such a thing would be too 'romantic', but otherwise the space was used in the ways they imagined. Objects were not only placed within the main double-height living area but also within the cosy alcove (under the balcony bedroom) wherein an eye-level shelf expressly designed for the display of objects ran around the top of the built-in seating. Like a film set, this 'room within a room' has only three sides, and at night the space was made more magical by 'fairy lights' in the latticed ceiling

(see Fig. 10.1 and Fig. 10.3), a feature sadly no longer there.

'At home': setting the stage

At home Ray and Charles mostly entertained close friends, including clients and consultants who had become friends. They preferred the group to be small, preferably four, and claimed to have only four full settings of cutlery.[20] Charles's well-known dislike of parties extended to a dislike of eating in restaurants unless one could hear all of the conversation, and the multipurpose alcove provided an excellent conversation area.[21] Ray, who had a rare ability to transform the rituals of eating and daily life into memorable events, was responsible for choreographing 'home' and hospitality, from setting the scene as a whole down to 'super simple' yet 'orgiastic feasts' set out on beautifully arranged tables.[22] If, as the Arts and Crafts movement preached, the laying of a table was an art form, Ray was one of its most notable practitioners. Together with her love of performance (she studied ballet with a Russian-trained ballerina and modern dance with Martha Graham[23]) and skills at layout, collage and interior design, it underpinned the chez Eames experience.

Before friends visited for an 'informal' evening at home (see Fig. 10.3), Ray oversaw a small team of Eames Office staff, ensuring that candles were burned down to the specified lengths, every pillow was puffed up to just the right degree and every object placed just so.[24] Don Albinson, who worked in the Eames Office from 1946 to 1959, likened these behind-the-scenes preparations to

Fig. 10.3. Conversation cum reading cum relaxation area, living room, Eames House, 1961. Left to right: Billy Wilder, Audrey Wilder, Charles Eames and Ray Eames. Photograph: Paul Fusco. © Paul Fusco/Magnum Photos.

those preceding a play or film shoot: 'It was all theatre. Every visit was totally staged. Ray storyboarded it all in her head, down to the newest object or a particularly lovely geranium plucked from a pot by the front door. Everything had to be "just so."'[25] Office members were under instructions to be out of the house well before guests arrived: seeing the 'stage hands' would lessen the magic of the performance. Albinson recalled:

Ray liked our cars to be well clear of the house and driveway before guests arrived. Well, on this

particular occasion, we were running late. Ray kept checking the time and began to chase us out of the door. She panicked, shouting 'Get out of the way!' They'll see you, they'll see you' — things like that. We were mid-way across the patio as Charlie drove up to the house with Billy and Audrey Wilder. Ray was clearly very upset but it was comical in a way. What could we do? There is only a narrow drive and you couldn't fail to see our cars parked there. Even if we had hidden in the bushes they would have seen the cars. And now they couldn't miss us running to them. 'Hey, Don', Charlie called, 'Good to see you. What are you doing up here?' He seemed genuinely surprised to see us. I wondered if he had any idea just how much work went into those 'informal' evenings but realized Charlie knew everything that went on.[26]

'At home': with the Wilders

Understanding that a designer couple might put extra effort into an evening when a photographer from *Look* magazine was shooting them and their home,[27] I asked Albinson if his remarks related to the evening featured in *Look.* He insisted that such preparations prefaced all 'impromptu' Eames entertaining, adding 'on each and every occasion everything was choreographed down to the nth degree.'[28] Billy Wilder credited much of the 'magic' and 'joy' of such evenings to Ray's 'flawless taste' and 'brilliant eye' and to the couple's 'warmth' as hosts.[29] Audrey Wilder, who entertained enough to understand that, even with hired help, it involved more than waving a magic wand, appreciated just how much sheer effort as well as decorating talent went into creating 'those visually delightful arrangements of objects' and the 'wonderfully relaxed atmosphere'.[30]

Figure 10.3 shows four people amidst the exoticism of the objects and arrangements of objects in the Eames House, each exotic in its own way: the Eameses (star designers), Billy Wilder (star director) and Audrey Wilder (model and former starlet, 'Glamourette' and singer with the Tommy Dorsey band). They become four more elements in the cultural mélange. Audrey's Hollywood-style glamour, for example, contrasts with the studiously

artistic clothing of Ray and Charles and the more conventional (though always stylish) clothing of her husband, adding yet another layer of 'extra-cultural surprise'. Design historians rarely discuss glamour in the same breath as Modernism, yet even the coffee table was glamourised at the Eames House; a one-off version of the Eameses' mass-produced plywood tables, it had been given a golden top of gilded brass, which, in turn, provided yet another surface for the changing displays of objects.

In terms of personal statement and use, the alcove was one of the Eameses' most successful creations. They appear to have used this custom-designed seating area more often than examples of their own mass-produced furniture that were also in the living area, namely the Lounge Chair and Ottoman (1956) and Sofa Compact (1954). The alcove seating was not the only one-off seating in the house: two Indian handcrafted chairs were added in the late 1950s (see Fig. 10.1), providing, like the Herman Miller items, further surfaces for the display of 'functioning decoration'.

'At home': a cross-cultural tea ceremony

The Eameses were fascinated by Japan. The light, simple structure of their house and the sliding partitions, tatami mats and paper lampshades therein testify to their debt to traditional Japanese design. Their fascination was part of a wider interest in Japan on the part of Westerners that dates back to the second half of the nineteenth century, when it tended to focus on prints and decorative arts objects.[31] By 1950, the interest was extremely wide-ranging, from film and fashion to Sumo wrestlers (about which the Eameses made a film in 1972). The Eameses welcomed a variety of Japanese visitors to their home, including the potter, Hamada, 'Tiger' Saito, editor of *Japan Today,* and Sokosen, later to be the grand tea master Soshitsu Sen XV.[32] Accompanying Sokosen was Japanese American Sōsei Matsumoto, who opened a tea ceremony school in Los Angeles in 1951, the year in which she participated in a tea ceremony at the Eames House (see Fig. 10.4) and starred in such a ceremony in a Hollywood movie.[33]

In postwar Japan, the tea ceremony, already acknowledged as increasingly distanced from everyday life, was self-consciously reconstructed as something essentially 'Japanese' and promoted as a form of cultural nationalism.[34] In the United States, interest in the ceremony came to stand for cultural pluralism, what philosopher Horace Kallen called 'the federation or commonwealth of nationalities'.[35] Fig. 10.4 suggests that the Eameses were aiming at an overall feeling of 'Japaneseness' but with a touch of 'commonwealth of nationalities'. Although they took considerable care to be authentic about some aspects—most notably by inviting Matsumoto perform the ceremony—they did

Fig. 10.4. Tea ceremony, Eames House, 1951. Left to right: Sōsei Matsumoto, Yoshiko (Shirley) Yamaguchi, Charlie Chaplin and Iris Tree. Photograph: Charles Eames © 1997 Lucia Eames (dba) Eames Office.

not fetishise the traditional, happily mixing it with 'modern', including the small low tables they designed for the Herman Miller Furniture Company (1950).

That Hollywood director King Vidor also invited Matsumoto to perform a tea ceremony in a film supports a reading of the Eames ceremony as theatre, as do photographs of Charlie Chaplin posing and gesturing with a fan.[36] Starring Japanese film actress and singer Yoshiko (Shirley) Yamaguchi, *Japanese War Bride* (1951, released 1952) highlighted contemporary discourse on racial integration and cultural pluralism. As the girlfriend, later wife, of Japanese American sculptor and designer Isamu Noguchi, a friend of the Eameses who had worked for Herman Miller since 1948, it was probably in Yamaguchi's honour that the Eameses hosted the tea ceremony. Yet, ironically, Yamaguchi, who had been brought up in China, proved unable to perform the ceremony with the degree of skill demanded by the director, King Vidor, and therefore he had to create a role in the movie for Matsumoto.

The participants in the Eames ceremony were as culturally disparate as the objects within the Eameses' 'functioning decoration'. Besides Noguchi, Matsumoto and Yamaguchi, they included Charlie Chaplin, British-born comic and Hollywood icon, Iris Tree, British 'Bloomsbury Set' bohemian poet whose thespian father, Herbert Beerbohm Tree, had introduced her to Chaplin in the 1920s, and American actor Ford Rainey, with whom Tree then had a relationship. Although both Matsumoto and Yamaguchi wore traditional Japanese dress, the former often wore Western dress, as on a different visit to the

Eames House.[37] Before she visited the United States for the first time in 1950, Yamaguchi felt as, if not more, comfortable in Chinese dress than Japanese dress, commenting that she was only taking 'two or three kimonos for the stage', a remark that also adds to a theatrical reading of this culturally complex event.[38] So too does the presence of Chaplin, the most famous performer in the Western world, who, like the Eameses, took extremely seriously the host–guest relationship.[39]

The attendance of Chaplin, a master of nonverbal communication, was sufficient in itself to transform the gathering into a multicultural Theatre of the Absurd. I use the term somewhat loosely, but certain of the Eameses' interests intersected with those of that particular development in European theatre of the late 1940s and 1950s in which time, place and identity were ambiguous and fluid. It was influenced by Dadaism and other avant-garde art movements, 'nonsense poetry', antirealism and Albert Camus's existentialist notion that life is inherently without meaning and therefore one has to create one's own meanings.[40] Besides Ray's strong involvement with avant-garde art in the 1930s, the Eameses were passionately interested in nonverbal communications, and their fascination with fluidity of identity is evident not only in the tea ceremony but also in their fascination with the circus and their modes of self-representation.[41] Nonverbal communication also interested many of the 'progressives' and Left-wingers in Hollywood, including the émigré German Marxist playwright, poet and theatre director, Bertolt Brecht, with whom Chaplin mixed at Salka Viertel's salon.[42] To speak of the Eameses' tea ceremony in terms of the Theatre of the Absurd and 'functioning decoration' is not to detract from it but rather to suggest the many and complex layers of meaning within it, from respect for Japanese traditions to radical commentaries on American ones, let alone issues of cultural pluralism, appropriation, 'authenticity' and politics.

This American domestic spectacle embraced the former enemy, Japan, and, through Chaplin, showed support for 'progressives' within the Hollywood community hounded by the Federal Bureau of Investigation (FBI) and the House Un-American Activities Committee and who were accused of being Communists or Communist sympathisers.[43] The attack from the religious and political Right was against liberals and liberalism as well as Communists and Communism, and it was as liberals that the Eameses supported Chaplin.[44] For a couple who normally stood aside from formal politics and certainly in later years eschewed direct connections between art and politics, this domestic tea ceremony is as explicit a political statement as one gets from the Eameses.[45] Despite the FBI conceding that there was no proof of Chaplin ever having been a member of the Communist Party, soon after the Eameses extended to him their hospitality, the country in which he had lived and worked for thirty-seven years denied him further hospitality, cancelling his re-entry permit to the United States in 1952.[46]

Noguchi, the child of an American mother and a Japanese father, had also fallen foul of the FBI when campaigning against internment camps established in the United States during the Second World War for Japanese

Americans and co-founding a group of antifascist artists, authors and musicians (1945). His deportation order was rescinded only after vehement protests by the American Civil Liberties Union.[47] After the war, Noguchi spent some considerable time in Japan; indeed, at the time of the Eames ceremony, he had recently returned from Hiroshima, where he had been discussing his role in the Peace Center project. He later wrote movingly about the uncertainty and fluidity of identity: 'With my double nationality and double upbringing, where was my home? Where were my affections? Where my identity? Japan or America, either, or both—or the world?'[48] Noguchi's notion of 'the world' was not dissimilar to Chaplin's 'One World' politics and the Eameses' 'hands across the world'— style liberal internationalism.[49] Tony Benn, British socialist politician and friend of Charles, recognised the Eameses' internationalism in their film *Tops* (1969), which, he argued, by means of showing 'mankind of all races, and from all over the world, and every culture, playing with a single simple toy' conveys the 'unity of humanity' in ways 'utterly pleasurable and absolutely unforgettable'.[50]

It is difficult to picture the altogether more irreverent and sardonic Billy Wilder at the tea ceremony. The very different type of 'at home' entertaining, where he and Audrey enjoy a cigarette, an alcoholic drink and good conversation, seems much more his style. But each one of the different imaginings and playing out of 'home' and hospitality explored above all have certain things in common. Conceptually they fall within the Eameses' understanding of the host–guest relationship, cultural pluralism and a liberal internationalism that saw people, regardless of culture or creed, as having more in common than differences, and visually they fit within the framework of the Eameses' 'functioning decoration' aesthetic of 'extra-cultural surprise'.

Notes

1. E. Demetrios, *An Eames Primer* (Universe Publishing, 2001), p. 155.

2. P. Kirkham, *Charles and Ray Eames: Designers of the Twentieth Century* (MIT Press, 1995), pp. 1–8.

3. See H.-R. Hitchcock and P. Johnson, *The International Style: Architecture Since 1922* (Museum of Modern Art, 1966) and T. Benton, *The Modernist Home* (V&A Publications, 2006).

4. C. Wilk, ed., *Modernism 1914–1939: Designing a New World* (V&A Publications, 2006), pp. 11–21.

5. A. Jones and E.A.T. Smith, 'The Thirty-Six Case Study Projects', in E.A.T. Smith, ed., *Blueprints for Modern Living: History and Legacy of the Case Study Houses* (Museum of Contemporary Arts, Los Angeles, 1989), pp. 41–82.

6. Kirkham, *Charles and Ray Eames,* p. 1.

7. J. Neuhart, M. Neuhart and R. Eames, *Eames Design: The Work of the Office of Charles and Ray Eames* (Thames & Hudson, 1989), p. 137.

8. E. Frances, 'If I Could Tell a Woman One Thing about Furnishing a Home . . .', *Family Circle* (March 1958), pp. 27–33.

9. Kirkham, *Charles and Ray Eames,* pp. 143–66; E. McCoy, 'An Affection for Objects', *Progressive Architecture* (August 1973), pp. 64–7.

10. P. Kirkham, 'Humanizing Modernism: The Crafts, "Functioning Decoration" and the Eameses', *Journal of Design History* 11/1 (1998), pp. 15–29.

11. Kirkham, *Charles and Ray Eames,* pp.143–59.

12. G. Nelson, *Display* (Whitney Publication, 1953), p. 65.

13. P. Smithson and A. Smithson, 'Eames Celebration', *Architectural Design* 36 (September 1966), p. 443.

14. Ibid.

15. Cited in McCoy, 'An Affection for Objects', p. 67.

16. D. Hayden, 'Model Homes for the Millions: Architects' Dreams, Builders' Boasts, Residents' Dilemmas', in E.A.T. Smith, ed., *Blueprints for Modern Living,* pp. 197–212.

17. Neuhart, Neuhart and Eames, *Eames Design,* p. 47.

18. Demetrios, *An Eames Primer,* p. 162.

19. 'Case Study Houses 8 and 9 by Charles Eames and Eero Saarinen, Architects', *Arts & Architecture* (December 1945), pp. 43–51.

20. M. Noyes, Letter to author, 1991.

21. Kirkham, *Charles and Ray Eames,* p. 157.

22. E. K. Carpenter, 'A Tribute to Charles Eames', *Industrial Design 25th Annual Design Review* (1979), pp. 12–13.

23. Kirkham, *Charles and Ray Eames,* p. 35; Demetrios, *An Eames Primer,* p. 66.

24. Carpenter, 'A Tribute to Charles Eames', p. 12.

25. D. Albinson. Interview with author, Pennsylvania, 2004.

26. Ibid.

27. J. Peter, 'A Visit with Designer Charles Eames', *Look* (20 June 1961), pp. 58b–58h.

28. D. Albinson. Interview with author, Pennsylvania, 2004.

29. Carpenter, 'A Tribute to Charles Eames', p. 12; B. Wilder, interviews with author, Los Angeles, 1993 and 1994.

30. A. Wilder. Telephone conversation with author, 1993.

31. See S. Wichmann, *Japonisme: The Japanese Influence on Western Art since 1858* (Thames & Hudson, 1999).

32. Neuhart, Neuhart and Eames, *Eames Design,* pp. 283, 167, 170.

33. Neuhart, Neuhart and Eames, *Eames Design,* pp. 154, 170; www.nea.gov/honors/heritage/fellows; B.L.C. Mori, 'The Tea Ceremony: A Transformed Japanese Ritual', *Gender & Society* 5/1 (1991), pp. 86–97.

34. C. C. Simpson, '"Out of an Obscure Place": Japanese War Brides and Cultural Pluralism in the 1950s', *A Journal of Feminist Cultural Studies* 10/3 (1998), p. 48; Mori, 'The Tea Ceremony', p. 87.

35. Simpson, '"Out of an Obscure Place"', p. 48.

36. Library of Congress, Prints and Photographs Division: LC-USZ6-2282–3.

37. Neuhart, Neuhart and Eames, *Eames Design,* p. 170.

38. M. Duus, *The Life of Isamu Noguchi: Journey without Borders* (Princeton University Press, 2004), p. 223.

39. Lambert, *The Ivan Moffat File,* pp. 229–30.

40. M. Esslin, *The Theatre of the Absurd* (Doubleday, 1962).

41. Kirkham, *Charles and Ray Eames,* pp. 148–59, 356–7.

42. Lambert, *The Ivan Moffat File,* p. 34.

43. J. J. Gladchuk, *Hollywood and Anti-Communism: HUAC and the Evolution of the Red Menace, 1935–50* (Routledge, 2006).

44. M. S. McAuliffe, *Crisis on the Left: Cold War Politics and American Liberals, 1947–1954* (University of Massachusetts Press, 1978).

45. Kirkham, *Charles and Ray Eames,* p. 372.

46. C. J. Maland, *Chaplin and American Culture: The Evolution of a Star Image* (Princeton University Press, 1991), pp. 280–6.

47. Duus, *The Life of Isamu Noguchi,* pp.164–85.

48. Ibid, p. 6.

49. Maland, *Chaplin and American Culture,* p. 276.

50. Kirkham, *Charles and Ray Eames,* p. 336.

Chapter Eleven

Italy's New Domestic Landscape, 1945–1972

Penny Sparke

In these complete rooms ready for use [the visitor] will ... be able to find ... fresh variety ... vitality (however diversely expressed), and freedom from sterile intellectualism.[1]

The 'complete' rooms referred to above formed part of the exhibition *Italy at Work: Her Renaissance in Design Today*, which toured the United States in 1951. Although the show's main agenda was the vital role played by traditional crafts—glass, ceramics, furniture, straw-work etc.—within Italy's energetic, postwar design programme, it also openly acknowledged that it was in the space of the interior that many of Italy's most significant material achievements came together. Furthermore, given the importance, stressed by the catalogue's author, of the architect to that country's 'design renaissance', the exhibition demonstrated that many of Italy's creative geniuses did not limit themselves to one area of production and that it was in the interior that the rich variety of their practices was visible. The interior—represented at that particular event by a foyer for a marionette theatre by Fabrizio

Clerici; a terrace room by Luigi Cosenza; a private chapel by Roberto Menghi; a living-dining room by Carlo Mollino and a dining room by Gio Ponti—was seen an important aspect of Italy's postwar renaissance. Indeed it played several important roles within it. They included bringing architecture in contact with the decorative arts and demonstrating the blending of tradition with modernity that was such a strong feature in the early post-1945 era. Whilst, on the one hand, it offered a means with which to provide the less well-off with functional living spaces, it also demonstrated the continuity of Italy's deeply rooted commitment to the idea of 'the good life'.

Together those themes defined the Italian postwar design phenomenon of those years, and they were all visible in the staged interiors that toured the United States in 1951 in the following ways: The ceramist Guido Gambone had supplied the floor tiles for Clerici's terrace, and the glassware in Ponti's space was provided by Venini; the modern aesthetic of Mollino's furniture items was sharply contrasted by references to the 'traditional liturgy' in Menghi's chapel; Mollino employed several examples of flexible furnishings as a solution to the problem of the 'modest apartment'; whilst the high level of decoration in Ponti's dining room would undoubtedly have appealed to a more affluent client and suggested a more middle-class lifestyle (see Fig. 11.1). In short, in 1951, the interior could be seen as being at the centre of many of the cross-cutting agendas that made up the Italian post war design programme.

In the discussion about the relationship of the designed interior with both 'modernism' and the broader concept of 'modernity' that runs throughout this book, post–Second World War Italy provides an interesting and illuminating case study. Between 1945 and the mid 1960s, enormous efforts were made on the part of manufacturers, working with architect-designers and local chambers of commerce, to develop a modern Italian furniture and furnishings movement which would have an impact internationally. At home, however, the modernisation of Italian society engendered a response to modernity which, where the consumption of furniture and furnishings was concerned, covered a spectrum from traditional forms to a more wholehearted embrace of the modern style. Most of the currently available studies of Italian design after 1945 have tended to emphasise the isolated, decontextualised, sculpturally defined designed objects which were visible in the international marketplace—the items of chic modern furniture, the avant-garde floor lamps, the sculptural kitchen machines and the elegant automobiles among them. This chapter sets out to demonstrate that the spatial and material culture of the interior (especially but not exclusively in the context

of domesticity) played a key role within Italian design, particularly of its manifestations on Italian soil from the 1940s to the 1970s, and arguably beyond. It was, it will be suggested, one of the key sites of Italian domestic (both in the sense of existing within national boundaries and of being 'at home') modernisation. It provided both a frame for the novel designs of the new generation of architect-designers that led to Italy being seen, by the 1960s, as a world leader in the area of modern design and, at the same time, it was also the main setting for the maintenance of traditional values in the home, one of the key themes in the early postwar years of Italy's own material modernity.

In the 1940s, the concept of architectural and design modernism that had been developed in the interwar years was seen as problematic in a country which had been led by a fascist dictator who had, to a significant extent, embraced the idea of the 'modern'.[2] Although tainted by those associations, some efforts were made, nonetheless, after 1945, to revive the ideological programme of modernism on Italian soil. Ernesto N. Rogers, for example, the editor, between 1946 and 1948, of the longstanding Italian architectural and design periodical *Domus,* was committed to the social idealism of prewar architectural rationalism, seeing it as the necessary underpinning for a reconstruction of the Italian home.[3] Northern Italy had experienced a 'housing crisis' since the early twentieth century, when, in Milan for example, over half the population had lived in one- or two-room dwellings.[4] In addition, over three million houses had been destroyed or damaged during the Second World War, and the idea

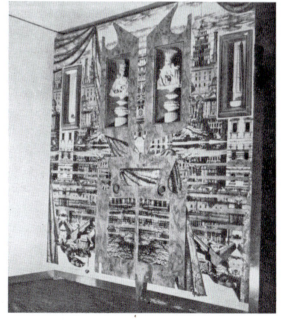

Fig. 11.1. Gio Ponti. Dining room at the Italy at Work: Her Renaissance in Design Today exhibition, held at the Brooklyn Museum, New York, in 1951. Illustrated in the exhibition handbook, authored by Meyric R. Rogers (Rome: Compagnia Nazionale Artigiana, 1951), p. 61.

of a 'home of one's own' became, as a result, an increasingly widespread aspiration.[5] The rationalist programme—linked to the new political, economic and social ideals of the new Republic—was evoked as a solution to that challenge. Rogers introduced the idea of *la casa umana* (the human house), which built upon architectural modernism, extending that programme, however, to focus on the human being at the heart of the architectural problem and also acknowledging the importance of maintaining a level of commitment to the past.

Many members of the generation of young architects—Paolo Chessa, Ignazio Gardella, Marco Zanuso, Vico Magistratti, Ettore Sottsass Jr., among others—who were entering the profession in the 1940s had imbibed the principles of architectural rationalism in the education they had received in the 1930s. In the years after 1945, which were dominated by the impact of rapid industrialisation and modernisation, those young practitioners set out to reconstruct Italy, focusing on the interior spaces of the new apartment blocks that were being built around the major cities and on items of light-framed and flexible furniture items which they designed specifically for those new spaces. So rapid was the industrial growth of those years that the design spotlight was focused on the innovative domestic products of the new, and renewed, manufacturing companies—Cassina, Artemide, Arteluce, and a range of others—many of them located in the traditional furniture manufacturing area of Brianza, north on Milan. As Eugenio Fossati, the president of Milan's chamber of commerce, was to explain in a 1961 furniture catalogue that illustrated baroque-framed mirrors alongside splayed-legged plastic-framed chairs (see Fig. 11.2 and Fig. 11.3), 'they [the manufacturers] have at their disposal the best equipments and a highly specialised labour, which is devoted, according to family tradition, to this activity. In Italy there is also a wide set of artists and architects whom work hard in order to secure the characteristics of high quality and taste to this sector.'[6] In 1946 Vico Magistretti and Ignazio Gardella, among others, showed a number of simple, flexible furniture designs at the RIMA exhibition in Milan. The latter furnished a 'Home for Three People', whilst the former exhibited a demountable bookshelf and chair.[7] The Milan Triennale of the following year also focused on the subject of the home, emphasising the idea of furnishings for the masses. Ettore Sottsass Jr. contributed a small chair with a steel rod structure and a carved wooden seat and arms.

In 1950, in the words of Vittorio Gregotti, 'realism came to an end.'[8] The focus on democratisation that had characterised the early postwar years and had been underpinned by the existence of, first, a Communist and, subsequently, a Coalition government, came, with the advent of Centre Party rule from 1948 onwards, to a sudden end. In its place, Ponti's middle-class-oriented 'good life' became more prominent.[9] Ponti used *Domus*, which he edited from 1948 onwards, as a mouthpiece for his ideas, focusing on the need to retain a link with the traditional crafts.[10] Design responded to the new consumerist climate of the 1950s, and the concept of Italian modernity took on more luxurious connotations at that time. Where product design was concerned, the Triennales of those years stressed the need to combine utility with beauty and contributed to the emergence of a highly distinctive, sculpturally defined Italian product aesthetic which was widely admired internationally.[11] The impetus given by those exhibitions to what subsequently became the orthodox story of the rise of modern Italian design, epitomised by the sensuous abstract forms that filled the pages of the magazine *Stile Industria* in the late 1950s and early 1960s, has been extensively documented.[12] Within that climate, the design of the middle-class domestic interior also took on a new significance, providing a means by which the young architects could supplement the incomes they received from the furniture manufacturers. Magistretti, Gardella, Carlo di Carli, Sottsass and many others took on numerous 'interior decoration' projects in those years.

Sottsass was especially prolific in this area, using it as a way of developing his own unique modern design language. He began designing interiors for wealthy clients in the early 1950s and continued until the contract he acquired from the electronics company, Olivetti, in the late 1950s, took over as his main source of income. The 1940s had seen his design for a room in a 1948 Turin exhibition and for the interior of a beer cellar in the same city in the same year, but his most innovative work was to be produced in the following decade, when all his preoccupations came together in that context. The architect's long-standing interest in colour, decorative surfaces, forms based on a grid structure,

Fig. 11.2. Hall mirror and console table, manufactured by Maspero & Cie., Como. Illustrated in *Mobili e Mobilieri D'Italia* (Milan Chamber of Commerce, 1961), p. 22.

Fig. 11.3. Two splayed-legged armchairs, manufactured by La Permanente Mobili, Como. Illustrated in *Mobili e Mobilieri D'Italia* (Milan Chamber of Commerce, 1961), p. 183.

space and light were brought together in his designed interiors, and he created numerous highly innovative spatial, material and visual compositions in them. As a 1953 article about the architect published in *Domus* explained, 'The need of knowing well his materials is very important for an architect and not only the "materials" but the real raw material of an architect: space. In the studio of Sottsass we found more traces of research in this field than is customary in an architect's office.'[13] An interior he created 'for a modern prince' of that year combined an antique chest with a number of small biomorphic laminated plastic side tables designed by the architect, whilst an interior in Turin, created in a rented

apartment in the same year, was more overtly modern and contained more of Sottsass's own furniture designs.[14]

In a 1957 interior, Sottsass exploited the ways in which the two-dimensional surfaces of walls and moveable screens, decorated with geometrical patterns, could be used spatially, and he combined them with three-dimensional objects—open shelving systems and cupboards among them. He covered their surfaces with geometrical patterning as well.[15] The designs owed much to the early twentieth-century *Gesamtkunstwerk* interiors of Josef Hoffmann and Charles Rennie Mackintosh and showed the backward-looking, yet overtly modern, face of Italian design in those years which manifested itself more widely in the architectural and decorative arts 'Neo-Liberty'movement.[16] Like the proto-modernist pioneers he admired, Sottsass experimented with the elements of his new design language across a range of media, from ceramics to paintings to furniture designs to lighting. It was in the interior, however, that that language was consolidated and tested. In a 1955 article in *Domus* entitled 'Interior without Walls', Sottsass revealed his desire to move beyond the interwar modernists' dedication to abstract space and to engage with a new level of materiality. 'In opposition', he wrote, 'to the neo-plasticists' idea of space as something created by abstract mathematical surfaces (and colours) we have here the new idea of real surfaces and real materials.'[17] The interior 'without walls' that he created depended on partitions and cupboards to articulate its spaces.

The year 1955 also saw Sottsass's creation of an interior which housed a number of modern paintings and sculptures. Another interior for a 'house on the hill' of 1957 relied once again on a grid, and he juxtaposed a baroque mirror with a Harry Bertoia chair.[18] In the same year, in a *Domus* article entitled 'Compositions of Walls', Sottsass explained the ways in which he constructed his interior spaces which involved combining two and three dimensions. He emphasised the subtle ways in which he controlled the use of light sources and his careful positioning of ceramic objects within it.

In 1958 the architect discussed 'the elements of interior decoration' in an article in *Domus.* In the specific interior he focused on in that discussion, the grid was present yet again visible both in the structure of the room itself as well as in numerous two- and three-dimensional details, including the wooden frame of a mirror. Stripes embellished the surfaces of furniture items, and wooden partitions and cabinets were employed spatially. The architect's ideas about the spatial use of colour and graphics had much in common with those that informed American abstract painting at that time. He combined those preoccupations, however, with an architectural interest in the manipulation of space through the use of partitions and furniture items.

Sottsass also designed a computer for Olivetti, the Elea 9003, in 1958. Whilst that new venture may seem to have marked a shift from spaces to objects, early computers consisted of groups of large cabinets assembled in a single space and, for their designer, they had, as a consequence, more in common with an interior than with a material artefact. Sottsass approached the design of the Elea as a spatial exercise first and foremost, ensuring that the heights of the cabinets allowed the operators to see each other and that they were linked visually through an emphasis on the vertical and horizontal lines that he introduced into the space they occupied as a means of unifying and emphasising the cabinets' material presence within it. Whilst Sottsass was working on interiors as an income source—1957 saw his grid-based design for the display of glass at the Triennale, and, in the following year, he created an interior for a dentist in Genoa—more importantly they provided him with an ideal medium in which to develop his visual, material and spatial ideas. Whilst he is, perhaps, best known for his typewriters and office furniture for Olivetti, his ceramic objects and his furniture items designed in the 1960s, in essence they also all 'belonged' to interiors, whether overtly or otherwise. An architect above all else, Sottsass's use of colour, pattern and form were all ultimately united in, and defined by, even if only conceptually, their spatial contextualisation. From his 'Grey' furniture series of 1970 to his design for the 1972 Museum of Modern Art's exhibition *Italy: The New Domestic Landscape* to his designs for the Memphis group from 1981 onwards, the vast majority of his designs required either a visible or an invisible interior frame because their forms and surfaces assumed, and were dependent upon, its existence.

Whilst Sottsass developed his own unique language of design through the 1950s and 1960s, which, arguably, depended upon the conceptualisation of a quite complex model of a modern interior that, in turn, was rooted in, above all, the early twentieth-century idea of the *Gesamtkunstwerk,* he was not alone in working in that way. Such was the strong architectural underpinning to Italian modern design in those years that many of the leading furniture and product designers also worked on interiors, and the objects they created depended strongly upon them. An image of a strikingly modern sofa by Ico and Luisa Parisi in a 1955 publication, for example, which depicted it positioned in an interior containing a picture with an antique frame around it, provided a more complete picture of Italian modernity—one which embraced both the past and the present in the context of the home—than one which

might have showed it in isolation (see Fig. 11.4).[19]

By the middle of the 1960s, the commitment to the past was less in evidence in the Italian modern interior, however, and a number of designers began to create integrated environments which were neither interior spaces nor objects but something in between. Joe Colombo, known above all for his innovative designed objects—among them his curved plywood armchair of 1964, his all-plastic 'Universale' side chair of 1965 and his range of lighting objects—also created a number of 'systems', or 'micro-environments',—among them his 'additional-system' armchair of 1967 and his 'square plastic system' of 1969.[20] Achille Castiglioni created a number of public sphere interiors into which he introduced his own designs, among them the Splügen Braü restaurant in Milan of 1960 and the Gavina showroom in Milan of a couple of years later.[21]

By the late 1960s, the decontextualised designed object, which had been so prominent in the early 1960s, had begun to lose its preeminence as groups of young Italian designers sought to side-step the, by then, confirmed role of the designer in the creation of conspicuous consumption and in the promotion of profit-seeking manufacturing companies. The so-called crisis of the object swung the balance back in the direction of environments and systems, and young architectural groups, such as Superstudio and Archigram, among others, aligned themselves with that approach. The movement that came to be known as 'Radical' or 'Counter' design renounced the object, seeking instead to reinstate the architectural and

Fig. 11.4. Ico and Luisa Parisi, divan. Illustrated in R. Aloi, ed., *L'Arredamento moderno* (Milan: Hoepli, 1955), p. 327.

environmental approach to design and to minimise its preoccupations with materiality and, by implication, materialistic values. The 1972 exhibition—*Italy: The New Domestic Landscape*—that was held in New York's Museum of Modern Art (MOMA), served as a moment for reflection on the progress of Italian design since 1945—in particular, over the preceding decade. The title suggested that the emphasis on the culture of the Italian home, which, for clear economic, social and cultural reasons, had been such a dominant theme in the immediate postwar years, was still relevant in the early 1970s.

That assumption was premised upon the continuing role and omnipotence of the architect and on the fact that the vast majority of the objects created by Italian designers were destined ultimately for the domestic arena. In creating a postwar modern design movement, Italy had also, by implication, created a model of modern domesticity, a modern 'lifestyle' which impacted first on the home market but moved, increasingly, into an international arena. The shift from specific interior spaces to transportable interior environments or systems served to facilitate that transference.

In its survey of the previous decade of design, the MOMA exhibition separated out objects from environments. Whereas, where the former was concerned, it recognised the impact of objects already in existence as well as the contemporary trend towards 'flexible patterns of use and arrangement' that emphasised their spatial context, the environmental projects had been designed and produced especially for the exhibition. They fell into two categories—those that reflected problem solving in the sociocultural field and those more radical projects which sought 'structural changes in our society'.[22] Several of the microenvironments that were shown at the exhibition acknowledged the continuing importance of the 'domestic landscape' but proposed radical changes to that familiar territory. They also recognised the important link between design and the way people live their lives and the need to recognise change in those areas, including 'more informal social and family relationships, and evolving notions of privacy and territoriality'.[23] As it had been when Rogers

was outlining his views about the *la casa umana,* the emphasis was still upon the dwelling, 'with explicit concern for the context of housing'.[24] Interestingly, although the emphasis in 1972 was on the future and behavioural change in the domestic sphere, the importance of 'individual and social memory' was still emphasised.[25]

Three 'house-environments' were displayed at the exhibition created by Gae Aulenti, Ettore Sottsass Jr. and Joe Colombo. The first consisted of a system of three different and flexible elements which, by being arranged differently, could be put to different domestic uses; the second, recalling in some ways Sottsass's design for Olivetti's Elea 9003 computer, consisted of a series of plastic moulded pods on wheels that contained different functionalities and could also be arranged flexibly; the third comprised, once again, a number of elements which facilitated basic domestic activities and could be rearranged as desired. In all three cases, there was little evidence of the traditional home but rather a suggestion of a future in which it was behaviours rather than images, objects or even spaces that mattered. Whilst the materials and aesthetic employed by the three architects expressed both a technological and a social utopianism which could only realistically be expressed in the context of an exhibition, their aspirations to use inhabited spaces as engines for social and cultural change and improvement echoed Rogers's words of two and a half decades earlier.

Despite not having been fully documented, it is clear from contemporary records that the designed domestic interior played a crucial role, therefore, in the development of Italian design in the period 1945 to 1972. It served as a test bed for many of the architects who were extending the range of their activities into new media, and it brought their disparate designs into a single setting; it provided a means of fulfilling many of the social, economic and cultural challenges presented by Italy's need to address modernity and become a modern society; it reflected the shift from a simultaneously backward- and forward-looking culture to one which, by the end of the period in question, embraced the progressive aspects of modernity more wholeheartedly and revived the ideological and aesthetic programme of modernism; and it served to offset the consumerist push towards excessive materialism by allowing designers to define their discipline as one which embraced the spatial and the environmental as well as the visual and the material. Although, perhaps because it tends to locate Italian design in an Italian context rather than in the more internationally oriented one which most historians of the subject have embraced, it has been relatively under-researched to date, the modern Italian interior of the years 1945 to 1972 can be seen to have underpinned much that went on in that period and to be more significant than has hitherto been fully acknowledged.

Notes

1. M. R. Rogers, 'Author's Preface' to *Italy at Work: Her Renaissance in Design Today* (Compagnia Nationale Artigiana, 1951), p. 50.

2. In the 1930s, Mussolini developed new towns—Sabaudia and Littoria—in the *novecento* style on the marshlands south of Rome.

3. *Domus* was founded by Gio Ponti in 1928.

4. M. Clark, *Modern Italy, 1871–1982* (Longmans, 1984), p. 165.

5. Clark, *Modern Italy*, p. 317.

6. E. R. Fossati, *Mobili e Mobilieri d'Italia* (Camera di Commercio, 1961), p. iv.

7. G. Ambasz, *Italy: The New Domestic Landscape, Achievements and Problems of Italian Design* (Museum of Modern Art, 1973), p. 316.

8. Ibid., p. 318.

9. Gio Ponti promoted a much more middle-class version of Italian modernity than Ernesto Rogers, who was a member of the Italian Communist Party.

10. Through his long career, Ponti continually promoted Italian crafts and artisanal traditions as a baseline for its modern design renaissance.

11. The Triennales began life in the 1920s in Monza but were transferred to Milan in 1933.

12. The magazine *Stile Industria* was founded in 1954 to promote the new products of Italian industry. Its stark photography presented designed artefacts as if they were works of art.

13. 'Form, Interiors, Objects', *Domus* 279 (1953), p. 3.

14. *Domus* 288 (1953), pp. 31–3.

15. *Domus* 327 (1957), pp. 20–2.

16. *Domus* 292 (1954), pp. 43–6.

17. *Domus* 306 (1955), p. 25.

18. *Domus* 330 (1957), pp. 5–13.

19. See R. Aloi, *L'Arredamento Moderno* (Hoepli, 1955), p. 327.

20. See I. Favata, *Joe Colombo and Italian Design of the Sixties* (Thames & Hudson, 1988).

21. See P. Ferrari, *Achille Castiglioni* (Electa, 1984).

22. Ambasz, *Italy*, p. 137.

23. Ibid.

24. Ibid.

25. Ibid., p. 139.

Chapter Twelve

Ship Shapes: Ocean liners, modern architecture and the resort hotels of Miami Beach

Alice T. Friedman

With the recovery of the US economy in the aftermath of the Second World War, the resort and tourism industries of Miami Beach, Florida, sought to develop a new identity in tune with the trends and spending habits of the burgeoning postwar consumer culture. The design of the new large-scale hotel complexes that emerged during the 1950s, a group of buildings most memorably represented by Morris Lapidus's well-known Fontainebleau Hotel of 1952–54 (see Fig. 12.1), can be analysed within the context of these economic and cultural developments, marking an important phase in an evolving tradition of local hotel design that began with a handful of modest art deco and streamlined moderne buildings in the 1930s and ultimately produced such South Beach monuments as the high-rise hotels of L. Murray Dixon's Raleigh, Caribbean and Grossinger Beach, Igor Polevitzky's Shelborne and Robert Swartburg's Delano of 1947.[1]

Thanks to a strong local economy and to the growing popularity of Miami Beach as a vacation destination, hotel architects had been extending their reach and increasing the scale and budgets of their buildings incrementally for three decades by the time that Lapidus—who had been trained in architecture at Columbia University in the 1920s, worked briefly in the New York office of Schultz and Weaver and embarked on a successful career as a commercial architect soon thereafter—began working in the area in the late 1940s. Their distinctive creations marched steadily northward along Collins Avenue, creating a wall of high-rise structures on the ocean front and a memorable urban skyline for the burgeoning city (see Fig. 12.2).[2] This movement picked up speed after the war as developers competed to acquire vacant lots and demolish existing real estate to create vast land parcels, mowing down the abandoned mansions of the super-rich jet-setters of the 1920s and replacing them with modern hotels. This was clearly the case with the Fontainebleau, whose enormous bulk loomed menacingly behind the existing Mediterranean Revival Firestone mansion throughout the entire period of construction, offering a vivid display of the inexorable process of change that was overtaking the area.

Fig. 12.1. Fontainebleau Hotel, Miami Beach, Gottscho and Schleisner Collection (Library of Congress).

Despite Miami Beach's history as a virtual laboratory for the design of up-to-date and commercially successful hotel architecture, nothing in the city's experience prepared contemporary observers for the enormity of the Fontainebleau or for the work that was to follow. The monumental scale of the buildings, their distinctive shapes and palatial isolation within extensive grounds were clearly unprecedented both in the local area and elsewhere.[3] Moreover, the range of services and amenities they provided under one roof was awe-inspiring, going well beyond the simple provision of guest rooms, parlours and dining areas to include expansive lobbies, dramatic staircases, card and game rooms, multiple restaurants and snack bars, ballrooms, shops, nightclubs, fancifully decorated cocktail bars, indoor and outdoor swimming pools, pool decks, tennis courts, beach cabanas, observation platforms, diving boards and landscaped gardens with Renaissance-style parterres decorated with multicoloured flowers.

Whilst the quality of Lapidus's design work has been a subject of heated debate among architectural critics ever since the hotels first opened (a debate which grew more

Fig.12.2. Miami Beach skyline (Historical Museum of South Florida).

heated in 1970 when a younger generation of postmodern architects sought to call attention to his architecture in an exhibition at the Architectural League in New York), there has never been any doubt about their popular success or of the signal role played by the architect in creating a clear and memorable brand identity for high-end tourism on Miami Beach.[4] As an architect and interior designer, Lapidus served as a highly effective merchandiser of this new, American vacation product, using techniques drawn from commercial architecture, graphic art and theatre design to create a cutting-edge approach to hotel design that not only appealed to a wide range of consumers but established the conventions of a building type and brand identity which would remain unchallenged for decades.

In 1952, when Lapidus began working on the Fontainebleau, he had completed only a handful of other buildings, all of them recent Miami Beach hotels designed in collaboration with more experienced architects. These included the Sans Souci Hotel of 1949 with Roy France, the Biltmore Terrace in 1951 with Albert Anis and the Algiers in 1952 with Henry Hohauser and Melvin Grossman.[5] Lapidus's previous experience was in the field of retail design and specifically in product display and store interiors; his work reveals considerable range and versatility, making use of an elegant, angular art deco manner at the Doubleday store in Detroit of 1932, and, in such examples as the Rainbow Shops in Brooklyn of 1942 and elsewhere, an ebulliently decorative neo-baroque approach in other projects. He was an expert merchandiser who appealed to the public through a combination of bold signage, dramatic lighting and imaginative—and sometimes profuse—ornament, highlighting people and objects through careful attention to sight lines, circulation and background setting. His success lay in his ability to capture the customer's attention quickly and decisively and to create a shopping experience that she would want to repeat.

In his postwar hotels, Lapidus cleverly seized on both the typology and the imagery of the great ocean liners, one of the era's most immediately recognizable and broadly appealing symbols, with its connotations of elegance, speed and excitement. Employing smooth white surfaces and sinuous curves on a monumental scale, and alternating these with large expanses of plate glass in the manner of Erich Mendelsohn's famous modern department stores in Germany, Lapidus updated the familiar art deco manner of Miami Beach, not through direct reference or quotation of recognizable nautical motifs, but by visual association and analogy. In this way he made it clear that his postwar hotels were new and modern and updated, but unmistakably connected to local traditions of popular entertainment and material luxury.

The bold image of the ocean liner, familiar to consumers from such sources as travel posters, movies, advertising and a wide range of fashionable products, represented not only the promise of glamorous travel and the spirit of discovery in faraway places, but also the most up-to-date engineering and technology: these huge ships provided travellers not only with access to exotic destinations, connecting the United States, Europe and South America, but they did so with impressive speed, competing with one another to cross the Atlantic in record time whilst offering elegance, entertainment and evident pleasure to passengers.[6] These events were covered by newspapers and magazines, which also published passenger lists of the most famous liners, replete with movie stars and famous personalities. Surprisingly flexible and multifaceted, the image of the ocean liner suggested at one and the same time both urban sophistication and an escape from the familiar—themes that Miami Beach's postwar developers wanted consumers to focus on.

Like hoteliers, the great steamship companies prided themselves on their new technology, offering guests access to telephones, elevators, radios, efficient plumbing, chilled water, heating and, of course, the latest in nautical engineering. They also offered an impressive array of interior furnishings and dramatic spaces, both public and private. Thus, Lapidus's hotel designs—which would soon come to include the Eden Roc (see Fig. 12.3) of

Fig. 12.3. Eden Roc Hotel, Miami Beach (collection of the author).

1955 and the Americana of 1956—made ample use of projecting balconies, rooftop terraces and huge swimming pools to allow guests to take advantage of the proximity to the ocean and of the warm tropical breezes whilst still maintaining a sense of protective isolation from their surroundings. High sea walls, stairs, circular driveways, shop fronts and deep setbacks served a similar function, creating a world within a world that enabled guests to leave postwar anxieties behind.

Then, as now, these hotels also offered guests a wide range of entertainment and sports activities within the confines of the resort property, from poolside eating and drinking to cabaret and musical theatre in the various hotel bars and cabarets, to massages and spa treatments on roof decks and pool terraces (experiences that were documented in a photographic spread by Henri Cartier-Bresson in *Life* magazine in January 1958), to golf and swimming, or shopping in the many small shops that dotted the hotel lobby and basement arcade. Indeed, as these enormous hotel complexes took shape at locations on the northern edge of the city (a development that further eroded the popularity of South Beach in the 1950s), there seemed to be less and less reason for tourists to venture 'ashore' to sample the wares of the city as a whole, a fact that was not lost on local restaurateurs nor on the scores of merchants whose upscale, Lincoln Road emporia suffered serious financial losses when moneyed tourists favoured the Lapidus-designed hotels and other resorts (such as the Deauville of 1957 by Melvin Grossman, who would go on to design Caesar's Palace, one of the first themed resort hotels in Las Vegas, in 1966, or the Carillon Hotel, 1957, by Norman Giller) located in North Beach.

During the 1950s, Lapidus became more and more adept at manipulating these nautical elements to create a series of distinctive and memorable images in his Miami Beach hotels. At the Eden Roc Hotel, for example, the massive silhouette of the building—its multiple projecting balconies sharply etched by dark shadows against smooth white walls—offered a romantic and evocative image, topped by a rounded tower that recalled the funnel smokestacks of a ship. Here the architect also used a wide variety of surface patterns, ornaments and colours, such as fish-scale screens across the windows, flanked by strips of variegated blue tiles that rise from the ground to the roof on the street front of the hotel, to create associations with the sea. Although such decorative devices were singled out for particular criticism by appalled modernists, they clearly fit the glamorous, travel-oriented ambience that Lapidus wanted to create in these buildings. Moreover, this imagistic and evocative mode of working and thinking,

which owes so much more to advertising and product design than it does to the internal theories or practices of modern architecture, served as Lapidus's starting point, reflecting his own experience as a designer of commercial spaces and product displays. As a merchandiser, he drew on a wide range of references to satisfy his clients, piling layer upon layer of images and associations to create visual experiences that consumers wouldn't forget. On both the large and small scale, in photographs and in real-time experience, his hotels thus became photogenic, recognizable and memorable.

Mainstream consumers encountered the distinctive image of the ocean liner and its message of modern luxury in a variety of media: by the postwar period, both image and message had even become something of a cliché, although they continued to be deployed in the travel industry with considerable success. One well-known mode of advertising, for example, popularised by the Cunard company, made use of comparisons with famous buildings and other well-known monuments to demonstrate the enormous size and power of the liners. Examples of such 'Cunard Comparisons' emphasised the scale and technological power of the new ships, using such graphically powerful and humorous juxtapositions as Christopher Columbus's three tiny sailing ships tucked inside the foyer and restaurant of the *Queen Mary* or the *Queen Mary* placed alongside the Eiffel Tower, the pyramid of Cheops, the Empire State Building and Cologne Cathedral. With such devices, these brochures made their case clearly and effectively; the formula was repeated in numerous variations from the turn of the century through to the end of the Second World War.

Given the popularity and success of such advertisements, it is perhaps not so surprising that one such image (see Fig. 12.4) provided the source material for Le Corbusier's famous illustration in *Vers une architecture* of 1924 comparing the SS *Acquitania,* one of the firm's flagship liners, to a handful of famous French monuments. Although his ultimate goal in reproducing this image was clearly very different from that of the original Cunard advertisers, it is nonetheless significant that Le Corbusier—like Lapidus and his clients some three decades later—was captivated by the idea of glamorous modernity that the sight of the ocean liner called to mind. As is well known, Le Corbusier used carefully chosen and edited photographs of nautical parapets, horizontal railings and ribbon windows receding into deep space, all culled from a variety of photographic and advertising sources, as well as selected views of spare interiors and machine parts to present a picture of clear, rational modern

The R.M.S. ''Aquitania'' in Paris. How her great length would compare with Notre Dame, Tour St. Jacques, Arc de Triomphe and the Opera House.

R.M.S. ''Aquitania'' at Lucerne.

Fig. 12.4. Plate from Cunard Comparisons (collection of the author).

design appropriate for the new world of the twentieth century.[7] Despite the fact that many popular images of ocean liners emphasised their decorative opulence and, in some cases, their rather retrograde notions of luxury, including potted palms, ornamental friezes, Rococo-revival staircases and furnishings and plush fabrics—such as might be found in the public rooms of the SS *Acquitania* itself (see Fig. 12.5)—Le Corbusier's distinctive visual manifesto drew on a cluster of powerful associations to inspire the popular imagination with a vivid image of modernity in the 1920s and 1930s.

Readers throughout the twentieth century—and, indeed, up until the time in the early 1960s that the ocean liner was effectively replaced by the jet airplane—no doubt recognised that both versions of the ocean-liner myth and its visual culture could coexist in a multivalent and many-layered symbol. Hollywood films in particular popularised images of the liners'

opulent public spaces, setting key scenes in grand ballrooms and on the steps of theatrical, multilevel staircases of the sort that one might find aboard the most elegant ships. Many film plots and scenarios took advantage of the theatrical vistas that permitted ocean-going travellers (and film goers) to observe the habits and fashions of their well-to-do neighbours at close range. Such was also the case with the grand hotels, shopping streets and boulevards of Paris and other elegant cities that became the focus of so much media and consumer attention in the period. By the 1950s, the glamour and theatricality of a carefully choreographed descent down a staircase had become such a popular cliché that it was used again and again in advertising, fashion and film. Whether we turn to fashion shots in the pages of popular magazines like *Life* or *Vogue* or to movies such as Billy Wilder's *Sunset Boulevard* (1950), in which the mad and aging silent-film star Norma Desmond slowly descends the staircase of her overdecorated mansion in a parodic display of movie-star glamour, we find the ingredients repeated again and again. Moreover, although the particular style of interior design and fashion sensibility were no doubt of importance to some observers, one suspects that, for many media-savvy viewers, it mattered far less whether the action took place aboard ship, in a grand mansion or in a luxurious hotel; the image and the experience of moving through space, enhanced by the scenographic treatment of the surroundings, were more important than the style of design.

Lapidus first experimented with these forms in a series of designs for remodelling

Fig. 12.5. The Palladian Lounge, SS *Aquitania* (1914).

a former troop ship for use as a cruise liner, published in the pages of *Interiors* magazine in December 1945.[8] Though unbuilt, his project—perhaps surprisingly in a far more modernist vein than we find in his more famous postwar hotels—clearly suggests the debt that Lapidus's later hotel work had to nautical architecture and interiors. Open staircases, wide vistas and large expanses of glass make their first appearance here. Moreover, it is notable that Lapidus convincingly deploys the popular streamlined moderne style that is characteristic of his earlier retail work. For him, modern architecture was just one among many evocative modes from which to choose. The critical question was how to attract the attention of consumers.

Thus, at Lapidus's resort hotels one often finds sleek, modern exteriors paired with highly decorated, expressionist interiors, seemingly drawn from an entirely different pattern book and design philosophy. With no particular theory to defend or modernist vision to uphold, Lapidus seems not in the least troubled by a lack of consistency or homogeneity in his work. On the contrary, he went out of his way to touch on every one of the many associations, fantasies and expectations that consumers might bring to the experience. The sleek street façade of the Fontainebleau recalled the bold form and the modern technology of an ocean liner, whilst the interior was a riot of period details jumbled together to create backdrops for photo-ready vignettes. Each offered a different scenario, enabling guests to take part in elaborate and playful fantasies. Lapidus was explicit about his design strategy:

My early training in drama and my experience in store and restaurant design gave me an inkling about what people thought and felt as they came into a room. People love to feel as if they are onstage when travelling or stopping at an elegant hotel ... In the Fontainebleau, I actually have the guests go up three steps to arrive at the platform, walk out on the platform, and then go down three steps ... everyone loves a dramatic entrance.[9]

Platforms, decks, mezzanines, dramatic staircases and multilevel lobbies made it possible to take in the view and to promenade in the resort wear that marketers of postwar fashion loved to show in their ads. Moreover, the Fontainebleau offered an array of amenities comparable to those on any ocean liner, including shops and boutiques that enabled vacationers to avoid the city altogether—indeed, these would contribute to the ultimate decline of once-popular shopping districts like Lincoln Road.

The Eden Roc was very similar in spirit. The façade on the ocean front is modern and boldly nautical, whilst the interior was, according to Lapidus, based on Renaissance models—although a Raphael or a Michelangelo would be hard pressed to see how the fluted columns capped with circles of light, or the giant fleur-de-lis on the floor, or the movie star staircase descending to the lobby—complete with fashionable conversation pit—fit that designation. Nor could one say with any certainty how the space-age 'Bacchus Lounge' in the basement, with its rusticated silver walls, lattice windows and classicizing relief panels was exactly consistent with that theme. Then again, for a generation used to flipping through magazines, watching movies and, by the mid 1950s, to channel surfing on television (albeit without a remote) such disjunctions were not especially problematic. Lapidus explained this in a well-known statement:

> I was convinced that just as a store had to be designed to make people want to buy what the merchant had to sell, so a hotel had something to sell also. What was that something? A home away from home? Absolutely not! Who wants a homey feeling on a vacation? The guests want to find a new experience—forget the office, the house, the kids, the bills. Anything that good old homey feeling that the old hotels used to see with a comfortable bed, a nice rocker on the veranda, a good solid nourishing meal. Not on your life! We were coming out of the war and the postwar period. People wanted fun, excitement, and all of it against a background that was colorful, unexpected; in short, the visual excitement that made people want to buy—in this case, to buy the tropic luxury of a wonderful vacation of fun in the sun. A sense of freedom from the humdrum lives the guests had—a feeling of getting away from it all.[10]

Lapidus's most significant design models clearly came not from architecture but from the worlds of merchandising and entertainment architecture: his hotels, restaurants and lobbies often recall the distinctive style of Dorothy Draper, whose use of historicist cartouches and overscaled ornament in her interiors of the 1940s combined touches of Old World opulence with modernist and surrealist imagery.[11] At the Americana Hotel of 1956 (now sadly lost to a new generation's hunger for new resort development), for example, the monumental staircase in the lobby surrounded a giant two-story terrarium containing a display of tropical plants and two live alligators. Lapidus had used animal and bird displays in his hotel work before (at the Algiers, there was an enormous cage filled with parrots at one end of the lobby), but here it seems to represent exactly the sort of overscaled and artificial décor that gave such works their bad reputation among so many critics and consumers. Like the colonialist theme of the Americana itself—the murals on the walls were meant to represent heroes of the Americas from the perspective of the United States—the conflation of type forms in one building that was part hotel, part natural history museum and part zoo would come to be ridiculed by a younger generation uninterested in postwar fantasies of silver-screen glamour and in the sort of competitive consumerism that played itself out in the display of evening gowns, jewels and furs in hotel lobbies and nightclubs.

Nevertheless, whilst many critics and consumers would view Lapidus's work as synonymous with the self-delusion and American isolationism that accompanied the rise of postwar consumer culture, for a certain group of wealthy American vacationers in the 1950s and early 1960s, these hotels were the ultimate tourist destination, precisely because they offered entertainment, imagination and convenience in a way that made it possible to leave the Cold War world behind, to dip into memories of an imagined past and to have the feeling that you could look into the technological future. Like Disney's theme parks, they combined travel, experience, theatre and modern technology to create fantasy worlds of experience that were distinctively American.

It was all great fun, parading around in fancy clothes, sunbathing on the pool deck or playing cards with friends on stage sets that were not only very different from anything one had previously encountered but were also strangely and reassuringly familiar from films, movie palaces and department stores. Wasn't such leisure and the freedom to enjoy people and things exactly what modernity had promised? Wasn't America a place where people could reinvent themselves—as many times as necessary? Let Le Corbusier make his modern world over in the stark image of an ocean liner's upper deck—for Lapidus and his clients, that journey into the future was nothing if it did not include the pleasures of the ocean liner's opulent lobbies, the grand staircases, elegant dining rooms, glamorous staterooms and the well-stocked boutiques that tourists had long imagined and dreamed of experiencing firsthand.

Notes

1. For the history of Miami Beach, see D. Dash Moore, *To the Golden Cities: Pursuing the American Dream in Miami and Los Angeles* (Harvard University Press, 1994), pp. 25–6; and A. Ambruster, *The Life and Times of Miami Beach* (Knopf, 1995), pp. 105–6. The best history of hotel architecture in Miami Beach is J. F. Lejeune and A. T. Shulman, eds., *The Making of Miami Beach: The Architecture of Lawrence Murray Dixon* (Rizzoli, 2000).

2. For a detailed overview of Lapidus's career, see his autobiographical writings, *An Architecture of Joy* (E. A. Seemann, 1979) and *Too Much Is Never Enough: An Autobiography* (Rizzoli, 1996).

3. For the history of hotels and their architecture, see M. Berger, ed., 'The American Hotel', *Journal of Decorative and Propaganda Arts* (Wolfsonian-Florida International University) 25 (2005), especially A. T. Friedman, 'Merchandising Miami Beach: Morris Lapidus and the Architecture of Abundance', pp. 216–53. See also A. K. Sandoval-Strausz, *Hotel: An American History* (Yale University Press, 2007); E. Denby, *Grand Hotels: An Architectural and Social History* (Reaktion Books, 1998); J. Limerick, N. Fergusson and R. Oliver, *America's Grand Resort Hotels* (Pantheon Books, 1979).

4. The controversy at the Architectural League is discussed in Lapidus, *Architecture,* p. 211.

5. For analysis of Lapidus's architecture and a catalogue raisonée, see M. Düttmann and F. Schneider, eds., *Morris Lapidus: Architect of the American Dream* (Birkhäuser, 1992). The work is also discussed at length in A. T. Friedman, 'The Luxury of Lapidus: Glamour, Class and Architecture in Miami Beach', *Harvard Design Magazine* 11 (Summer 2000), pp. 39–47.

6. For the ocean liner's history and design typology, see A. Weallans, *Designing Liners: A History of Interior Design Afloat* (Routledge, 2006).

7. See B. Colomina, *Privacy and Publicity: Modern Architecture as Mass Media* (MIT Press, 1994).

8. M. Lapidus, "Public Rooms for Tomorrow's Ships," *Interiors* 105 (December 1945), pp. 60–65.

9. Lapidus, *Architecture,* p. 164.

10. Lapidus, *Architecture,* p. 129.

11. Thanks to a recent exhibition at the Museum of the City of New York, there has been a revival of interest in Draper. See C. Varney, *In the Pink: Dorothy Draper, America's Most Fabulous Decorator* (Pointed Leaf Press, 2006); and D. Albrecht, *The High Style of Dorothy Draper* (Pointed Leaf Press, 2006).

Chapter Thirteen

Nationalism and Design at the End of Empire: Interior design and the ocean liner

Anne Massey

The process by which the design of the interiors of the *QE2* progressed from 1963 until its launch in 1969 illustrates a move which can be characterised as 'From Chintz to Formica'—a shift in the way that British identity was represented by its national flagship. At the time of the launch, the British design press were dismissive of preceding liner interior design and looked to the *QE2* for a long-awaited confirmation of modern movement design principles in Britain. As the *Architectural Review* editorial commented in the introduction to its special issue on the *QE2* in 1969:

> In 1914 a serious critic would have dismissed derisively the mock interiors of the 'Aquitania'. A generation later he would have found a change of attitude towards style, but little to recommend, in the design of the 'Queen Mary'. Yet both these ships became in many ways the embodiment of their respective age—an embodiment glamorised by the ephemeral nature of ships. Whether the QE2 will be to the 1970s what the 'Aquitania' was to the 1920s will largely depend on factors outside the control of those responsible for her design. The

> design quality of the QE2 will continue to bear fruit long after the tribulations that accompanied her first sea trials have been forgotten.'[1]

An analysis of the interior design of the *QE2* reveals the ephemeral and multifaceted nature of modernism itself as an interior design style. The *QE2* was a 'Swinging Ship', which used modern design to represent a new Britain. As *Design* magazine commented in 1969: 'the QE2 is a floating Swinging London, a Hilton à la Kings's Road offering five extra days in London before you even get there.'[2] At the dawn of the age of postmodernity, it is striking how much official involvement there was in the design of the *QE2*. No longer regarded as the preserve of the chairman's wife and society decorator, interior design had grown in significance as a means of representing the modern nation state at the end of Empire.

Ocean liner design as a vehicle for modernity and modernism

It would be difficult to imagine a more fitting symbol of modernity than the ocean liner.

From the earliest days of the *Great Britain* and the *Great Eastern,* crowds clamoured to view the mammoth achievements of the Industrial Revolution with the application of steam power replacing sail and iron replacing wood. Such technological innovations enabled comparatively reliable mass travel around the globe to serve the needs of burgeoning empires and a booming emigration trade from Europe to North America and Australia in particular. The popular press during the nineteenth century was full of admiration for this new technology, usually coupled with a fawning description of the interiors, which privileged luxury and grandeur and neglected the dreadful conditions of the majority who travelled in steerage class and the crew. The sheer scale and speed of these new types of vehicle made an impact and added to and reinforced the discourse of modernity in the popular press.

When this development is considered against the backdrop of the growth of reforming modernism, ocean liners are often used as evocative symbols of sleek functionalism, for example in the work of Le Corbusier.[3] This lead was followed by some ship line owners; for example Sir Colin Anderson of the Orient Line employed Brian O'Rorke to produce modern interiors for ships destined for Australia. Anderson used the fashionable features of modernist design to promote the company, most notably in his lecture at the Royal Society of Arts in 1966, published in the *Journal of the Royal Society of Arts* in May of that year, just after the new design team for the *QE2* had been announced. Anderson compared the interiors of the *Orion* (1935) with that of

the *Viceroy of India* (1929) to illuminate the progressiveness of his firm:

> *She has now run her appointed course and has been duly broken up, so she can no longer stand as a witness to the truth of my contention, when the whole project was being argued about before her building ever started, that if she was ahead of the taste of her time when she came into service she would end up her span still well abreast of fashion. But this was exactly what happened.*[4]

This was a discourse around modernism and British ship interior design which was to reverberate from the mid 1960s onwards. When *Architectural Review* devoted a special issue to the *QE2* in 1969, the *Orion* was singled out as putting into practice the design philosophy of the modern movement 'as long ago as 1935'.[5]

However, for most ship lines, the style of the *Orion,* whilst feted in the design press, did not have universal appeal. For example, when Cunard was looking for a designer for the *Queen Elizabeth* in 1936, the Chairman visited the *Orion* but found:

> *The ship is essentially designed and decorated as a hot weather ship and everything had been subordinated to giving an effect of coolness. The decoration has been reduced almost to a minimum and is mostly carried out in veneered plywood ... The general style is I think, too plain for an Express Atlantic steamer and would be considered mean by many of our passengers ... The furniture in the ship looks cheaper and simpler than ours.*[6]

In the following month, Grey Wornum, architect of the Royal Institute of British Architects headquarters in London, was selected to design the *Queen Elizabeth,* after pressure from Neville Chamberlain, the Chancellor of the Exchequer, to appoint a British architect following the use of American Benjamin Morris for the *Queen Mary.* This was in a style which oozed tradition, quality and 'conservative' modernism. And when Cunard began developing the next major liner, initially called the *Q4,* in 1963, the interior design was, at first, to follow in the steps of past Cunard traditions.

Phase 1: Chintz

An informal design advisory board was created to consider the interiors of the new luxury liner, which was to become the *QE2.* This consisted of the wife of the chairman of Cunard, Lady Brocklebank; the Vice-Chairman and Dan Wallace, the naval architect, with advice from Jean Monro.

Jean Monro was a professional interior decorator who followed in her mother's footsteps and designed interiors using decorative fabrics, most notably chintz, and drew from period styles. She had begun her ship work in the late 1950s for the Union Castle line, and most notable of her interiors were the designs for the *Windsor Castle.* During the early 1960s, she was working for Cunard on the refits of the *Carmania* and *Franconia* in her trademark style. Hence, she was invited to advise Cunard on the latest ship. For two years the group toured hotels in Europe and the United States, travelling by liners already in service and studying those

under construction. During the early 1960s, the leading examples, apart from *Carmania* and *Franconia,* were P & O's *Canberra,* in service from 1961 with design coordination by Hugh Casson, and the Orient Line's *Oriana* of 1960, coordinated by Brian O'Rorke and Misha Black. Other examples, which may have presented more competition, included the French *France* of 1962, the American *United States,* the Dutch *Rotterdam* and Italian *Leonardo da Vinci.* So it is clear that the western world was investing heavily in ocean transport as flagships for the nation. Each of the lines accentuated the national identity of the home country.

In Britain, there were concerns about the self-appointed design committee not exploiting appropriate British design. After questions were asked in Parliament, Cunard was forced to defend its position by the new Labour government, voted in a year before and perhaps anxious to refresh the national identity of Britain, exemplified by Harold Wilson's 'White Hot Heat of Technological Revolution' and the insecurity of rapid decolonisation.[7] In February 1965, Cunard met reluctantly with the Council of Industrial Design to view the portfolios of eight selected and approved designers. Lady Brocklebank was reserved in her comments after the meeting: 'There was no intention that they should not be consulted. We are in full agreement with the Council that this ship should reflect what is best in British design, but it will be some months before we reach finality and appoint the design team, including those responsible for co-ordination.'[8] However, Cunard needed to acquiesce to official pressure, because the completion of the *QE2* was reliant on a loan of £17,600,000 from the government. When questions were asked in Parliament about the design of the ship, Roy Mason, Minister of State at the Board of Trade, replied:

> Cunard know the importance I attach to standards of industrial design in a ship of this kind and are taking full advantage of the wide range of new fittings and equipment now available in Britain. But under the terms of the loan we have no power to insist on any particular interior design or the appointment of any particular designer.[9]

In October 1965, the full list of designers appointed was announced by Cunard. This included Jean Monro and her friend, decorator Evelyn Pinching; the society interior designers David Hicks and Michael Inchbald; veterans of the Festival of Britain and probably recommendations of the Council of Industrial Design, Dennis Lennon and James Gardner plus exhibition and yacht designer Jon Bannenberg and industrial designer Gaby Schreiber, who had designed the interiors of British Overseas Airways Corporation aircraft. The team was criticised in the British press for being a heterogeneous group which would lack a unified vision. However, Lady Brocklebank defended the choice, stating: 'It is an exciting project and we have got the best people for the job.'[10] Lady Brocklebank attempted to provide design leadership for the QE2, despite media hostility.

However, the situation rapidly changed, and only one month later, Lord Brocklebank was forced to retire due to ill health and so his wife could no longer be involved with the project. As his successor, Sir Basil Smallpeice

commented: 'Not surprisingly, in view of Liverpool's dearth of management experience in the field, Lady Brocklebank had taken upon herself the responsibility for these matters. Although the chairman's wife, she had no official position in the company, and it was an untenable arrangement.'[11] Smallpeice came from an accountancy background and led a significant change of direction for Cunard, which was much more commercially driven. At a meeting at the shipbuilder's, John Brown & Company, in December 1965, Smallpeice:

> reviewed the recent happenings in the Cunard Company and outlined their new selling policy whereby emphasis would be on the hotel rather than on the transport function. He stated that it was vital to Cunard that the delivery date for no. 736 be achieved if Cunard's recovery programme were to be successful. Sir Basil stated that as a result of a current survey it might prove advantageous to alter the number of classes of accommodation or the type of accommodation, but any changes would be superficial.[12]

The survey Smallpeice referred to was by the Economist Intelligence Unit, conducted mainly in the United States, where the majority of passengers would hopefully originate. Passengers indicated in the survey that they would be more comfortable with no class divisions on board, as opposed to the three which Cunard had been designing for since the birth of the company in 1840. This presented some major problems for the shipbuilders, John Brown, who had signed the contract to build the new Cunard in the old format in 1964.

An extension of three months was granted by Cunard, and work began on converting a three-class ship into a two-class ship, with the option for integration between the two remaining classes into one. Smallpeice had discussions with the chairman of the Council of Industrial Design, Sir Duncan Oppenheim, late in 1965 and, in early January 1966, announced that 'Q4 will get the professional touch'[13] with James Gardner already appointed to style the exterior of the ship and Dennis Lennon to coordinate the total design of the interior.

Phase 2: Formica

The conversion was a challenge, given the revision of the class segregation on board, whereby public rooms such as the dining room or library no longer had to appear in triplicate. The new approach meant that the tourist class and cabin class could be merged, giving the opportunity, for example, for the Double Room—a merging of the cabin class and tourist-class lounges, previously arranged on two separate decks, one above the other, to be a double-story room with a wide sweeping staircase. Further changes in the design team also took place and were announced in February 1966. Theo Crosby and Stephan Buzas joined the existing team of eight, and Hugh Casson, then professor of interior design at the Royal College of Art, was appointed, with some students to design the teenage and children's rooms, as they had done successfully on P & O's *Canberra*.

This may look like jobs for the boys, and it is striking how the majority of women

involved at various times with the interior design of the *QE2* were associated with the amateur and with the domestic. For example, John Barry in the *Sunday Times* reviewed the conflict on 28 February 1965, just after Cunard had visited the Council of Industrial Design, with the headline: 'Design Men Fear the Q4 Will Be Too Olde Worlde.'[14] Women's involvement with the interior design of the *QE2,* which began as high profile, resulted in Jean Monro's resignation from the project in May 1966, possibly because she had been relegated from interior design consultant to designer of cabins with no responsibility for the public rooms. Similarly, Evelyn Pinching was charged by the new design coordinators to design the crew accommodation and the lower-class swimming pool, the hierarchy of gender reflecting the hierarchy which still characterised the ship's interior layout. She was replaced by Jo Pattrick. In April 1967, when work was well underway on the interiors, the *QE2* was featured in the new *Weekend Telegraph Colour Magazine.* The new model of the ship is featured, surrounded by members of the Cunard Board. This features Lady Tweedsmuir: 'Cunard's first woman director who is advising on the practical aspects of the Q4 from the passenger viewpoint'.[15]

The magazine also featured the new design team, including Dennis Lennon, now responsible for the design of all passageways and cabins and connecting staircases, to give the overall interior unity. Jon Bannenberg was assigned to the public lounge, room suites and entertainment facilities; David Hicks the night club that converts to a lounge by day and Michael Inchbald the main lounge and library. The design process was tightly controlled, and an internal memo by Cunard's managing director, Philip Bates, of May 1966 clearly set out the working arrangements whereby all decisions regarding the interior design were reported to the Chairman, Deputy Chairman and Managing Director of Cunard. As design coordinators, Gardner and Lennon were responsible to Cunard for 'the visual character and design treatment' and for keeping the naval architect, technical director and new project director fully informed of progress. The approved plans were then sent to John Brown, if they had problems, then they contacted the naval architect at Cunard. Meetings took place in London with James Gardner and Dennis Lennon and the naval architect to iron out problems. The design process was a torturous one; the archives of the shipbuilder, John Brown in Glasgow, reveal frustration at the seemingly ever-changing interior designs. For example in December 1966, John Brown wrote to Cunard about changes to the first-class lido lounge/nightclub and casino: 'Reduction of the width of the doors to stairway about frame 68 is noted and we are proceeding accordingly in respect of the sliding panel fire door but it should be borne in mind that according to our present information 305 persons have to escape through the doorway which appears to be 6' 3" wide.'[16] However, it should be borne in mind that the design team had been introduced to the project at least three years after its inception, when the major structural decisions had been made.

Despite this obvious clash of cultures, the interior design of the QE2 was a harmonised, British brand of modernism with acknowledgement of the pop palette and novel materials of Swinging London. One uniting feature was the use of Formica for most passageways and some cabin-class rooms. Formica won the exclusive contract to supply all laminates, as the company had recently developed a new, textured finished to line walls and ceilings that resembled fabric or parchment rather than the usual smooth laminate. Of the two million square feet on the ship, over half was covered in Formica in different surface patterns—for example light blue paisley for the tourist bathrooms and brown stripes for the first-class bathrooms. Wood panelling was reserved for use in the first-class areas.

Cunard was keen to publicise the ship, and, as part of this promotion of the QE2 as modern, there was an exhibition at the Council of Industrial Design's Headquarters in Haymarket entitled *QE2—A First Look Inside the New Cunarder* from 21 February until 23 March 1968. Princess Margaret opened the exhibition and enthused:

> this new Cunarder will show that design in Britain is not only exciting and full of vigorous common sense but is always out in front, leading the field. A great ship like Queen Elizabeth 2, *must inevitably be looked upon as a sort of flag-ship for the nation. It just might have turned out to be a 'grandmotherly, chintzy hotel.'*[17]

The media reception of the designs was positive and much in accordance with Princess Margaret's remarks. The *Daily Telegraph* commented: 'There's nothing of the old lady about the new *Queen Elizabeth 2*. She is smart, crisp and modern, using new colours and fabrics and materials.' And the *Times,* so critical of the earlier design approach, was entirely positive: 'The impression is of good 1960s hotel design compared with good 1930s design of the old Queens. Moulded wood, wrought metal, folkweave, and damask are out; plastic, tweed, leather are in; green, brown, and gold are out; oatmeal, sun yellow, dark blue, and magnolia are in.'[18]

The *QE2* first sailed to New York, and *Life* magazine reported: 'Far better than most modern resorts, the QE2 encapsulates its customer in a comfortable world of chrome, veneer, mirror, inset brass and stainless steel.'[19] The first public space that the passengers encountered was the circular 'Midships Lobby' by Dennis Lennon (see Fig. 13.1). Traditionally, this had been a grandiose space, with sweeping staircases and carved wood panelling. On the *QE2,* it was chrome contrasted with navy hide-covered walls and apple green hide-covered seating, surrounding a trumpet-shaped, white column which spanned out to meet the silver-painted, segmented ceiling, illuminated by spotlights. The carpet was ink blue.

The public staircases were in similar modern style. As *Design* magazine commented: 'The public stairs on the QE2 are a far cry from the extravagant sweeping steps and elaborate rococo balustrades once beloved of Hollywood musicals and ocean liners. Pure function has replaced those flights of fancy;

Fig. 13.1. Dennis Lennon, Midships Lobby, *QE2*, Cunard, 1969 (collection of the author).

instead of carved curlicues and ormolu nymphs, two parallel bands of coloured reinforced plastic hurtle down the stairwells in a square spiral.'[20] But wasn't this one fantasy replacing another? The construction of Britain at the forefront of technological innovation, the young, modern leader of a commonwealth, rather than the musty patriarch of an empire. It wasn't Hollywood, but it was James Bond and Pinewood Studios. The four sets of stairs connecting the main public areas came in four colours typical of the pop era—red, ochre, blue and white—which were echoed in the colour schemes for the interiors of the lifts. The 'Double Room' by Jon Bannenberg, so called

because it provided a double-height room between the upper and boat decks, featured smoked brown glass which was used to frame the dance floor and add contrast to the balustrades and aluminium planked ceiling (see Fig. 13.2). *Design* magazine was critical of the apparently jarring colour scheme and materials, but admitted: 'the saving feature of the room is undoubtedly its carpet, a lush herringbone of puce and damson, specially woven by Kosset.'[21]

One of the 'most spectacular of the public interiors' to be selected by *Architectural Review* in its special issue in 1969 was the first-class lounge, or 'Queen's Room', by Michael Inchbald. This was basically

Fig. 13.2. John Bannenberg, Double Room, *QE2*, Cunard, 1969 (collection of the author).

square in layout, with white fibreglass tulip-shaped columns which merge into the white fibreglass ceiling. White fibreglass troughs for plants were used to frame the sunken dance floor. The end wall was decorated in fibreglass blocks, veneered in walnut with mirror between. The chairs were designed by Inchbald but drew heavily on Saarinen pedestal prototypes. Upholstered in beige leather, the chairs harmonised with the coffee tables in polished aluminium topped with walnut—the trumpet shape of the columns was again echoed.

The 'Lookout' by Theo Crosby, at the bow of the ship, used dark colours with cedar-veneered walls and olive-green carpet. Visual relief was provided by the pop art red chart reader matched by a vermillion piano on the opposite side. The 'Britannia Restaurant'—by Dennis Lennon and featuring a red, blue and white colour scheme—sat eight hundred, and the more select 'Columbia Restaurant' by Dennis Lennon sat five hundred first-class passengers.

Cunard successfully used modern design to express a new national identity and

Fig. 13.3. The *QE2* at Gibraltar, 2005. *Source:* Bruce Wealleans.

moved away from country-house chintz and embraced the modern, more commercial world of Formica. But this was not everlasting, reforming modernism; it was fashionable modernism which did not stand the test of time. The *QE2* has retired to Dubai as a hotel, much in the same spirit as the *Queen Mary* at Long Beach, California (see Fig. 13.3). The Formica has now been stripped out to make way for more traditional wood panelling, perhaps indicating that it is modernism which hasn't stood the test of time or the style no longer expresses British national identity. Or perhaps, in the age of globalisation and postmodernity, the apogee of national identity has passed with the demise of imperialism.

Notes

1. *Architectural Review* 145/868 (1969), pp. 397–8.

2. *Design* (April 1969), p. 37.

3. See A. Wealleans, *Designing Liners: A History of Interior Design Afloat* (Routledge, 2006), p. 3 for a discussion of Le Corbusier's use of ocean liner imagery.

4. C. Anderson, 'The Interior Design of Passenger Ships', *Journal of the Royal Society of Arts* (May 1966), p. 484.

5. *Architectural Review,* p. 397.

6. Unpublished manuscript, Percy Bates in Memo to Chairman, Lord Brockelbank, 14 September 1936, University of Liverpool Cunard Steam-Ship Company Archives.

7. *Sunday Times,* 28 February 1965, p. 4.

8. 'Between 1945 and 1965 the number of people under British colonial rule shrank from seven hundred million to five million. Within a generation some twenty-six countries, comprising the vast bulk of the British Empire became independent. A number of factors ... helped to precipitate this collapse: loss of prestige in Asia accompanied by post-war military weakness, emergent nationalism in the colonies, global opposition to imperialism and its retreat on nearly all fronts, fiascos such as Suez and scandals such as Hola, Britain's recurrent economic crises and its move towards Europe, the democratic preference for welfare at home rather than ascendancy abroad.' P. Brendon, *The Decline and Fall of the British Empire, 1781–1997* (Jonathan Cape, 2007), p. 599.

9. *Sunday Times,* 28 February 1965, p. 5.

10. As quoted in N. Potter and J. Frost, *QE2: Queen Elizabeth 2, The Authorised Story* (Harrap, 1969), p. 126.

11. Ibid.

12. B. Smallpeice, *Of Comets and Queens: An Autobiography* (Airlife, 1980), p. 197.

13. Unpublished manuscript, UCS1/107/433 Ship No 736 Minutes of Cunard Meetings: Diary Note of Meeting 17 December 1966, Glasgow University John Brown Archive.

14. *Sunday Times,* 2 January 1966, p. 6.

15. *Sunday Times,* 28 February 1965, p. 4.

16. *Weekend Telegraph Colour Magazine,* April 1967.

17. Unpublished manuscript, UCS1/16/32 John Brown Letter Books No 736, Letter from Technical Director, John Brown's to D. N. Wallace dated 1 December 1966, Glasgow University.

18. Potter and Frost, *QE2,* pp. 130–1.

19. Ibid.

20. *Life* (1969), p. 46. University of Brighton Design Archives.

21. 'Queen Elizabeth 2', *Design* (April 1969), p. 51.

22. Ibid., p. 244.

Part Four

The Late Twentieth-century Interior (1970–present)

Part 4 The modern interior IKEA style. Photograph courtesy of Inter IKEA Systems B.V. 2008.

Introduction

Trevor Keeble

The final decades of the twentieth century witnessed a flourishing of the designed interior caused by a number of shifts in the areas of professional design and architectural thinking; enhanced academic interest and critical enquiry; and, perhaps most significantly of all, the rise of a tenacious and increasingly global consumer economy.

The early years of the 1970s saw the consolidation of the sustained critique of modernism which had been articulated first in Robert Venturi's 1966 book *Complexity and Contradiction in Architecture.*[1] Venturi's rejection of the modernist dictum of 'less is more' in favour of a postmodern response that 'less is a bore' might be read today as a clarion call to all those interior designers whose work had been sublimated to little more than an 'interior' expression of a modernist architecture. Through an emphasis upon the ephemeral rather than the enduring aspects of the built environment, and the communicative possibilities rather than the functional determinants of architectural space, the emergent *Language of Post-Modern Architecture,* as Charles Jencks would later style it, offered terms of reference in which the interior might be valued and expressed in more meaningful ways.[2] Whilst many buildings that would come to exemplify this new mode of thinking would in fact add up

to little more than dressed-up versions of their older modernist siblings, the reconsideration and design of interior spaces in relation to both their architecture and one another was integral to this debate.

Although postmodern thinking developed outside the areas of architecture, design and the built environment, its embrace of, and engagement with, popular culture enabled the interior to find a new expression. It is no coincidence that the paintings and sculptures of the Pop artists Andy Warhol, Richard Hamilton and Claes Oldenburg were often inspired by domestic spaces and objects. The attempt to move away from the reified discussions of the modernist era allowed for a critical examination of 'other' things. Nowhere was this more evident or influential than in the work of Peter Reyner Banham.[3] A former research student of Nikolaus Pevsner, Reyner Banham's investigation of the often seemingly banal, 'undesigned' aspects of life facilitated a broader understanding of what constituted design. This was extremely important in allowing a reevaluation of interior designs, spaces and objects. Working as an academic, writer and journalist in the United Kingdom and the United States during the 1970s, Reyner Banham was instrumental in the formation of design history as an academic field in its own right, and he became the first patron of the Design History Society in 1977.

The 1970s and 1980s also witnessed the development of a range of new modes of critical academic enquiry. The emergence of a largely Marxist social history, and political and academic feminism, meant scholars were turning their attention quite literally to areas of our lives that had previously been overlooked. The effect of this was to validate new questions and subjects for academic attention, the interior among them. Indeed, the combination of postmodern critical discourses, and the fragmenting and pluralising of academic interest, led to the formation of new fields and disciplines for which the interior—and, perhaps most importantly, the domestic interior—would be an important subject. Design history, the discipline from which many of the contributions to this volume have emerged, sat alongside cultural and media studies, gender studies, and visual and material culture. In its early years, it paid only passing attention to the significance of interior design. Due undoubtedly to its often complex and collective 'authorship', its domestic or commercial contexts and its transient and evolutionary nature, interior design resisted the attention of design historians for a number of years, focused as their attention was on working within a canon of 'named' designers and the products of the industrial world. It was not really until the fundamental shifts of the second half of the 1980s, when the academic arts and humanities began to place greater emphasis upon the roles and contexts of consumption rather than production, that design history began to widen its remit. The development

of material culture studies was central to that shift and has provided a significant number of studies of social practices within the domestic interior in recent years. Although, as Alison Clarke has noted in her contribution to this volume, style and aesthetics have been thoroughly neglected as aspects of this broader investigation into social practice.[4]

That shift in academic focus and the move towards a more interdisciplinary understanding of enquiry shed light upon a number of hitherto marginalised design objects of study such as fashion and dress, interior design and craft practices, each of which had, in its own way, previously fallen foul of the dominant dogma of modernism. An ongoing concern with issues relating to gender has informed the critical position of each of these areas. The disciplinary maturing of its treatment and understanding of gender, heavily influenced by concurrent developments within the fields of dress history and fashion theory, has opened up for design history the critical and historical space of the designed interior in a way never possible before. This has taken place across other disciplines too. The interdisciplinary consideration of gender has revealed somewhat incidentally, for example, a history of Victorian retail interiors, the pubs and café spaces frequented by the 'Dilly boys' of *Queer London* and the boutiques and salons of London's Kings Road.[5] This 'spatialisation' of history—that is the locating of historical subjects within the spaces and contexts in which they existed—has been emphatically consolidated since the early 1990s, when the increasingly dominant discourses of cultural and historical geography began to seek new objects of study.

Despite the methodological developments that occurred in the late twentieth century, most academic attention has been focused on earlier periods. Relatively little academic consideration has been given to interiors and spaces designed and experienced during the post-1970 period. Notable exceptions include a number of broader surveys, already mentioned in this volume, such as Anne Massey's *Interior Design since 1900,* Penny Sparke's *An Introduction to Design and Culture: 1900 to the Present,* Stanley Abercrombie's, *A Century of Interior Design, 1900–2000* and Jonathan Woodham's *Twentieth-Century Design*[6]; thematic surveys including Lesley Jackson's *Twentieth-century Pattern Design: Textile & Wallpaper Pioneers* and Gareth Williams's *The Furniture Machine: Furniture since 1900*[7]; topographic surveys including Pilar Viladas's *California Beach Houses,* Beth Dunlop's *Miami: Trends and Traditions* and Herbert Ypma's, *London Minimum*[8]; and monographs of designers such as Deyan Sudjic's *John Pawson Works,* Práce Evy Jiřičné's *In/exterior: The Works of Eva Jiricna,* Catherine McDermott's (ed.) *Plans and Elevations/Ben Kelly Designs,* and Deyan Sudjic's, *Equipment Stores: Architect John Chipperfield* and *For Inspiration Only/ Future Systems.*[9]

Modernism continued to inform interior design in a number of ways, however, not least, perhaps, in the rather ascetic and strictly rationalised ambience of minimalist design. With their overtones of a pared-down Japanese aesthetic, minimalist interiors of the 1980s and 1990s offered a highly publicised oasis of calm in both domestic and retail spaces that seemed to continue the modernist tradition of imposing order and regulation upon their inhabitants. Perhaps more persuasively, a neofunctionalist and technological form of design and architecture developed throughout the period which, it might be argued, extended the modernist project much more fundamentally. This could be seen in the late 1970s and early 1980s work of Norman Foster and Richard Rogers that became known for a time as 'British High-Tech'. Projects such as the Centre Georges Pompidou (Richard Rogers and Renzo Piano, completed 1977) and the Hong Kong Shanghai Bank (Norman Foster Associates, completed 1986) demonstrated a modernist preoccupation with 'rationalised' design. Using technology as the generative principal of design, new buildings were created which, like their modernist precedents, sought to minimise the distinction between interior and exterior. Although reluctant ever to acknowledge it, the High-Tech architects worked with a highly stylised aesthetic that often used technology in a fetishistic and emblematic manner. Within the interior, this proved particularly successful as evident in the Joseph shop interiors by Eva Jiricna and the domestic interiors of Future Systems.

The maturing of the technological approach to architecture and design saw the continuation of another modernist preoccupation of earlier years: the abiding comparison between architecture and transport. It is perhaps in the design of transport termini such as railway stations and airports that this mode of design has reached its most significant achievements. In projects such as Stansted Airport (Norman Foster Associates, completed 1991) and the Waterloo International Terminal (Nicholas Grimshaw & Partner, 1993), the architects formerly grouped together under the banner of High-Tech developed a sophisticated and rationalised model of the interior which, although still defined largely by architectural structure, also worked very clearly on its own terms.

The 1970s also saw the flourishing of the radical and antidesign debates that had been initiated in the previous decade. Concerned to explore the popular consumerism of everyday culture and the language and imagery of mass media, the antidesign critique of modernism evident in the designs, writings and installations of groups of young architects such as Archigram and Superstudio argued for a more socially aware form of design practice. Much of this critique originated in the Italian design schools of Milan and Florence, and it was in the former city that the highly influential group of architects and designers known as Studio Alchimia came together. Including Ettore Sottsass, Jr., Alessandro Mendini, Andrea Branzi and Michele De Lucchi, Studio Alchimia sought a critical engagement with design through the reevaluation of everyday objects. Although the group had significant critical impact through exhibitions at the Milan Triennale of 1979 and the Venice Biennale of the following year, its work tended to be polemical rather than necessarily propositional.

Having spent the previous twenty years designing products and furniture for Olivetti, Sottsass, in particular, wished to address these issues through design rather than academic discourse and discussion concerning design, and it was with this aim in mind that in 1980 he drew together the collective that would come to be known as Memphis. Under Sottsass's leadership, Memphis became the most influential design collective of the 1980s. Working within an era of rapidly expanding global communication and media, the influence of Memphis can be seen throughout the developed world. Although the designers steadfastly rejected an understanding of their work in terms of style, the various objects that they designed shared a number of characteristics. As designers who understood their practice as being culturally situated, Memphis design sought to juxtapose materials and forms to challenge conventional understandings. Brightly coloured laminates were combined with expensive Italian marbles, and established furniture forms, such as chairs and tables, were challenged by the omission, for example, of a fourth leg or the oblique positioning of its other elements. Perhaps the most significant impact of Memphis upon interior design was the manner in which the group's works reinvigorated and legitimised the notion of decoration. Always concerned to challenge received notions of 'good taste', Memphis used colour, and the surfaces on which it appeared, to reject all trace of modernist 'honesty'.

One of the designers to benefit most from Memphis's strident example, perhaps, was Philippe Starck. The self-styled enfant terrible of French design, Starck was, by the end of the 1980s, the most famous designer in the world, having designed projects throughout Europe, Japan and the United States. Although he had been one of a number of designers commissioned by President Mitterand to decorate the apartments of the Elysée Palace, it was the 1984 interior that he designed for the Café Costes in Paris that demonstrated his early signature style.[10] Featuring a three-legged chair that would later be produced by Italian firm Driade, the interior was decorated in pastel shades with occasional decorative accents and motifs. The furniture was angular in form and combined with the central staircase at the top of which was a large plain-faced clock used to create the effect of an updated 1920s ocean liner. Though relatively modest in hindsight, this interior reiterated decorative, stylistic and self-referential possibilities for the interior which previous years of modernist dogma had worked hard to deny.

The work of Philippe Starck differed from his Italian counterparts in that there was in it no hint of academic or critical position. This has left critics and historians unable to place him within any trajectory or canon. In a retrospective of his work at the Design Museum in London, the title of the show even questioned 'Is Philippe Starck a Designer?' Whilst this was a largely rhetorical exercise, the questioning of Starck's status as a designer testified to the breadth of his interests and the ease with which he worked with style and decoration, and nowhere was this more apparent than in his interior design. Throughout the 1980s and 1990s, Starck created a number of 'high'-style interiors that were represented and mediated throughout the world. Through commissions such as the Royalton (1988) and the Paramount (1990) Hotels in New York, Starck developed a theatrical ensemble of his owns designs that celebrated and revelled in polished surfaces, colourful mismatched furniture and yards of draped fabric. The spaces of those interiors were articulated and punctuated with lightness and darkness worthy of a stage. Starck's work constituted the ultimate postmodern understanding of the interior as image. Part designer, decorator, *ensemblier* and celebrity, Philippe Starck returned to and celebrated the difficult and unashamed plurality of the interior tradition of the premodern era. Whilst he cuts a lone figure in the interior design culture of the late twentieth century, it could be argued that the spectacular nature of his work combined with the challenging forms of Memphis to liberate a generation of designers from the constraining self-consciousness of good taste and modernist ideals.

In 1993, Droog Design was formed in the Netherlands by designer Gijs Bakker and art historian Renny Ramakers. The Droog Design 'platform' has grown significantly into a network of international designers for whom design is both process and cultural commentary and embodies concept, originality, practicality and wit. Much of Droog's design has focused upon the objects, furniture, and furnishings of the interior, and, whilst as a group of designers, they do not design interiors as such, their work exists and is presented within the context of interior 'ensembles'. This was the concept that underpinned Jurgen Bey's design for the exhibition *Simply Droog* (2003), where objects and furniture items were situated within the schematic outlines and plans of nine different interiors. Droog have made the critique of the design and manufacturing process central to their concerns, and in so doing have explored the interaction and engagement between design production and consumption. Developing many of the critical themes of their Italian antidesign predecessors, Droog have used exhibitions to develop what might be described as an 'expanded' design sensibility that invites the engagement of the consumer. This can be seen in the 2005 exhibition *Value for Money* shown in Milan and Amsterdam. Participant designers and visitors were asked to reflect upon the function, form, meaning, look, comfort and durability of the domestic objects on show and consider the role and value of their 'design'. This attempt to encourage a greater consideration and understanding of design as part of a broader economic and cultural process marks an important theme of contemporary design in the early twenty-first century and is particularly significant for consideration of interior design because it chooses to locate itself within the context of everyday life. Whilst Droog Design is, like Memphis, quick to deny any collective style or aesthetic, its work has had a tremendous influence on contemporary mainstream domestic style and furnishing.

One of the most significant opportunities to emerge during the final two decades of the twentieth century for both professional and amateur interior designers and architects was the redevelopment of existing buildings and sites. During the 1980s, the United Kingdom witnessed a dramatic, and often nostalgic, shift in public attitudes towards the historical built environment. Coupled with the strident redevelopment of post-industrial sites such as warehouses, docklands and factories and the comprehensive gentrification of previously poor urban areas such as Notting Hill and Islington in London, interior designers

and architects found extensive opportunities in both redesignating and redesigning those buildings for new purposes. That work, which intervened and interacted with existing design contexts, was integral to the signifying and referential practices of postmodernism, and some of its most high-profile interior design achievements are to be found in postmodern buildings.[11] One such project is the design and development of the Musée d'Orsay in Paris. Designed by Gae Aulenti and ACT, the redevelopment of a former railway station on the bank of the River Seine offered one of the most spectacular unfurlings of postmodern interior design. The presentational gallery interior of heavy masonry blocks, frames and platforms offers a playful counterpoint to the lightly decorated iron and glass single-span structure of the nineteenth-century railway architecture in such a way as to highlight both the change and diversity of scale and purpose in the building.

At the Royal Academy on London's Piccadilly, Norman Foster Associates created the Sackler Gallery within a hitherto overlooked 'nonspace' between existing buildings, the earliest of which dated back to the seventeenth century. With a glazed roof which draws light into its spaces, the three-story steel-and-glass structure provides circulation, connection and display space and, in doing so, creates an almost architecture-free interior. Designed to emphasise the materiality of the environment rather than any technological achievement of its design, the most striking aspect of this interior results from the ways in which inhabitants are brought up close to the formerly exterior facades and architectural details of those buildings which form its boundaries. By turning exterior walls into an interior scheme, Foster's design appropriated an authentic decorative language to very great effect.[12]

This less apparently technological and historically sympathetic approach to interior architectural intervention was demonstrated once again by Foster Associates at the beginning of the twentieth-first century, when the firm created the Great Court at the British Museum in London. In erecting an immensely detailed glass canopy across a large courtyard site, which formerly housed only the British Library Reading Room amongst a number of interstitial low-rise offices and other service spaces of the museum, the design creates a truly magnificent interior that fundamentally reworks the spatial relationships throughout the complex building. At the heart of this space, now almost objectlike within the building's core, sits the equally magnificent domed interior of the former Reading Room.[13]

The 'brown-field' regeneration of disused urban spaces and buildings has been central to the cultural regeneration of London since the mid 1980s. On the south side of the River Thames, for example, Herzog and De Mueron's redevelopment of the former Bankside Power Station into the Tate Modern has been fundamental to both the extension of the resurgent Tate 'brand' and its activities and the regeneration of London's Southbank. Making a feature of the large empty former turbine hall, Herzog and de Meuron created a low-key interior within a difficult building. By using a pared-down industrial aesthetic that draws only occasionally upon original features, the design provides something of

a cipher of the building's previous existence alongside the anonymous white spaces of its galleries.

The redevelopment of museums and galleries has yielded many of the most notable interiors of the late twentieth century. Whilst the anonymous 'white cube' has predominated in the design of gallery spaces, museums have come increasingly to understand the importance of interior design in the presentation of their collections. The development of museological debates during the 1990s articulated a rejection of the static presentation of objects behind glass in favour of a more interactive and environmental approach. One of the most successful examples of this can be seen in the Primary Galleries at the Victoria and Albert Museum in London. Designed principally by Casson Mann, the project to present British decorative arts and design from the sixteenth to the nineteenth centuries saw the abandonment of the beige-coloured hessian panels and plinths on which the collection had previously sat in favour of a more precise and reflexive presentation that makes demands of its visitors.

Working at the heart of the curatorial process, the interior design team was key to the ways in which critical decisions concerning access, information, presentation and viewing were made. The sophistication of the design is perhaps most apparent in its treatment of interior architectural fragments, such as an 'Adam' ceiling and an eighteenth-century museum room. The ceiling is suspended as a solitary fragment within the space of the gallery without any attempt to reconstruct some notion of its original context, other than a very subtle mirroring of its area in a change of floor surface beneath it. The music room, presented ostensibly as a period room in its entirety, reveals on its exterior the rough-hewn structure and joinery beneath its gilded surface. These presentations open up and spatialise a dialogue for the visitor concerning the ways in which interior spaces and surfaces have been historically articulated, experienced and produced.[14]

Not surprisingly, the lessons learnt through the interior design of the cultural sector have been well developed by retailers. The 1980s saw the emergence of a very strong commercial and retail design sector. The increasing understanding and significance of branding and marketing, and the resultant conditions of 'design convergence', meant that interior design took on a new and fundamental importance in the role of commerce and business. On a relatively small scale, one-off shop interiors provided designers with spectacular opportunities to create unique environments for their clients. The list of high-profile shops through which many designers of the 1980s began to establish their reputations is extensive and includes in London alone diverse examples such as Jigsaw by Nigel Coates, One Off by Ron Arad and Joseph by Eva Jiricna. That retailers sought to express themselves so evidently and stylistically during this period testifies to the ways in which interior design was becoming increasingly understood as a strategy for successful commerce in this period. One of the most significant of these strategies was the use of minimalism, as already mentioned. Working with his sometime collaborator Claudio Silvestrin,

renowned minimalist John Pawson designed a space redolent of the art gallery for the Cannelle patisserie on London's Fulham Road. Creating a minimal façade through the use of etched glass, the window-wall held a single clear box that linked the street and interior. Within it was a heavily decorated and preciously presented cake upon an ornate glass stand. The restraint of the minimal design created an almost surreal encounter with the goods of the patisserie, and such considered and precise presentation served, in the manner of the art gallery plinth, to reify these goods in the mind of the visitor.[15] The interior design of the retail and service sectors was, however, much more broadly experienced on the high street. The success of companies such as Fitch & Co during the 1980s was due largely to the corporate work they undertook for retailers and banks such as the Midland Bank and Next.

The reciprocal flirtation between the retailer and the museum and gallery has been very evident in the interior design practices of the recent past. Nowhere has this rather hybridised entity between the space of the museum and the space of the shop been more in evidence than in the creation of the Niketown.[16] Since the late 1990s, Niketowns have appeared in the prime retail districts of the capitals and major cities of the developed world. These outlets, designed as brand flagships throughout the world, constitute a sophisticated development in Nike branding and retail operations that seek to localise the global brand. The interiors are designed to reference the cities and environments in which they are located and constitute multimedia installations that bring together items of corporate sporting memorabilia, such as signed running shoes presented in museumlike glass cabinets, film footage and outsize photographic images of sportsmen and women in action. Throughout the interiors, slogans on the walls narrate the building for the visitor by informing them that the football section is 'for those who view life in 45 minute halves'.[17] The realisation of sport advertising, branding, media and history within the space of the interior serves to mask the explicitly commercial nature of these sites. The intensely experiential nature of these shops effectively supplements and imposes meanings on the goods purchased there, and these in turn become part of that place.

Whilst the consideration of design and presentational contexts for retailing are certainly not new to the late twentieth century, this period witnessed a changing understanding of the role of retail, consumption and consumerism. In recent years, the act of shopping has become a more explicitly cultural activity in which consumers seek to define themselves and their identities. For a retailer such as Selfridges, design and 'cultural' engagement has provided a very useful tool in the development and consolidation of market position. This development, which initially focused upon extending the stores' activities northward to cities such as Leeds and Manchester, took a highly publicised turn when it created a new purpose-built store in Birmingham, designed by Future Systems. This patronage of high-style architecture clearly reflects Selfridges's desired position within the retail sector and manifests its identity with aplomb. Not

unlike Nike, the store has sought to deepen its cultural resonance and has established itself as a site for the exhibition and display of contemporary art practice. Through the installation of work by artists such as Samuel Fosso, David LaChapelle and Brian Eno, Selfridges has very consciously attempted to hybridise the shop and gallery interior.[18]

The final decades of the twentieth century witnessed the dramatic rise of a global consumer culture, and it is in the context of consumerism that the modern interior perhaps found its most pervasive and broadly formulated form. The expanding consumer experiences offered by high-street and out-of-town retailers during the 1980s and 1990s meant that the opportunities for interior design to make decisions and choices about how homes were conceived and made were more broadly felt than ever before. Because domestic consumption provided the opportunity for expression and identity, the domestic space became the focus of both popular and academic interest and enquiry at that time. In hindsight, it is difficult now not to interpret the BBC's documentary series *Signs of the Times* (1991) as capturing something of that moment when a combination of media interest, insatiable nosiness and the consumerist need to measure ourselves against others came together. The series of six programmes about 'real people's' homes provided snapshot images narrated by voiceover answers to the unheard questions of the programme makers. The programmes, which addressed themes such as people who lived alone, people who lived together, and mothers and daughters echoed with the scrutiny and judgement of both the programme makers and viewers. For a TV audience not yet accustomed to the reality television shows that would emerge in subsequent years, the experience of watching those people open up their homes, and in turn themselves, was often excruciatingly painful to watch. What the programmes did, however, better than any academic treatise was evidence the fundamental proposition of French philosopher Pierre Bourdieu that 'taste classifies the classifier'.[19]

The commercial and media infrastructure of domestic furnishing and provision also developed significantly in the United Kingdom during these years. Stores such as Habitat and Heals expanded and were joined by retail park companies such as Ikea. By the end of the 1990s, these stores had capitalised on Web-based technologies and were selling online, effectively rendering no home beyond their influence. Magazines such as *House and Garden* continued throughout the period, and new ones joined them to become highly influential in the construction and dissemination of interior tastes and styles. Not surprisingly, these magazines ordered themselves into a hierarchy that reflected professional concern, consumer wealth, aspiration and market demographics. As such, *Blueprint* magazine, for example, discussed interiors alongside industrial design and architecture in its address to design professionals, whilst *World of Interiors* offered a much more refined presentation of 'unknown' interiors of high style than those offered by *Elle Decoration* which took a much more consumerist approach to interiors and styling and included plenty of product-oriented editorial and discussion.

This range of magazines reflects the spectrum of interior interest from amateur householder to design professional during recent years and, to some extent, expresses the expanding nature of that spectrum. The increasing prevalence and opportunities for interior design during the 1980s and 1990s naturally drew people into the sector, and this had a significant effect of stratifying and fragmenting it both in professional and educational terms. It could be argued that the popularisation of the term 'interior design' to include domestic furnishings and decoration was one of the key factors in the dissemination of the term 'interior architecture' to the United Kingdom. Though it was used more extensively on the continent, interior architecture was not commonly used within either the design profession or design education until the early 1990s, when the need to 'define' more specifically the kinds of large-scale activities, such as the reformulation of existing buildings, led to the use of the term. It is hard, however, not to interpret this change as addressing broader anxieties about the nature and status of interior design. Whilst there was certainly a need to better define the new kinds of work being undertaken by 'serious' interior designers, the change might have been motivated by professional anxieties rooted within modernist dogma and prejudices and that of 'serious' interior designers' need to differentiate themselves from the 'others'. This change in sensibility became significant for higher education in the early 1990s and was marked by a need on the part of university courses to clarify their own positions. Hence, in 1992, the University of Brighton course became BA

(Hons) Interior Architecture, clearly aligning itself entirely with architectural form, whilst the course at Kingston University remained BA (Hons) Interior Design, running alongside the undergraduate course in furniture and product design.

The mid-1990s emergence of television makeover shows further blurred the distinctions between different types of interior design practices. Combining 'real people', 'real homes' and arguably 'real designers', programmes such as the BBC's *Changing Rooms* further disseminated interior design understanding and knowledge and proved immensely popular. Subsequent programmes such as Channel 4's *Grand Designs* and *Property Ladder* present a much more 'serious' consideration of domestic design and building by focusing on full-scale house-building projects and property development and renovation, respectively. This emphasis upon the profession, trade and business of domestic design is still, however, very much rooted in a consumer context with issues such as financial investment, risk and profit being fundamental to the programmes' narratives.[20]

The shifting effects of professional versus amateur, good versus bad taste have resonated throughout the popular representation of interior design during the past decade. When, in the mid 1990s, the Swedish retailer Ikea cried for the women of Britain to 'chuck out your Chintz', it reiterated quite explicitly the modernist sensibilities and prejudices upon which the firm had been established. These clearly associated progress with their own 'clean' and undecorated products and furniture. Whilst it is unlikely to feature any product from Ikea within its glossy pages,

Wallpaper magazine, founded in 1996, offers a very similar negotiated representation of 'authoritative' interior design and taste. The magazine, which has probably done more than any other to situate the interior at the forefront of a 'lifestyle' nexus of fashion, consumerism, food, culture and entertainment, purveys a highly informed judgement and sensibility that projects 'good' design in its own image. Whilst it is published very evidently for the coffee table, it clearly reflects professional notions of international high style and taste.

The essays that make up this final section of *Designing the Modern Interior,* each in its own way, represent some of the challenges and opportunities for the design and study of the modern interior. Concerned with the consumption and experience of interiors in Japan, the judgements and feelings of domestic householders, the critique of domesticity through fine art practices and the challenges posed to interior design by the needs of sustainability and the environment, the essays represent the breadth of context in which the objects, spaces and discourses of the interior now find themselves at the beginning of the twenty-first century.

In 'The Dark Side of the Modern Home: Ilya Kabakov and Gregor Schneider's Ruins', David Crowley demonstrates the centrality of the domestic interior to the artistic exploration and reconsideration of Soviet and fascist legacy. In order to uncover an alternate formulation of the 'modern' home, Crowley explores the ways in which two artists have placed domestic spaces and objects at the heart of their critique of what it meant to be living within the totalitarian societies of the Soviet and Nazi eras. Considering the ways that these artworks of ordinary things and spaces materialise memory, Crowley reveals the manner in which the artists expose and explore the very specific conditions of domestic past, present and value.

'Locating the Modern Impulse within the Japanese Love Hotel', written by Sarah Chaplin, examines a highly unique form of the modern interior, the love hotel bedroom. Concerning herself, in particular, with the modernity of the bed, the electric lighting and the mural as they come together to create that interior, Chaplin reveals the very specific ways in which Japanese culture encountered notions of modernity through the interior. The chapter provides yet another, perhaps perverse, version of the modern interior which rejects the natural light, simple forms and spatial designations of modernism in favour of temporally regulated artifice.

Alison Clarke turns attention to the views and values of the domestic householder in 'The Contemporary Interior: Trajectories of Biography and Style'. Drawing upon findings of the Mass Observation Homes directive (October 2006), for which she was the principal investigator, Clarke reveals an increasing transience within contemporary domesticity which is marked and recorded through style. By considering the ways in which respondents entwined their stylistic and biographic memories and understanding of their homes, Clarke uncovers a micro-level understanding of style and typology as it is both imagined and lived within the interior. Anne Chick's 'Living the Sustainable Life: A Case Study of the Beddington Zero Energy Development (BedZED) Sustainable Interior', places upon the modern interior the most

pressing demand and challenge of twenty-first-century society, that of environmental sustainability. Through the case study and analysis of the BedZED project located in South London, Chick offers a neofunctionalist progeny of modernism. Exploring the ways in which the environment of the interior is controlled through the specification of environmentally sound materials, the regulated use of energy and natural resources and design features such as the 'sunspace', the sustainable interior is characterised as a technologically realised entity every bit as progressive and polemic as its modernist antecedents.

Notes

1. R. Venturi, *Complexity and Contradiction in Architecture* (Museum of Modern Art, 1966).

2. C. Jencks, *The Language of Post-Modern Architecture* (Academy Editions, 1977).

3. P. Reyner Banham, *Theory and Design in the First Machine Age* (Architectural Press, 1960).

4. For an interesting but typical example of a material culture approach to interiors, see R. St. George, 'Home Furnishing and Domestic Interiors', in Chris Tilley et al., eds., *Handbook of Material Culture* (Sage, 2006).

5. E. D. Rappaport, *Shopping for Pleasure* (Princeton University Press, 2000); Matt Houlbrook, *Queer London* (University of Chicago Press, 2005); C. Breward, D. Gilbert and J. Lister, *Swinging Sixties* (V&A Publications, 2006).

6. A. Massey, *Interior Design since 1900* (Thames & Hudson, 2008); P. Sparke, *An Introduction to Design and Culture: 1900 to the Present* (Routledge, 2004); S. Abercrombie, *A Century of Interior Design, 1900–2000* (Rizzoli, 2003);

and J. Woodham, *Twentieth-Century Design* (Oxford University Press, 1997).

7. L. Jackson, *20th Century Pattern Design: Textile & Wallpapers Pioneers* (Mitchell Beasley, 2002) and G. Williams, *The Furniture Machine: Furniture since 1900* (V&A Publications, 2006).

8. P. Viladas, *California Beach Houses* (Chronicle, 1996); B. Dunlop, *Miami: Trends and Traditions* (Monacelli Press, 1996); and H. Ypma, *London Minimum* (Thames & Hudson, 1996).

9. D. Sudjic, *John Pawson Works* (Phaidon, 2000); P. E. Jiřičné's, *In/exterior: The Works of Eva Jiricna* (Proster, 2005); C. McDermott, ed., *Plans and Elevations/Ben Kelly Designs* (Architecture, Design and Technology, 1990); D. Sudjic, *Equipment Stores: Architect John Chipperfield* (Wordsearch, 1993); D. Sudjic, *For Inspiration Only/Future Systems* (Academy, 1996).

10. Massey, *Interior Design since 1900,* p. 208.

11. The critical literature on the design, remodelling and regeneration of buildings is limited; however, G. Brooker and S. Stone's *Rereadings. Interior Architecture and the Design Principles of Remodelling Existing Buildings* (RIBA Enterprises, 2004) provides an excellent analysis and discussion through case study.

12. Brooker and Stone, *Rereadings,* pp. 117–19.

13. Massey, *Interior Design since 1900,* pp. 228–9.

14. A. Walker, 'Object Lessons', *Blueprint* (October 2001), pp. 32–5. See also C. Wilk and N. Humphrey, eds., *The Making of the British Galleries at the V&A: A Study in Museology* (V&A Publications, 2004).

15. 'Minimalism on the High Street', *Blueprint* (December/January 1989), pp. 44–5.

16. Massey, *Interior Design since 1900,* pp. 237–8; Robert Goldman and Stephen Papson, *Nike Culture* (Sage, 1998).

17. 'Do They Mean Us?' *Blueprint* (July/August 1990), pp. 50–1.

18. 'Shopping Vs Art', *Blueprint* (June 2006), pp. 85–6; 'Selfridges Heart Is in Las Vegas', *Blueprint* (May 2005), p. 27; 'Selfridges Installs Eno's Sound and Vision', *Designweek* 22/5 (1 February 2007), p. 7.

19. P. Bourdieu, *Distinction: A Social Critique of the Judgement of Taste* (Routledge & Kegan Paul, 1984).

20. See V. Narotzky, 'Dream Homes and DIY: Television, New Media and the Domestic Makeover', in J. Aynsley and C. Grant, eds., *The Imagined Interior. Representing the Domestic Interior since the Renaissance* (V&A Publications, 2006).

Chapter Fourteen

The Dark Side of the Modern Home: Ilya Kabakov and Gregor Schneider's ruins

David Crowley

The modern home is, conventionally, bathed in the light of order. Adolf Loos's vision of a 'New Zion' stripped of its nostalgic ornament; Le Corbusier's *fenêtre en longeur;* and Pierre Koenig's glass curtain walls and open plans constitute steady steps in the progress of the rational, improved home from its Enlightenment origins. But they do not represent the only kind of modern dwelling. In fact, such domestic utopias might be an inadequate measure of twentieth-century modernity. The 'most terrible century in Western history' provides many images of broken homes.[1] Windowless bomb shelters, the maternity wards of Heinrich Himmler's *lebensborn* programme, ghetto towns like Terezín and the ruins of war-torn cities like Beirut constitute landmarks in an alternative and unwritten history of the modern home. How might these homes be understood not as 'accidents' of history but as its design? And, if viewed in this way, what are the aesthetics of these ruins of history?

Ruins have, of course, long been aestheticised by being seized as symbols through which to reflect on the irresistible passage of time. Their broken state invites comparison with the frailties of the body, whilst the weeds that thrive in their cracks testify to the triumph of nature over culture. Many eighteenth- and nineteenth-century aesthetes—famously Wordsworth, Piranesi, Diderot and Michelet—found a melancholic pleasure in contemplating the ruin as utopia in reverse.[2] This sensibility is by no means exhausted today. Recently, for instance, the depopulated centres of America's rust belt cities have been viewed in a similar fashion.[3]

But it is important to stress that two new orders of ruin emerged in the course of the nineteenth and twentieth centuries which laid a claim on modernity. Linda Nochlin has observed that the French Revolution marked the first moment in history in which architectural fragments appeared 'as a positive rather than a negative trope'. The ruin was drafted to symbolise the march of progress:

[T]he fragment, for the Revolution and its artists, rather than symbolizing nostalgia for the past, enacts the deliberate destruction of that

past, or, at least, a pulverization of what were perceived to be its repressive traditions. Both outright vandalism and what one might think of as a recycling of the vandalized fragments of the past for allegorical purposes functioned as Revolutionary strategies.[4]

It is perhaps not surprising that Russian intellectuals—schooled in a society created by revolution—have allegorised destruction as progress. Mikhail Yampolsky has written, 'Destruction and construction can be understood, in certain contexts, as two equally valid features of immortalisation.'[5] The erection of a new monument on the site of an old one is an act of double commemoration or, as he puts it, immortalisation.

It is, perhaps, more difficult to limn the ruins produced by industrial warfare, although of course many have tried.[6] The products of this order of modernity—the results of mechanised violence—seem less innocent or optimistic. The ruins of Rotterdam, Leningrad, Dresden, Warsaw, Hiroshima, Mostar and even New York could and cannot function as what Simmel called the 'naturalised artefact' because their origins are in catastrophe.[7] Their status as symbols is overshadowed by their status as indices of events. As Andrew Hersher has argued of the modern ruin in another context:

Damage is a form of design, and the traces of damage inflicted by political violence— a facade stippled by the spray of bullets, a penumbra of smoke around a hole where a door or a window once was, or a pile of rubble no longer identifiable as architecture at all—are at least as significant as any of the elements from which buildings are constructed for living, for the living.[8]

In this sense, the ruins produced by violence are far more 'legible' than those produced by the effects of entropy. Comparing the kinds of objects which provoke nostalgic reverie such as the pressed flower in the scrapbook with souvenirs of deathlike relics, Susan Stewart has written: 'they mark the horrible transformation of meaning into material more than they mark, as other souvenirs do, the transformation of materiality into meaning.'[9] This contrast also structures the differences between the entropic ruin and the debris of modern war.

It is not surprising that the image of the house in ruins, and its accompanying figure, the displaced person, was a persistent theme in Europe after 1945. It formed the mise-en-scène for novels by Heinrich Böll, Marek Hłasko and Graham Greene as well as films by Roberto Rossellini, Grigori Chukrai and Andrzej Wajda. The destruction of the home was a powerful allegorical form through which artists and writers could reflect not only on the difficult conditions of the present, but also on the problems of remembrance and forgetting. The condition of house in fragments—decayed and riddled with spatial and temporal uncertainties—seemed much like the condition of memory itself facing the recent horrors of war and, in the East, the pressure of an ideology which claimed to already know the past and the future. Equally, the utilitarian modern homes promised to Europe's displaced peoples—in the new geography of East and West in the aftermath of war and mass destruction—were criticised as being inadequate precisely because they could not inspire memory work of dreams.[10]

Humankind seemed to be stripped of its humanity when displaced from home. In 1945, General Patton, for instance, expressed higher regard for the Germans in their bombed out ruins than the Jews who had survived the camps and were now searching for homes and families in Europe's ruins: '[General] Craig … told me he had inspected another Jewish camp yesterday', he wrote in his diary,

> in which he found men and women using adjacent toilets which were not covered in any way although screens were available to make the toilets individually isolated, which the Jews were too lazy to put up. He said the conditions and filth were unspeakable. In one room he found ten people, six men and four women, occupying four double beds. Either these Displaced Persons never had any sense of decency or else they lost it all during their internment by the Germans.[11]

Housing not only provides shelter; in the authoritarian mind, it makes people orderly, tidying lives and bodies.

Whilst the image of the home in ruins may have been at its peak in the 1940s and 1950s, it has been a persistent theme in twentieth century culture. What should we make the image of the home in ruins at the end of the century? What perspective might be taken on the debris of domestic life in the twentieth century? In the remains of this short essay, I will turn to the work of two artists, Gregor Schneider and Ilya Kabakov, both of whom have created homes from and with the debris of modern life. Kabakov's 'Ten Characters', an installation based on the form of the communal apartment, and Schneider's *Totes Haus u r* (Dead House u r) are powerful commentaries on the catastrophes which shadow modernity in the 'medium' of the home.

It would surely be possible to read the domestic spaces exhibited by both artists as autobiographies or even psychological portraits. Kabakov has described his early installations in his Moscow studio as 'an experiment of biography in the installation genre' in which he 'became a character of himself'.[12] And Schneider's seemingly compulsive and secretive behaviour as well as the assault on his own home—the basis of the Dead House—has encouraged many to follow this line. Paul Schimmel has called the *Dead House* 'life's echo'.[13] Such readings reproduce one of the principal myths of the century: that the home is a mirror of the individual and a container of private memory. As Ivan Illich puts it, 'to dwell means to inhabit the traces left by one's own living, by which one always retraces the lives of one's ancestors.'[14] But Schneider and Kabakov's artistic archaeologies draw attention to a wider and perhaps more disturbing set of modern ambitions of domestic perfection.

Undiscarded things

Ilya Kabakov, active in nonofficial art circles in the Soviet Union from the 1960s, emerged into the consciousness of the West in the late 1980s, his art drawing attention to the textures of life and the residual utopianism of the Soviet Union at the time when it was being dismantled. His first major installation exhibited in the West in 1988 was 'Ten Characters', an extension of the themes he had been exploring in albums and paintings made since the 1970s.[15] His installation—a series of cell-like rooms off a shabby corridor poorly lit with electric light bulbs—presents the possessions and living spaces of ten absent Soviet citizens. In their absence, their lives are described in a series of vivid extended texts (often in the heterogeneous voices of official reports, newspaper articles, diaries and ad hominem reflections) and, of course, their possessions. The viewer is invited to be both a psychologist and an archaeologist, extracting meaning from the debris of life and fragmentary reports. In this work, Kabakov recreated a communal apartment *(komunalka),* the most distinct space in the domestic landscape of the Soviet Union, domestic exotica for audiences in Washington, Paris and London.

The *komunalka* is a fascinating historical artefact: it remains both a symptom of the radical hopes and, in the event, the failure of the Soviet dream world. In the aftermath of the October Revolution, the 'bourgeois' conception of home as a private space—both socially and spatially—was rejected in a series of decrees issued from 1918 nationalising land and abolishing private ownership of property. Collective modes of housing were not only adopted as a matter of exigency, but also proclaimed as the democratisation of space.[16] Large prerevolutionary apartments, once occupied by the wealthy and their servants, were subdivided to provide homes for a number of working-class and peasant families. In his Moscow diaries, Walter Benjamin

described, employing a characteristically surreal metaphor, how these private homes had become common property and were now overpopulated by numerous families and their meagre possessions; 'Through the hall door one steps into a little town'.[17]

The *komunalka* was an instrument with which to create the new collectivity. It was to be the first stage in a new domestic landscape which would be furnished with *dom komunii* (communal houses), glass and steel building-machines which would accommodate hundreds of adults and children meeting their basic needs with collective facilities like public canteens and on-site boarding schools. Minimal allowances of private space were to be provided to foster the kind of communalism lauded by communist ideologues and inhibit the private possession of things. In fact, the desire for such things was expected to disappear when all human needs were satisfied by the perfect environment.[18] Andrei Platonov, in his novel *The Foundation Pit* (1930), described the 'All Proletarian Home' as a step towards Communism itself. His hero, predictably an engineer who is—less predictably—riddled with doubt, designs a

single building that was to replace the old town where … people lived fenced off from one another on their private plots: in a year's time the entire local proletariat would leave the old town and its petty properties and take possession of the monumental new home. And in another decade or two, some other engineer would construct a tower, in the very centre of the world, where the toiling masses of the whole earth would happily take up residence for the rest of time.[19]

Such new collective homes were never (or hardly ever[20]) built. And whilst the mass housing schemes promoted by Nikita Khrushchev and his successor Leonid Brezhnev dramatically altered the face of cities and the living patterns of society, they did little to break up the institution of the family (in fact, in the form of the single-family apartment, they did much to reinforce it). Moreover, the *komunalka*—the first phase in the campaign against bourgeois domesticity— remained a lasting feature of domestic life in the Soviet Union. In 1989, for instance, one- quarter of the population lived in *komunalkii,* sharing a common kitchen, a common toilet and a common telephone in an apartment subdivided by flimsy partitions, sometimes little more than curtains.[21]

Conventionally, art historians have turned to Kabakov's 'Ten Characters' as a comment on the forms of horizontal surveillance which operated not only in the communal apartment but throughout Soviet society. Constantly aware of one's movements and opinions being detected by others, the individual modifies his or her behaviour. Life is reduced to one of vigilance and performance or, as Boris Groys puts it elegantly, 'the communal turns everyone into an artist.'[22] For the purposes of this essay, another feature of the installation calls for attention: the debris from which Kabakov fashions his art. One space—once occupied by a cosmonaut who seemingly has flown into space by means of a catapult—is a 'spectacle of total devastation'[23] (see Fig. 14.1). A massive hole in the ceiling created by an explosion detonated at the moment of takeoff has left the room littered with plaster fragments whilst the former occupant's possessions are strewn all around. The room

itself, bathed in the red light of propaganda posters, is a temple for Soviet dreams of futurism, of transcendence.[24] After the departure of this anonymous Gagarin, all that remains is junk.

Another room—occupied by 'The Man Who Never Threw Anything Away'—is far more orderly and retrospective in tone (see Fig. 14.2). Scraps of paper and film, slithers of packaging, rags, tins and jars are carefully arranged in vitrines and hung on the wall. Each has a label attached to it, in the style of a museum catalogue, with a number and an inscription. The room itself is short and narrow, like a corridor, and contains two doors, one of which is permanently locked. This is the living space of an individual, but no furniture is visible, except a small divan.

Svetlana Boym, in her brilliant study of the myths of everyday life in Russia, describes the *komunalka* as the place where 'domestic trash' triumphed.[25] Far from being a new commonwealth in which the frictions caused by attachment to possessions were eased by the benefits of collective life, things (and often the social divisions they represent) announced their presence loudly, if sometimes mysteriously, in the communal apartment. This is Kabakov's own description of the corridor:

Despite regular cleaning … there was always a heap of undiscarded things. No-one knew whom these things belonged to, what they were used for, nor was it known whether the owners of these things still lived in the apartment or if they had already left. These things were scattered in all the corners, hung on the walls, stood along the entire length of the hallway. Because of all this, the apartment

Fig. 14.1. Ilya
Kabakov, The Man
Who Flew Into
Space From His
Apartment, 1981–88,
mixed media
installation, 110 x
95 x 147 inches.
Photo: D. James
Dee, Collection of
Musée National
d'Art Moderne,
Centre Georges
Pompidou, Paris.
Courtesy Ronald
Feldman Fine Arts,
New York.

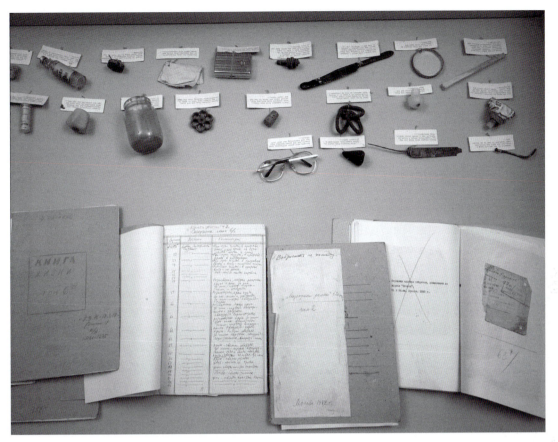

Fig. 14.2. Ilya Kabakov, 'The Man Who Never Threw Anything Away (detail), 1981–88' mixed media installation: 8 hanging clusters of objects, 10 collages, 1 fifteen panel text album with collage, and 1 vitrine containing 9 scrapbooks and 27 object labels dimension variable. Photo: D. James Dee. Courtesy Ronald Feldman Fine Arts, New York

took on the appearance of a mysterious cave, full of stalactites and stalagmites, with a narrow passageway between them leading to the constantly open kitchen door ... Near the large discarded things—big wardrobes, cast-iron stoves, couches and other household junk -, smaller things were piled up on all sides and on top of the other ones—pipes, crates, boxes, old buckets, bottles, both broken and complete.[26]

Recycling and garbage were prominent in the ecology of late Soviet socialism: a greasy tide of filth seeped into public spaces such as common hallways, streets, parks and beaches; whilst shortage turned citizens into skilled fixers of broken things, adept at the everyday arts of bricolage. Only when things were completely exhausted (itself never a certain state) could they be dumped. But Kabakov's debris—collected by the pseudonymous figure of the 'The Man Who Never Threw Anything Away'—is neither a practical resource nor is it without value. It evidently operates within the memorial economy rather than the economic one.

But what is being memorialised in this collection of things? Might this room operate as what Mikhail Epshtein, writing at same time, described as a 'lyrical museum', a home for things cycling between the warehouse and the dump? The collection of the ordinary stuff of everyday life, he says, is a response to modernity: 'Our ancestors would hardly have thought of trying intensely to understand surrounding Things or of creating a memorial for them because the homes they lived in were such "memorials." The Thing was meaningful from the start when it was inherited ... and meaningful at the end when it was passed on.'[27] In the Soviet Union, the figure of the collector—an activity laced with pathos—is rendered poignant by the fact that he was a representative of a social system which made the greatest possible claim to free mankind from the weight of the past and from the alienating effects of things. But Kabakov's collector does not preserve fragments of a prerevolutionary world (say in the manner of Chatwin's fictional Utz or Dombrovsky's Keeper of Antiquities[28]); he collects the debris of Soviet socialism. Even before the end of the Soviet experiment in 1991, Kabakov sensed how this dream world could become a ruin; how the future could become the past; and how utopia could become trash.

Dead House u r

Much distinguishes Kabakov's installation from Gregor Schneider's project, the Dead House. The Russian artist's prolixity and his interest in the structures of ideology, reason and progress are very distant from the obdurate preoccupations of the young German artist. Nevertheless, Robert Storr, writing in *Art Forum* in 2001, saw in Schneider's work at the Venice Biennale that year 'evidence of the delayed but growing influence in the West of Ilya Kabakov's gritty, dystopian fantasies'.[29]

In the mid 1980s, Schneider, then a young man, began remodelling his own three-story family home in Rheydt, a district of Mönchengladbach. By removing and duplicating walls, he created twenty-two rooms as well as numerous passages and dead ends. Massive structures—suggesting inverted houses—were built into existing rooms. Doors to bedrooms were hidden behind heavy, brick walls which Schneider could move, albeit with difficulty, like a sliding door, to welcome (or incarcerate) his guests. Entire rooms could rotate on their axes. Many of the spaces created by these radical modifications were cramped and oppressive, punctuated with holes which penetrated through floors and what Schneider calls 'in-between rooms'. Blind windows were built directly in front of actual windows facing the outside world. Cupboards functioned as doorways into secret rooms. Hidden lights and ventilators produced the illusion of daylight and fresh air. And, like Kabakov's lyrical museums, the Dead House became a kind of exhausted *kunstkammer* filled with decaying photographs, rolled up carpets, stuffed animals and dingy antiques. In these ways, it was a kind of mutant home formed from the corpses of other homes nearby, many of which were abandoned when the authorities forced their occupants to move so that the coal-rich ground could be mined.

Schneider's dead ends, blind windows and cells within rooms suggest spaces of burial and torture, extraterritorial zones where the 'rules of life' are suspended and violent forces unleashed (some floors were lined with lead, whilst some walls were dressed with sound-proofing materials). This is perhaps where the bloodshed or loss suggested by the project's title, *Totes Haus u r*, occurs. But the project also pointed to birth. *u r* ostensibly refers to the first and last letters of the street on which it stands, Unterheydener Strasse. But *ur* also means origin. Homes are conventionally sites of social and biological reproduction. In its decomposed state, Schneider's house combined the symmetry of womb and tomb (poles that Freud famously conjoined in his essay on the Uncanny).[30] In the mid 1990s, Schneider said:

> I dream of taking the whole house with me and rebuilding it somewhere else. My father and mother would live with me there; the older relatives lie dead in the cellar. My brothers live upstairs, here and there live women and men who have no other place to go. Somewhere in the corner sits a large woman who's always having babies, churning them out into the world.[31]

Schneider figured aspects of this particular nightmare in the form of portrait photographs concealed within the walls: each generation sealed, invisibly, in layers of plaster, brick and cement.

In the 1990s and the early years of the new century, Schneider's elements of the Dead House were carefully removed from its Rheydt site and reinstalled within the white walls of galleries throughout Europe and North America (see Fig. 14.3 and Fig. 14.4). The Dead House achieved its greatest exposure at the Venice Biennale in 2001 when the artist represented Germany. This setting brought one of the Dead House's most potent themes to the fore: the German pavilion had been remodelled in 1938 by the Third Reich in order to conform to the neoclassical idiom. Architect Ernst Haiger replaced the iconic columns and a modest gable of the small classical temple with four massive flat pilasters carrying an austere architrave. It represented an unmistakable projection of fascist aesthetics onto the international stage.

In this particular setting, Schneider's Dead House was unmistakably drawn into the orbit of German history (somewhat inevitably following Nam June Paik and Hans Haacke's treatment of the historic space in 1993 in their installation 'Germania').[32] Schneider created a claustrophobic labyrinth within the Pavilion and set a common glass-paned door from Rheydt into its grand entrance, a gesture which perhaps points to the complicity of ordinary homes in the reproduction of Nazism and even as the site of the execution of its crimes (see Fig. 14.5). This has repeatedly been the accusation made of German society. But the idea that a house is somehow guilty of crimes seems illogical, a category error which confuses mind and matter. Yet the places in which tremendous violence has been generated are often demolished in order to exorcise their ghosts (or to deny ghost-hunters). In 1946, for instance, the garden of the Reich's Chancellery, the site of Hitler's bunker, was razed and the area levelled by the communist authorities which now controlled

Fig. 14.3. Gregor
Schneider, Totes Haus
u r, Deutscher Pavillon,
49. Biennale von
Venedig, Venezia 2001,
© Gregor Schneider /
VG Bild-Kunst, Bonn

Fig. 14.4. Gregor
Schneider, Totes Haus u r,
Deutscher Pavillon, 49.
Biennale von Venedig,
Venezia 2001, © Gregor
Schneider / VG Bild-
Kunst, Bonn.

the Eastern sectors of the city. The bunker was buried (again). Similarly, in 1952, the Bavarian government blew up the ruins of the Berghof, Hitler's *heimatschutzstil* home on the Obersalzberg. In an effort to stop the site becoming a site for Nazi and neo-Nazi pilgrims, the building could not be allowed to remain (though this intention to suppress memory was somewhat undermined by the choosing to commit this domicide on the anniversary of Hitler's death, 30 April).

But of course Schneider has not destroyed the Dead House, but expanded and mutated it. In a strange twist, his secret rooms and false floors seem to echo the desperate places fashioned by Europe's Jews in which to hide in Germany and the occupied countries of the Second World War. These were, as we know, too rarely safe homes. 'Street by street, house by house, inch by inch, from attic to cellar', wrote one survivor of a German ghetto-clearing in occupied Poland, 'The Germans became expert at finding these hiding places. When they searched a house they went tapping the walls, listening for the hollow sound that indicated a double wall. They punched holes in ceilings and walls.'[33] Entering into the constricting passages and false rooms was an uncertain experience, particularly for those who visited the 'original' incarnation of the Dead House in Rheydt; it produced the uncanny double effect of hunting and being hunted.

The Dead House was, in this regard, a strange kind of countermonument, a celebrated genre of public artworks through which Germany was asked to confront the Holocaust in the 1980s. Far more typical were those schemes which—by means of disappearing columns or as street cobbles carrying the names of Jewish cemeteries on their underside—asked Germans to reflect on the absences in their midst.[34] This phenomenon sought to address the aesthetic problem of the monument, historically an object associated with triumphalism, by seeking to produce a sense of anguished reflection on the part of its viewers. Such countermonuments have attracted a good deal of controversy. As Richard Esbenshade put it in 1995, 'The celebration of counter-memory or counter-history begs the question of *who* is doing the remembering and the rewriting of history.'[35] A far more disturbing (and tactically irresponsible) countermemorial is perhaps one which simulates the conditions in which people became prey.

Inconclusive material

Historian Eric Hobsbawm has represented the late twentieth century as an era of disconnect: 'The destruction of the past, or rather of the social mechanisms that link one's contemporary experience to that of earlier generations, is one of the most characteristic and eerie phenomena of the late twentieth century.'[36] Living in a 'sort of permanent present lacking any organic relations to the public past', the 'historical memory is no longer alive' in modern societies. Hobsbawm's observation made in 1994 was intended to reaffirm the role of the historian as a political and social conscience. What kind of connection with the past is made in Kabakov's and Schneider's homes? After all, eeriness is precisely the sensation generated by both installations.

Both Kabakov and Schneider explore the ways in which ordinary things might materialise memory, an enquiry which was all the more powerful for exploring the debris of the home. In environments in which homes were experiments for either the deconstruction of domesticity (the Soviet Union) or its perversion (Nazi Germany), these artists produced spaces for an examination of the trash produced by modernity. The facticity and durability of material has long been claimed as its value. Hannah Arendt argued, for instance, that it was these qualities which

> gives the things of the world their relative independence from men who produced and use them … From this viewpoint, the things of the world have the function of stabilizing human life, and their objectivity lies in the fact that … men, their ever-changing nature notwithstanding, can retrieve their sameness, that is, their identity, by being related to the same chair and the same table.[37]

But in societies which have been forced through the mill of history, the 'sameness' of that chair or table might be the very cause of disturbance.

Notes

1. Isaiah Berlin cited by Eric Hobsbawm, *Age of Extremes: The Short Twentieth Century, 1914–1991* (Abacus, 1995), p. 1.

2. C. Merewether, 'Irresistible Decay: Ruins Reclaimed', in M. S. Roth, C. Lyons and C. Merewether, eds., *Irresistible Decay* (Getty Research Institute for the History of Art and the Humanities, 1997), pp. 1–13. See also C. Woodward, *In Ruins* (Vintage, 2002).

3. J. J. Higgins, *Images of the Rust Belt* (Kent State University Press, 1999).

4. L. Nochlin, *The Body in Pieces: The Fragment as a Metaphor of Modernity* (Thames & Hudson, 1995), p. 8.

5. M. Yampolsky, 'In the Shadow of Monuments', in N. Condee, ed., *Soviet Hieroglyphics* (BFI Publishing, 1995), p. 100.

6. The damaged yet preserved state of the Kaiser Wilhelm Gedächtniskirche in Berlin, for instance, represents a humanistic view of the ruin.

7. G. Simmel, 'The Ruin', in Kurt H. Wolff, ed., *Essays on Sociology, Philosophy and Aesthetics* (Harper & Row, 1965), pp. 259–66.

8. A. Hersher, 'The Language of Damage', in *Grey Room,* 7 (Spring 2002), p. 69.

9. S. Stewart, *On Longing. Narratives of the Miniature, the Gigantic, the Souvenir, the Collection* (Duke University Press, 1993), p. 138.

10. A. Vidler, *The Architectural Uncanny, Essays in the Modern Unhomely* (MIT Press, 1994), p. 64.

11. G. S. Patton, 21 September 1945, in M. Blumenson, ed., *The Patton Papers, 1940–1945* (Da Capoi Press, 1998), p. 759.

12. I. Kabakov, *Der Text als Grundlage des Visuellen/The Text as the Basis of Visual Expression,* Z. Felix, ed. (Oktagon, 2000), p. 269.

13. P. Schimmel, 'Life's Echo', in *Gregor Schneider* (Charta, 2003), pp. 103–18.

14. I. Illich, *H2O and the Waters of Forgetfulness. Reflections on the History of 'Stuff'* (Dallas Institute of Humanities and Culture, 1985), p. 8.

15. It was first mounted at Ronald Feldman Fine Art in New York in 1988.

16. M. Bliznakov, 'Soviet Housing during the Experimental Years, 1918 to 1933', in W. C. Brumfield and B. A. Ruble, eds., *Russian Housing in the Modern Age: Design and Social History* (University of Cambridge Press, 1993), pp. 85–149.

17. W. Benjamin, 'Moscow', (1927), in *One Way Street* (NLB, 1979), pp. 187–8.

18. On the early Soviet critique of the commodity, see C. Kiaer, *Imagine No Possessions. The Socialist Objects of Russian Constructivism* (MIT Press, 2005), particularly pp. 1–88.

19. A. Platonov, 'The Foundation Pit' (1930), in C. Kelly, ed., *Utopias* (Penguin, 1999), p. 21.

20. On attempts to produce new experimental collective housing schemes in the 1960s, see M. Rüthers, *Moskau bauen von Lenin bis Chruscev. Öffentliche Räume zwischen Utopie, Terror und Alltag* (Böhlau, 2007), pp. 248–61.

21. See K. Gerasmiova, 'Public Privacy in the Soviet Communal Apartment', in D. Crowley and S. E. Reid, eds., *Socialist Spaces: Sites of Everyday Life in the Eastern Bloc* (Berg, 2003), pp. 207–30.

22. B. Groys, D. A. Rose and I. Blazwick, *Ilya Kabakov* (Phaidon, 1998), p. 63.

23. Kabakov, *Der Text als Grundlage des Visuellen,* p. 332.

24. For a brilliant analysis of this space, see B. Groys, *Ilya Kabakov. The Man Who Flew into Space from His Apartment* (Afterall, 2006).

25. S. Boym, *Commonplaces. Mythologies of Everyday Life in Russia* (Harvard University Press, 1994), p. 123.

26. Kabakov, *Der Text als Grundlage des Visuellen,* p. 300.

27. M. Epshtein, 'Things and Words: Towards a Lyrical Museum', in A. Efimova and L. Manovich, eds., *Tekstura* (University of Chicago Press, 1993), p. 164.

28. B. Chatwin, *Utz* (Cape, 1988); Y. Dombrovsky, *The Keeper of Antiquities* (Harvill, 1988).

29. R. Storr, 'Harry's Last Call', *Artforum* (September 2001), p. 159.

30. 'To some people the idea of being buried alive by mistake is the most uncanny thing of all. And yet psychoanalysis has taught us that this terrifying fantasy is only a transformation of another fantasy which had originally nothing terrifying about it at all, but was qualified by a certain lasciviousness—the fantasy, I mean of intra-uterine existence.' S. Freud, 'The "Uncanny"', in *Art and Literature (Collected Works)* (Penguin Books, 1985), p. 366.

31. Gregor Schneider in an interview with Ulrich Loock in *Gregor Schneider* (Charta, 2003), pp. 99–100.

32. The marble floor of the pavilion interior was smashed into fragments at Haacke and Paik's instruction. The visitor had to walk with great care over the uneven and unstable surface. As they moved, their steps were amplified and broadcast back into the echoing space. Here was a national pavilion—and, by extension, a nation—without solid foundations. See D. Gamboni, *The Destruction of Art: Iconoclasm and Vandalism since the French Revolution* (Reaktion, 1997), p. 166.

33. Henry Orenstein cited by Daniel Jonah Goldhagen, *Hitler's Willing Executioners: Ordinary Germans and the Holocaust* (Abacus, 1997), p. 395.

34. See J. E. Young, *The Texture of Memory: Holocaust Memorials and Meaning* (Yale University Press, 1993) and J. E. Young, *At Memory's Edge: After-images of the Holocaust in Contemporary Art and Architecture* (Yale University Press, 2007).

35. R. S. Esbenshade, 'Remembering to Forget: Memory, History, National Identity in Postwar East-Central Europe', *Representations* 49 (Winter 1995), pp. 72–96.

36. E. Hobsbawm, *Age of Extremes: The Short Twentieth Century, 1914–1991* (Abacus, 1995), p. 3.

37. H. Arendt, *The Human Condition* (University of Chicago Press, 1999), p. 137. I am grateful to Paul Betts for alerting me to this passage in Arendt's book.

Chapter Fifteen

Locating the Modern Impulse within the Japanese Love Hotel

Sarah Chaplin

In 1920s Japan, an architect named Wajirō Kon developed an observational practice that he called *kōgengaku* or 'modernology', the purpose of which was 'to record and analyse contemporary custom before it became history'.[1] Provoked by the Kanto earthquake in 1923, which had destroyed much of contemporary life in Tokyo and forced upon its inhabitants a reconstruction of their lifestyle, Kon's research was about 'capturing custom as it was being lived and experienced before it hardened into habitual convention'[2] and, as such, was 'capable of disclosing the interior life of contemporaries by locating the social meaning they invested in them'.[3] Kon's work was criticised by Jun Tosaka for being phenomenological formalism, but Harold Harootunian has argued that Kon's work on the *gendai,* or contemporary, was important because it articulated the tendency for everyday culture to 'develop before one's eyes' in the form of gestures, attire and conduct.

If Kon were practising *kōgengaku* today, he would no doubt be frequenting some of Japan's 30,000 or so love hotels, which disclose many contemporary customs in the making. Just as in the 1920s, when those overlooked aspects of everyday life proved a rich hunting ground for evidence that a modern sensibility was emerging on many levels, in the late twentieth century the love hotel provides a similar context in which to discover that which has tended to remain downplayed simply because it is not considered to be important. This is the defining characteristic of the everyday and one might argue, of modernity. Kon looked upon the city as a 'storehouse of memory' and concerned himself with recording what he called a 'moving present' *(ugoki tsutsu aru).*[4] By focusing on the trivial, Kon got close to notions of everydayness in 1920s Tokyo, but perhaps not close enough: Harootunian concludes that, 'while Kon's phenomenological investigations brought him into a close relationship to the details and commodities dominating modern everyday life, his method prevented him from looking beyond the surface to discover what lay beneath them.'[5] This stems in part from Kon's emotional relationship towards his subject matter: he was perhaps too optimistic and idealising in a way that typified the Taisho era in which he lived.

As a product of the late twentieth century, the love hotel interior belongs to a less idealised and upbeat period of Japanese history and therefore offers powerful insights into the changing nature of the Japanese relationship both to its own culture and to other cultures, which have become embodied in its design and use. Whilst Kon's work in the 1920s was largely synchronic, dealing with a moment in time, the love hotel demands a more diachronic approach: it emerged following a ban on licensed prostitution enacted in 1958, had its definitive period in the mid 1970s, was legislated against in 1985, struggled to survive the 'lost decade' of the 1990s and has emerged as a sophisticated extralegal category in the twenty-first century. In other words, for the last fifty years, the love hotel interior has functioned continuously as a democratic and accessible place at the service of the general public, but its means of doing so have changed significantly. It is thus a useful cultural barometer for measuring modernity, making it possible to gauge some of the effects of changing life circumstances in Japan and the beliefs, preferences and practices that accompany them.

These changes in circumstance and attitude span a time when Japan was recovering from defeat in the Second World War, enduring the American occupation which followed and dealing with the cultural, political and economic shift in values and priorities that inevitably ensued. The Japanese were importing and consuming a huge quantity of new goods and ideas, as well as developing their own spheres of modern industrial production. At the same time, they were recalibrating their cultural position with respect to dominant Western values and their own sense of cultural and moral inferiority. It was a time of rapid growth and growing economic prosperity, but

Japanese people were nevertheless coming to terms with the trauma and psychological after-effects of the Second World War.

Emerging in the midst of this difficult context, the love hotel demands to be examined as a complex and situated figure of modernity which encompasses more than the immediate parameters of everyday life that Kon studied under the auspices of his 'modernology'. Miriam Silverberg addresses this when she asserts,

A new cultural history needs to explore how new attitudes toward food, dress, and sexuality had profound implications regarding Japanese attitudes toward self, others and the state. In other words, to recount the adoption of Western clothing, bread for breakfast, and new attitudes toward sex, without associating them with new social practices that went far beyond dressing, eating, or kissing, is to avoid problematising the Japanese experience of modernity.[6]

The love hotel interior provides a means to explore, problematise and moreover schematise new social practices, and thereby locate them within popular culture.[7] This is because the kinds of social practices, which go beyond 'dressing, eating, or kissing' are not simply evident in the love hotel interior, but are in some senses *produced* there. Given the love hotel's specific purpose as a space set aside for sexual relations and the innovative spatial, visual and material configurations which were introduced to enable competing establishments to attract sufficient custom, the bedroom interiors display a panoply of typical features, which has changed significantly over time. That is to say, the love hotel interior, through its specific formation in late twentieth-century Japanese society, has served as a site of transgression, where new forms of intimacy and courtship are able to be performed, creating a space in which traditional social and cultural mores and identities can be challenged and alternatives may be developed and practised.

Just as Walter Benjamin in his *Passegenwerk*[8] sought to analyse the emergence, development and decline of the Paris arcades as a space of modernity, capturing them just at the point at which they were likely to disappear, the love hotel interior charts a similar dialectic, functioning now as a prominent yet dwindling aspect of Japanese culture. Like the Parisian arcade, the love hotel interior is a space set apart from normal urban life, a space of loosening, of becoming, that gives those who occupy it opportunities to alter the nature of their relationships with themselves and others (see Fig. 15.1). In both settings, meanings and identities are in constant circulation and under a constant process of revision, which in turn informs their visual, spatial and material parameters, and thus characterises the interior environment.

Fig. 15.1. Maria Theresia Rooms, Osaka, offering choice of 'romance' or 'adventure'.

Compared to the arcade, the love hotel interior, whilst just as concerned with constructional innovation, imported imagery, luxury goods and new practices of consumption, is experienced as more private and therefore requires to be framed somewhat differently. Whereas the arcade allowed the exercising of a distinctive new public persona in relation to consumption, the love hotel interior has facilitated the development of new forms of private persona in the context of a highly articulated consumer society and is therefore not just more internalised. Altogether more 'interiorised'. That is to say, issues of the individual and the ways in which they work through their own relationship to others, to society and to the globalised context in which they live are, on the one hand, highlighted by the love hotel interior, in its referencing of other spaces and places. On the other hand, the love hotel interior achieves its sense of interiority by negating patterns of spatiality and behaviour that are external to its purpose.

The love hotel interior is radically modernising in the sense that it has brought to the fore many of the attributes of modern design well before the Japanese domestic interior was able to follow suit. Love hotel proprietors were early adopters of Western furnishings and consumer technologies long before these were incorporated into the average Japanese home, which makes the love hotel as a type progressive and modern. Three items in particular—beds, electric light and wall-mounted imagery— came to the fore in the design of the love hotel interior and contributed to its modern identity.

Modern = bed

The Western-style bed was, and still is, the focal point of the love hotel interior (see Fig. 15.2). Even by the 1950s, very few Japanese people had experienced Western-style beds; although they had been available in Japan since the 1920s, when experiments in 'cultural living' or *la vie simple* very often incorporated the high-up double bed, the majority of Japanese still rolled out their futons on tatami-matted floors each night, because, for most people, cost and lack of space precluded dedicated bedrooms. Consequently, the bedroom, and specifically the bed, remained an alluring and unattainable image of a truly modern lifestyle well into the late twentieth century.

The first time Western-style beds were introduced in any great quantities was during the 1960s, particularly during the run-up to the 1964 Tokyo Olympics, when new Western-style hotels and motels were being built to accommodate visitors to the Games from overseas. Japanese businessmen who had travelled abroad would also have experienced Western-style beds, and a preoccupation with a new way of sleeping grew during this developmental period. Love hotels began to use the Western bed as the main way of differentiating themselves from other types of accommodation, particularly the traditional inns or *ryokan,* which retained the futon. Nowadays, many business- and tourist-class hotels offer both *washitsu* (Japanese style) and *yōshitsu* (Western style) rooms to guests, where the bed is the main point of distinction, since green tea, *yukata* robes, slippers, and other Japanese elements of hospitality are

Fig. 15.2. Joyful Club, Osaka, an older establishment offering vestiges of traditional hospitality in the form of slippers. Photograph: Sarah Chaplin.

usually available in both. Specifically, love hotel interiors in the definitive period of its development during the early 1970s tended to favour large divans covered with patterned valanced bedspreads, a sign of luxury in a changing economic context. Much as the introduction of chairs had already made sitting on the floor seem very backward during the Meiji period, the idea of sleeping raised above the floor held particular kudos for Japanese in the Showa period.

The sophistication and appeal of the Western-style bed was not limited to its elevation above the floor and the new types of bedding involved, but was also associated with its permanence and presence in a room. Sand comments that, 'in a *tatami*-matted house, any room could serve as a sleeping chamber, and as a result, no room bore specifically erotic overtones in the manner of the Western bedroom or boudoir.'[9] The Japanese were used to beds that disappeared during the daytime, and, unlike the love hotel, their beds did not occupy space as the main figurative element. Traditional futons also constituted sleeping as something that took place side by side rather than together under the same set of covers. The love hotel bed is almost without exception the focal point of the room as depicted in the love hotel guides, photographed from the ideal view upon entering the room. Such a permanent and central feature was deeply unfamiliar, and the sheer emphasis on the bed as the prime object in the space was erotic in itself: 'the general absence of a native tradition of marking a private space in the home for the conjugal couple only enhanced the eroticism of bedrooms and beds.'[10] The Japanese were also not accustomed to placing the

head of a bed against a wall, since futons were generally laid out in the middle of the room, with space all around them. This new positioning of the bed allowed for much innovation in the relationship of bed to wall, particularly in the form of mirrors and headboards, and this exotic spatialisation of the bed also led to the development of spatial arrangements between other relatively new items of furniture. Bedside tables, television consoles, lighting controls etc., all took up positions relative to, or integral to, the bed, augmenting its centrality in the room. As such, the status of the bed moved from an image to a technology in the development of the love hotel interior.

By the late 1970s, love hotel owners started to become more competitive and ambitious, installing imported European-style beds, ornate Louis XIV styles, four-posters or oversized sleigh beds at great cost, which they put in their best rooms. As the need to differentiate one love hotel from another, and indeed to differentiate one room from another, grew more intense, specially designed novelty beds started to emerge in the early 1980s, an extravagance which further distinguished the love hotel from other kinds of overnight accommodation. Even today, there are still a few rooms sporting a bed in the shape of a clam shell, a space rocket, a car or a boat, but these have since fallen out of favour and are only found in the unrefurbished establishments.

The type of bed to emerge as peculiar to the love hotel was the *dendō* or *engata* bed, a circular revolving contraption which was invariably surrounded by mirrored panels and was electrically operated. For a time during the 1970s, the *dendō* was thought to be the quintessential ingredient in a love hotel interior, effectively rendering the bed as not a place to sleep but as a rotating erotic stage or adult toy with pornographic and kinaesthetic potential, thereby explicitly signalling the bed's primary purpose for sex. By the mid 1980s, the authorities took the view that this kind of perverted use of technology needed to be legislated against, and the *dendō* became the main item that was prohibited in the 1985 revision to the Law Regulating Businesses Affecting Public Morals,[11] along with mirrors over one square metre that were designed to reflect a body in a supine position. Proprietors invariably responded by removing the electric motors from the circular beds, and the *dendō* now only remains in vestigial form in a handful of love hotels that have not undergone wholesale refurbishment. This kind of bed is now therefore regarded as old-fashioned, but it was in its heyday the primary means by which to achieve an ultramodern aesthetic for the love hotel.

Modern = electricity

The connotations of modern interior space and electric lighting are prefigured in Japanese design history by Jun'ichiro Tanizaki in his 1931 essay *In Praise of Shadows,* in which he deplored electric light as undermining an appreciation of Japanese material culture, arguing that it cast Japanese skin, lacquerware and other esteemed items too harshly compared to simple candlelight. He claimed, 'so benumbed are we nowadays by electric lights that we have become utterly insensitive to the evils of excessive illumination.'[12] He managed to occidentalise and demonise

electric light, characterising it as something that is vulgar and lacking in sensitivity, and associating it with lowbrow Japanese culture: 'the gaudy kabuki colours under the glare of western floodlamps verge on a vulgarity of which one quickly tires.'[13] Edward Seidenstecker reports that, in the Yoshiwara at the turn of the twentieth century, it was not flood lamps but chandeliers that glittered in the reception areas of many brothels, which could also account for Tanizaki's negative valuation of electric lighting.[14] There is an obvious continuity between entertainment, the floating world of Edo and the development of the love hotel, which can be evidenced in the use of light. Bright lights were clearly synonymous with sexuality in Japan, and, by comparison, Tanizaki achieved a link between dimness and aesthetic refinement, particularly of traditional Japanese handicrafts.

There is hence a necessary connection between modernity and bright, artificial light. Whilst most ordinary Western-style hotel bedrooms in Japan feature a simple overhead pendant light and a bedside reading light, today's love hotel designers make use of a whole array of different lighting effects— including rope lights, fairy lights, Christmas lights, backlit stained glass or images, downlights and uplights—to the extent that the average bedroom interior appears as richly wrought as a well-lit film set (see Fig. 15.3). Love hotel guidebooks depict rooms with their coloured lighting effects in full use and list as one of their marketable features how many lighting scenes a room can achieve. The deployment of excessive lighting and the occupant's ability to control it scenographically is clearly an important element of the success of a modern love hotel interior.

Fig. 15.3. Candybox Rooms. Photograph: Sarah Chaplin.

Like the *dendō,* there is one popular form of illumination that has come to epitomise the love hotel interior: the black light fantasy, or BLF. Ultraviolet lighting was already a staple of the nightclub and discotheque, and its use in the love hotel interior also came to the fore at a time when special effects were becoming more and more dominant in the film industry.

As a special effect, the black light fantasy not only renders flesh in an erotic and flattering light, but it has the effect of doubling the spatial experience in that it can transform one bedroom setting into something entirely different and exotic, bringing into focus motifs or scenes that have been painted in ultraviolet reflective paint onto the walls, typically conjuring up images of underwater worlds or distant galaxies. Atsushi Katagi notes that 'this transforms the role of the wall from separation and isolation into creation and expansion of the private space.'[15] Some love hotels' reputations are based on having a BLF in every room (*Casa Swan* in Umeda and *Köln* in Shibuya), whilst many others feature one or two rooms that have ultraviolet lighting. Although the technology is no longer new, the BLF remains an important feature in the love hotel interior repertoire and moreover is still diversifying in terms of its application, becoming part of a suite of coloured lighting effects that can now be produced using light-emitting diode technology.

Modern = mural

An established part of the love hotel interior is the *moodie,* which is effectively a large mural that is either painted, constructed (for example,

plaster bas reliefs, three-dimensional elements organised in a vitrine or a stained-glass panel) or projected onto a wall surface within the room. In an environment where actual views out or openable windows were rare, the love hotel began to deploy the *moodie* during the definitive period of its development as a way of providing an artificial view of elsewhere, which could be consistent with the rest of the room's theming or, in the case of the BLF version, a departure from it.

Typical subject matter for the love hotel *moodie* reveals a changing preoccupation and familiarity with other places over time. The earliest love hotels derived their imagery from historical Japanese images of samurai, geisha, irises and recreations of familiar Hokusai and Utamaro masterpieces. As the Japanese began to become active as tourists overseas as well as on their home turf, Japanese imagery was superseded by a preference for romantic places in Europe, Neuschwannstein castle in Bavaria being a popular motif (found in *Piaa* on the outskirts of Osaka and *Ōjo* in Tokyo). Love hotels in the 1980s drew from popular Western clichés, such as forests and palm-fringed beaches (for example *Yasuda* in the Higashi-Kanto area), and began to conjure up destinations of which only a few Japanese had direct experience, such as Egyptian pyramids. More recently, the trend has shifted towards photographic backdrops of other cities, New York's skyline and the Golden Gate Bridge being popular choices.

This widening repertoire of other places is evident in the development of supplemental subject matter in erotic prints or *shunga* during the eighteenth century. Timon Screech shows how, as 'travel increased and places known only by hearsay entered the realm of actual experience',[16] these images departed from the standard setting of the Yoshiwara and started depicting copulating couples against a great variety of different backdrops which were intended to heighten the erotic charge of the main image, employing devices to create a sense of spatial extension or inclusion of elsewhere. Typically, *shunga* showed views of Mount Fuji and other significant landmarks painted on screens, which had the effect of associating sexual acts with journeys and travelling, and hence a spirit of adventure and the possibility of new encounters, which carried a frisson in its own right. The love hotel has simply taken this technique a stage further and, through the *moodie,* is able to make reference to a wider spectrum of other places and journeys, maintaining for the Japanese the association between travel and sex. The realm of experience is today enlarged not only through travel, but also vicariously through the media, and many *moodies* contain imagery that borrows from the landscape of film, including James Bond and Disney scenes. There are, however, very few instances of *moodies* depicting naked or copulating bodies, with the exception of *shunga* art used as wallpaper in room 410 and an erotic *moodie* in room 411 of Hotel Adonis in Uehonmachi, which is a sadomasochism-orientated love hotel.

In many recent love hotels interiors, whilst the traditional *moodie* appears to have been omitted, it is still present in other forms: a third of rooms now have an open aspect, allowing in daylight, and, in some cases, an actual view of a cityscape replaces the depiction of an urban scene, bringing the room into much closer proximity with its actual location, thereby revoking the former strategy of removing the gaze from the everyday and the here and now. A second contemporary manifestation of the *moodie* is given by the TV plasma screen or data projection screen for computer gaming, which offers an animated, interactive way for customers to participate more fully in an act of escapism—albeit one that seemingly replaces or foregoes the sexual encounter rather than augmenting it. Shoichi Inoue commented in a 1989 article on the love hotel interior that there had been a shift from the desire to be enclosed or incarcerated within a hermetic world to a desire to include, even if vicariously, a sense of the beyond, providing a release from the confines of the actual space.[17] Now, it is clear that the vicarious sense of elsewhere is being replaced by an acceptance of the love hotel being congruent with the everyday, and thus there are fewer cues that are intentionally designed to transport the room's occupants into an imaginary realm.

One reason the *moodie* grew in importance as a key ingredient of the love hotel interior was as a substitute for large mirrors, which the 1985 legislation change had effectively outlawed. The long-standing association between mirrors and love hotels dates back to their precursors, the *tsurekomiyado,* which were adapted for amorous use through the introduction of mirrored surfaces.[18] As such, mirrors are synonymous with the eroticisation of space, giving rise to a preponderance of reflective surfaces that epitomised the love hotel interior during its definitive phase. These were often decorated with patterns and motifs that obscured portions of their reflective surface, ostensibly to make women feel aroused but not objectified. Shoichi Inoue has argued that opulence in the design of love hotels was intended to make women feel they were being treated well, but it is more likely that the overtly sexual orientation of early love hotel interiors was originally geared towards satisfying male sexual instincts with a prominent emphasis on the visual. By the mid 1980s, when the mirrors were called into question by the state, they were also proving unpopular with the love hotels' female clientele. As Suzuki argues, as women began to become more active in the decision-making process where love hotels were concerned, it became apparent that they found an abundance of mirrors sexually inhibiting,[19] and many establishments began to refurbish rooms accordingly. The strong visual orientation of the love hotel interior has thus gradually diminished, with today's interiors much more restrained visually with respect to their sexual overtones.

Conclusion

The locus of the modern impulse in relation to the experience of a typical love hotel bedroom has changed significantly over the last fifty years. Over this time, the design of a love hotel interior has challenged many of the modernist tropes that characterise interior design in the twentieth century. The modern interior tends to be associated with an abundance of natural light, a sense of visual connectedness to the exterior world, a limited colour palette, a preference for simple forms

and materials and clear spatial designation of use. The love hotel interior exhibits a marked preference for artificial lighting, views of outside being confined to representations, rich colours and sumptuous, and often fake, materials and temporal rather than spatial designation of use. It is a perverse, yet sharply tuned, format which has favoured novelty over familiarity.

The love hotel may therefore be characterised as both a product of modernity in terms of its rationality of ends, but simultaneously a product of postmodernity in terms of its means of achieving these. It developed during a late capitalist phase in history and has been thoroughly worked over by postmodern experience, which has been dominated by issues of consumption and identity. Harootunian regards Japan as having a particular relevance of in this regard: 'the Japanese experience showed … that modernity was always a doubling that imprinted the difference between the demands of capitalism and the force of received forms of history and culture.'[20] Constructing a cultural history of the love hotel is thus one way of both probing this difference and calling into question these received forms.

Notes

1. H. Harootunian, *History's Disquiet: Modernity, Cultural Practice and the Question of Everyday Life* (Columbia University Press, 2000), p. 130.
2. Ibid., p. 130.
3. Ibid., p. 131.
4. Ibid., p. 128.
5. Ibid., p. 133.

6. M. Silverberg, 'Constructing a New Cultural History of Prewar Japan', *Boundary 2* 18/3 (Duke University Press, 1991), p. 87.

7. A. Gordon, ed., *Postwar Japan as History* (University of California Press, 1993), p. ix.

8. W. Benjamin, *The Arcades Project* (Belknap Harvard, 1999).

9. J. Sand, *House and Home in Modern Japan: Architecture, Domestic Space and Bourgeois Culture, 1880–1930* (Harvard University Asia Center, 2003), p. 343.

10. Ibid., p. 343.

11. *Fuuzoku Eigyou Tou no Kisei Ooyobi Gyoumu no Tekiseika Tou ni Kansuru Houritsu.*

12. J. Tanizaki, *In Praise of Shadows* (Leete's Island Books, 1977), p. 36.

13. Ibid., p. 24.

14. E. Seidenstecker, *Low City, High City: Tokyo from Edo to the Earthquake, 1867–1923* (Penguin, 1983), p. 172.

15. A. Katagi, 'Leisureland of Sex: Design Theory of the Leisure Hotel', *City Quarterly* (Urban Design Research, Autumn 1989).

16. T. Screech, *Sex and the Floating World: Erotic Images in Japan 1700–1820* (Reaktion Books, 1999), p. 266.

17. S. Inoue, 'The Passage of Mankanshoku: What the "Fashion Hotels" Have Lost', *City Quarterly* (Urban Design Research, Autumn 1989).

18. A. Suzuki, *Do Android Crows Fly over the Skies of an Electronic Tokyo? The Interactive Urban Landscape of Japan* (Kosaido, 2002), p. 34.

19. Ibid., p. 39.

20. Harootunian, *History's Disquiet,* p. 111.

Chapter Sixteen

The Contemporary Interior: Trajectories of biography and style

Alison J. Clarke

My favourite room is the extension. The significance of the room is two-fold. Firstly it was paid for with my inheritance after the sudden death of my mother. Her framed photo has pride of place in the window and I always think of her when I am in that room. Secondly, the colour scheme and furnishing stems from travels; my husband to Stockholm, where he loved the simplistic, clean lines of the hotel he stayed in; [and] a family holiday to Seville, where we loved the ochre and burnt-sienna colours of the walls.

Response to *Homes* Mass Observation Directive, Autumn 2006; female, 47, North of England, M3412

Since the 1943 publication of the ground-breaking Mass Observation[1] social survey *An Enquiry into People's Homes,* notions of the home interior, its decoration and spatial layout have shifted ever further from practical issues of structure, function and storage. Instead, in the twenty-first century, emphasis is commonly placed on the expressive, emotive and social relational aspects of the interior both in popular discourse (as revealed in the excerpt quoted above from a 2006/7 Mass Observation *Homes* enquiry) and current academic research.[2]

The original 1943 Mass Observation wartime study (sponsored by the Advertising Service Guild) was unique in explicitly setting out to discover the kinds of homes 'British workers' really wanted and was highly influential in establishing a series of guidelines, based on in-depth qualitative research, that would shape postwar social housing policy.[3] Respondents to the 1943 *People's Homes* survey spoke of simple desires: to have heated bedrooms (to allow their daytime use as playrooms for children), space enough for a piano and access to outside space (preferably a garden). Notably in the 1943 survey, the term 'interior design' refers specifically to the spatial aspects of layout rather than furnishings or decorative features.

Many of the study's findings merely substantiated presumptions regarding the British relationship to the home; indeed it was a testament to British predilection for privacy, with respondents emphasising the importance of having one's 'own front door' and avoiding the noise and gaze of neighbours. Other findings proved a surprise for the researchers. The reluctance of residents to offer any subjective opinion regarding their homes and interiors caused a serious stumbling block for the survey; 'for a great many people ... the idea that they might either like or dislike their home is a novel one', the report concluded.[4] Similarly, when given the opportunity to forego practical concerns and envisage instead the 'home of their dreams', the researchers' were sorely disappointed. The incongruity of this concept for informants whose homes and personal trajectories were so 'taken for granted' and fixed as to be unworthy of reflection is perhaps unsurprising (and rather frustrating for the commercially motivated sponsor of the directive). For the few informants who dared to dream, such as a woman from Metrotown with two teenage children and a husband in the army, the extent of her aspiration was summarised in her musings over a home with two lavatories, a bow window, a refrigerator ('of course people in our circumstances can't have it') and paint ('so you can just sponge it down') in a warm parchment tone as opposed to traditional wallpaper.[5]

In stark contrast, the Mass Observation *Homes* directive of 2006/7 not only elicited descriptions of dream homes from over 80 per cent of its respondents,[6] the majority did so with startling enthusiasm and attention to detail as illustrated by the following extract:

My ideal home would be ... a Victorian Gothic Mansion. BIG SOLID WALLS! Large cosy fireplaces. No fussy interiors. Soft leather upholstery. Large library. Art studio. Large solid family kitchen—with Aga and solid wood table. Each bedroom to have walk-in dressing room and bathroom ... Large stylish dining room—for entertaining! Playroom for Georgia. Swimming pool and steam room. Gym. Double, no—triple—garage.

Female, 47, Middlesborough F3592

Direct historical comparison cannot easily be made between evidence gleaned from a wartime 1940s survey of predominantly working-class residents of state housing during a time of rationing and a mixed demographic of respondents from twenty-first-century Britain. Nevertheless, there has been an undoubted shift from conceptualising the home interior as a relatively static entity (in terms of familiarity, tradition and adherence to class-prescribed genres of décor) to one defined by late twentieth century ideals of tireless modernisation and projected aspiration.[7]

The social historian Raphael Samuel has observed that this 'distinct hankering for dreamscapes, discovering decorative possibilities in the most unpromising settings, aestheticizing the most humdrum objects of everyday life and beautifying kitchens and bathrooms' had its origins in the increasingly gentrified Britain of the 1970s and 1980s.[8] Furthermore, in his analysis of the growing taste for 'retro' alterations and 'periodized' styling typical of this period (from refurbished Georgian sash windows to reproduction Victorian oak panels), Samuel aligns the process of retrofitting to 'that revolution in expectations which in the 1950s and 1960s changes the living environment from a fixed property into one on which individuals could make their mark'.[9] As was observed widely in the left-wing press of the late 1980s and in the newly established academic discourses of cultural studies, the home and related consumerism had replaced political activity as the focus of social life and change.[10]

This chapter considers the implications of this shift in the materiality of the contemporary interior from one of stasis to one of increasing transience in which individuals are 'free' to make their mark. Whilst Samuel viewed the unprecedented desire for 'retro' home improvement and historical styles as part of the macropolitics of Thatcherite Britain, here I explore how genres of style are understood at the micro level of individually narrated histories of the home and its interior. By analysing the sole-authored, written responses of participants from a national Mass Observation survey (returned late 2006/2007) the chapter offers a glimpse, from a broader forthcoming study, into the ways in which individual and familial biographies become integrally tied not just to objects (their acquisition and divestment) but to specific typologies of architecture and constellations of interior design. These genres, styles and typologies are layered together by respondents in their musings over ideal homes and in the actions, agencies and materialities of lived interiors. Style, it is suggested, is not just a visual device but a means of controlling temporality and charting life courses; part of the process Gregson refers to as the 'enduring, transience and holding' process that defines dwelling.[11]

The intertwining of objects, memory, social relations and contemporary home interiors is well developed as an established field of research in material culture, sociological and anthropological research.[12] Similarly, recent studies have explored the everyday practices of the home; its technologies and products as a means of exploring the interrelation of domestic routines and the use of everyday consumer items beyond the visual.[13] Most significantly, though, the home is increasingly viewed as a site of dispersal and 'ridding' as much as one of containment and stasis. This literature (emerging predominately in the social sciences) whilst justifiably moving away from a perceived overemphasis on the purely visual aspects of homes and their contents, almost entirely discounts style itself as a relevant aspect in the practice of ordering temporality and shaping life trajectories. In such studies, the style of things, and the making of aesthetic competences, is either entirely neglected as an aspect of social practice or understood only in terms of the making of self-identity, Bourdieuian reflection of social class or the manipulation of the design industry.[14]

Unlike ethnographic or sociological study of the home interior, where researchers dictate the terms and priorities of description, the Mass Observation directive invites an open literary and visual response from its panel of respondents. Consequently, they are able to appropriate a range of literary genres that may change according to the subject of the directive and even change within the same directive response; some may respond 'through exposition, others with narrative, some write as if writing a letter to a friend, and occasionally a few may write a poem as a part of the directive'.[15]

In this respect, a striking feature of the responses to the Mass Observation *Homes* study is the tendency of respondents to choose a narrative genre in which biography is intertwined with trajectories of styles and aesthetic genres and architectural typologies are inseparable from their personal and familial histories. As Street points out, Mass Observation data have limitations in being used as straight 'knowledge transmission', as their exceptional value lies in the partiality of the data generated; in this case partiality offers the researcher an opportunity to understand the contemporary interior not just as part of a broader sociological phenomenon but also as a trope of narrative construction.[16] Furthermore, in contrast to the majority of existing home-related studies (that due to ease of methodology and theoretical focus) deal exclusively with women or couples, the Mass Observation *Homes* directive includes an extensive range of male respondents.[17]

Biographies of style

I believe that it is a mistake to become too attached to a place to the point where you become old and infirm and your previously nice property disintegrates around you. The trick is to know when to move.

French Polisher, male, retired,
Bedfordshire, G3126

The undermining of self through the loss or redistribution of personal possessions brought on through institutionalisation and/or aging, is well established within material culture studies.[18] As revealed in the proceeding quote from a retired French Polisher (who

has painstakingly restored the interior decor of his 1930s home for decades), whose narration includes an ideally timed exit from an envisaged degeneration in which the agency of the disintegrating home takes over from that of the tendered interior. For it is not just loss or rearrangement of objects of memory or sentiment that affects personhood, it is also the making and breaking up of constellations, biographies and related competencies of style (as well as what Gell describes as 'dispersed personhood') that needs to be accounted for in understanding the home interior of the twenty-first century.[19]

The retrospective narration of a 'style biography' is not just the imposition of order, through formal stylistic analysis, on a series of dwellings and life stages or the self-conscious rendering of the self.[20] Rather, it reveals the ways in which styles (these can be fantastical or 'real'), and their contradictions, have agencies and temporalities within and of themselves as revealed in the following case study typical of the narrative responses to the Mass Observation directive.

Executive mock tudor meets scandinavian mid-century modern

Respondent T3775 is a married 70 year-old retired man of Swedish origin who spent much of his early working life as a translator inhabiting temporary, prefurnished accommodation moving from city to city. T3775 locates the beginning of his own style biography with the purchase of what he describes as a 'jerry-built' 1929 bungalow that he moved to from a furnished company home (his first marital home) in 1975. Whilst for his daughter the bungalow stands as an idyllic family home, T3775 has entirely ambivalent memories of the first family home expressed almost entirely through reference to its shoddy materiality and failure to respond to nurturing repairs and reconstruction. More than thirty years on, the respondent reflects on the demise of his relationship with the 1929 bungalow, much as one might reflect on a failed romantic relationship. Seduced by its 'nice proportions', its nonexistent insulation and the architecturally unsound extension ultimately caused years of discomfort: 'We did what we could to insulate and change it, but gave up in the end', he laments. Most significantly, the failures and misfortunes that came to be embodied in the housing type of the 1929 bungalow led T3775 and his wife to make an uncharacteristic decision, in 1990, to buy a 'new-build' home in a small builders' development (see Fig. 16.1). The comparatively low maintenance of the efficiently insulated new home had one major drawback: 'the builder had provided the house with what they called an "inglenook"' or, as the respondent continues, '[a] monster in brick that totally dominated the room and completely ruined a wall that could have been

Fig. 16.1. The 'executive-style' mock Tudor house happily inhabited by an advocate of Scandinavian modernism whose rendering of its interior transforms its biographical aesthetic significance.

Fig. 16.2. A 'monster in brick'; Mass Observation respondent T3775's description of the inglenook fireplace that has asserted its agency as a fondly endured 'interior eyesore' in his home for over fifteen years.

perfect for a very large bookcase' (see Fig. 16.2). Furthermore, citing his Swedish origins as a possible explanation, T3775 declares himself entirely unable to understand the 'sooo conservative' British obsession with the open fireplace.

Sixteen years after moving into the house, the detested inglenook remains a testament to a broader compromise of style; it is pitted in direct opposition to a pressing need to shelve their ever-growing collection of books—by definition an impingement on their intellectual pursuits. Yet whilst the external aspects of the neo-vernacular architecture bothers them little ('outside was mock-Tudor ... But we bought it anyway'), the 'monster in brick' and

the cheap 'builder's wife' bathroom fittings have proved less easy to accommodate. The bathroom fittings were hastily changed for simple Modernist versions, but, aware that the neighbour has already removed its inglenook feature, T3775 considers it as a project pending. In the meantime, a well-positioned flat-screen television and other electronic media continue to disguise the interior eyesore.

The new-build home was purchased after a long deliberation over importing a Swedish prefabricated house, an idea abandoned only when a plot of land proved impossible to find. For despite the respondent's avid interest in Danish mid-century modern furniture, and

Scandinavian principles of design in general, the 'mock-Tudor' home he and his wife eventually came to inhabit is actually the stylistic antithesis of their collective ideal. Significantly, the dream home described by T3775 is far from a flight of fancy conjured up merely in response to a Mass Observation survey; he designed his dream residence many years ago, and the details of its features are well rehearsed. A 'house that does not look like a clone of million other houses', the *u*-shaped bungalow 'heavily influenced by Danish architects' would be 'cheap to run and built using recyclable material'. Most importantly, it would house a library and, in opposition to the aesthetics of a 'builder's house', it would be 'practical' and 'well-designed'. Whilst the floor plan of the interior space would be altered enormously, in the ideal home, T3375's Scandinavian furnishings and white walls remain unaltered.

In the lengthy process of searching for an alternative family home to the doomed 1929 bungalow, T3375 used this Danish architectural ideal as a means of negotiating a compromise with the lived experience of the British housing market and (in his perception) the limited typologies of architecture available. Hence, a self-declared 'cultured' man (he expresses pride in personally knowing several leading Swedish artists and of owning their work) devoted to Scandinavian Modernism came to happily inhabit a speculative 'executive-style' new-build mock Tudor home—the epitome, in stylistic terms, of the British conservatism he deplores.[21]

This contradiction (which is referred to consistently throughout the respondent's narrative) is offset by the stylistic consistency of the home's interior. T3375 sees the interior as just that—a play of light and space which, viewed through a softened lens, can just about summon up the aesthetic of a Danish mid-century architect rather than that of a Midlands' builder. He connects his predilection for Scandinavian furnishings with an innate sense of design consciousness: 'Coming from Sweden I am used to good design and high quality.' After moving to the house and searching furniture shops from Sheffield to London, T3375 and his wife failed to find anything they considered useful, nicely designed or appropriately priced—commenting that the styles in British furniture shops looked identical to those on offer twenty-five years hence. Thwarted in their attempts to purchase a piece of well-designed, durable modern furniture, they settled for a 200 year-old mahogany dining table. Like the 'good design' of Scandinavian modernism, the solid antique table (which 'looks lived in') offered a form of authenticity lent by its antique temporality otherwise absent from their slightly whimsical stylistically neohistorical builder's home. Whilst the dining table offered a solid physical materiality (and an enduring investment), the discovery (whilst surfing online) of a nearby specialist outlet dealing solely in secondhand Danish furniture was one of sheer serendipity for an ex-pat Swede with a hankering for designers such as 'Hans Wegner and the other Danes'. The entire house is now furnished using the Danish Furniture Store (DFS) and pieces picked up from junk and antique shops in Sweden (see Fig. 16.3). The aesthetic has spread to their daughter (who has also chosen a house, her father comments, that

Fig. 16.3. The durability of 1970s Danish furniture is used to transcend the ephemeral 'thin slice of wood over cheap chip board' furniture culture that the Mass Observation respondent considers endemic in contemporary Britain.

is generally assumed to have been 'designed by a Dane or a Swede') who inherits her parents' DFS cast-offs as well as shopping there herself. The son has also taken the first steps to adopting the style for his home, receiving a cast-off Ikea bentwood armchair from his parents as they 'up-graded' to a 'genuine' Scandinavian-designed leather easy chair. Every day, T3357 checks the DFS website to see if there are any new good furniture 'catches'.

T3357 contrasts the well-built and stylistically enduring design of Danish furniture with failed democratic design visions of the famous Swedish furnisher, Ikea, whose items, he notes, consist of little more than 'a thin slice of wood over cheap chip board'.

Like the 'jerry-built' 1929 bungalow where he began his married life, Ikea furniture has a cheap transience that can now only be justified in the shelving of books (with the furniture acting only as an invisible means of supporting something more significant).

The use of Ikea furnishing in making temporary, ephemeral or peripheralised space has been well documented in relation to a range of interiors and their users, including au pairs and newly cohabiting householders.[22] In this respondent's description of a style trajectory in the latter stages of life, Ikea design is almost expunged from the interior; stripped of any aesthetic significance, it is confined to a specific genre of furniture— the bookcase. Unlike the interesting 1790 mahogany collapsible card table, purportedly used in horse-drawn carriages in eighteenth-century Sweden, Ikea furniture has no provenance, no charm; its temporality no longer has a place in this interior.

Although the house's interior style has evolved as one of enduring value (in the form of collectible antiques, the materiality of solid mahogany and aesthetic pedigree of classic twentieth-century design), the configuration of these styles is subject to a relentless editing process in which even admired items are weeded out and replaced. A 1960s Danish writing desk takes pride of place one month, but a 'new home' (via the auction house) may be beckoning weeks later. Whilst formed from a series of 'designerly' and classic pieces, this interior is far from static as its overarching aesthetic principles are used as means of constant divestment. Items that contradict the style habitus, even if they are of potential sentimental value, are ruthlessly discarded as a means of breaking ties with antecedents or forging them with descendents.

T3357's mother's favourite piece of furniture (a reproduction bow-fronted eighteenth-century French chest of drawers that he grew up with) was sent to auction immediately after the mother's death. A similarly recalcitrant stylistic legacy, a suite of solid black furniture his father had made as a bachelor, 'followed us until his death', commented the respondent, whereby it was soon after dispatched.

In her study of Norwegian homes, Garvey focuses on the movement, rearrangements and reprocessing of home interiors as a means of inhabitants reordering their emotional selves.[23] Rather than the individual items of the interior holding specific and cherished values, the constellations and process of reordering generate value within the interior.

In the case of T3357, it is style divestment as well as the rearrangement of furnishings that generate a perpetual transience in an otherwise orderly interior. So rigorous is the household practice of furniture circulation and riddance that items that suddenly become unwanted are not shifted to an intermediate 'holding' space (such as the attic or shed, as is typical household practice), but rather they proceed directly to auction, charity shops or the homes of offspring: 'many people seem to buy new furniture and move the old into the garage. We prefer to keep cars in the garage and take superfluous furniture to the daughter's.' Considering T3357's ambivalence towards his own inherited furniture, we can only assume his daughter is more fully entrenched in the family interior aesthetic.

The typical academic response to T3357's 'style biography' might be to explain it away as an exemplary illustration of Swedish modern design summoned up as effective 'cultural capital' narrated by a member of the creative middle classes. But as Halle's classic study of art in US homes argues, there are limitations to a 'top down' Bourdieuian theoretical model of power and aesthetic knowledge; 'many meanings emerge or crystallize in the context of the setting in which the audience views the works (house, neighborhood, and the family and social life woven therein)'.[24] Furthermore, as observed in previous ethnographic studies, adherence to specific styles, in both fashion and furnishings, is as much tied to the immediacy of social relations as to a priori dispositions of taste (as indicated by static data provided by Bourdieu's questionnaire responses).[25] Here we see how taste is not just culturally reproduced but materially 'passed on' in the divestment of specific objects of family furniture in the making of offsprings' new homes.

Stylistic divestment

'The ridding of things', writes Gregson, 'is about the redistribution and potential revaluation of things'. Furthermore, the process of ridding and the transience it generates is as critical as keeping in the social practice of dwelling in the twenty-first century.[26] The increasing impact of the fashion industry on home design and the shift of the interior from a static, normative phenomenon to one of expressive value has made style (and related competencies) ever more crucial.[27] What we see in the case study presented above, and in a range of style biographies ranging from single mothers in Northumbria to recently bereaved widowers in Surrey, is the telling of their lives through trajectories of style. This practice is not only confined to those with formal aesthetic knowledge, or even enthusiasm for matters of design. On the contrary, as Woodward points out in her study of women's wardrobes, it is often those who declare the least competency in such matters that invest the most.[28] Whilst one respondent describes how the austere, newly unornamented style of his interior is dictated by the boisterous habits of his Alsatian dog, another respondent describes a trajectory incorporating 'Victoriana opulence' and 'vintage 1940s' with 'contemporary

uncluttered'. An ever complex and rapid system of style obsolescence is a defining feature of a late capitalist society.[29] Similarly, the social pressure to command new forms of aesthetic competence generates an array of mechanisms, commercial and social relational, to deal with associated anxieties.[30] Samuel's description of the rise of home decoration, and attention to nostalgic neohistorical details and fantasy in 1980s Britain, indicated an unprecedented shift in consumption that rendered the 1943 Mass Observation survey *People's Homes* a truly historical document. In the twenty-first century, genres of style, the interchanging of identifiable periods, the identification of typologies of housing (from 1930s semis to Victorian terraces) is bolstered by the increasing popularisation and domestication of design historical knowledge (through media, estate agents, online auction websites and related popular cultures). Unhinged from preexisting hierarchies of cultural capital, this new vernacular of style is interwoven in the processes of riddance that has come to define contemporary dwelling, be it the project of 'making-room' or decluttering or passing on.

In his study of houses in Northern Botswana, Morton describes how homes are built through layerings of materials (from recycled sacking to corrugated iron), social and kin relations, competencies and processes of remembering that far exceed the understanding of the house as a merely static container for 'memory or biography' but rather as an ongoing, active constituent of 'relatedness'.[31] These vernacular houses, he argues, occupy a dimension he describes as 'otherplaceness' and 'othertimeness' in that the house refers beyond itself; 'sites of dwelling as accretions of tasks and objects built up over time ... constantly refer outwards to other times, seasons, events.'[32] The occupants of British dwellings, as they rearrange, declutter, modernise and retrofit their interiors, use style in constant processes of remembering and expelling.

Biographies of style, revealed through narration of the self and interior, expose the processes of stylistic divestment and reveal style as a temporal phenomenon that static description (typical of much art and design history) otherwise overlooks. This process of internalising stylistic genres as a process of dwelling, as a temporal phenomenon, reveals the contemporary interior as a live element in the construction of biography. Whilst the agency of style in relation to personhood is an established theoretical claim of anthropological studies,[33] the intertwining of style and biography as practiced in the everyday processes of provisioning and riddance moves the interior beyond that of a 'snapshot' image (a moment in the construction of a home). Instead it necessitates longitudinal approaches in which we acknowledge houses and their interiors 'as material entities that are fluid both spatially and temporally' and, as such, have 'particular connections with the way people locate memories; activate them, and make them meaningful as part of life'.[34]

Notes

1. For an extensive exploration of the history and significance of Mass Observation's social research, see N. Hubble, *Mass-Observation and Everyday Life* (Palgrave Macmillan, 2006).

2. See, for example, A. Money, 'Material Culture and the Living Room: The Appropriation and Use of Goods in Everyday Life, *Journal of Consumer Culture* 7/3 (2007), pp. 355–77; I. Woodward, 'Domestic Objects and the Taste Epiphany', *Journal of Material Culture* 6/2 (2001), pp. 115–36; N. Makovicky, 'Closet and Clutter; Clutter as Cosmology, *Home Cultures* 4/3 (2007), pp. 287–309; R. Hurdley, 'Dismantling Mantelpieces: Narrating Identities and Materializing Culture in the Home', *Sociology* 40/4 (2006), pp. 717–33.

3. See D. Jeremiah, *Architecture and Design for the Family in Britain, 1900–1970* (University of Manchester, 2000).

4. *An Enquiry into People's Homes* (Advertising Service Guild, 1943), p. 53.

5. Metrotown was the pseudonym for an undisclosed West London borough living in 'better-style working class Flats', *An Enquiry into People's Homes* (Advertising Service Guild, 1943), p. x.

6. The *Homes* directive (October 2006) was supported by funding from the focused study 'Envisaging the Contemporary Interior', part of the Arts & Humanities Research Council Centre for the Study of the Domestic Interior at the Royal College of Art, London. The author acted as principal investigator for this focused study.

7. See A. Clarke, 'The Aesthetics of Social Aspiration', in D. Miller, ed., *Home Possessions* (Berg, 2001), pp. 23–46; A. Clarke, 'Taste Wars and Design Dilemmas: Aesthetic Practice in the Home', in C. Painter, ed., *Contemporary Art in the Home* (Berg, 2002), pp. 131–52.

8. R. Samuel, *Theatres of Memory: Past and Present in Contemporary Culture* (Verso, 1994), p. 95. In the chapter 'Retrofitting', Samuel describes the transition of British home decoration and improvement from a project of modernisation in the 1950s and 1960s to one of aestheticisation, in the form of the 'neo-vernacular' in the 1980s.

9. Samuel, *Theatres of Memory,* pp. 75–6. Unlike many academics and commentators of this period, including P. Wright, *Living in an Old Country* (Verso, 1985), who viewed the upsurge in the heritage industry and the populism of 'living history' as a reactionary response to social change, Samuel's work championed people's taste for popular history.

10. F. Mort and N. Green, 'You've Never Had It So Good—Again!', *Marxism Today* (May 1998), pp. 30–3; M. Featherstone, 'Lifestyle and Consumer Culture', *Theory, Culture & Society* 4/1 (1987), pp. 55–70.

11. N. Gregson, *Living with Things: Ridding, Accommodation, Dwelling* (Sean Kingston Publishing, 2007).

12. See, for example, Miller, *Home Possessions;* D. Miller, *The Comfort of Things* (Polity Press, 2008); D. Miller, 'Things That Bright Up the Place', *Home Cultures* 3/3 (2006), pp. 235–49.

13. For example, E. Shove, M. Watson, J. Ingram and M. Hand, *The Design of Everyday Life* (Berg, 2008); S. Pink, *Home Truths: Gender, Domestic Objects and Everyday Life* (Berg, 2004).

14. For example, in Shove et al., style and aesthetics are arbitrarily separated from inhabitants' relations to the physical materiality of the home interior and simplistically aligned with the external forces of 'market manipulation' rather than broader on-going competencies of individuals. See Shove et al., *The Design of Everyday Life,* p. 64.

15. D. Bloome, D. Sheridan and B. Street, *Theoretical and Mass Observation Issues in Researching the Mass-Observation Archive,* Mass Observation Archive Occasional Paper 1 (University of Sussex Library, 1993), p. 7.

16. For an extensive exploration of Mass Observation and respondents' use of directives as an empowering form of history-making, see B. Street, *Writing Ourselves: Mass Observation and Literacy Practices* (Hampton Press, 2000).

17. The Mass Observation project has recently sought to increase representation of men in its panel of respondents, This directive, when compared to other academic studies of home across disciplines, was surprising in that it attracted almost equal numbers of men and women (42% men, 58% women) when the figures were adjusted to take into account the gender representation of the active Mass Observation panel as a whole (171 men, 309 women). Although gender is not prioritised here in relation to the construction of 'biographies of style', in the broader ongoing study, this will form part of the analysis.

18. J.-S. Marcoux, 'The "Casser Maison" Ritual: Constructing the Self by Emptying the Home', *Journal of Material Culture* 6/2 (2001), pp. 213–235; F. Parrott, '"It's Not Forever": The Material Culture of Hope', *Journal of Material Culture* 10/3 (2005), pp. 245–62.

19. A. Gell, *Art and Agency: An Anthropological Theory* (Oxford University Press, 1998).

20. A. Giddens, *Modernity and Self-identity* (Polity Press, 1991).

21. Prime Minister Margaret Thatcher was condemned by the Left in the 1980s for buying a 'sham' neohistorical pastiche new-build home. See J. Moran, 'The Curse of Mr Barratt', *New Statesman* (9 October 2006). In notable contrast, her predecessor, the Conservative Prime Minister Edward Heath inhabited an 'authentic' Georgian house in the conservation area of Salisbury Cathedral, Wiltshire.

22. Z. Burikova, 'The Embarrasment of Co-Presence: Au pairs and Their Rooms', in *Home Cultures* 3/2 (2006), pp. 99–122; A. Clarke, 'Window Shopping at Home: Classifieds, Catalogues and New Consumer Skills', in D. Miller, ed., *Material Cultures* (Chicago University Press, 1998), pp. 73–99.

23. P. Garvey, 'Organized Disorder: Moving Furniture in Norwegian Homes', in D. Miller, ed., *Home Possessions* (Berg, 2001), pp. 47–68.

24. D. Halle, *Inside Culture: Art and Class in the American Home* (Chicago University Press, 1993), p. 11.

25. For an anthropological analysis of how couples, neighbours, peer groups and families generate style and 'taste' as a dynamic aspect of immediate social relations (as opposed to mere reflections of a priori class positions), see A. Clarke and D. Miller, 'Fashion and Anxiety', *Fashion Theory* 6/2 (2002), pp. 191–214.

26. Gregson, *Living with Things,* p. 126.

27. For analysis of the growing market for seasonally changing home interior goods, and the 'merge' between 'real' homes and 'retail' homes, see M. Brodin, 'Building Privileged Trajectories in Interior Decoration Stores', in H. Brembeck et al., eds, *Little Monsters; (De)coupling and Assemblages of Consumption* (Lit Verlag, 2007), pp. 51–66.

28. S. Woodward, 'Looking Good, Feeling Right: Aesthetics of the Self', in S. Kuechler and D. Miller, eds., *Clothing Material Culture* (Berg, 2005), pp. 21–40.

29. See V. I. Postrel, *The Substance of Style: How the Rise of Aesthetic Value Is Remaking Commerce, Culture, and Consciousness* (Harper Perennial, 2004).

30. Clarke and Miller, 'Fashion and Anxiety', 2002.

31. C. Morton, 'Remembering the House: Memory and Materiality in Northern Botswana', *Journal of Material Culture* 12/2 (2007), pp. 157–79.

32. Ibid., p. 166.

33. Gell, *Art and Agency.*

34. Morton, 'Remembering the House', p. 177.

Chapter Seventeen

Living the Sustainable Life: A case study of the Beddington Zero Energy Development (BedZED) sustainable interior

Anne Chick

From government and industry to the individual consumer, there has in recent years been a growing realisation that we must all consider our 'ecological footprint' and our legacy for future generations. The issues of sustainable design are now recognised by a growing number of business, community and environmental leaders as a key driver in innovation and social sustainability change. This chapter will explore the issues of sustainable design as they relate to the design of the modern interior through a case study of the United Kingdom's largest carbon-neutral eco-estate, the Beddington Zero Energy Development, or BedZED. This multi-award–winning development is one of the most coherent examples of a built environment project that encourages sustainable living in the United Kingdom and was created to provide a holistic solution to the problems of sustainable urban living.[1] This chapter examines the ways in which the BedZED partners translated a notion of a sustainable lifestyle into a cohesive design with particular focus on the materials and design features of the domestic interior spaces (see Fig. 17.1).

Sustainable architecture in development

During the 1970s, the oil crisis and rising costs of natural gas led architects to investigate ways of moving away from dependence upon, and wasteful use of, fossil fuels and raw materials in the design and development of their buildings. This work led to designs based upon bioclimatic principles that could reduce the energy requirements of housing whilst guaranteeing comfort through the use of passive energy sources.[2]

As environmental debates intensified, the criteria of sustainable design became more multifaceted within the arena of sustainable architecture, where the goal was to reduce the collective environmental impacts incurred during the production of building components, the construction processes and, perhaps

Fig. 17.1. BedZED was a prototype development that aimed to produce affordable, attractive and environmentally responsible housing and work space.

more importantly, during the lifecycle of the building itself. The emphasis upon efficiency of heating and cooling systems, alternative energy sources, choosing an appropriate site for the building, the way in which building materials are reused or recycled, on-site power generation through solar technology, ground source heat pumps, wind power and other methods, rainwater harvesting for gardening and washing and on-site waste management became central to considerations of sustainable design.[3]

Over recent years, architects' motivations and scope have gradually broadened with their experience of designing for sustainability. The result has seen a substantial broadening of sustainable architectural goals to enable lifestyles which have a significantly reduced long-term impact on the environment, society and economy.[4] Perhaps not surprisingly, this approach has attracted the sometimes-

disparate interests of governments, developers and sustainability lobby groups.

Sustainable living

One of the principal challenges to environmental design of the early twenty-first century is the need to reduce the levels of energy and environmental resources that we consume, whilst at the same time improving the quality of life for all. It is perhaps no surprise, then, that there is a growing body of evidence testifying to a range of significant environmental and social impacts associated with how individuals in the developed world currently live. Whilst it is by no means a universal feeling, many agree these impacts urgently need to be addressed. However, twenty-first-century human nature being what it is, it has been found that people resist making changes to their lifestyle if they feel that their quality of life will be undermined or reduced in some way.[5] However, with busy, complex lives, the question of exactly how people can change their behaviours and evolve a sustainable lifestyle remains fundamental to sustainable design debates.

Sustainable living can be defined as a lifestyle that aims to operate without exhausting any natural resources or challenging any ethical considerations. The development of a sustainable lifestyle addresses the key human needs of housing, clothing, food, health care, education, energy, transport and leisure.[6]

Ecological footprinting

The question facing sustainable design has been how to measure and reduce a consumer's ecological impact. Ecological footprinting is used globally as an indicator of environmental sustainability. Per capita ecological footprint is a means of comparing consumption and lifestyle and checking this against nature's ability to provide for this consumption. It can be used to explore the sustainability of individual lifestyles, goods and services, organisations, industry sectors, neighbourhoods, cities, regions and nations and has been fundamental to emergent understandings of design for sustainable living.[7]

Ecological footprint analysis compares human demand on nature with the biosphere's ability to regenerate resources and provide services. It does this by assessing the biologically productive land and marine area required to produce the resources a population consumes and absorb the corresponding waste using prevailing technology. This quantitative approach can also be applied to an activity such as the manufacturing of a product or driving a car. Increasingly, ecological footprints have been used as justification of the argument that many current lifestyles are simply not sustainable, and this approach was used to inform the design, development, management and maintenance of the BedZED community.[8]

The typical UK ecological footprint is 6.29 hectares per person (based on a four-person household); this footprint is three times the global per capita target. If everyone on the planet consumed as much as the average UK citizen, we would need three planets to support us. The consequences of this have been demonstrated by BioRegional: 'If we in the UK decided to live within our fair share of the Earth's resources, we'd need to reduce our ecological footprint by two-thirds.'[9] This

target, supported in the twenty-second report by the Royal Commission on Environmental Pollution, published in the year 2000 and funded by the government, recommended that the UK population should reduce fossil fuel use by 60 per cent by 2050 to stabilise carbon dioxide in the atmosphere.[10]

The BedZED development

The reduction of overall ecological domestic footprint was the central goal of the BedZED development. Key to this ambition was the aim to assist inhabitants to change the default decisions of their daily lifestyle to ones which are sustainable. Since BedZED residents had not been selected because of their eco qualifications, a factor which tends to be prevalent with 'eco village' projects, this ambition remains significant to the development of BedZED, the large proportion of which is designated for social and key workers and is let on the basis of affordable rent in line with the Peabody Trust mandate.[11]

Creating a sustainable economy and lifestyle requires more than incremental improvements in environmental efficiency; it demands radical innovation and social changes. The ideas of, and solutions for, sustainability are complex transformations that take place between multiple stakeholders, involving both social and technical innovation. This was the task which the project partners designing BedZED were to tackle. Designed to minimise its ecological impact both in construction and to help residents live within their fair share of the world's resources, some of the key operational aims of BedZED were the overall elimination of carbon emissions due to energy consumption and to reduce:

1. water consumption by 33 per cent
2. power consumption by 60 per cent
3. space heating needs by 90 per cent
4. private fossil fuel car mileage to 50 per cent of UK average[12]

BedZED was developed as a prototype design that aims to produce affordable, attractive and environmentally responsible housing and work space. Located in Wallington, South London, BedZED is a mixed-use, mixed-tenure development comprising 100 homes, community facilities and work space for 100 people. The homes are a mixture of sizes (one-bedroom and two-bedroom flats, maisonettes and town houses) and a single show flat so that visitors may see what it is like to live at BedZED.[13]

Originally developed by the Peabody Trust in partnership with Bill Dunster Architects and BioRegional Development Group as the environmental consultants, BedZED has been occupied since March 2002. The Peabody Trust manages the housing at BedZED, whilst the other partners are still based in the development. This team worked together to show that eco-construction and developing sustainable lifestyles can be easy, accessible and affordable and can provide a good quality of life. Importantly, in doing this the development brings together a number of proven methods — none of which are particularly high tech — of reducing energy, water and car use and encouraging sustainable living.[14]

BedZED consists of high occupation density and repetitive terracing made possible by integrating work space and housing within a compact cross-section. The work space roofs are gardens for the adjacent dwellings, giving most units a private garden at densities that would normally allow only a balcony. The work spaces are in the shade zone of the dwellings and are lit by large triple-glazed north windows set between the roof gardens, leaving the houses to benefit from the southern sun and useful passive solar gain.[15] The relationships between the living accommodations and the work spaces ensure that shading is minimised and the winter sun can penetrate deep into all of the living areas.

Designed to make maximum use of natural daylight, the project questions the dependence on conventional space heating, reducing energy demand through conservation and passive solar design. A 300-milimetre overcoat of super insulation to the roofs, walls and floors keeps in the warmth so that sunshine, human activity, lights, appliances and hot water provide all environmental heating needs. Triple-glazed, argon-filled windows with low-emission glass, large panes and timber frames further reduce heat loss, and well-sealed windows and doors, together with the concrete construction, make the development, to all intents and purposes, practically airtight.[16]

The creation of sustainable and comfortable interiors is fundamental to the BedZED development. The interior environments of the development benefit directly from specifically designed large and playful exterior 'windcowls' which provide wind-powered natural ventilation and heat recovery up to 70 per cent to help prevent the houses from overheating. Stale air is also drawn out from kitchens, bathrooms and toilets, removing odours and excess moisture by these windcowls.[17] The 130-kilowatt combined heat and power unit fuelled by the waste of tree surgery generates electricity for both the houses and offices. A by-product of this returns hot water to the spaces via a small district heating system.[18]

Energy consumption remains central to the experience of the BedZED residents. When questioned, two-thirds of BedZED residents said it was important to them to use renewable energy. However, the other third said the cost of electricity was more important. Leaseholders were more likely than tenants to say that it was important to them to use renewable energy, as they had bought properties due to the estate's sustainability credentials.[19]

Where possible, BedZED was built from natural, recycled or reclaimed materials. All the wood was approved by the Forest Stewardship Council or comparable internationally recognised organisations to ensure that it came from a sustainable source. To reduce the overall energy of BedZED, construction materials were selected for their low embodied energy (the energy required to manufacture a product) and sourced within a 35-mile radius of the site where possible. The energy expended in transporting materials to the site was therefore minimised.[20]

Distinctive architecture

During its relatively brief existence, the BedZED development has become an iconic statement of innovative and striking architectural design. Its highly distinctive external features and details offer low-technological answers to the ambitious aims of the project. Principally, these aims were to reconcile higher-density living with an improved quality of sustainable lifestyle whilst developing an eco-construction and design that resulted in particular building physics and internal environment.

A delightful characteristic is created through the playoff between the heavy mass of the traditional materials and the elegance of the windcowls. They have given the development a sense of place and create a positive landmark in the area. The use of timber as a construction material has been steadily returning to favour amongst architects. This has been aided by the building profession's acknowledgement that timber holds many environmental credentials that other construction materials cannot compete with, if a life-cycle approach is adopted.[21] Architects are increasingly using timber as an exterior and interior visual focus and indicator of a building's sustainability credentials. BedZED was an early UK pioneer of this approach in domestic homes with its use of timber cladding, framed windows, flooring, ceilings and kitchen units. Although principally specified for environmental reasons rather than aesthetic design, wood is central to the aesthetic form of BedZED (see Fig. 17.2).[22]

BedZED domestic interior spaces

At first glance, it might seem that the interior design and detailing of the BedZED houses did not receive the same amount of care and

Fig. 17.2. A pared down design allows occupants long-term flexibility in interior layout.

attention as the architectural exterior. This is not, however, the case. When designing the interiors, a conscious decision was made to pare down the internal fit out and finishes according to sustainability principles. From the outset of the development, the client had expressed a desire to leave the interiors relatively design neutral in a bid to ensure that residents would be able to impose themselves and their own identities upon their homes. Initial resident surveys showed that they were generally 'enthusiastic about the design and layout of their homes' with only the single exception concerning the 'amount of storage space provided as many felt this was inadequate'.[23] Partitions were installed that could be easily moved or removed during the lifetime of the building, giving occupants long-term flexibility in interior layout. Finishing materials were avoided altogether where possible, and this makes for an interesting design feature. For example, blockwork (walls or other features built of precast concrete or breeze blocks) in work space units is simply painted without plaster finish, whilst blockwork party walls in dwellings are plastered.[24]

The buildings make interesting and sustainable use of timber. The mezzanine floor in the work space is made of reclaimed timber floor boards, and the timber floor 'sunspaces' in the dwellings are made from local ash. Interior planed skirtings, cover strips and timber doors are softwood under various certified environmental schemes such as the Forest Stewardship Council. Tiles were sourced from a British manufacturer that uses British clay. Linoleum flooring was used in kitchens and bathrooms.[25] Linoleum is a linseed oil–based product with a very low environmental impact, offering the same performance as unplasticised polyvinyl chloride vinyl flooring.[26]

A standard Peabody Trust kitchen consists of medium-density fibreboard units with parana pine frames and a Formica work surface. The kitchen units installed in BedZED were made to be extremely durable, cost effective and have minimum environmental impact, including maintaining a 'healthy internal environment by minimizing off-gassing'—a process whereby materials emit potentially volatile and harmful gases through evaporation.[27] As BedZED homes are designed to be low-allergy homes, avoiding the use of formaldehyde-emitting and volatile organic compounds–emitting products where possible has meant the standard medium-density fibreboard carcass was replaced by birch-faced plywood. For the kitchen unit doors, 18-milimetre birch-faced ply was chosen. A number of options for the work surface finish—including recycled plastic and tiles—were explored; however, a block

beech work surface was chosen. The small sections required for this surface enabled the use of off-cuts of timber which would otherwise be wasted. Whilst the materials for the BedZED kitchen units added about 20 per cent additional costs to the standard Peabody Trust model, research has shown that higher initial investment is reflected in a low-maintenance and longer-life product (see Fig. 17.3).

Fundamental to the design of BedZED and indeed all forms of sustainable building is the controlled provision of services and utilities. The households and businesses located at BedZED are fitted with low-energy lighting and energy-efficient appliances to reduce electricity requirements. Kitchens are fitted with well-located electric and water metres for residents to monitor their consumption.

Water, too, is used sparingly, and rain is collected on the roofs. A typical toilet uses up

Fig. 17.3. BedZED homes are designed to be low-allergy homes and encourage sustainable behaviours.

to nine litres of water per flush and accounts for a third of a typical UK household's annual water consumption.[28] In BedZED, toilets are designed to use half the amount of water in a normal flush. The fitted water-efficient 'dual flush toilet' allows the user to select a reduced flush or a full flush. Approximately 20 per cent of UK domestic water is used for bathing and showering.[29] Water-saver showers are used rather than power showers. These showers simulate the effect of a power shower but without the high flow rate.[30] This is achieved by aerating the water flow so that the showers operate at approximately half the water use of a power shower. Water-efficient appliances and kitchen sinks are also in use at BedZED. In the United Kingdom, washing machines use approximately 14 per cent of domestic water.[31] Smaller and well-designed kitchen sinks as well as aerated taps can save over sixteen litres of water per person per day.[32]

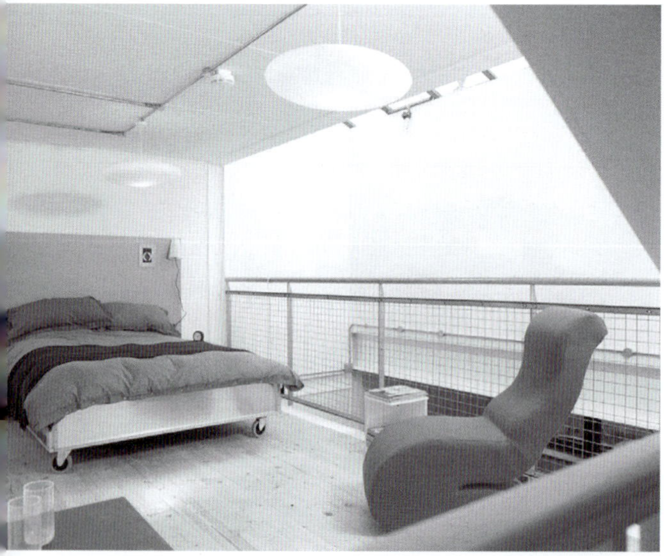

Fig. 17.4. The work space roofs are gardens for the adjacent dwellings, giving most units a private garden, at densities that would normally allow only a balcony.

Other internal features that encourage sustainable behaviour are a set of containers for different types of waste built into the kitchen. There are multimaterial recycling points on site for metal, glass, paper, card, textiles and shoes as well as community composting on the BedZED allotments.

Designed from a holistic perspective, it is clear that living in BedZED requires commitment by residents to its aims and ambitions. Residents are provided with a handbook and information service by Peabody Trust and BioRegional about their home and estate, including practical sustainable lifestyle guidance.[33] Further information concerning sustainable interior design choices—including environmentally considered floor coverings, furniture, upholstery and domestic paints—is made available (see Fig. 17.4).[34]

BedZED sunspaces

The physical and visual interconnections between interior and exterior space are a fundamental aspect of the BedZED design. The skilful section and location of the dwellings allows the warmth of the winter sun to stream through the 'sunspaces' and deep into the living areas. High natural light levels are promoted by the sunspaces, and skylights bring light directly into the depths of the homes. In the upper dwellings, the sunspace provides views of private footbridges covered in climbing plants, which pass over the mews between the block, and of the 'skygardens', small plots of land which residents can plant with whatever they choose, whether vegetables, plants, flowers or grass.[35] This feature plays a vital role in the management of the internal climate of the dwellings. During the summer months, the sunspace area heats up during the day whilst the rest of the flat remains cool. As the temperature drops in the evening, the double doors can be left open to allow the build-up of heat to spread through the rooms. In the winter, the triple-glazed doors can be kept closed to keep the rest of the dwelling warm (see Fig. 17.5).

Conclusion

Demand for BedZED homes has been exceptional ever since their completion. This interest has continued to increase so that the homes command a premium above market rates.[36] Resident surveys have demonstrated that the most frequently given reasons for wanting to live at BedZED are the 'modern green lifestyle' and the 'innovative design'. Key design features remain central to residents' appreciation of the buildings and include, in particular, 'the sunspace, the gardens, and the sense of space in the homes'.[37]

BedZED demonstrates that the provision of sustainable building infrastructure can lead to sustainable behaviour. However, more research is required to examine how specifically the provision of a sustainable home can influence a range of behaviours (which make up a lifestyle), particularly in relation to behaviours that would require action on the part of the resident.[38] BedZED has also demonstrated that providing information on the sustainability features of homes to residents is extremely important in driving both desired behavioural changes and demand for these features.

Fig. 17.5. Strong connection between the outside architecture and the inside domestic spaces created by the sunspaces.

Lowenstein points out that, by encouraging sustainable lifestyles through the design of buildings and facilitation of information exchange schemes, BedZED has extended the sustainable building ethos into the whole infrastructure of modern living. Broader debates and new arguments are now occurring regarding density levels, affordable homes and city regeneration within a sustainability context due to the very notable success of BedZED. Lowenstein has argued that the influence of a development such as BedZED has seeped into mainstream thinking so that 'the concept of sustainable cities is moving closer to envisaging, planning and realizing more nuanced environments'.[39]

A key reason for embarking on the BedZED project was to demonstrate to a sceptical house-building industry how sustainability is possible and can really make a difference for society and its future.[40] There is an increasing body of literature and research on the benefits of building sustainable homes, but this has yet to convince house builders, particularly in the private sector, to participate. As the Upstream Consultancy emphasises: 'In order for developers to build sustainable homes to create sustainable lifestyles there needs to be credible evidence that this adds value to the business. To develop truly sustainable projects, private and public developers must ensure that schemes are not only environmentally and socially sustainable, but that they are also economically viable.'[41]

Due to the success of BedZED, the business case for sustainable homes is gaining credibility, but it is still not as proven or well evidenced as it needs be to make a tangible change to contemporary house building. There is a continuing need for a variety of research, especially relating to the private sector, to provide more robust, in-depth and quantitative evidence for the business case for sustainable homes.

Notes

1. P. Desai and S. Riddlestone, *Schumacher Briefings 8: Bioregional Solutions: For Living on One Planet* (Green Books, 2007), p. 92.

2. D. Chiras, *The Solar House: Passive Heating and Cooling* (Chelsea Green Publishing, 2002).

3. I. Holm, *Ideas and Beliefs in Architecture and Industrial Design: How Attitudes, Orientations, and Underlying Assumptions Shape the Built Environment* (Oslo School of Architecture and Design Press, 2006).

4. T. Williamson, A. Radford and H. Bennetts, *Understanding Sustainable Architecture* (Spon Press, 2003); L. Tilder, 'Ten Shades of Green: Architecture and the Natural World', *Journal of Architectural Education* 60/4 (2007), pp. 60–1.

5. J. Collins, G. Thomas, R. Willis and J. Wilsdon, *Carrots, Sticks and Demons: Influencing Public Behaviour for Environmental Goals* (Department for Environment, Food and Rural Affairs, 2003).

6. A. Darnton, *Driving Public Behaviours for Sustainable Lifestyles (Report 2)* (Department for Environment, Food and Rural Affairs, 2004).

7. Global Footprint Network, *Ecological Footprint: Overview* (17 October 2006). http://www.footprint network.org/gfn_sub.php?content=footprint_ overview, accessed 10 January 2008.

8. Desai and Riddlestone, *Schumacher Briefings 8,* p. 28.

9. Ibid.

10. Royal Commission on Environmental Pollution, *Energy — The Changing Climate,* chapter 4, paragraph 4.51 and Table 4.1, June 2000.

11. Eco-village members are united by shared ecological, social or spiritual values. An eco-village is often composed of people who have chosen an alternative to centralised power, water and sewage systems. They see small-scale communities with minimal ecological impact as an alternative. D. Christian, *Creating a Life Together: Practical Tools to Grow Ecovillages and Intentional Communities* (New Society Publishers, 2003); Peabody Trust, *Our Aims* (2006). http://www.peabody.org.uk, accessed on 10 January 2008.

12. Bioregional Development Group, *BedZED Monitoring Data* (2007). http://www.bioregional. com/programme_projects/ecohaus_prog/

bedzed/bz_monitoring.htm, accessed 7 January 2008.

13. B. Dunster, *General Information Report 89: BedZED—Beddington Zero Energy Development, Sutton* (BRECSU, 2002), p. 8; C. Twinn, 'BedZED', *Arup Journal* 1 (2003), pp. 10–16.

14. Peabody Trust, *Our Aims.*

15. Dunster and BioRegional, *General Information Report 89,* p. 9.

16. Ibid., p. 11; Twinn, 'BedZED', p. 12.

17. Twinn, 'BedZED', p. 14.

18. Dunster and BioRegional, *General Information Report 89,* p. 13.

19. Peabody Trust, *Report for Property Standards Panel: BedZED Resident Survey Results* (Peabody Trust, April 2004).

20. Peabody Trust, *BedZED (Beddington Zero Energy Development) Factsheet* (2005). http://www.peabody.org.uk, accessed 2 January 2008.

21. O. Lowenstein, 'Wood in Architecture', in K. Hall, ed., *The Green Building Bible: All You Need to Know about Ecobuilding, 3rd Edition, Volume 1* (Green Building Press, 2007), p. 68.

22. N. Lazarus, *Beddington Zero (Fossil) Energy Development: Construction Materials Report: Toolkit for Carbon Neutral Developments—Part 1* (BioRegional Development Group, 2002), p. 22.

23. Peabody Trust, *Report for Property Standards Panel.*

24. Lazurus, *Beddington Zero,* p. 11.

25. Ibid.

26. J. Potting and K. Blok, 'Life-cycle Assessment of Four Types of Floor Covering', *Journal of Cleaner Production* 3/4 (1995), pp. 201–13.

27. Lazurus, *Beddington Zero,* p. 23.

28. Water Regulations Advisory Scheme, *Conservation of Water: An IGN for Architects, Designers & Installers* (WRAS, 1999), p. 22.

29. Environment Agency, *Conserving Water in Buildings: Showers and Baths* (Environment Agency, 2001).

30. J. Organ, Interview with the author on 7 January 2008.

31. Environment Agency, *Conserving Water in Buildings.*

32. N. Grant, *Water Conservation Products: A Preliminary Review* (2002). http://www.elemental solutions.co.uk.

33. Peabody Trust, *Report for Property Standards Panel.*

34. J. Organ, Interview with the author on 7 January 2008 at BedZED.

35. Dunster, *General Information Report 89,* p. 19.

36. Upstream, *The Gaps in the Existing Case for Building Sustainable Homes to Encourage Sustainable Lifestyles* (November 2005), p. 65. Sponge Sustainability Network, http://www.up streamstrategies.co.uk/uploadedfiles/Sponge_ Sustainable Lifestyles_Business Case. pdf, accessed 20 January 2008.

37. Twinn, 'BedZED', p. 16.

38. Upstream, *The Gaps in the Existing Case,* p. 77.

39. O. Lowenstein, 'Architectural Trends', in K. Hall, ed., *The Green Building Bible: All You Need to Know about Ecobuilding, 3rd Edition, Volume 1* (Green Building Press, 2007), p. 63.

40. Twinn, 'BedZED', p. 10.

41. Upstream, *The Gaps in the Existing Case,* p. iii.

Notes on Contributors

Penny Sparke (Editor) is Pro Vice-Chancellor (Research and Enterprise) at Kingston University and Director of the Modern Interiors Research Centre. She has published widely on design and culture and writes and speaks internationally on design in the academic community and for the media. Her publications include: *As Long As It's Pink: The Sexual Politics of Taste* (Pandora 1995); *An Introduction to Design and Culture in the Twentieth Century, 1900 to the Present* (Routledge 2004) (new edition) and *Elsie de Wolfe, Interior Decorator* (Acanthus Books 2005). Her most recent book, *The Modern Interior,* was published by Reaktion Books in 2008.

Anne Massey (Editor) is Professor of Design History at Kingston University and has published widely on aspects of twentieth-century visual and material culture. Her publications include: *The Independent Group: Modernism and Mass Culture in Britain, 1945–1959* (MUP 1995); *Interior Design of the Twentieth Century* (Thames & Hudson, World of Art Series 2008, 3rd edition); *Hollywood Beyond the Screen* (Berg 2001) and *Designing Liners: A History of Interior Design Afloat* (Routledge 2006). She is currently working on *Chair,* a new book in the Objekt series for Reaktion Books.

Brenda Martin (Editor) is Curator of the Dorich House Museum at Kingston University. Her publications include: 'A House of Her Own. Dora Gordine and Dorich House' in *Women's Places: Architecture and Design, 1860–1960* (Routledge 2003); 'Photographs of a Legacy' in *The Modern Period Room, 1870–1950* (Routledge 2006) and 'An Artist at Home: Studio Residences and Dora Gordine' in *Embracing the Exotic: Jacob Epstein and Dora Gordine* (Papadakis 2006). Her research contributed to the first monographic study of Dora Gordine, *Dora Gordine: Sculptor, Artist, Designer* (Philip Wilson 2007), and she was the curator of the first major retrospective exhibition of Dora Gordine's work at the Kingston Museum and Dorich House Museum in 2009.

Trevor Keeble (Editor) is Head of the School of Art and Design History at Kingston University, London. His PhD, *The Domestic Moment: Design, Taste and Identity in the Late Victorian Interior,* was awarded in 2005 by the Royal College of Art. He has contributed essays on the history of domestic interiors to a number of publications, including: *The Modern Period Room* (Routledge 2006); *The Imagined Interior* (V&A Publications 2006); *Women and the Making of Built Space in England, 1870–1950* (Ashgate 2007) and *Design and Culture* (Sage forthcoming).

Emma Ferry is Senior Lecturer in Visual Culture at the University of the West of England and also lectures at Kingston University. Her publications include: '"Decorators May Be Compared to

Doctors:" An Analysis of Rhoda and Agnes Garrett's Suggestions for House Decoration' in *Journal of Design History* (2003); '"… Information for the ignorant and aid for the advancing": Macmillan's Art at Home Series, 1876–83' in *Design and the Modern Magazine* (MUP 2007) and "A Novelty among Exhibitions:" The Loan Exhibition of Women's Industries, Bristol 1885' in *Women and the Making of Built Space in England, 1870–1950* (Ashgate 2007).

Fiona Fisher is a postdoctoral researcher in the Modern Interiors Research Centre at Kingston University. She worked in consumer magazine publishing for over ten years before returning to education in 2001. She completed a BA in the History of Art, Architecture and Design in 2004. Her PhD, *In Public, in Private: Design and Modernisation in the London Public House, 1872–1902,* was awarded by Kingston University in 2008. She is currently developing her PhD for publication.

Sabine Wieber is a design historian and lecturer in Art History at Roehampton University, London. Her research concentrates on German and Austrian modernism with particular attention to the domestic interior as an important cultural site of modern identity. She is currently preparing a monograph on central European Salon Culture 1870 to 1930, as well as serving as curatorial advisor on the international loan exhibition *Madness and Modernity: Mental Illness and the Visual Arts in Fin-de-Siècle Vienna* at the Wellcome Collection, London (April to June 2009). Her publications include: 'The Allure of Nerves: Class, Gender and Neurasthenia in Klimt's Society Portraits' in *Madness and Modernity* (Lund Humphries 2008) and 'Munich Historicist Interiors and German National Identity, 1871–1888' in *International History Review* (2007).

Christopher Reed is Associate Professor of English and Visual Culture at the Pennsylvania State University. His publications include: *A Roger Fry Reader* (University of Chicago Press 1996); *Not at Home: The Suppression of Domesticity in Modern Art and Architecture* (Thames & Hudson 1996); *Bloomsbury Rooms: Modernism, Subculture and Domesticity* (Yale University Press 2004) and the catalogue for the exhibition *A Room of Their Own: The Bloomsbury Artists in American Collections* (Cornell University Press 2008). He is currently involved in researching a new project concerning constructions of occidental forms of masculinity through attitudes towards Japanese art and design.

Elizabeth Darling is an architectural historian and senior lecturer in the Art History Department of Oxford Brookes University. Her work focuses on twentieth-century British architectural history with a particular interest in interwar modernism, social housing, and gender. Her revisionist history of British architectural modernism, *Re-forming Britain: Narratives of Modernity before Reconstruction,* was published by Routledge in 2007. Her current research focuses on the arena in which progressive ideas about design and space were developed and disseminated in 1920s Britain and on producing an in-depth study of the work and life of the architect–engineer Wells Wintemute Coates.

Irene Nierhaus teaches Art Sciences and Aesthetic Theory at the University of Bremen in Germany. Her specialisms are visual and spatial culture in art, architecture, film and graphics, housing and interiors from the nineteenth century to the present. Her publications include: *Arch 6: Raum, Architektur und Geschlecht* (Sonderzahl 1999); 'Statt/Stadt Rom: Zu Mitte und Rand im

Rom der Moderne' in *Imaginäre Architekturen. Raum und Fiktion in Kunst und Gestaltung* (Reimer 2006) and, with Elke Krasny, *Urbanografien: Stadtforschung in Kunst, Architektur und Theorie* (Reimer 2008).

Hilde Heynen is head of the Department of Architecture, Urbanism and Planning, KULeuven in Belgium. Her research specialisms are architectural theory, urban theory and architecture and gender. Her recent publications include: *Architecture and Modernity: A Critique* (MIT Press 1999); *Back from Utopia. The Challenge of the Modern Movement,* co-edited with Hubert-Jan Henket (010 2002) and *Negotiating Domesticity. The Production of Gender in Modern Architecture,* co-edited with Gülsüm Baydar (Routledge 2005).

Charles Rice is Associate Professor of Architecture and Director of Research Programs in the Faculty of Design, Architecture and Building at the University of Technology Sydney. He is author of *The Emergence of the Interior: Architecture, Modernity, Domesticity* (Routledge 2007). He has co-edited special issues of the *Journal of Architecture* on 'Walter Benjamin and Architecture' (with Andrew Benjamin, vol. 12, no. 5, 2007) and 'Constructing the Interior' (with Barbara Penner, vol. 9, no. 3, 2004). Most recently he has published '"So the flâneur goes for a walk in his room": Interior, Arcade, Cinema, Metropolis' in *Intimate Metropolis: Urban Subjects in the Modern City* (Routledge 2009).

Peter Blundell Jones was trained as an architect at the Architectural Association in London. He has been involved in practice, criticism and teaching for most of his professional life and has been Professor of Architecture at the University of

Sheffield since 1994. In 1973–4 he wrote his first book on the German architect Hans Scharoun, and he has remained a leading expert on this subject area. Recent publications include: *Gunnar Apslund* (Phaidon 2006); *Modern Architecture through Case Studies, 1945–1990* (Architectural Press 2007) and *Peter Hübner: Building as a Social Process* (Axel Menges 2007).

Pat Kirkham is Professor of Design History at the Bard Graduate Centre for Studies in the Decorative Arts, Design and Culture, New York. She writes widely on design, gender and film. Her publications include: *Charles and Ray Eames: Designers of the Twentieth Century* (MIT Press 1998); *Women Designers in the USA, 1900–2000: Diversity and Difference* (Yale University Press 2002). She has just finished co-editing a special issue of *Studies in the Decorative Arts* entitled 'Issues in Interior Design History' (2008) and is currently editing *A History of the Decorative and Applied Arts and Design 1400–2000* (Yale University Press). Her book on Saul and Elaine Bass will be published in 2009 by Laurence King Publishing.

Alice T. Friedman is Grace Slack McNeil Professor of the History of American Art at Wellesley College, Massachusetts, where she has taught since 1979. Her research specialisms are architecture, gender and social history. She has written widely on these subjects and is the author of *Women and the Making of the Modern House: A Social and Architectural History* (Harry Abrams 1998). Her current research focuses on mid-century modern architecture and includes a book-length study entitled *American Glamour and the Evolution of Modern Architecture,* which will be published by Yale University Press in 2010.

David Crowley teaches Cultural History at the Royal College of Art in London. He has a particular interest in the history of architecture and design in Eastern Europe in the nineteenth and twentieth centuries. His publications include: *Socialist Spaces: Sites of Everyday Life in the Eastern Bloc* (co-edited, Berg 2002) and *Warsaw* (Reaktion Books 2003). He was on the curatorial team of *Modernism: Designing a New World, 1914–1939* (V&A Museum 2006) and was consultant curator of *Cold War Modern: Art. Design 1945–1972*, which was shown at the Victoria and Albert Museum in London in 2008 and will be shown at the Museo di Arte Moderna e Contemporanea di Trento in Rovererto and the National Gallery in Vilnius in 2009. He is currently writing a book on the interconnected histories of communism and photography.

Sarah Chaplin is Deputy Director of the Urban Renaissance Institute at the University of Greenwich. She trained as an architect and runs a design consultancy, *evolver,* with her husband. She is a board director of the Academy of Urbanism, a national organisation dedicated to identifying best practice in urbanism and fostering learning from place. Her publications include: *Japanese Love Hotels: A Cultural History* (Routledge 2007); 'Heterotopia Deserta: Las Vegas and Other Spaces' in *Designing Cities: Critical Readings in Urban Design* (Blackwell 2003) and *Curating Architecture and the City,* co-edited with Alexandra Stara (Routledge 2009).

Alison Clarke is Professor of Design History at the University of Applied Arts, Vienna, and managing co-editor of *Home Cultures: Journal of Architecture, Design and Domestic Space* (Berg). Her most recent research (WWTF 2008-2011) focuses on kinship and the visual and material culture of interiors in a comparative ethnography of Austria and Britain. Previous related publications include: 'The Aesthetics of Social Aspiration' in *Home Possessions: Material Culture behind Closed Doors* (Berg 2001); 'Taste Wars and Design Dilemmas: Aesthetic Practice in the Home' in *Contemporary Art in the Home,* edited by C. Painter (Berg 2002) and 'Coming of Age in Suburbia; Design and Material Culture' in *Designing Modern Childhoods: History, Space and the Material Culture of Children* (Rutgers University Press 2008).

Anne Chick is Director of the Sustainable Design Research Centre at Kingston University. She is Adjunct Professor in the Faculty of Environmental Design at the University of Calgary, Canada, and co-founder of Greengaged (www.greengaged. com), a not-for-profit organisation and network that disseminates sustainable design information. Her recent publications include: 'Closing the Loop: The Role of Design in the Success of Six Small UK Recycled Product Manufacturers' in *Design & Manufacture for Sustainable Development* (Professional Engineering Publishing 2004); 'Beyond-the-Box Packaging Solutions and Assessment of Packaging Practices' in *Paper or Plastic: Searching for Solutions to an Overpackaged World* (Sierra Club Books 2005) and 'The Ecopreneur and Sustainable Development' in *Entrepreneurship for Everyone* (Sage Publications 2008).

List of Illustrations

Select Bibliography

Abercrombie, S., *A Century of Interior Design, 1900–2000: The Design, the Designers, the Products, and the Profession,* New York: Rizzoli, 2003.

Adler, H. A., *The New Interior: Modern Decoration for the Modern Home,* New York: Century Company, 1916.

Adorno, T. W., *Minima Moralia. Reflections from Damaged Life,* London: Verso, 1951.

Albrecht, D., *The High Style of Dorothy Draper,* New York: Pointed Leaf Press, 2006.

Aldrich, M., ed., *The Craces. Royal Decorators 1768–1899,* Brighton: John Murray and the Royal Pavilion, Art Gallery and Museum, 1990.

Ambasz, E., ed., *Italy: The New Domestic Landscape, Achievements and Problems of Italian Design,* New York: Museum of Modern Art, 1973.

Ambruster, A., *The Life and Times of Miami Beach,* New York: Knopf, 1995.

Aslin, E., *The Aesthetic Movement: Prelude to Art Nouveau,* London: Elek Books, 1969.

Atterbury, P., and Wainwright C., eds., *Pugin: A Gothic Passion,* London: V&A Publications, 1994.

Attfield, J., and Kirkham, P., eds., *A View from the Interior: Women and Design,* London: Women's Press, 1989; 1995.

Aynsley, J., and Grant, C., eds., *Imagined Interiors: Representing the Domestic Interior since the Renaissance,* London: V&A Publications, 2006.

Banham, J., Porter, J., and MacDonald, S., *Victorian Interior Style,* London: Studio Editions, 1995.

Banham, R., *Theory and Design in the First Machine Age,* London: Architectural Press, 1960.

Baranski, Z. G., and Lumley, B., eds., *Culture and Conflict in Postwar Italy,* London: Macmillan, 1990.

Beckett, J., 'The Abstract Interior', in *Towards a New Art: Essays on the Background to Abstract Art 1910–1920,* London: Tate Gallery, 1980.

Bell, C., *Since Cézanne,* London: Chatto and Windus, 1922.

Benjamin, W., *The Arcades Project,* ed., Rolf Tiedemann, tr. H. Eiland and K. McLaughlin, Cambridge, MA: Harvard University Press, 1999.

Benjamin, W., *Moscow Diary,* Cambridge, MA: Harvard University Press, 1986.

Benjamin, W., *Reflections. Essays, Aphorisms, Autobiographical Writings,* New York: Schocken, 1978.

Benjamin, W., *Selected Writings, ii,* Cambridge, MA: Harvard University Press, 1999.

Benton, C., ed., *Documents: A Collection of Source Materials on the Modern Movement,* Milton Keynes: Open University Press, 1975.

Benton, T., *The Modernist Home,* London: V&A Publications, 2006.

Berger, P. L., Berger, B., and Kellner, H., *The Homeless Mind. Modernization and Consciousness,* New York: Vintage Books, 1974.

Berman, M., *All that Is Solid Melts into Air. The Experience of Modernity,* London: Verso, 1982.

Bloch, E., *The Principle of Hope* [translation of *Das Prinzip Hoffnung* 1959], Oxford: Blackwell, 1986.

Bloom Hiesinger, K., *Art Nouveau in Munich: Masters of Jugendstil,* Munich: Prestel Verlag, 1988.

Blundell Jones, P., *Hans Scharoun,* London: Phaidon Press, 1995.

Brandwood, G., Davison, A., and Slaughter, M., *Licensed to Sell: The History and Heritage of the Public House,* London: English Heritage in Association with CAMRA, Campaign for Real Ale, 2004.

Branzi, A., *The Hot House: Italian New Wave Design,* London: Thames & Hudson, 1984.

Bremback, H., et al., eds., *Little Monsters; (De) coupling and Assemblages of Consumption,* Berlin: Verlag, 2007.

Brendon, P., *The Decline and Fall of the British Empire, 1781–1997,* London: Jonathan Cape, 2007.

Brumfield, W. C., and Ruble, B. A., eds., *Russian Housing in the Modern Age: Design and Social History,* Cambridge, MA: Cambridge University Press, 1993.

Büchli, V., *An Archaeology of Socialism,* London: Berg, 1999.

Büller, L., and Den Oudsten, F., 'Interview with Truus Schröder', in P. Overy, et al., *The Rietveld Schröder House,* Cambridge, MA: MIT Press, 1988.

Cacciari, M., 'Eupalinos or Architecture', *Oppositions,* 21 (1980), pp. 106–16.

Cantacuzino, S., *Wells Coates; A Monograph,* London: Gordon Fraser, 1978.

Carpenter, E. K., 'A Tribute to Charles Eames', *Industrial Design 25th Annual Design Review,* New York: 1979.

Chiras, D., *The Solar House: Passive Heating and Cooling,* White River Junction: Chelsea Green Publishing, 2002.

Coates, W., 'Furniture To-day, Furniture To-morrow: Leaves from a Meta-Technical Notebook', *Architectural Review,* 73 (July 1932), pp. 31–4.

Collins, J., Thomas, G., Willis, R., and Wilsdon, J., *Carrots, Sticks and Demons: Influencing Public Behaviour for Environmental Goals,* London: Department for Environment, Food and Rural Affairs, 2003.

Colomina, B., *Privacy and Publicity: Modern Architecture as Mass Media,* Cambridge, MA: MIT Press, 1994.

Cooper, J., *Victorian and Edwardian Furniture and Interiors. From the Gothic Revival to Art Nouveau,* London: Thames & Hudson, 1987.

Crook, J. M., *The Greek Revival: Neo-Classical Attitudes in British Architecture 1760–1870,* Brighton: John Murray, 1972.

Crowley, D., and Reid, S. E., eds., *Socialist Spaces: Sites of Everyday Life in the Eastern Bloc,* Oxford: Berg, 2003

Darling, E., and Whitworth, L., eds., *Women and the Making of Built Space in England, 1750–1950,* Ashgate, 2007.

Darling, E., *Re-Forming Britain: Narratives of Modernity before Reconstruction,* Abingdon: Routledge, 2007.

Darnton, A., *Driving Public Behaviours for Sustainable Lifestyles (Report 2),* London: Department for Environment, Food and Rural Affair, 2004.

Dash Moore, D., *To the Golden Cities: Pursuing the American Dream in Miami and Los Angeles,* Cambridge, MA: Harvard University Press, 1994.

De Wolfe, E., *The House in Good Taste,* New York: Century Company, 1913.

Denby, E., *Grand Hotels: An Architectural and Social History,* London: Reaktion Books, 1998.

Desai, P., and Riddlestone, S., *Schumacher Briefings 8: Bioregional Solutions: For Living on One Planet,* Totnes: Green Books, 2007.

Dixon, R., and Muthesius, S., *Victorian Architecture,* London: Thames & Hudson, 1978.

Driller, J., *Breuer Houses,* London: Phaidon, 2000.

Düttmann, M., and Schneider, F., eds., *Morris Lapidus: Architect of the American Dream,* Basel: Birkhäuser, 1992.

Duus, M., *The Life of Isamu Noguchi: Journey without Borders,* Princeton, NJ: Princeton University Press, 2004.

Eastlake, C. L., *Hints on Household Taste in Furniture, Upholstery and Other Details,* 4th edition, London: Longmans, Green, 1878 [1868].

Elwall, R., *Bricks and Beer: English Pub Architecture, 1830–1939,* London: British Architectural Library, 1983.

Esslin, M., *The Theatre of the Absurd,* Garden City, NY: Doubleday, 1962.

Evans, R., 'Rookeries and Model Dwellings', in *Translations from Drawing to Building and Other Essays,* London: Architectural Association, 1997.

Evans, R., 'The Developed Surface: An Enquiry into the Brief Life of an Eighteenth-century Drawing Technique', in *Translations from Drawing to Building and Other Essays,* London: Architectural Association, 1997.

Everdell, R., *The First Moderns: Profiles in the Origins of Twentieth-Century Thought,* Chicago: University of Chicago Press, 1997.

Fales, W., *What's New in Home Decorating?,* New York: Dodd, Mead, 1936.

Favata, I., *Joe Colombo and Italian Design of the Sixties,* London: Thames & Hudson, 1988.

Ferriday, P., ed., with an introduction by Sir John Betjeman, *Victorian Architecture,* London: Jonathan Cape, 1963.

Forty, A., *Objects of Desire: Design and Society 1750–1980,* London: Thames & Hudson, 1986.

Fossati, P., *Il Design in Italia, 1945–1972,* Turin: Einaudi, 1972.

Frankl, P., *New Dimensions: The Decorative Arts of Today in Words and Pictures,* New York: Payson and Clarke, 1928.

Franklin, J., *The Gentleman's Country House and Its Plan,* London: Routledge & Kegan Paul, 1981.

Friedman, A. T., *Women and the Making of the Modern House: A Social and Architectural History,* New York: Harry N. Abrams, 1998.

Furneaux-Jordan, R., *Victorian Architecture,* Harmondsworth: Penguin, 1966.

Garrett, R., and A. Garrett, *Suggestions for House Decoration in Painting, Woodwork and Furniture,* London: Macmillan, 1876.

Gamboni, D., *The Destruction of Art: Iconoclasm and Vandalism since the French Revolution,* London: Reaktion, 1997.

Gell, A., *Art and Agency: An Anthropological Theory,* Oxford: Oxford University Press, 1998.

Georgakas, D., 'Hollywood Blacklist' in M. J. Buhle, P. Buhle and D. Georgakas, eds., *Encyclopaedia of the American Left,* Urbana: University of Illinois Press, 1992.

Gere, C., and Hoskins, L., *The House Beautiful: Oscar Wilde and the Aesthetic Interior,* London: Lund Humphries/Geffreye Museum, 2000.

Giedion, S., *Space, Time and Architecture,* Cambridge, MA: MIT Press, 1941.

Giedion, S., *Mechanization Takes Command: A Contribution to Anonymous History,* New York: W. W. Norton, 1947.

Girouard, G., *Sweetness and Light, the 'Queen Anne' Movement 1860–1900,* New Haven, CT: Yale University Press, 1977.

Girouard, M., *Life in an English Country House, a Social and Architectural History,* New Haven, CT: Yale University Press, 1978.

Girouard, M., *The Victorian Country House,* New Haven, CT: Yale University Press, 1971; 1980.

Girouard, M., *Victorian Pubs,* New Haven, CT: Yale University Press, 1984.

Gladchuk, J. J., *Hollywood and Anti-Communism: HUAC and the Evolution of the Red Menace, 1935–50,* New York: Routledge, 2006.

Gordon, A., ed., *Postwar Japan as History,* Berkeley: University of California Press, 1993.

Grassi, A., and Pansera, A., *Atlante del Design Italiano 1940–1980,* Milan: Fabbri, 1980.

Greenhalgh, P., *Modernism in Design,* London: Reaktion, 1990.

Gregotti, V., *Achille Castiglioni,* Milan: Electa, 1985.

Gregson, N., *Living with Things: Ridding, Accommodation, Dwelling,* Wantage: Sean Kingston, 2007.

Grieve, A., *Isokon,* London: Isokon Plus, 2004.

Günther, S., *Interieurs um 1900,* Munich: Wilhelm Fink Verlag, 1971.

Halle, D., *Inside Culture: Art and Class in the American Home,* Chicago: University of Chicago Press, 1993.

Harootunian, H., *History's Disquiet: Modernity, Cultural Practice and the Question of Everyday Life,* New York: Columbia University Press, 2000.

Harrison, B., *Drink and the Victorians: The Temperance Question in England, 1815–1872,* London: Faber and Faber, 1971.

Harrod, T., *The Crafts in Britain in the 20th Century,* New Haven, CT: Yale University Press, 1999.

Haweis, M. E., *The Art of Decoration,* London: Chatto & Windus, 1881.

Hayden, D., 'Model Homes for the Millions: Architect's Dreams, Builders' Boasts, Residents' Dilemmas', in E. A. T. Smith, ed., *Blueprints for Modern Living: History and Legacy of the Case Study Houses,* Los Angeles: Museum of Contemporary Arts, 1989.

Hays, K. M., *Modernism and the Posthumanist Subject: The Architecture of Hannes Meyer and Ludwig Hilberseimer,* Cambridge, MA: MIT Press, 1992.

Heynen, H., and Baydar, G., eds., *Negotiating Domesticity: Spatial Productions of Gender in Modern Architecture,* London: Routledge, 2005.

Hitchcock, H. R., and Johnson, P., *The International Style, Architecture since 1922,* New York: W. W. Norton, 1995 [1932].

Hobsbawm, E., *Age of Extremes: The Short Twentieth Century, 1914–1991,* London: Abacus, 1995.

Hoffman, H., *Modern Interiors in Europe and America,* London: The Studio, 1930.

Holm, I., *Ideas and Beliefs in Architecture and Industrial Design: How Attitudes, Orientations, and Underlying Assumptions Shape the Built Environment,* Oslo: Oslo School of Architecture and Design Press, 2006.

Jeremiah, D., *Architecture and Design for the Family in Britain, 1900–1970,* Manchester: Manchester University Press, 2000.

Jervis, S., *High Victorian Design,* Suffolk: Boydell, 1983.

Jervis, S., *Victorian Furniture,* London: Ward Lock, 1968.

Kahle, K. M., *Modern French Decoration,* New York: G. P. Putnam's Sons, 1930.

Keeble, T., Martin, B., and Sparke, P., eds., *The Modern Period Room: The Construction of the Exhibited Interior 1870–1950,* Abingdon: Routledge, 2006.

Kelly, C., ed., *Utopias,* Harmondsworth: Penguin, 1999.

Kerr, R., *The Gentleman's House: Or How to Plan English Residences from the Parsonage to the Palace,* London: John Murray, 1871 [1864].

Kiaer, C., *Imagine No Possessions. The Socialist Objects of Russian Constructivism,* Cambridge, MA: MIT Press, 2005.

Kirkham, P., *Charles and Ray Eames: Designers of the Twentieth Century,* Cambridge, MA: MIT Press, 1995.

Kirkham, P., ed., *The Gendered Object,* Manchester: Manchester University Press, 1996.

Kuechler, S., and Miller D., eds., *Clothing Material Culture,* Oxford: Berg, 2005.

Labaco, R., ed., *Ettore Sottsass, Architect and Designer,* London: Merrell, 2006.

Lambert, G., *The Ivan Moffat File: Life among the Beautiful and Damned in London, Paris, New York, and Hollywood,* New York: Pantheon Books, 2004.

Lanchester, E., *Charles Laughton and I,* London: Faber & Faber, 1938.

Lapidus, M., *An Architecture of Joy,* Miami: E. A. Seemann, 1979.

Lapidus, M., *Too Much Is Never Enough: An Autobiography,* New York: Rizzoli, 1996.

Le Corbusier, *Towards a New Architecture,* tr. F. Etchells, 1927, reprinted New York: Praeger, 1960.

Lejeune, J. F., and. Shulman, A. T., eds., *The Making of Miami Beach: The Architecture of Lawrence Murray Dixon,* New York: Rizzoli, 2000.

Limerick, J., Fergusson, N., and Oliver, R., *America's Grand Resort Hotels,* New York: Pantheon Books, 1979.

Loftie, W. J., *A Plea for Art in the House,* London: Macmillan, 1876.

Lowenstein, O., 'Architectural Trends', in *The Green Building Bible: All You Need to Know about Ecobuilding;* 3rd edn, i, Llandysul: Green Building Press, 2007.

Luthmer, F., *Malerische Innenräume moderner Wohnungen: In Aufnahmen nach Natur,* Frankfurt: Heinrich Keller, 1884.

Lux, J. A., *Das neue Kunstgewerbe in Deutschland: Ein Versuch,* Leipzig: Klinkhardt & Biermann, 1908.

Macleod, R., *Style and Society, Architectural Ideology in Britain 1840–1914,* London: Royal Institute of British Architects, 1971.

Maland, C. J., *Chaplin and American Culture: The Evolution of a Star Image,* Princeton, NJ: Princeton University Press, 1991.

Marchand, S., and Lindenfeld, D., eds., *Germany at the Fin de Siècle: Culture, Politics and Ideas,* Baton Rouge: Louisiana State University Press, 2004.

Martin, B., and Sparke, P., eds., *Women's Places: Architecture and Design 1860–1960,* London: Routledge, 2003.

Massey, A., *Interior Design of the Twentieth Century,* London: Thames & Hudson, 1990.

Matich, O., 'Remaking the Bed. Utopia in Daily Life', in J. Bowlt and O. Matich, eds., *Laboratories of Dreams. The Russian Avant-Garde and Cultural Experience,* Stanford, CA: Stanford University Press, 1996.

McAuliffe, M. S., *Crisis on the Left: Cold War Politics and American Liberals, 1947–1954,* Amherst: University of Massachusetts Press, 1978.

McKellar, S., and Sparke, P., eds., *Interior Design and Identity,* Manchester: Manchester University Press, 2004.

Miller, D., ed., *Home Possessions,* Oxford: Berg, 2001.

Moholy-Nagy, S., 'Steel, Stocks, and Private Man', *Progressive Architecture* (January 1958), pp. 128–9.

Mori, B.L.C., 'The Tea Ceremony: A Transformed Japanese Ritual', *Gender & Society,* 5/1 (1991), pp. 86–97.

Muthesisus, S., *The High Victorian Moment in Architecture 1850–1870,* London: Routledge & Kegan Paul, 1972.

Nash, P., *Room and Book,* New York: Scribners, 1932.

Naylor, G., *The Arts and Crafts Movement: A Study of Its Sources, Ideals and Influences on Design Theory,* London: Studio Vista, 1971.

Neuhart, J., Neuhart, M., and Eames, R., *Eames Design: The Work of the Office of Charles and Ray Eames,* London: Thames & Hudson, 1989.

Nicholson, V., *Among the Bohemians, Experiments in Living 1900–1919,* Harmondsworth: Penguin, 2003.

Orrinsmith, L., *The Drawing Room: Its Decoration and Furniture,* London: Macmillan, 1877.

Painter, C., ed., *Contemporary Art in the Home,* Oxford: Berg, 2002.

Peabody Trust, *Report for Property Standards Panel: BedZED Resident Survey Results,* London: Peabody Trust, April 2004.

Pevsner, N., *Pioneers of Modern Design,* Harmondsworth: Penguin Books, 1960 [1936].

Pevsner, N., *Some Architectural Writers of the Nineteenth Century,* Oxford: Clarendon Press, 1972.

Pink, S., *Home Truths: Gender, Domestic Objects and Everyday Life,* Oxford: Berg, 2004.

Potter, N., and Frost J., *QE2: Queen Elizabeth 2, The Authorised Story,* London: Harrap, 1969.

Praz, M., *An Illustrated History of Interior Decoration, from Pompeii to Art Nouveau,* London: Thames & Hudson, 1964.

Rathke, E., *Jugendstil,* Mannheim: Bibliographisches Institut, 1958.

Reed, C., ed., *Not at Home: The Suppression of Domesticity in Modern Art and Architecture,* London: Thames & Hudson, 1996.

Repp, K., *Reformers, Critics and the Paths of German Modernity,* Cambridge, MA: Harvard University Press, 2000.

Rice, C., *The Emergence of the Interior: Architecture, Modernity, Domesticity,* London: Routledge, 2007.

Rybczynski, W., *Home: A Short History of an Idea,* New York: Viking/Penguin, 1986.

Samuel, R., *Theatres of Memory: Past and Present in Contemporary Culture,* London: Verso, 1994.

Sand, J., *House and Home in Modern Japan: Architecture, Domestic Space and Bourgeois Culture 1880–1930,* Cambridge, MA: Harvard University Press, 2004.

Sandoval-Strausz, A. K., *Hotel: An American History,* New Haven, CT: Yale University Press, 2007.

Screech, T., *Sex and the Floating World: Erotic Images in Japan 1700–1820,* London: RoutlegeCurzon, 2005.

Seidler, H., 'Our Heritage of Modern Building', in *Harry Seidler: Houses & Interiors 1, 1948–1970,* Melbourne: Images Publishing, 2003 [1954].

Sennett, R., *The Fall of Public Man,* London: Penguin Books, 2002.

Shove, E., Watson, M., Ingram, J., and Hand, M., *The Design of Everyday Life,* Oxford: Berg, 2008.

Simmel, G., 'The Ruin' in K. H. Wolff, ed., *Essays on Sociology, Philosophy and Aesthetics,* New York: Harper & Row, 1965.

Smallpeice B., *Of Comets and Queens: An Autobiography,* Shrewsbury: Airlife Publishing, 1980.

Smith, E.A.T., ed., *Blueprints for Modern Living: History and Legacy of the Case Study Houses,* Los Angeles: Museum of Contemporary Arts, 1989.

Smithson, A., and Smithson, P., eds., 'Eames Celebration', *Architectural Design* (September 1966), pp. 432–71.

Somol, R., 'Dummy Text, or the Diagrammatic Basis of Contemporary Architecture', in *P. Eisenman:*

Diagram Diaries, London: Thames & Hudson, 1999.

Sparke, P., *As Long as It's Pink: The Sexual Politics of Taste,* London: Pandora, 1995.

Sparke, P., *Elsie de Wolfe: The Birth of Modern Interior Decoration,* New York: Acanthus Press, 2005.

Sparke, P., *Ettore Sottsass, Jr.,* London: Design Council, 1982.

Sparke, P., *Italian Design, 1870 to the Present,* London: Thames & Hudson, 1988.

Spigelman, A., *Almost Full Circle: Harry Seidler,* Sydney: Brandl and Schlesinger, 2001.

Stansky, P., *Redesigning the World. William Morris, the 1880s, and the Arts and Crafts,* Princeton, NJ: Princeton University Press, 1985.

Stanton, P., *Pugin,* London: Thames & Hudson, 1971.

Stern, F., *The Politics of Cultural Despair: A Study in the Rise of the Germanic Ideology,* Berkeley: University of California Press, 1961.

Stewart, S., *On Longing. Narratives of the Miniature, the Gigantic, the Souvenir, the Collection,* Durham, NC: Duke University Press, 1993.

Street, B., *Writing Ourselves: Mass Observation and Literacy Practices,* Hampton: Hampton Press, 2000.

Summerson, J., *Victorian Architecture, Four Studies in Evaluation,* New York: Columbia University Press, 1970.

Tanizaki, J., *In Praise of Shadows,* New Haven, CT: Leete's Island Books, 1977.

Taylor, M., and Preston, J., *Intimus: Interior Design Theory Reader,* New York: John Wiley, 2006.

Taylor, P., *Modernities: A Geohistorical Approach,* Cambridge, UK: Polity Press, 1999.

Thompson, P., *William Butterfield,* London: Routledge & Kegan Paul, 1971.

Tilder, L., 'Ten Shades of Green: Architecture and the Natural World', *Journal of Architectural Education,* 60/4 (2007), pp. 60–1.

Todd, D., and Mortimer, R., *The New Interior Decoration: An Introduction to Its Principles, and International Survey of Its Methods,* London: B. T. Batsford, 1929.

Tosh, J., *A Man's Place: Masculinity and the Middle-Class Home in Victorian England,* New Haven, CT: Yale University Press, 1999.

Van Herck, K., '"Only Where Comfort Ends, Does Humanity Begin": On the "Coldness" of Avant-garde Architecture in the Weimar Period", in H. Heynen and G. Baydar, eds., *Negotiating Domesticity. Spatial Productions of Gender in Modern Architecture,* London: Routledge, 2005.

Varney, C., *In the Pink: Dorothy Draper, America's Most Fabulous Decorator,* New York: Pointed Leaf Press, 2006.

Vidler, A., *The Architectural Uncanny, Essays in the Modern Unhomely,* Boston: MIT Press, 1994.

Wainwright, C., *The Romantic Interior: The British Collector at Home 1750–1850,* New Haven, CT: Yale University Press, 1989.

Watkin, D., *The Rise of Architectural History,* New York: Architectural Press, 1980.

Wealleans, A., *Designing Liners: A History of Interior Design Afloat,* London: Routledge, 2006.

Wharton, E., and Codman Jr., O., *The Decoration of Houses,* London: B. J. Batsford, 1897.

Wichmann, S., *Japonisme: The Japanese Influence on Western Art since 1858,* London: Thames & Hudson, 1999.

Wilde, O., 'House Decoration', in *Essays and Lectures by Oscar Wilde,* London: Methuen, 1908.

Wilk, C., ed., *Modernism 1914–1939: Designing a New World,* London: V&A Publications, 2006.

Williams, R., *Keywords: A Vocabulary of Culture and Society,* London: Fontana Press, 1976.

Williamson, T., Radford, A., and Bennetts, H., *Understanding Sustainable Architecture,* London: Spon Press, 2003.

Wölfflin, H., 'Principles in Art History,' in D. Preziosi, ed., *The Art of Art History: A Critical Anthology,* Oxford: Oxford University Press, 1998.

Woolf, V., *To the Lighthouse,* London: Hogarth Press, 1927.

Yorke, M., *The Modern House,* London: Architectural Press, 1934.

Index